THE BEST MINERS
IN THE WORLD

THE BEST MINERS
IN THE WORLD

Stories from Canada's Sullivan Mine

W.R. (Bill) Roberts

"Through this portal have gone
the best miners in the world."

– Bud Hart, 1985

Hardrock Publishing
Penticton, British Columbia, Canada

THE BEST MINERS
IN THE WORLD

Stories from Canada's Sullivan Mine

By W.R. (Bill) Roberts

Third Printing: November 2008 Copyright ©2004 W.R. Roberts

Hardrock Publishing
#237 – 805 Comox Street • Penticton, BC Canada   V2A 8G5
Ph (250) 276-5360 • www.hardrockpublishing.ca

Library and Archives Canada Cataloguing in Publication

Roberts, W. R. (William R.), 1943-
    The best miners in the world: stories from Canada's Sullivan Mine / W.R. Roberts;
Susan Bond, editor.

Includes index.
ISBN 0-9735591-0-1

    1. Sullivan Mine (B.C.)--History. 2. Miners--British Columbia--Kimberley--
Biography. 3. Miners--British Columbia--Kimberley--History. 4. Mines and mineral
resources--British Columbia--Kimberley--History. 5. Kimberley (B.C.)--Biography.
6. Kimberley (B.C.)--History. I. Bond, Susan, 1953- II. Title.

HD8039.M72C347 2004   338.2'09711'65   C2004-904683-7

Editor: Susan Bond
Design: Desktop Graphics

Distributor:
Sandhill Book Marketing Ltd.
Unit 4 – 3308 Appaloosa Road • Kelowna, BC Canada   V1V 2W5
Ph (250) 491-1446 • Fax (250) 491-4066
Email info@sandhillbooks.com • www.sandhillbooks.com

Printed and bound by: Houghton Boston, Saskatoon, Saskatchewan

This book is dedicated to all those who worked in the Sullivan,
and especially to the seventy-three men who gave their lives in the mine.
I would have been proud to call any of them "pard."

CONTENTS

PHOTOGRAPHS & ILLUSTRATIONS

Except where otherwise indicated,
all photographs and illustrations are courtesy
of the Kimberley Heritage Museum.

*The Sullivan Mine is located
at Kimberley, British Columbia,
Canada.*

FOREWORD

When Bill Roberts asked me to read a draft of *The Best Miners in the World*, I had no idea what an interesting read lay before me. I wasn't too far into the stories of some of the more colourful characters at the Sullivan when I realized that only a miner could have accurately recorded the various accounts that follow in these pages.

As a member of the Sullivan Mine & Railway Historical Society, I am working to preserve the physical history and technological achievements over the life of the Sullivan. Bill has captured the human history of the mine. These miners' stories represent the lives of thousands of people over four generations.

Underground mining, like logging, can be a hazardous business and the close calls and the fatalities tend always to be part of what people remember. As a former General Manager of Cominco's Kimberley Operations and the Teck Cominco executive responsible for the Sullivan until closure in 2001, I am very thankful there were no fatalities in the last fourteen years of the Sullivan's life.

Management takes some "bouquets" and some "bricks" in the pages that follow, quite deservedly so. As an engineer myself, I loved the comments about engineers. Some of us took twenty years for the miners to train, others were impossible!

This book is an absolute "must read" for anyone who had any association with the Sullivan or Kimberley, and will appeal to anyone who likes history or a good yarn, whether they know anything about mining or not. Bill has included a glossary of terms at the back for those who want to understand the mining jargon in the text. He has also included a list of all those who made the ultimate sacrifice at the Sullivan.

I commend Bill for the incredible amount of time he spent interviewing miners over many years to put this accounting together. He has brought the history of the famous Sullivan Mine to life.

R.M. (Mick) Henningson
Senior Vice President, Mining (ret.)
Teck Cominco

INTRODUCTION

"It has been said that the best thing to come out of a mine is a miner." So wrote *Kimberley Daily Bulletin* editor Carolyn Grant in an article marking the closure of the Sullivan Mine in 2001.

As a Sullivan miner myself for thirty-six years, I have to agree. But I would add this: "The next best thing to come out of a mine is a story told by a miner."

Wherever they meet, miners swap tales, and the best ones are told again and again. Invariably, when an old favourite gets yet another hearing, often over a beer after shift, someone says, "Somebody should write a book." So, in the mid-1980s, I decided to do just that when I realized the oldtimers were dying off and their recollections of the Sullivan would go with them.

I pretty much knew who all the good storytellers were so I started to arrange interviews. Taking a tape recorder along, I would sit down with a miner, usually at his kitchen table, and ask four basic questions: where and when did you start mining; what were your working conditions; how were you paid; and what were your best and worst times as a miner. Of course, once we got going — and the tape recorder was no longer an intimidating presence — the stories would tumble out, sometimes with help from the miner's wife who would remind her husband of a name or a date.

It was a privilege to listen, and watch faces crinkle with laughter at one memory or eyes tear at another. Mining is a hard way to make a living. In their retirement years these were guys that dragged little wheeled carts to keep them supplied with oxygen; who apologized when they coughed and hacked into a handkerchief, battling for breath to feed lungs damaged by the dust and fumes they had inhaled over the years; who gestured with hands and fingers grown arthritic after being broken and bashed over time; and, most often, guys who hardly ever heard me properly the first time I asked a question because their hearing was shot by decades of drilling and blasting.

But there was never any whining or complaining. They considered the hazards and their consequences part of the job, and to a man they said they would do it all again. They were proud of what their skill had achieved, and the filter of memory had left them recalling the best times not the worst — the laughs they shared and the bonds they forged underground. In the end, humour and camaraderie overcame the fears and anxieties of working in a hostile and uncompromising environment. At times I found myself very moved, and ever so proud to call myself a hard rock miner.

The stories that follow were transcribed directly from the tape recordings and have undergone very little editing. They reflect a true picture of life underground and will take you from the 30s and 40s, into the 50s and 60s when the Sullivan was in its richest and most productive phase, and right up to the 90s and the last years of the mine.

I'm sure many of the stories have been enriched by lively imagination, but I don't think that's important. Some of the men who speak from these pages are natural storytellers, and embellishment is the right of a good storyteller. I believe in the old adage that says: "Don't let the truth get in the way of a good story." And, regardless of the accuracy of every detail, you will be left with an understanding of what it was to be a hard rock miner.

Almost twenty years have passed since I started gathering the interviews that have finally become this book. Much has changed in that time. The Sullivan has closed and many of the oldtimers who talked with me have passed on. I'll never swap a story or share another round with Red Foster, Alf Jolie, John Ekskog, Billy Masich, Bob Varley, Alf Olsen, Ed Pendry, Dory Arnfinnson or John Chernoff.

The Best Miners in the World tells the stories of twenty-three hard rock miners who worked in one of the world's greatest underground mines. My only regret is that I didn't start this chronicle sooner. There are so many more stories that should have been told.

Bill Roberts
Kimberley, British Columbia, Canada
April 2004

ACKNOWLEDGEMENTS

This book would not have been possible without the help of many people. My thanks go, first of all, to the miners who told me their stories. Without them, there would be no book.

I am grateful to the staff at the Kimberley Heritage Museum, especially Marie Stang whose help in finding photos and charts was no less than fantastic. Having sole responsibility for the museum and Teck Cominco's vast array of photographs, Marie guarded them with her life. She is not to be trifled with as she carefully protects these valuable documents.

Thanks to Brian McKenzie for providing permission to use Cominco's archives and photos, and to Mick Henningson for reading the book in manuscript form, making valuable comments and writing such an encouraging Foreword. He is a man who really appreciates miners.

My gratitude to my editor, Susan Bond, has no bounds. She is a true professional. Susan has mining blood in her veins. Her grandfather is in one of the photographs in the book — the barman up a very tall ladder, a truly dramatic picture. Her insistence on accuracy was fierce. At times she reminded me of a mining partner who wants to drill one more hole when I was ready to load and blast. But in the end her care and finesse proved to be just what the book needed. I owe a lot to Susan, thank you.

Most of all, though, I want to acknowledge my wife, Sandra. Without her computer skills, patience and constant support, I would have been lost. What's all this stuff about sentence structure and punctuation, I asked myself? Well, I soon found out, especially each time I heard, "Bill, come in here! What does this mean?" as she transformed my handwritten pages and the audio tapes into readable text. Sandra knew how important this book was to me as a way of giving miners a face and a voice. She had faith in the project and encouraged me throughout its long gestation. She knows what it's like to be a miner's wife. To my "Pard," I say thank you.

The Mighty Sullivan

The Sullivan was truly a mighty mine.

It was big. More than two miles long and nearly half a mile deep, the Sullivan required forty-two miles of rail track and ten miles of roads to move 164 million tons of ore during its productive life.

It was rich. The Sullivan produced 18.5 billion pounds of lead, 17.5 billion pounds of zinc and 297 million ounces of silver worth more than $20 billion over the its hundred years of existence; the Sullivan and its related operations employed more than 60,000 people; and it spawned a city of 7,000 that now has an independent life of its own.

And, for a mine, it lasted a long time. Discovered in 1892 and a continuous producer from 1900 until closure in 2001, the Sullivan has a history that encompasses three centuries and spans four generations.

How the Sullivan Was Born

What about the orebody itself? How did it come to be, and how long ago?

These are difficult questions because the orebody was formed long before there were people on Earth. However, geologists who have studied the Sullivan and similar orebodies in other countries have pieced together the evidence to form as detailed a picture as possible. In this sense, geologists are like detectives.

The Sullivan orebody is located at the western edge of the Rocky Mountain Trench and on the eastern flank of the Purcell Mountains in the southeastern corner of British Columbia. It is in the shape of a saucer that has been turned upside down and tilted. The "saucer" is thickest near the centre, about 328 feet deep, and thins outward in all directions to an average of 68 feet deep.

The saucer-shaped orebody lies in layers of sedimentary rock called the Aldridge Formation. This formation — about 12,000 feet thick and roughly 500 miles long by 100 miles wide — began to form about 1,500 million years ago, long before plant or animal life appeared on land. (The age of the dinosaurs was at its peak about 150 million years ago and mankind has been here for only about two million years.) The layers of the Aldridge were deposited under a great sea or gulf that was surrounded by low-lying hills.

When it was about one-third deposited, a steep fault, or plane of weakness, began to reach up through the Aldridge sediments to the sea floor. Movement along this fault caused the sediments to break up into small chunks of material, forming the "conglomerate" that lies under most of the orebody.

Fluids began to percolate up this fault plane. At first, they brought mainly boron to the sediments, and these boron-enriched sediments later became the "chert" or tourmalinite we now know. Then things changed dramatically. Large amounts of hot metal-rich fluids poured out onto the sea floor. The most common metal was iron, but lead, zinc, silver, tin, cadmium, indium, antimony and trace amounts of a few other metals were also present. These were deposited, largely as sulphides, to form the orebody we came to know as the Sullivan.

The orebody was nearly flat when it was formed and, over time, more Aldridge Formation deposits and other overlying formations were laid down on top of it. Evidence suggests that eventually the orebody was buried under at least five miles of sedimentary rock.

Then, as huge forces started to uplift the land, the sea withdrew. These forces tilted or folded the rocks and the orebody within. Under the relentless effects of wind, rain and Ice Age glaciers, most of the five miles of overlying rocks were eroded away until, after all those millions of years, a little bit of the southernmost part of the Sullivan was exposed for four 19th century prospectors to find.

Nobody knows how many other orebodies may have been exposed and completely eroded away before our time. We guess that most of the North Star orebody opposite the Sullivan was eroded by the time it was found. On the other hand, some orebodies may not have been exposed on the surface at all and are still deep below. Some knowledgeable people believe another Sullivan is waiting to be discovered.

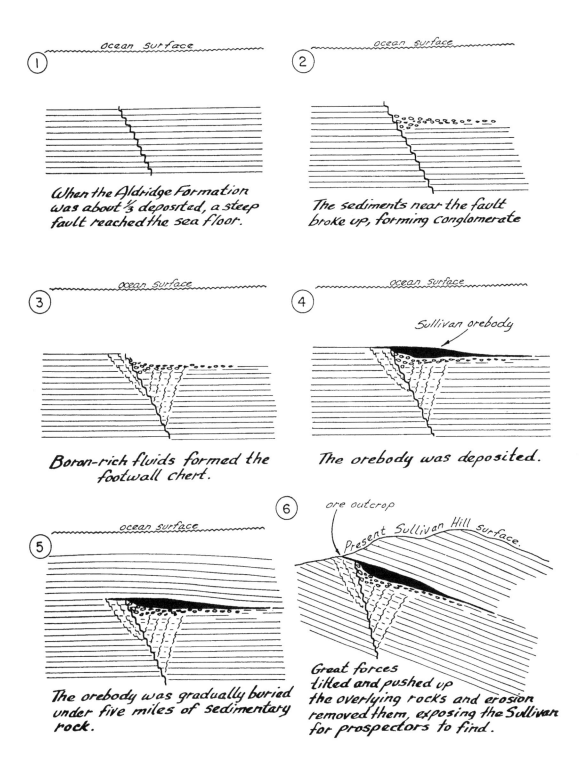

1. When the Aldridge Formation was about ⅓ deposited, a steep fault reached the sea floor.

2. The sediments near the fault broke up, forming conglomerate

3. Boron-rich fluids formed the footwall chert.

4. *Sullivan orebody* — The orebody was deposited.

5. The orebody was gradually buried under five miles of sedimentary rock.

6. *ore outcrop* — *Present Sullivan Hill surface.* Great forces tilted and pushed up the overlying rocks and erosion removed them, exposing the Sullivan for prospectors to find.

Cominco Communicator

Inside the Sullivan

As I entered the dark pervasiveness of the mine, I often thought of it as a huge, living entity, its black innards lit only by the narrow cone of light shining from my headlamp. It was a good place to use the term "tunnel vision."

Like any living thing, a mine breathes in good air and exhales used air, through its intake and exhaust fan "lungs." A mine has its own smells. Blasting smoke and dust ride along on the fresh air coming in, and every type of ore has its own smell that joins the mixture on its journey of circulation throughout the mine.

This huge creature makes noises that conjure up all sorts of images. The pinging of an airline might sound like a call for help, instead of a demand for air to a drill somewhere. Muck cascading down an orepass to a waiting train below, or an unseen blast and its following concussion, might sound as if a calamity is about to break loose.

The one noise that makes everyone take note is the sound of a bump. When the ground talks, everybody listens, then takes a look above their heads. The distinctive crack of a bump is quite different from the sound of a blast. Because the ground in a mine acts as a conductor, a ground shift miles away can sound like it's right beside you. And when it is beside you, you know it. There's the crack!, a puff of dust, and as the ground around you moves, down fall rocks, big and small, but hopefully not where you are standing.

Just like a living thing, a mine can lash out. You have to treat it with respect.

From Tramping to Homesteading

Miners started showing up to work in Kimberley towards the end of the 19th century. The North Star Mine, where the ski hill is now, was the centre of mining activity at the time, but as it petered out, a much bigger orebody across the narrow valley of Mark Creek was being discovered..

In the beginning, the Sullivan depended on a restless breed of miner known as a "tramp miner." Many came from overseas looking for a better way of life, others just wanted adventure. A lot came west from mines back east, or travelled up from the United States. These men brought the skills the Sullivan needed. Most had worked in coal mines in Europe or eastern Canada. The ones coming up from the south had hard rock mining experience from gold and silver mines in the western States. Wherever they came from though, they brought with them a tremendous work ethic.

But tramp miners are a restless bunch. The majority had great skills but no loyalty to any company. When they got the urge, they moved on. It didn't take much: they didn't like the place where they were working, they might have a disagreement with management; their wife might have hated the camp; or — and this was usually the reason — "I hear that such and such a mine is paying better bonus." Before you knew it, the tramp miner was hitting the road once again.

In Kimberley, though, a great many of the trampers stayed and put down roots. Perhaps the town appealed to them, with its outdoor life that's hard to beat, or maybe the Company seemed like a pretty good outfit to work for, or — the big one — "The old lady and the kids don't want to move no more." And, of course, the Depression helped to give the Sullivan a steady workforce because jobs were so scarce then.

Whatever the reason, a lot stayed, and over the years their sons followed in their footsteps. They were content to work in one spot for the rest of their lives and a

Early miners at the portal at 4800 Level, the first place opened into the Sullivan orebody.

whole new type of miner evolved, the "homestead miner." Eventually, the Sullivan had third- and fourth-generation miners. Now that's homesteading.

The pull of an exceptional mining community like Kimberley, where it seemed the ore could last forever, is strong. There's security, family, friends, and money to be made. Once a miner makes a contract bonus, he's hooked. Soon he's married with kids and a mortgage. Now he's locked in. But he's making just as much or more than what a university-degree job would pay him. And he's doing something he loves, something that not too many people can do.

A great many people who try mining don't stay with it for very long. The demanding physical labour, ever-present danger and darkness and confinement soon weed out those who can't cut it. The guys that can find they have pride in their ability and skill. They're part of a special breed. Most miners enjoy the sense of danger and risk, the rush of adrenalin when you go in to "pull that round." At the end of the shift, when you've drilled and blasted, there is a sense of contentment. And the best thing is that you get to do it all again tomorrow.

Of course, the carrot on the stick is the contract bonus system, money paid for busting your ass, where you can prove to yourself and others that you can give it hell. If it wasn't for contract, I don't think many people would be miners. Contract pay makes up for the hard work, and the danger that goes with it.

The Mining Hierarchy

Mine management could be compared to the army. The mine manager is the general who is responsible for the overall operation of the mine. There are usually a couple of superintendents that are designated to specific mining operations.

The production superintendent is responsible for getting the broken ore out of the mine and meeting quotas. He plans how to evenly draw down the broken ore reserves in order to maintain stability of the ground around where production people are working. The development superintendent is responsible for planning and overseeing the actual mining and long-hole drilling: the advancement into un-mined ground. These superintendents answer to the mine manager.

Section foremen are the majors and at one time were the real power in a mine. They rarely answered to anyone. Superintendents were nothing to these guys and a smart mine manager would often defer to his foremen. They held the pulse of the mine in their hands and they could make a mine manager look good or bad depending on whether or not they respected him.

The shift bosses are the sergeants in this army. They are the liaison between the foremen and the men, all of whom are aspiring to be a foreman someday. They are the front-line supervisors, usually reporting only to the foreman.

Then there is the support staff, usually including people that spend most of the shift outside. These include engineers in the planning department and geologists. The engineers would usually have underground surveyors working for them and they would supply maps and long-hole drill patterns to the miners and drillers. The geologists would check out broken ore being produced or check out core hole samples to see where to start developing.

No mucking machines or scoops here in 1913. Just the "muckstick" shovel. The geologist's pick in the fellow's hand indicates he is likely a supervisor.

1913
HAND MUCKING IN A STOPE

The Consolidated Mining & Smelting Co. of Canada, Limited.

Men employed at SULLIVAN MINE, April 15th 1920

MINE

Name	Age	Nationality	Class of Employment	Surface or Underground
Holland, J.S.	38	Canadian	Rockhouse Boss	S
Lucey, A.	49	"	"	S
Switzer, F.	28	"	"	S
Beach, F.	18	"	Crusherman	S
Moore, P.	25	Irishman	"	S
Morrison, L.	21	Canadian	"	S
Burry, F.	49	Polish	Ore Sorter	S
Cameron, P.	28	Canadian	"	S
Cox, A.	48	English	"	S
Cox, G.	18	"	"	S
Dubord, T.	20	Canadian	"	S
Hill, P.	51	Scotch	"	S
Hudy, W.	23	Uranian	"	S
Johnson, C.	40	Foreman	"	S
Knutson, E.	38	Norwegian	"	S
Laird, C.	40	Irish	"	S
Letoile, A.	28	Canadian	"	S
Looke, V.	35	English	"	S
Malmloff, C.	27	Canadian	"	S
Murray, C.	18	"	"	S
Makowski, V.	39	Polish	"	S
McKenzie, P.	35	Canadian	"	S
Morley, B.	23	Scotch	"	S
Price, M.	39	Welsh	"	S
Radke, H.	50	German	"	S
Simpson, G.	22	Scotch	"	S
Sjoberg, A.	43	Swedish	"	S
Todhunter, J.	55	English	"	S
Wachuk, J.	46	Polish	"	S
Wigh, N.	27	Danish	"	S
Zympta, J.	45	Polish	"	S
Johnson, P.	38	Swedish	Master Mechanic	S
Bennett, C.	45	Canadian	Boss Blacksmith	S.
Draper, S.	54	English	Blacksmith	S
Guertin, L.	32	Canadian	"	S
Madison, L.	45	"	"	S
Johnson, M.	44	Swedish	" helper	S
Nicholl, S.	25	Canadian	" "	S
Plant, G.	35	English	Boss Machinist.	S.
Pratley, H.	32	"	Machinist	S
McPhee, H.	24	Canadian	Drill Doctor	S
Johnson, W.	26	Norwegian	Machinist Helper	S
Dahlgren, G.	29	Swedish	Electrician	S
Kirby, H.	26	American	" helper	S
Hanson, C.	45	Norwegian	Tramman	S
Walters, C.	21	Canadian	"	S
Caire, F.	35	German	"	U
Coon, R.	25	American	Motorman	U
Creslinsky, D.	22	Polish	"	U
Palombe, D.	24	Italian	"	U
Switzer, H.	20	Canadian	"	U
Vanstone, W.	45	Canadian	Timberman	U
Clemo, J.	35	English	"	U
Blayney, T.	45	Welsh	Hoistman	U
Gallante, O.	30	Italian	Nipper	U
Luciano, S.	25	Italian	"	U
Moffatt, R.	35	English	Pipeman	U
Schoonen, J.	26	Dutch	Powderman	U
Usher, J.	63	Canadian	Hoistman	U
Selby, C.	43	"	Pipeman	U
Myrene, O.	56	Swedish	Trackman	U.
Clarke, A.	29	Scotch	Shifter	U
Coldwell, W.	30	Canadian	"	U

- 8 -

Name	Age	Nationality	Class of Employment	Surface or Underground.
Barnicoat, O.	33	English ✓	Miner	U
Brodey, S.	40	Ukranian	"	U
Cairns, J.	41	Scotch ✓	"	U
Drewry, G.	45	Canadian ✓	"	U
Hilley, F.	24	Rumanian	"	U
Davies, S.	24	Welsh	Mucker	U
Enquist, S.	36	Finlander	"	U
Freed, L.	36	Russian	"	U
Ferby, W.	30	Austrian	"	U
Gallante, C.	23	Canadian	"	U
Hudson, E.	26	American	"	U
Hastings, T.	27	Irish	"	U
Heywood, A.	34	American	"	U
Horihoren, J.	45	Russian	"	U
Jennings, A.	24	English	"	U
Johnson, G.	20	Canadian	"	U
Kentler, D.	23	American	"	U
Kostenyuk, G.	22	Austrian	"	U
Kohnako, J.	26	Polish	"	U
Kozak, M.	20	Austrian	"	U
Lavoie, L.	30	Canadian	"	U
Lloyd, G.	28	English	"	U
Lecuyer, G.	48	Canadian	"	U
Lindsay, A.	26	Scotch	"	U
Lokinuk, H.	18	Russian	"	U
Lisiewich, M.	23	Ukranian	"	U
Melneruk, A.	23	Ukranian	"	U
Misavish, G.	30	Austrian	"	U
Malco, A.	28	Galician	"	U
Miller, J.	22	American	"	U
McKinnon, T.	22	Canadian	"	U
McDougall, J.	24	Canadian	"	U
Matthews, M.	47	English	"	U
Moran, J.	39	Canadian	"	U
Purcell, H.	21	English	"	U
Pascutti, A.	32	Italian	"	U
Peterson, R.	37	Swede	"	U
Ridub, L.	26	Galician,	"	U
Ross, F.	42	Canadian	"	U
Radisum, M.	30	Serbian	"	U
Janick, D.	25	Austrian	Miner	U
King, T.	42	English ✓	"	U
Kochelnik, G.	24	Russian	"	U
Korchinsky, J.	30	Ukranian	"	U
Kis, J.	23	Austrian	"	U
Kozemko, S.	24	Ukranian	"	U
Leshchynsky, A	27	Austrian	"	U
Lepoudre, F.	24	Belgian	"	U
O'Brien, E.D.	20	Canadian ✓	"	U
Pretchnuk, S.	22	Polish	"	U
Plytko, P.	25	Ruthenian	"	U
Veroski, L.	40	Polish	"	U
Tretheway, J.	30	English ✓	"	U
Tuff, G.	31	American ✓	"	U
Trounson, W.	38	English ✓	"	U
Tzar, M.	27	Austrian	"	U
Veroski, J.	28	Polish	"	U
William, J.	40	Italian	"	U
Worla, J.	39	Lithuanian	"	U
Atkins, F.	27	English	Mucker	U
Bellyk, H.	28	Russian	"	U
Bradburn, J.	42	English	"	U
Burton, A.	36	English	"	U
Bores, S.	40	Austrian	"	U
Blumson, H.	23	English	"	U
Batistella, L.	36	Italian	"	U
Brown, J.	28	American	"	U
Bourque, H.	26	American	"	U
Betts, G.	32	"	"	U
Collins, C.	20	English	"	U
		Ukranian	"	U

From Cominco archives

1913

LOADING V-CARS

Loading V-cars 1913.

So all in all, there's a lot of people involved in a mine, just like an army. It's just a matter of getting everyone marching in the same direction.

Now a young fellow doesn't start out as a miner. He has to work his way up starting from the bottom. The bottom will mean mucking on the belt, that is shovelling spillage from the belts back on to the belt, or mucking out sump pits. This is strenuous backbreaking work with no bonus pay.

From the belts, he'll go into a section to work as a nipper [gofer], a pipeman or he'll work on the track gang, all at the bottom of the pay scale. He'll stay doing these jobs until there is an opening as a long-hole driller, a trammer, or maybe on the timber gang. Now he will start making a bit of bonus or contract.

Along the way there just might be a call for development miners. Being a miner in the truest sense is not for everyone. If you like to highball it and live on the edge at times, this is the job for you. With this job you only get out of it what you put into it. This is where the money is. Miners are "king of the hill" in the pecking order of a mine.

As development miners start to burn out, they are usually rewarded with an easier job such as being a slusher miner or maybe working on the timber gang. But to a miner, there are only two jobs that qualify for the name and these are the development miners and the slusher miners. Everyone else has their own separate and distinct job that defines them. In other words, working in a mine doesn't mean that you are a miner.

Learning the Ropes

Miners learn from each other, and they look after each other.

A rookie miner's school colours are black and blue because he's going to take a lot of beating while learning his skills. The experience that an older miner shares with a younger one is what keeps the youngster out of harm's way. The most important first lesson for a rookie is: "Keep your mouth shut and listen."

The veteran can show him how to drill properly with a jackleg or a stoper, how to build a proper set-up to work from, how to support bad ground with timber and rock bolts so it doesn't cave in on him, and how to read the ground.

The ability to read the ground is probably the most important thing a miner can learn. If you don't understand the ground where you're working, sure as hell you're going to get nailed.

The sound of the rock when you check it with a scaling bar, or when you turn on your drill, is all important. If it sounds drummy or hollow, you know it's not far from coming down. You learn that dry rocks in a wet heading are usually loose and have to be brought down before they tag you. You learn it's not good when you're drilling up holes and the water is coming out behind you. That means there's loose rock over you that has to be brought down. These are the things you learn to watch for.

Most miners have a great respect for the danger around them. There are always close calls. A piece of loose that could crush you falls inches from where you're standing. Or falling loose takes out the staging you're standing on, sending your drill and steel rod down the raise, and you're just able to grab a rope tied to a footwall steel. Or you're spread-eagled sliding down a raise, hoping to snare a footwall steel with your foot and not your nuts.

But miners learn how to put a handle on their fear. Sure as God made little green apples, your miner is going to laugh about his close call later, or at least grin, knowing he got away with it one more time. "Son of a bitch. I almost bought it there," he'll say, or, "It's the small ones that hurt. The big ones you don't feel." Half the time, survival is just dumb luck. The other half it's sixth sense and agility.

Instinct is what can really save a miner's butt. Instinct roams around in a miner's body, looking for danger, always on guard, ever alert. When it senses something, instinct shoves all those little neck hairs up and tells the miner, "Hold it. Something is not right here." It might be a rock falling on its own, a puff of dust, maybe a change in air pressure, or the sound of a crack or bump in the ground that catches the attention of Mr. Instinct. It's probably one of the best tools a miner has. I'm sure I'm not the only guy who was working underground when instinct came into play and warned of some catastrophic event about to occur.

Finally, the young miner learns from the older miner what hard work is and to always do his best. Once he's learned those lessons he starts to acquire the pride that comes from working in one of the most difficult environments man has ever ventured into — and he earns the acceptance of a great bunch of people.

When the older miners finally accept the young guy, there is no ceremony or diploma or anything like that. They might start talking to the rookie about things unrelated to the job. Downtown, they might invite him to sit down and have a beer. You know you've been accepted when the old guy is not telling you what to do on the job anymore. He trusts you to do it right. But real acceptance comes when he calls you "pard."

When you have worked with miners, most of them anyway, you come to really appreciate them, their helpfulness, their honesty, the bonds they forge with each other. Oh sure, there are moments when you don't share each other's point of view, but in the end you find that really doesn't matter. You are measured by your effort and integrity when it comes to getting the round out. That's what it's all about.

Terror on the Track

Miners are supposed to be a tough bunch but here's a little story that shows we can be spooked just like anyone else...

There were seven of us who got off the man-skip on 3500 Level that fateful night. As the skiptender belled himself and the skip away, we made our way over to the large double doors that lead to the drift. Opening one, we fell into single file as we walked down between the train tracks. We were on our way to the doghouse for a cup of coffee before heading to our separate work areas.

As we followed Jack "Twiggy" Hunt, all three hundred pounds of him, I found myself wanting to break out into a hearty "Hi ho, hi ho, it's off to work we go." From my place in the middle of the procession, I felt for all the world like one of the Seven Dwarfs.

So there we were, making our way down the track, lunch buckets and drill oil bottles in hand, bags of bits slung over our shoulders, making some small talk but mostly watching our footing with our headlamps pointing down, when all of a sudden Twiggy lets out a scream of terror that resounds in my memory to this day.

For a big man, Twiggy moved with the speed of an Olympic sprinter that night. As he turned to flee, he barrelled into Jack Glennie behind him and from there it was the classic domino effect as we all went down like bowling pins. I poked my head out from beneath the pile of cussing humanity to see what terrifying calamity was about to befall us.

I shone my light down the drift. Coming toward us was a pair of the most devilish eyes you would hope never to see again. They were a dark burning red and below them were huge glistening teeth that looked like tusks. It was truly a fearsome apparition. I let loose with an involuntary shriek that added to the panic as the others spotted the furry behemoth descending upon us.

We were a pile of the Sullivan's finest — rugged, tough, hard rock miners — clawing and bellowing amidst our scattered lunch buckets, bit bags and oil bottles, completely devoid of dignity as our imaginations ran away with us.

What caused all this commotion, you might ask? Well, it was a packrat, just a plain ordinary packrat, but in that frightful moment it seemed to us that it was the size of a buffalo — and a man-eater to boot!

The packrat himself didn't want anything to do with us. I guess he could see we had enough on our plates as we struggled to disentangle the pile. About ten feet from us, he turned and climbed up the wall of the drift and onto the air and water pipelines hanging about six feet off the ground. He walked along the pipes until he got by us, then he came down the wall and moved back to the middle of the track.

As he waddled off, bathed in the light of seven lamps, I'm sure he turned and showed those fearsome teeth once again, only this time it looked like a grin.

As we finally, and sheepishly, continued on our way to the doghouse, Jack Glennie swore us to secrecy. We all agreed never to divulge to anyone what had happened. However, since all of the fellows but me have passed on, I feel it's my duty to let it all out now. How in hell could I not? It's a good story.

How to Pull a Round

I expect other miners will doubt whether this process will break ground but I assure you it works. I've done it a few times in my life.

The cut in the centre of the back is probably the most important part of the whole round. You start by drilling the "big hole," a couple of inches in diameter and a bit larger than the holes to follow. It is the first to be blasted.

Four cut holes, drilled to surround the big hole, are progressively further away from the centre cut. No. 1 would be two inches away, No. 2 would be three inches, No. 3, four inches, and No. 4, five inches. They go next in the blasting sequence.

The four square-up holes, Nos. 5 and 6, are placed an equal distance higher and lower from the cut. Four easer holes, Nos. 7, 8 and 9, are spaced equally from the square-up holes. Then they go in sequence. All the other holes — your breast holes, back holes, knee holes and the lifters — are the last to go.

With the advent of I-cord, a slow-burning igniter cord, the need for individual ignition of a fuse for each hole was eliminated. Using I-cord, we

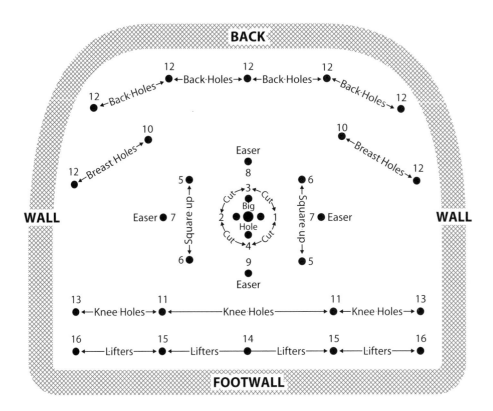

Desktop Graphics illustration

would measure off equal lengths of cord for each hole and put a twist, called a pigtail, in the middle of the resulting bundle. When tying in the fuse with attached blasting caps, we would crimp the igniter end of the fuse to the I-cord, starting with the holes to be blasted first closest to the pigtail and working out in sequence. We would light the pigtail, and the I-cord would burn outward, lighting the fuses one by one as it went.

Electric blasting caps made it a whole lot easier. Each cap had a number on it from one to twenty. The miner would run B-line, a high-explosive igniter cord, to the numbered caps inserted in the blast holes and crimp them, lower numbers going first and working outward from the centre as before. An electric blasting cap was tied to the B-line and an electric blast line was run out to a safe distance where the miner could set it off electrically, a much safer method.

This is an example of how a round is drilled and blasted. By blasting in sequence from the centre, the big hole gets bigger and bigger until the whole round has gone and you have a nice pile of muck (ore) to show for your efforts.

Crushing & Conveying: An Underground Ore Factory

Once the round is pulled, what do you do with the muck? Very simply, you crush it into small pieces in the mine and then send it on to the concentrator where it is separated into its component parts. From there, the concentrates go to Trail for smelting.

Early mining at the Sullivan was conducted in the upper portion of the orebody, that is, above 3900 Level where the orebody is thickest.

(The levels were named based on their elevation above sea level. For instance, 2400 Level was deeper than 3900 Level by 1500 feet.)

The sinking of Nos. 1 and 2 incline shafts gave access to the thinner but more uniform part of the orebody below 3900 Level.

To effectively handle ore from both the upper and lower sections, a crushing and conveying system became an integral part of the Sullivan. Broken ore is extracted from drawholes and/or draw points using slusher hoists or scoop trams and is dumped into ore passes that lead to one of three crushing chambers. All ore is crushed through primary jaw crushers and secondary cone crushers, at an average rate of 450 to 500 tons an hour, from an original size of up to three cubic feet to yield a product grading 80 per cent finer than one and a half inches.

Ore mined above 3900 Level is crushed to 5-inch size in the 3800 crushing chamber. The ore is then transported via a conveyor belt to a bin where it is divided into minus 2-inch ore and plus 2-inch ore. The larger ore undergoes further crushing and then is mixed with the smaller ore and conveyed to the crushed ore bin.

Ore mined below 3900 Level is crushed to minus 5-inch in the 2850 and 2500 Level crushers. It is then moved via a series of conveyor belts from the lowest parts of the mine up to the 3800 Level crushing chamber, where it is crushed to fine pieces.

The main conveyor system at the lower level is a series of seven conveyor belts totalling over 5000 feet in length and covering an elevation gain of 1380 feet on a 17-degree incline.

From the 3800 Level crushing chamber, all ore passes into a crushed ore pocket where it is loaded onto electric trains, each carrying approximately 600 tons, for transportation to the concentrator on the surface nearly four miles away. The first half of the trip is underground, along the 3700 Level adit, which is the main haulage tunnel for crushed ore, and the remainder is on the surface.

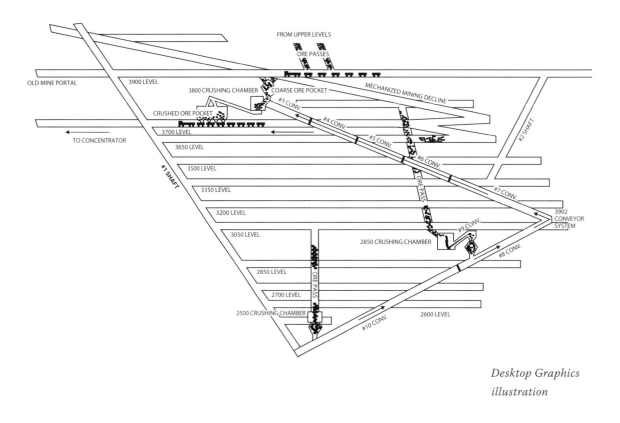

Desktop Graphics
illustration

THE DRILLER'S TROUBLES

B.A. Price, 1917

The ground is as hard as the devil,
The steel won't cut at all.
The smith knows a lot about temper,
The boss ought to give him a call.

One piece is so hard and brittle,
The next one's soft as lead.
If he don't give us stuff we can work with
I'll bend a length over his head.

My partner blocked up like a farmer,
The bar's coming down by the feel.
The air hose water is leakin',
And I'm most wet as a seal.

The machine takes oil like a furnace
And blows it all over the face.
Some son-of-a-gun has swiped my wrench
And left a bum one in its place.

We'll never get the round in by tally
It's a cinch that the shifter is sore.
If the muckers had gotten the dirt out,
We'd have finished it long before.

The powder and caps are rotten.
The fuse is a genuine fake.
The air is chock full of water
And the blasted ground won't break.

There's no need in sweatin' your life out.
This job is awfully tough.
So I think its time to taper off,
I guess she's deep enough.

MINERS' STORIES

HARRY "RED" FOSTER

Hello, this is Red, and I'm smiling at you...

I'm sure when Red woke up in the morning he was already laughing. He wasn't a big man physically — maybe five feet six inches and 150 pounds — but his sense of humour and his smile were huge. "Hello, this is Red, and I'm smiling at you" is how he would answer the telephone, no doubt a telemarketer's dream. He smiled all day long.

Red was a storyteller. He loved relating the past to me, including stories about people and situations in Kimberley that I dare not pass along, stories he would share only if I turned off the tape recorder. We would sit at the kitchen table and roar with laughter, taking care that the missus couldn't hear. But when he talked of tragedy, he was very respectful. I could sense the emotion when he spoke of those times.

Red took the job of mining very seriously. He worked in the Sullivan until he was forced to go on pension at the age of sixty-five, but he would have worked underground until the day he died if the Company had allowed it. As it happened, he did work for Cominco after retirement when the Company hired him to go to Greenland as a Supervisor/Instructor at the Black Angel Mine. As a pensioner, he also had a drilling and blasting business on the side. Basements, roads, smoke stacks, whatever you wanted blasted, he would do it. Red had the oldest blasting certificate in British Columbia and the second oldest in Canada. It's hard to find anyone nowadays who used black powder for blasting, as he did.

Hundreds of Kimberley residents remember Red as the man who taught them to square dance when they were children. For many years, Red and his wife Winnifred held square dancing classes in McDougal Hall. At Christmas, he would don a Santa suit and put smiles on the faces of a lot of children as he and his trusty elf, George "Haggis" Williams, made their rounds of homes in town.

Red was a phenomenon. Once you met him, you never forgot him. Certainly he wouldn't forget you. To me, he was the ultimate miner and one of the inspirations for this book. Maybe when I'm about to croak, I'll pass along those stories that didn't make it on to the tape.

I started in the mines in 1920, in Staffordshire, England, when I was thirteen. The age limit them days was thirteen. The age limit had changed after World War I [1914-18], as it was twelve during the war. The young miners had to wear a badge on their jackets saying that you were under age. This rule came from the Coal Mine Federation.

When you first went into the mines you had to be initiated. The old guys would grab you and down came your pants. They would have a rag with that black axle grease and smear it all over your private parts. You couldn't get it off at the mine because there was no such a thing as a shower at the mine. You had to wait until you got home to wash it off, but that's how you got initiated. Everybody went through it. That was seventy years ago.

English Coal Mining: Horses & Orphans

So two days after my thirteenth birthday, my job was to hook up cars to go to the surface. Each of these cars held 800-weight of coal. I would hook up four cars at a time, so that was 3200-weight of coal going up a 900-foot vertical shaft, and the hoist never stopped for anything.

When you went down in the morning, they put gates on the cars, eight men to a car, so that was thirty-two men going down each trip; only one stop, 900 feet down, and these skips was moving. The officials were already down. These were the fire bosses.

The fire boss would go into the working places and check for methane gas before anybody was allowed to come down. He would put his initial and date on the timbers to signify that this area was checked. These fire bosses put in long hours. They were there before anybody else and were the last people out of the mine. These fire bosses were recognized as the best underground and it was a privilege to be one. When the fire bosses were finished, they would put the gates on the cars so the men could start to be lowered from surface.

When the men were all lowered, the gates would be removed and coal would be starting to go up. Once emptied at surface, they would be sent back down, loaded with brick, mortar and lime. This was used for building material. The hoists never stopped.

This one morning, I brought a pit pony up to hook up six cars loaded with brick, mortar and lime. It was 8:30 in the morning and I got this goddamn lime in my eyes. It was burning the shit out of me. They wouldn't stop the skip from hauling to take me to the surface. I finally got out around lunchtime. They took me to the office where I sat for most of the day waiting for the goddamn ambulance. It was after four before it showed up. It was horse drawn and took me to the hospital. There was no such thing as first aid at the mine to look after you. Them bunch of bastards them days didn't care a bloody damn about the workingman, even a kid like me. I never saw daylight for two bloody weeks in that hospital.

But you never squealed, no, never squeal. They wanted to know what happened. I never told them that me and this other kid was throwing this wet lime at each other. We balled it up like snowballs and was having a snowball fight. That's how I did it, but I never squealed. The foreman asked me how it happened. I just told him that a car came off the track and I got splashed in the eyes. You couldn't tell him the truth because he would fire you, but he knew us kids was horsing around. It was hard to get a job them days and we needed the money at home. My father was killed in the mines in 1910 and my mother was left with six kids to bring up, God bless her.

I was making four and six pence for a seven-hour day, but it involved eight. We worked from seven till two on day shift, and on afternoon shift we went down about five, but that didn't include the time you were on the skip, only when you were at the face and had started working. You would work until two minutes to quitting time. We never went by the watch. We went by signal, an air horn. The signals for the skip were: one to stop, two for down, three for up, four for travel with men on board — you would get off at your level and walk to your job — five was for fire boss on board, six was for snacktime or lunchtime, seven for quitting time, and eight for cars off the track in the incline. There was a guy called a rail dog, whose responsibility was to get the cars back on the track as fast as possible. It usually took five or six guys to help him to get a car back on the track. These inclines were thirty degrees, so we had to be careful when we went out into the incline to catch a ride out if we were early, because the cars were moving right up until the signal came to start hoisting the men to surface. Them cars were just missing us by inches, they were.

When I got to go mining at the face, we worked on a 50-yard face. It was called a long-wall face, with a 25-yard wall on each side of us. This one time, the wall came down on a guy called a methane chaser. His job was to keep the methane gas ahead of the guys working the ribs or sides by means of blowing air into contaminated areas. I was working with this guy at the time. I must have been about sixteen. He died as a result of the cave-in.

The tools we used were picks, rakes and shovels. We wore kneepads in the small headings [work faces] off to the side of the incline. These were usually five, six feet high at the most. There was about six inches of dirt in the middle. What we would do is take out the bottom half, which was two and a half feet, using our kneepads or working on our sides, picking and shovelling. The guy at the face would push the coal to the guy behind him and that fellow would drag it out on a sled to the incline and load it into the cars provided for us.

We would go in twenty-five yards and timber as we went. The top coal above the dirt seam was worth more than the bottom half so as we went out twenty-five yards, we would knock out the timbers and let the back cave to where we had undermined. We would mark the cars that this was top coal, and we got a little more money for it. We did this for a thousand yards in and a hundred feet up. We left a 10-foot pillar to the workings above us.

There was no such thing as electric fans. All we had was compressed air blowing through steel pipes for ventilation. The heat down there was fierce and the noise from the blowing air was so bad that you couldn't hear anything going on around you, just as well at times.

At the end of the shift, the streets would be full of guys coming off shift and heading to their houses. There was usually a tub of hot water in the kitchen where you would wash in the winter. In the summer, you would wash in the backyard. You really looked forward to that tub of hot water in the winter because by the time you got home, your clothes would be frozen to you because you sweat like hell at the face. Hell, we never wore long underwear. It would have been too hot. All we wore was an old jacket and scarf around our neck. You were numb by the time you got home.

We didn't have hardhats them days. All we had was ordinary street caps. For lights, all we had was safety lamps, nothing like now where you have your light on your head. You would just hook the safety lamp on a timber so you could see. If it went out before lunch, there was a guy that would come along and light it for you. That was his job. If your light went out after lunch, you would just have to work with what light you got from your partners. It was a real bastard.

I was about nineteen and I was working as a face miner for this contractor, a big Irish bastard. The back [roof] behind us was working; it was snapping and popping, and three or four times I took off running. That Irish son of a bitch told me, "You run when I run, and not until." Him being a contractor, we had to work steady because we only got paid by how much coal we got to surface. This one day, the back came down. It covered a large area. Four guys got it. I could see him waving his arms and his big ass running. That was good enough for me. I took off after him.

We had to wait about ten minutes for the skip to come and get us and take us to surface. When we got to surface, he says, "Where's your goddamn box of tools?" I told him that I had left them there. "You know that I gotta pay for them so I expect you to dig them out tomorrow or you're going down the road kicking horse turds, my young bucko," he tells me. It took a lot of digging, but I did manage to find them. I gotta tell you, I was real nervous being there where those four guys bought it.

The horses came up to the surface for one week a year. There were about ninety horses in the mine I was in. They were well treated underground. They were fed molasses, good feed and somebody always made sure they had fresh water. They came up the first week of August and that's when we got a week off for holidays. When you got them to the surface, you would take them over to the pasture and turn them loose. It was something to see. They would run and buck, roll on the ground, fart, the whole thing. It was wonderful to see. These horses were a little bit bigger than a Shetland pony but they would last about ten years underground.

I had this old horse. His name was Boss. Oh, he was a good horse. He used to pull those six cars like a racehorse. One time somebody put seven cars on. When old Boss took up the slack he could tell by the sound of the six chains that there was an extra car on. That old son of a gun just stopped until that car was taken off. Everybody tried to fool him, but you couldn't.

When I first started in the mines in England, I talked to a lot of the oldtimers and they told me how they got into the mines. There was always a church near the mine that had an orphanage. Miners would go to the orphanage and pick out a kid around eleven or twelve and take him into the mine. If he were any good, they kept him, and if he wasn't, they would send him back. The ones they kept they had complete control over until they were twenty-one. The kid got to work on the face and learned how to mine, but he got no wages. The kid lived with a miner in his house. It was nothing but slavery. Most of the miners were deeply religious, even though they kept the young kids as slaves. Them churches were nothing but a bunch of hypocrites. A miner them days was allowed a pint of beer a day underground, but if they got caught swearing, his beer was cut off. But treating kids as slaves was all right. Jesus Christ, what a bunch of bullshit that was.

The coal miners had a background. They liked to sing, sing hymns, while they were working in the mine at the face. There were always three or four guys harmonizing. It sounded wonderful. It was said that during the week they were too tired to screw and on the weekend, too drunk to screw.

Speaking of coal miners, Bill Fraser was a guy that came from Alberta. I guess when they weren't farming over the winter, they would mine coal on their property. He told me they had a coal seam in a coulee where they drove a tunnel in to get at the coal. I guess the whole family got in on it.

Him and Don Elliot were working together in a slusher sub up here in the mine. They just had it all scraped out when I came into the sub to see them. Well, I looked down the sub and here's Bill on his goddamn knees, shovelling what was left on the footwall with a shovel. He was a coal miner all right. I'll never forget that. I was surprised that he didn't have kneepads. I guess he had some at home. He told me the seam of coal they had on the farm was only three foot high so kneepads were needed. He said his kneepads came in real handy when he dug out his footings for the addition he put on his house. Yeah, he was a good guy, very quiet and gentle.

Tramp Mining in Canada

I put ten years in the coal mines, five in England and five in Canada. I came to Canada after I came back from Australia, 1930. When I first got here, I landed in Vancouver and went to Calgary. A guy that had a boxcar load of sheep hired me on. I told him that I had worked with sheep in Australia and he hired me on the spot. I was a sheepherder for all one summer. It was a goddamn good job but when winter came, now that was another story. I had never experienced any weather like that in my life. It was time for me to move this little English ass. I quit, and moved on.

In 1930, I rode the rails to the gold mines around Kirkland Lake [Ontario]. I got a job there at Teck Mines. I was making about $3.50 a day. There was no union, and the workers would bribe the bosses to try to keep their jobs. Then there was the timekeeper who was taking money from the men, but they fired him. I just wanted to get paid for what I did. There were a lot of foreigners coming in and they were afraid for their jobs so, just out of fear, they paid these bastards off. One thing about these foreigners, their countrymen would take them in and stake them to a job. The Canadians wouldn't do that.

I put in around six months there and got the hell out of there as fast as I could. I couldn't believe how they treated men there, just like dirt. I don't think I have ever seen so many assholes in one place.

When I was hoboing, after I left Kirkland Lake, I got talking to some guys along the way and they asked me if I knew a guy named Bob McKelvey, who was the mine manager at the Little Long Lac Mine [gold mine near Geraldton, Ontario], and by God I did. So I went down to see him and see if I could get a job. Them trains that I was hoboing on would be a mile long, with maybe 400 fellows on it. I used to carry all my mining gear with me in a little pack. I used to take my hobo clothes off when I went into town and put on my going-to-town clothes.

When I got to the mine, this little guy told me I would never get a job around there. He'd been hanging around for six months trying to get on. So I went into the dry [change room] and asked a miner there about McKelvey and he told me he was an underground boss. I asked what he looked like and he said, "A big guy with a moustache." I told the miner that I knew McKelvey when he was just a kid working at the mine in Kirkland Lake during the summer holidays. He asked me if I was looking for a job and he said he would see McKelvey when he came out from underground. I told him to tell McKelvey that Red Foster was looking for him. When he saw me, he said, "You little red-headed bastard. Are you still alive? I thought you would be dead by now." He called me into his office and said he was pretty busy, it was Friday, but told me to be back on Monday and he would have a job for me. He told me to bunk in the dry for the weekend and that he would get some food up to me.

When I got my job, it was to push these cars along the track in the mine. I went to work on afternoon shift, from seven until two in the morning. Jesus Christ, he put me mucking and tramming, cleaning the track and ditches. We had about five hundred feet of bloody track. There were three of us: me, a scrawny little bugger, and two great big Ukrainian bastards. We had three cars to fill and get out. We pushed them by hand, which wasn't too bad. The drift ran at two per cent so the water would drain. We would go to the station and switch the cars. They'd go first and I would come last.

Well, I had been hoboing and hadn't eaten too good for two weeks and wasn't in good shape. By the time I got to the station, they were waiting for me. Their cars were empty and they were ready to go back in again. Christ, I had to stop quite a bit because I was so bloody weak. I had these big boots on and had worn holes in my socks. If they had given me a job just mucking, I'd been a lot happier. I stuck with the job for three weeks and then I got called in the office and was asked if I'd like another job. McKelvey said, "I'll give you a job mucking in the stope." I said that I'd take it. I said, "In all my life, I've never backed down on a job, and I got to do it this time 'cause I haven't been eating too well. I've been on the road and haven't been eating too well so I'm pretty weak. Thanks, I'll take the job." He and I grew to be the best of friends.

I left Ontario and ended up close to Estevan, Saskatchewan. I had heard there was coal mines there and that there was a good chance I would get on, being an experienced miner. So I moved on to Estevan. It was piss poor there too. I didn't do too bad because I was a face miner, getting top money. You know that song "You Load Sixteen Tons"? Well, it was like that.

I've seen guys come in there, farmers ya know, this was the Dirty Thirties, remember, and it was damn harsh. These poor buggers were making nothing. I was single so I was lucky, but these guys had families, and this was a real miserly, god-awful company to work for, so what the hell do you do? They had you by the short ones, the bastards.

It was room and pillar mining. There were usually twenty-five guys working in a room. You got forty-nine cents a ton, and you bought your own powder, blasting caps, fuse and carbide for your lamps. You had to load two-ton cars. You would put a little extra on the sides for weight at the scales.

I've seen some of those poor bastards who come in to dig coal rent a house for two dollars a week, eight dollars a month, from the company. This would be a four-room house. You got the electricity for nothing, and you weren't allowed to take coal from the boxcars. You were allowed to take the crap coal from the slag heaps for two dollars a ton. You loaded it and took it home on your own with wheelbarrows, in bags, any way that you could.

In the spring, if you owed the company money, you could make extra money by going down in the mine after shift and clean up the horse shit between the tracks. The big-hearted bastards would allow you to take it home and put it in your gardens. Big deal, eh? Some guys couldn't quit because their wives were pregnant, and the company had a medical plan. Jesus, they had you coming and going.

There was two guys, John Kerr and Joe Cole, crackerjack miners they were. They would go down in the mine after shift when nobody else was in the mine and shovel coal. They made forty-nine cents a ton and the company made six dollars. God, could they shovel. One month, they made ninety dollars clear. Some of those poor bastards were only getting two cars a shift, and if you didn't have enough out by the tenth of the month, you were fired. Then the company cops would kick you out of the house. They were a heartless bunch of bastards. And people wonder why there are unions.

The riot in Bienfait, a coalfield close to Estevan, was the reason I came west. Them goddamn mine owners were real pricks. They treated the workingman like dirt. We were trying to get a union in so we were called Reds, Commies, and all that stuff. Hell, most of the guys had no idea what a Commie or a Red was, just trying to be treated like a human being, that's all.

Old Harvey Murphy, he was organizing up in the Crowsnest area for the United Coal Workers of America. He told me some years later that he knew some of the guys that were trying to get us organized, Ivan Belange and the McLean brothers. These guys were labelled as agitators, that was the word them days, agitators, and they were blacklisted from the mines.

The mine I worked at, we decided that we wanted our own weighman at the collar, alongside the company weighman, to weigh our coal at the scales. There's no way we could trust the bastards to pay us what we had coming. So we hired one of the McLean brothers to be our weighman, and he was to be paid by us and not the company. We paid him two cents a ton. Jesus Christ, he was only there two days before the bosses got the Mounties to kick him off the property and throw him in jail for trespassing. What a chicken shit bunch of bastards. Big Ivan called a meeting and we all showed up and put enough money together to get McLean out of jail.

The mine owners had big-time lawyers working for them. Christ, we couldn't afford a lawyer, even a bad one. It was pretty much us against the world at that time. Everybody was against us: the owners, the politicians, the police. It was like we were no one, not even part of this country. Not nice times at all. We were only making about two bits an hour, and them bloody mine owners did every underhanded thing they could to stop us from getting organized.

So we all got together, all the miners, and marched up the main street of town [September 29, 1931]. The bloody mine owners called out the fire truck and had their men turn the hoses on us. Then the Mounties on horses came down from the other end and got us in the middle. Christ, these bloody Mounties were brought in from the training depot in Regina, in boxcars, along with their horses. It was like the mine owners were the only Canadians there. Well, this big Irish guy rushes the fire truck, jumps up on the cab, rips his shirt open, and yells at the cops, "Shoot, you bastards. Shoot."

And you know what? The bastards did. They killed three of us and shot up a lot of other guys. Killed the Irish guy. This was not one of the RCMP's finest moments.

Bienfait was the centre of the mining area at the time and if you go there today, you can see where they buried the three guys that were killed, all in one big grave. There's a great big tombstone, and on it were the words "Murdered

By The Mounties." Some embarrassed big shot had the word "Mounties" taken off so what's on there now is "Murdered By The" and a big yellow streak down it. The miners in that area will never forget that terrible time.

Just after the strike there was a bunch of us sitting around in the bunkhouse, just bullshitting, and in came the bloody Mounties. They started pointing at different guys, "You, you, and you. Outside, now," and started pushing them outside and questioning them, and not too gently either. A lot of guys were deported to Duck Lake [Saskatchewan], the guys they figured were the leaders, and some were sent back to Ireland where they came from, all at government expense.

Yeah, that song "Sixteen Tons of Number Nine Coal" really summed up what it was like. You would go up to the mine in the morning in your diggers — work clothes — and stand at the gate of the mine. If there was a long whistle, it meant there was work; a short whistle, you went home 'cause there was no work. You would come back at noon and do the same thing. After the strike, we got thirty-three cents an hour. That was if you were on straight day's pay, up from twenty-five cents. If you were a miner working at the face, you got paid only forty-six cents a ton, so you really had to move your ass to make any money. Most of the time we were only working two days a week.

I left the coalfields of Saskatchewan and headed back to Ontario, where I worked in different hard rock mines for about five years. I was top in seniority, shift-bossed for a couple years, but, hell, I wanted the hell out of there. Living in them bloody camps away up north just didn't appeal to me, nothing to do but sleep and work. It was the shits.

The war [World War II] was well on by now. This was 1943. I heard they were looking for miners out west, particularly coal miners. [Miners in Canada were exempted from military service during the war.] I sent a letter to the Selective Service Board and told them of my interest in getting a job in a coal mine. I got a letter right back from them telling me to be in Coleman, Alberta, on June 11. I wrote back and told them I needed a holiday to go spend some time with my young family. They didn't care. They sent a letter right back with the train fare. The board also sent a letter to the mine manager where I was working at the time, instructing him to lay me off so I could make haste to Alberta. The mine manager called me to his office and told me I was laid off at the end of the week but that he would pay me for two weeks' work. He asked me if I liked shifting. I told him that I didn't care for it, and that I would rather be back on the face, working with the guys. I wasn't meant to be a supervisor.

When I got to Coleman, the board sent me to Michel. This was where I was going to work, at one of the many mines there. I was hired on by old Barney

Caulfield. He told me that I was to be working on the timber gang. I told him that I got a family coming from back east and that I was going to need a place to stay. I told him I would like to find a place in Fernie because I didn't like the looks of Michel. He told me that wouldn't work because all the buses were full, no room.

Barney told me to go down by the Michel Hotel and go across the creek where there was a bunch of company apartments. So I go down and have a look. Jesus Christ, the walls were knocked out, no windows, filthy, just like a goddamn pig pen. Christ, he told me I could have my choice of the ones that were empty. There was no way I was putting my family in one of these places. Oh shit, I was mad. I marched up to the company office looking for him. "Where is that little son of a bitch?" The office people pointed down the hall. When I found him, I slammed my fist down on his desk. "Look, you sawed-off little bastard, if you think I'm moving my family into one of those goddamn pig pens, I'll refuse to work here, and that's the way it is." Jesus, he lived in Fernie.

So I was staying in the Michel Hotel, sharing a room with some big Italian guy. I was up in the room, sitting on the side of the bed, asking myself what the hell am I doing here. About one at night, a train comes in, right across from the hotel. I started packing. The Italian guy looks up from his bed to see what the hell I'm doing. I told him to tell the hotel manager that I would send what I owed him, two lunches and a one-night stay. I went to the caboose at the end of the train, introduced myself to the trainman, and asked about

Red Foster, second from right.

catching a ride to Cranbrook. No problem, he tells me, so I get on and make myself comfortable. He says he'll appreciate the company.

The Sullivan: A Beautiful Mine

When I got to Cranbrook, I went and made my presence known to the Selective Board. Well, they gave me shit and told me to get back to Michel, and the stipulation was that anybody that had worked in a coal mine in the last ten years has to go back. I told them I had been working in hard rock mines the last few years and wanted to try getting on in Kimberley, at the Sullivan Mine. The Selective guy says, "How about working at Michel until the fall and if you find a job to go to, go ahead and take it." I said fair enough, and that's what happened.

I think the guy that hired me was Doug Campbell, in the fall of '43. The first few days they had me nipping, pipe fitting, little bullshit jobs. I could see that this was a beautiful mine, compared to the ones I had just come from. The jobs they had me doing were not what I had in mind. So I told them I had hired on as a miner, not a nipper. The foreman told me that some guy had gone home and wasn't going in that goddamn place again and he sent me to see Pop Dietz, he was shifting down on the first level, and that he would put me to work.

Old Pop took me into this heading where there was this raise to drive at seventy degrees. Well, I had to set up a liner on a bar. Those goddamn liners weighed 150 pounds. The hardest part was getting the liner up high enough to drill the goddamn back-holes and packing steel up to the set-up. We used special steel for a six-inch change.

Miner's bar and arm in a raise using a hand crank.

That's all we were getting, six bloody inches to a steel, Jesus, Jesus. It would take us three to four shifts to drill a five-foot round and blast it. We were in that chert rock, one of the hardest rocks known. That chert would take the gauge right off the drill steel so when you put in a new steel, it would bind in the hole. Christ, it was a pain in the ass. We were always packing in new steel and packing away used ones. It wasn't like today, where all you pack is the bits

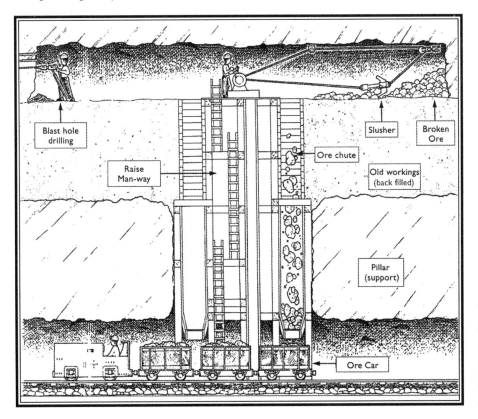

Traditional method used to remove ore from a stope.
Sunshine Precious Metals Inc.

for the steel. Hell, no, them days the bits were part of the steel. Jesus, it was hard work, especially when you had to pack it a hundred or so feet up a raise. But, God, I loved every day of it.

I worked in the stopes just the odd shift. They were only working the stopes on Saturdays. Old Jock McClaren, he asked me on a Friday if I wanted to come out the next day, which was Saturday. I told him that I would come out, providing he doesn't put me in no stope. Old Jock asked me why I didn't like being in the stopes. I said, "I don't work in the stopes because you have to use those goddamn liners and tripods. They're just too bloody slow." Old Jock says to me, "You'll never make a miner." I says to him, "You can't tell me

I'm no miner. I can out-mine you and most of the bloody guys here." He had me mad. I worked a few shifts in the stopes just to show him that I could do it, but it was just too bloody slow for me.

I got a phone call from old Jock one day when I was at home. He wanted to know how I would go about starting up a new stope. I says, "Why don't you go up to the mine and ask one of those know-it-all engineers how to do it?" He says, "I can't, Red. I'm in Vancouver with all those know-it-all engineers, and one of them gave me your number and told me to phone you." I guess that straightened him out whether I knew how to mine or not.

They wanted to know how we mined in the stopes in the old days, so I told them. I told them that first you had to drive the drawhole, then drive the raise out of it. You start drilling in the chert and when you hit ore, you started opening the raise up wider and into turn-backs, and on the last turn-back you would hit the footwall, and then drive it up to the hanging wall. Then you would start slashing the sides out to fifty feet wide. When you got that first lift drilled off and blasted, you would go to the other side and take the other lift. While one guy was drilling, his partner would be scraping the blasted round. You couldn't see a goddamn thing with all the fog and dust. Crazy bastards, we were.

When we were barring in the stopes, we used three 20-foot ladders. These were special-made ladders, ya know. They were made of two by four and had no knots in them, select timber, all of them specially dressed. They had a colour code painted on them, which was red. These ladders were painted red for four feet at each end. Nobody else was allowed to use them, except barmen in the stopes. You would put them together with a four-foot overlap. You were only allowed

A.K. Bond (top) and unidentified partner barring down the back in a stope. Note ropes supporting the ladders. Barmen made 25 cents an hour more than anyone else.

– 32 –

to go three ladders high, forty-eight feet straight up. Each ladder had four ropes tied to those wedge eyebolts in the wall of the stope. I really liked doing this. Hell, you were making barman's pay and nobody pushed you. You took all the time you needed. It was your life and everybody realized that. Hell, there were ropes all over the place.

I went up this ladder one day with a 10-foot scaling bar. When I got to the top, there was this great big crack! just above my head and I couldn't get down that ladder fast enough. The big fear, besides having a slab fall directly on you, was that it would hit one of your ropes and throw you off. Sometimes when a rope got hit, you would just wrap your arms around the ladder and hope you don't get knocked off, and that the other ropes would hold. You got one hell of a ride on her.

I just come here when Murph Wells got blasted. I think what happened was that some guys were slushing higher up, and had drilled and blasted some large muck. One of the shots, with cap and a stick of powder, fell into the chute Murph was pulling and went off, blinding old Murph. I don't know if he was lucky or not. He's been blind for fifty years but, boy, did he ever adapt, using machinery and building things, making cabinets for Christ sake, and quality work.

Christ, this one time we were on afternoon shift, it was around ten. We were all sitting on the coaches in the old timber yard back of 92 Drift, waiting to go out. The shifters had already gone out. Somewhere away up above us, where they were backfilling, a bulkhead got taken out, and behind the bulkhead was hundreds of thousands of gallons of water. You should have seen the goddamn water. The bloody water was coming down 100 Drift and it was coming so fast that it never took its time to go down No. 1 Shaft. It shot past the drift to the shaft and headed down the main line. Nobody knew what the hell to do.

Johnny Hume, who was on the motor pulling the coaches, put it in gear and away we went. When we got to 124 Shops, we had to stop. It had bust all the planks off the sidewalks and we couldn't go any further. The water was coming over the coaches. Some of the guys jumped off and landed in the ditches. We walked to where there was no water because it had all gone down the main line and got out another way. Some guys did go out on the main line and they said they beat the water. They run faster than the water was coming up. It would have been a real bastard if the water had gone down No. 1 Shaft instead of going all the way outside, about seven thousand feet from where it started. There would have been a wall of water at least six feet high.

The 3900 haulage drift and 124 shops area. Ore train on left and shops on right, including drill shop, mechanical, electrical and car repair.

Water took a few guys over the years. There was Hap Richardson and young Brown. They went up this raise where I had been working. I took about three rounds out of it, and on the last round, I had to blast the cut over the face and it went into the backfill. Anyway, Hap and young Brown had been up the raise to do some surveying and were coming down when the backfill broke through. Hap got hung over a pipe and young Brown went right down to his death, around a hundred and fifty feet. They tell me when they found him he didn't have a stitch of clothes on him. The water pressure and backfill just tore them right off him.

We had another up on the 4600 Level. There used to be an incline that took you up, then there was another incline cutter that came down at what we called the Top Mine. Old Dave Erickson and Frank Lafortune, they were up on that goddamn gravel chute and they had been sitting there and they didn't know the water and gravel was coming down the chute. When it broke through, Dave Erickson got killed. Frank got down into the drift and ran quite a ways into a dead end. He never had a lamp. Some guys that were working close by heard the noise and went to investigate. They found one hell of a mess. They happened to go into the drift and they heard Frank hollering, so they went and found him. He was scared because the water was building up. Hell, you can imagine what it would have been like without a light. I was up there later, cleaning up the mess with a mucking machine, and I found a lamp belt broke off with the battery still on it, and I don't know if it was Frank's or old Dave's.

Old Hardrock [Alec MacDonald], he was something. He used to wear his hardhat right down almost over his eyes. It looked like he had no hat liner in it. You could hardly see his eyes. And his breath, boy-oh-boy-oh-boy, that was something else. It would make your eyes water. You tried not to stand too close to him when he spoke. Thank Christ it wasn't very often. I changed beside him in the dry for years and he never spoke to me out there; in fact, he never spoke to anyone.

He used to dress beside me in the dry and he never put dry clothes on. Just Monday morning he had dry clothes, only because they had all weekend to dry out. He would just throw his wet clothes in the bottom of his locker when he came off shift and never give them a chance to dry out. Just wouldn't hang them up to let the air circulate. Nope, couldn't be bothered. Every morning he would put on those damn wet clothes and go to work.

One time I was working with Hardrock in this backfill sub. There was water coming off the face and he was digging a trench for the water to run down. The goddamn face caved in while I was back at the hoist. All this water and mud just exploded from the face and picked up Alec and pushed him down to the muck pile. He was buried up to his shoulders and giving me shit to hurry up and get him scraped out. I couldn't use the scraper because of where he was, so I had to dig him out with a jenny. All the time he was giving me shit to hurry so nobody would see him like this. I finally got him dug out.

He had a big cut on his cheek where he had hit an eyebolt. I told him that he had better go to first aid and have it looked at. He didn't want to go but he went. He was on the coaches when I got there as it was the end of the shift and we were ready to go home. He had this big bloody bandage on his face and he was madder than hell 'cause everybody going by was commenting on it. You know what he did? He ripped all the bandages off before we got outside so the guys waiting to go underground wouldn't see it. God, he was a tough old bastard, just didn't want anybody to see him hurt.

Dick Shannon had just been made a foreman when this barman that was working for him fell down a raise and got killed. Fell a hell of a long ways. This guy was working with Joe Shaw. The way I got it, this guy got his scaling bar stuck and was trying to fish it out or some bloody thing and lost his balance and away he went, away down the raise over a turn-back and landed on the muck pile.

Dick told me himself, he did, that he went down on ropes to recover the guy. I guess the raise was a 70-degree one, with muck stuck on the sides. When he got to the guy, he tied a rope around him and then tied it to himself. He pulled himself and the dead guy up the raise using only the hand rope and footwall steel, up and over the turn-back. Christ, muck was falling off the sidewalls and footwall. He told me he was scared. He said he was telling himself that he was nothing but a stupid old bastard all the way up the raise. But it was too late to stop now. He had to finish the job, and he did. Nothing but guts.

Just after old Dick had done this, Diamond, the president of CM&S, had come to the mine and wanted to meet old Dick. I was shifting at the time. Jay Colthorpe, who was the mine superintendent then, brought Mr. Diamond underground to meet old Dick. We were in the shifters' shack and in comes old Dick. Jay Colthorpe calls Dick over and says, "I want you to meet Mr. Diamond." Mr. Diamond puts his hand out, "How are you, old Dick?" Nothing. Then he said it again, "How are you, old Dick?" and Dick said, "I'm just bloody fine," and walked out. I'm thinking to myself, Jesus H. Christ, what a miserable old bastard. The president of the Company comes to see you and congratulate you for a brave act and you don't have time to talk to him. Some guy he was.

I was working for McQuarrie, along with old Hardrock as my partner, and we started that 3901 Shaft. Hardrock was in a big sub running a mucking machine and I was to scrape the muck to him so he could load the cars.

When we went in, Hardrock says to me, "Foster," he says, "There's gonna be no highballing in here." And I said to him, "Christ, if there's no money to be made, I won't highball it either, but I will if there's money to be made." So we started going. I'm scraping like hell and Hardrock is loading cars like a son of a bitch. Pretty soon, we could see that we could make some good money here. The next thing I see is old Hardrock picking up a big bloody twelve by twelve and hauling it up to where we're going to be placing it. I says to him, "Holy Christ, you don't have to do that. We got a goddamn tugger here to do that." "I can't be bothered," he mumbles. "It takes too bloody long." He was quite a man. Jesus, we made money. Christ, we were making sixteen dollars a day over day's pay.

This one time when I was working for McQuarrie, he pulled me out of this sub I was driving and sent me to help out a bunch of guys that were spare shifters who were working in a backfill raise. There was a big push on to get this job done. This was on a Friday afternoon shift, so I go in there and find out that we were only getting day's pay. Hell, it should have been barman's pay at least, so I was losing money. At lunchtime, I go in to see McQuarrie about the pay. "This is what I'm paying you and that's that."

So Monday day shift I didn't go and see him at the start of the shift, like we would normally do, I just headed to the job. I'm up the raise when McQuarrie shows up at the bottom of the raise. I shone my light down the raise at him, and he yells up at me, "You're not going to get it, you little bastard." I says, "I'll not ask you, you potbellied old bastard." He starts climbing up the raise and yells again, "You're not going to get it, you little bastard." "I'll never ask you, you potbellied old bastard," I yell back at him. When he gets to the top, his face is red and he's puffing like a bastard. He says, "Sit down. We're going to talk." I says, "It's wages you want to talk about, isn't it?" "Yes," he says. "Look," I tell him, "I found out you were changing the spare shifters' pay to barman's pay but not mine. That's nothing but discrimination and that's that. Besides, I'm losing money in here and I'm really pissed off." "I'll tell you what," he says. 'I'll make it up to you someday if I get a chance. I'll make it up. That's a promise."

Oh Christ, about three months later, Nick Seredick and me were barring in this pillar and it was snapping and cracking and popping, making all kinds of loose I was barring on slid down my bar and landed right on my goddamn foot. I never thought to look at it. It was sore all right but I carried on, just trying to ignore it, you know what it's like. Old McQuarrie came in. I was limping around and he notices that I seem to be in some discomfort. "What's the matter with your bloody foot?" he asks. I tell him, "I better sit down and take my boot off." We had to cut my boot off because my foot had swollen all up. "Jesus Christ, look at your bloody foot. Why in the hell didn't you tell me about it? I want you to go and sit in the steel shop until quitting time, and if anybody asks what the hell you're doing there, you tell them I told you to stay there, and if they got a problem with it to come and see me."

The next day I couldn't stand on it, so I stayed home. I went to work

Miner barring a side wall.

the next day and McQuarrie calls me aside and says, "You weren't at work yesterday." I told him, "I couldn't make it. I couldn't even get my shoe on because my bloody foot was so big and sore, never mind stand on it." He said, "I was looking for you. Don't tell anybody but I paid you for yesterday." You see, he made it up to me like he said, even though he and I never got along. He stuck to his word. He was an old miner and knew that a guy's word is very important.

I liked the stoper. You could do a lot of work with them. The first time I saw a stoper was up in Red Lake, Ontario. That was in 1934. Them stopers had a collar on the chuck. I've never seen any since. Compared to what we had when I first went mining, they were a real godsend.

This five-machine jumbo was used in driving the 3700 Portal in the late 1940s.

My last shift in the 3700 Portal, I crushed my goddamn foot. We were pulling the jumbo out. This jumbo had two decks on it. Each deck had three jacklegs on it, six guys on it drilling at a time. As we were pulling it out, the steel truck behind it was supposed to be hooked up to the coupling on the jumbo but it some how had uncoupled. I was standing behind, in where I thought was a good place. When the operator stopped the jumbo, the steel car just kept on coming and the wheel got my foot, ran right over it. Jesus H. Christ that hurt. Sore, my God it hurt. It crushed my veins and no blood was getting through. I didn't want them to take that boot off until I got to the hospital. When they cut my boot off, my foot looked like a bloody balloon. I was laid up for a time with that, I can tell you. My square dancing was put on hold for awhile.

Did you ever see the different types of blasting that we used to use underground? Well, I'll tell you. There was black powder. In the coal mines, mostly you'd make up your own shot. You'd take brown paper and wrap it around a stick or a pipe about one and a half inches in diameter, and then tie both ends of the paper with string. You'd pack it nice and tight then you would pour the black powder in, much like one of those old muzzle-loader guns. You would push this into the drilled hole with a pipe, then tamp it in to the bottom of the hole. Then you would put in a squib about six inches long. A squib is like a firecracker with a burning time of about two minutes. You'd light that, then get the hell out of there. When you lit that, it would shoot up the barrel and set off the powder and away she goes.

Black powder is no good when it's wet so we used to put grease all over the brown paper to make it waterproof, just in case the pipe had a crack or a hole in it or got caught going in the hole. Them bloody squibs were damn expensive. They were about seventy-five cents apiece, and that was a hell of a lot of money them days, especially when we were buying our own. You'd only blast one hole at a time. Blast, hand muck it out, then do it all over again.

B-line came in around 1939 or '40. That's the first time I saw it. Then anodets came in. That was an electrical ignition system, then anoline. With anoline, you could only blast with NCN, which was a mixture of fertilizer and coal oil. You couldn't use forcite powder because it would explode before it got to the bottom of the hole, and so you wouldn't get a good blast. Some of the powder wouldn't go because it would be cut off before it got to the bottom, that's because of the sensitivity of the forcite, especially the seventy-five per cent. The forty per cent wasn't too bad. Those percentages are nitroglycerine content.

So with anoline, you would put one stick of powder in the bottom of the hole with your anoline cap in it, then blow the NCN on it. I've tried using anoline on forty per cent forcite and almost a hundred times out of a hundred, all I would get is a blue flame shooting out of the hole. With B-line, it desensitizes down to the cap. That shows you how quick forty per cent powder will go. It travels at sixteen milliseconds per foot. I gotta tell you, things sure as hell changed over my time in the mines, and for the best, 'cause now a guy can really give her hell.

Probably one of the strangest things I was ever involved in was being called to help to get this hung-up raise down. The muck had been in there so long it had oxidized. When it gets to this point, it's a real bastard to get down. The muck turns all spongy and absorbs the shot, just doesn't break worth a shit, lots of noise and dust but no action.

Luck was on our side. We had a blasting expert, who worked outside in the office, with previous military experience. This student of modern warfare came up with the idea that we were going to attack the raise using military mortars. I guess he had some success using them at the Iron Plant, knocking the build-up off the walls in the furnaces. So we set these mortar tubes up at the bottom of the raise. We didn't know where the hell to stand to set these things off. Christ, we had no idea where the shell would end up after it bounced around up the raise. When it came back down, would it get us?

What we did was we tied a string on to the trigger and went away hell and gone down the drift and let her rip. We set off four or five of them with no result. We had to go back to traditional warfare, pushing blasting buggies loaded with powder with 16-foot two by fours tied together. Jeeze, it sounded like a good idea at the time.

The last shift? Not yet

I worked until I was sixty-five. I would have worked longer if they had let me. On my last day, I went to the foreman and told him that I wanted to run a stoper on my last shift. I went with Springhill Bill. The shifter said there was a job in a slusher sub where some eyebolt holes needed to be drilled.

Well, Jesus H. Christ, I go in and set up the stoper. The foreman, Terry Bloomer, came in especially to see me drill my last hole. Well, I threw open the throttle and the bit slid off a slip and the goddamn machine landed on top of me. I'm embarrassed all to hell. I get up and start a hole and, wouldn't you know it, the bloody steel got stuck in the hole so I had to ratchet it out of the hole. When I got it out, the hoses on the drill wrapped around my leg and I was thrown to the ground again. Bloomer said, "For Christ sake, Red, put it down before it kills you." I said, "No goddamn way. I'm going to drill a hole even if it kills me." I did get a hole drilled, much to the amusement of Bloomer and Springhill Bill.

Old Dick Shannon, he told me himself that he didn't have many friends from the mine when he retired. I was retired myself by then. He told me, "You know, Foster, when I'm coming down the street, guys would cross over to the other side so they won't have to talk to me. They won't boogery hell talk to me." I said, "You know why, don't you Dick?" "Yeah, I do now but it's too late," he says. "I was probably too hard on them and they took it bad."

That son of a bitch, I worked for him when he was shifting. He had a British habit of saying to workmen, "You're no boogery good. I got somebody to replace you." So he said that to me one time, and I remembered that saying over in the Old Country and how it was meant to degrade a miner. He said it to me outside, in front of a bunch of guys, and walked away. I caught up to him and stood nose to nose with him and said, "You old miserable son of a bitch, you ever say that to me again, we'll go at it right here, and I don't give a shit what happens." He never used that again with me. Oh, he was a mean, miserable son of a bitch.

A Greenland miner at 68

On my sixty-eighth birthday, I went to Greenland for Cominco with a buddy of mine, Hound Dog Garinger. We were to be mining technicians at Cominco's Black Angel Mine. Hell, I would have gone if I was ninety.

We flew from Montreal to Denmark, then on to Sondrestrom, Greenland, on a freight plane, and this was no jet plane, just an old gas-motor thing, all the way from Montreal to Sondrestrom. This way the Company saved money. By doing this, they didn't have to pay to put us on a commercial jet to Denmark and then on to Greenland.

About the only good thing this flight had going for it was we could drink all the free beer we wanted. When we arrived in Sondrestrom we were both a little worse for wear. Being a freight plane, we couldn't land on the regular runway. We had to land away back in the far reaches of the airport. Two customs officers came on the plane and told us not to leave, and said they had ordered a taxi to come and get us. We had to stay there for four days drinking beer because of the weather.

When we left Montreal we had pretty much spent all our money on those little pay-for-view television sets that they have all through the terminal and in the bar. When we landed in Sondrestrom, I had just a few bucks left.

There was this large American air force base just across from the terminal so Hound Dog and I thought it would be a good idea to go over there and see what's going on. We walked across the runway and over to this big workshop. There was this American fellow in there working on his Volkswagen. He asked how in the hell did we get there so I told him. He said that if security would have seen us, there would have been lights flashing all over the place and people tearing about in jeeps looking for us 'cause this was a restricted area. They would have probably thought that Hound Dog and I were saboteurs and all hell would have broken out.

It was pretty damn cold. I was all muffled up, lots of warm clothes, but Hound Dog wasn't. He never complained, tough old bastard he was. Well, we ended up in this American canteen and it just happened to be happy hour, just our luck. We took a cab back to Sondrestrom with some Yanks and we all got out at a bar. We had a few drinks and then I left to go to my room.

Hound Dog stayed, he borrowed a couple bucks off me to do some gambling. He got back to the room about eight in the morning and woke me up. It was time for breakfast anyhow. He said he had had all kinds of money, broke all the guys at the table except for two darkies. He said he had money sticking out of everywhere, but lost it all. They were playing blackjack or something. He got scared that they were going to roll him, so he lost it all. I didn't know whether to believe him or not, but I was going over in that direction after breakfast to get a haircut and Hound Dog said he'd come along to keep me company. When we got there, a couple of American airmen were there. They asked him how much he got away with. He said he lost it all. One airman said, "You couldn't have lost it all. You had money sticking out of everywhere."

So it was true, and he had no money left. I ended up buying his next few meals. Easy come, easy go.

The weather finally broke in Sondrestrom so we loaded up on a helicopter and flew halfway. We stayed overnight in this fishing/canning village where they put us up in a bunkhouse. The weather forced us to stay another four days so I got to look around a bit. I really found it interesting. I never saw an Eskimo before. They didn't like to be called Eskimos. They wanted to be called Greenlanders. The Greenlanders used to come into the camp from all around the area to visit relatives and friends. We'd put them up in the bunkhouse and feed them. Nicest people you could ever hope to meet.

Out of all the windows where the Greenlanders lived hung this bag. I didn't know what the hell this was all about, so I asked. Well, it was a bag of seal meat and every once in awhile, when the urge hit them, they would haul up the bag, saw off a piece and chew on this bloody raw seal meat. It was offered to me but I never took them up on it. Being an old Englishman, I liked the shit cooked right out of everything. Nope, never went near it.

The day we landed at the Black Angel was the day after New Year's. The next day Garnet Coulter, the general mine foreman, took us into the mine to show us around. There was a guy on the jumbo and a guy at the face that was a Greenlander and right after that shift, the Greenlander disappeared. Hound Dog, John Mickelson and I were sitting in my room having a few drinks when somebody hammered on the door. It was the village Burgermeister and he was looking for this Greenlander. They were going through all the rooms looking for him. They just figured he was drunk somewhere but they never found him. They followed his tracks down to a seal hole out on the ice and that was that.

The last guy to have seen him was down at the office. He was very distraught, crying and all that. I guess from what I heard he wanted to get home to his family, these people were very dedicated to their family. Garnet wouldn't let him go, told him that he couldn't let him go, short of men or something. I guess he hadn't got home for Christmas or the New Year, so he just took off. We didn't know if he just fell through the ice because of the darkness, or did it on purpose. I guess that's something we'll never know.

I had a couple of Greenlanders working for me on transportation, hauling ore while I was shifting. This one day, they were late. The rest of the crew had already come down on the aerial tram. The aerial tram is about a mile and a half long and almost eight hundred feet above the ocean. So, Christ, I had to go back up and get them. I figured they had just slept in and were in the doghouse. So up I go, and here they are waiting for me at the station. The buggers had the nerve to tell me they were cleaning up a spill under a chute. I've been around long enough to tell when a guy has just woken up. I wasn't mad or anything, just pretended that I was.

Gondola cable stretches over the fjord from mine portal to base camp at Black Angel Mine in Greenland.
*Courtesy
Peter Klewchuk*

Man-carrying gondolas used to transport workers to the mine portal at Black Angel Mine.
*Courtesy
Peter Klewchuk*

One of the guys was Asoph and the other guy's name was Germanus. So when we were coming down on the skip, I got to bullshitting with them. I asked them how old they were. One said he was twenty-four and the other was twenty-six. I told them I was older than both of them put together. They thought I was bullshitting them when I told them that I could still out-work them. We had a good laugh about that, even though we couldn't understand each other very well. I had to write my age down on a piece of paper 'cause we couldn't understand each other. These guys were really good-natured and great workers.

These same two guys didn't show up for work one night at seven, which was starting time. They finally showed up at midnight. I had to explain to them about how important it was for them to show up at the right time. The Greenlanders had absolutely no idea or concept of time. I had to go get an interpreter and go through him to get all this done. I told him to tell them that I was going to pay them for the whole shift but not to do it again, and for Christ sake, don't tell anyone or the whole works of them would be doing it. It was really hard to be mad at these guys 'cause they're always smiling at you.

One time, there was a rock fall up on the mine side, right where we got on the gondola. This big bloody slab came off the wall and knocked the cable off the pulley on the gondola. We were in the gondola, out in the middle of the bay, about a good seven hundred feet in the air, and we're not going anywhere. With the cliffs on the other side that we were going to, the cable had so much sag in it, we were almost vertical. Besides that, there was about a forty mile an hour wind blowing. We were stuck there. Not a good feeling at all, I can tell you. There was this great big son of a bitchin' Swede, one of the people that installed the gondola. Well, he came down the cable on a man sling. He pulled himself hand over hand all the way to us. With his tools and knowledge, he had us back on track in no time. When he got done, we hauled him in with us. He was one cold Swede, I'll tell you.

When I got back to Kimberley, I heard that Garnet Coulter, our foreman at the Black Angel, was sporting a big black eye. I had just talked to him on the phone and he never mentioned it to me, but from what I heard, this big John Mickelson and he got into it. They were both supposed to come out together and I guess they had some spare time while they were waiting and got into the whiskey. Big John was an acting shift boss and worked for Garnet. And so, being a pair of bull-headed bastards, they went at it. Then again, that goddamn Garnet could really piss you off.

Tony Keane was mine manager at the Black Angel, head of the whole operation, but that's not what Garnet thought. I went to Tony one day and asked him, "Who in the hell is in charge around here?" He says, "Well, I am, Red. Why?" "Well, I thought that bloody Garnet was 'cause he's always telling me this and telling me that. Jesus Christ, Tony, I went up to the mine to get a jackleg to take down to the mill to drill some holes and old Garnet got mad at me." Tony said he would look into it for me. I guess Garnet told Tony that he's the boss at the bloody mine and don't take anything without his permission. Jesus Christ, that's the way Garnet was. Yep, as far as Garnet was concerned, Cominco had made a mistake by not putting him in charge. What a guy.

Garnet was out, gone home to Kimberley for days off. This big John was acting shift boss and was drunk on the job, drunker than a bastard most of the time. I came into the shifters' shack this one time and answered the phone. Somebody was looking for Johnny. I told the caller I didn't know where he was, but I had an idea. I used to come down on the gondola at about three in the morning. The shift was over at six. I went into the lunchroom and here's Johnny, drunker than a bastard, stumbling around. The wastepaper basket was full of bottles. What a bloody mess he was. All the other shifters were coming in to report their men off work. I told John that he best get rid of the bottles. He just looked at me and laughed and promptly keeled over and passed out. John was really a real good man, just had some problems, and being so goddamn isolated, that didn't help either.

Big John and this Greenlander by the name of Jonas had one hell of a fight one time. This John was no dummy. He had gone to university in Copenhagen and had trained as an engineer. This fight took place the night we landed. John and Jonas started out peaceful enough, just having a couple of beers and twisting wrists. This Johnny was a powerful bugger and put Jonas down just like nothing. Jonas didn't like that so he hauled off and punched Johnny in the face. Then they really went at it, wrestling, punching, kicking, a real good mix-up. It didn't bother me. I was a spectator.

Well, when it was all over, John had got the best of Jonas and we had to take Jonas to the hospital that was fourteen miles away. Boy, he was in an awful way. Big John had done one hell of a number on him. John had put the boots to him, kicked him in the nuts. Jonas spent a few days in the hospital. Nothing was said about it. Tony Keane was out on days off, so it was kept quiet.

Carl Shonsta was brought in from Kimberley to build a chute for loading ore cars underground. Carl was probably one of the best timbermen in the Sullivan at that time so his knowledge and expertise was well appreciated. They were being brought in by helicopter from Sondrestrom to the mine. The pilot landed in this village so that everyone could get out and have a leak. When the pilot landed, the helicopter was surrounded by all these Greenlanders, women, kids, dogs, the whole bloody village, all standing there chattering and talking to him. So here's old Carl standing there, looking for a place to take a whiz. There's no trees, bushes, nothing, so he takes off running, looking for a place to take a leak. Out he goes on to the tundra. He turns and, to his horror, finds the whole village running after him, the goddamn dogs, kids, the whole bloody works of them, hot on his trail. They just wanted to see what he was about. He out ran them and by the time he had relieved himself, they caught up to him and escorted him back to the helicopter, all yakking away at him on the way back.

Did you know that the Company paid the Greenlanders half the pay that a Dane got? The reason they did this was that the Danes was taxed fifty per cent of their wages, which went to Denmark, and the Greenlanders paid no tax, so that's how the Company got around that. If the Danes stayed two years, they got all their tax money back. They got leave every three months. I was talking to some of the Danes and asked them what they did with all this money. They told me that they would go back to Denmark and buy a farm, maybe a hundred acres or so, and that would set them up so they wouldn't have to do this type of work any more. They really appreciated this opportunity.

Hound Dog and I lived in the bunkhouse in separate rooms right beside each other. This one night Hound Dog and I headed off to work and when we got there, we found out that the Danes had called a strike. They were looking for improvement in wages so everybody had stayed in their rooms. Nobody else in the whole camp was at the dry ready to go to work but Hound Dog and me. John Mickelson was at the dry, he was shifting at the time, and he tells us that we should be all right because we don't belong to the union. I said that I wouldn't work within a half a mile of a scab worker and headed back to the bunkhouse. I'm an old union man and believe in them with all my heart, 'cause I've seen what it was like before they were around to protect the worker.

What the Company did while this strike was on was close the beer parlour. No beer for the workers. So this one day, Hound Dog and I were sitting in his room bullshitting each other and a knock came to the door. In came these stewards, or bull-cooks, with beer for the staff. They were told to store it in this room because this is where they had always stored it. That was before Hound Dog had moved in. They were told to store it here for safekeeping, all eighteen dozen.

You could almost see the wheels in Hound Dog's head turning. I'm sure he thought he had hit the motherlode. "Lock the door," he says. "I think they made a mistake," I pipe in. "Bullshit, quick, lock the door." "Just how long do you think it will take you to drink all this beer?" I ask. He did some figuring on his fingers and said, "Two days ought to do it." Well, Hound Dog never got a chance to drink all that beer. The stewards came back just as he was about to start drinking and they took it away, but they were good enough to leave a dozen for the Hound Dog.

When we were waiting to come out, we were sitting in the waiting room at the camp. The chopper was late. We were sitting around this oil heater, just bullshitting, drinking beer, you know. Well, I never noticed that my goddamn feet were sweating. We loaded up on the chopper and took off. We were about a half hour out when I noticed that my feet were frozen. I guess the heater in the chopper was screwed up and had kicked off and I hadn't noticed. I suppose with all that booze in me I just never paid attention but, boy, they were hurting now. We went to base and were loaded up on a bigger chopper that was to take us to our destination. You know, my goddamn socks were frozen to me in my big bloody overshoes, yet this Dane who was flying out with us, all he had on were just ordinary leather shoes. He wasn't dancing like I was. His feet never sweated. That was the trick I guess, but, oh God, my feet were sore.

All in all, the more I think about my life, it's been damn interesting. I can remember the Germans in their zeppelins flying over and dropping bombs on England by hand, and then I got to see a man land on the moon.

I remember using black powder for blasting in the mines and then using forcite, NCN and slurry, and blasting with electricity instead of using spitters to light the fuse. I can remember lying on my side to chip at a coal seam and using pit ponies to haul the coal. Then came the new drills and bits. I saw trucks and front-end loaders underground, and drills you plug into an electric connection. I've seen it all.

But most of all, I was fortunate enough to have been a miner. I got to work with some of the best people in the world. I would have mined forever if I could have.

ALF JOLIE

No safety, no toes...

Alf was a solid miner of the old school who worked hard and played hard. He worked in a lot of the main infrastructure of the Sullivan Mine, such as No. 1 Shaft and the 3700 Portal. He was close to the guys he worked with. He hunted and fished with them, and they all partied hard together. He was a good all-round miner who didn't mind helping a new miner by sharing his vast experience.

I started in 1936. There was about eight of us mucking up a cave-in just off the mainline where you go into No. 1 Shaft. We mucked that caved-in rock across to where No. 1 Shaft is now.

This was all hot-muck country, even then. I was with Pratt when he got burned. A drawhole came down in this area when we were working a sub. He went up the drawhole and it came down. At that time, all we had was ordinary boots. They didn't care what you wore them days. Pratt, all he had on was leather boots that came halfway up his ankle. They filled up with hot dust. We got his boots off and stuck his feet in the ditch that had water in it. He was hopping round pretty good, a real hotfoot.

Miners with bar and arm set up and drilling a drift round. The drill is set up on a rail car jumbo.

We were using the old bar and arm drill that was for drifting. But you should have seen this son of a bitch we had for a mucking machine. It was an Arbuckle. Jeeze, it had eleven gears, and another seven gears on the bucket. It would turn right around on you. It would go all over the place. It was the only mucking machine they had here at the time. Sometimes it would get away on ya. There was so many goddamn gears on it you couldn't stop it from spinning around once it got started. When it started doing this, you picked a space and jumped to get away from it, then ran over and turned the air off. So one guy had to stay at the air header to turn the air off when it started spinning.

We cut out all the 04 Stope storage area, and all the shops and services area, with this stuff — liners and bars and this decrepit old mucking machine. Then they gave us those hydraulic bars and arms that had to weigh 40,000 pounds. The bar was mounted on the bottom of a flat car, with big water and air lines on it. They used three steel to a hole, big steel that they sharpened at the blacksmith shop. These liners were 260 pounds. Two of us would lift them up on a ladder to put the next arm on the bar for the higher holes.

I was in that 3700 Portal from start to finish. We finally got the Eimco mucking machine. That was a good machine. They brought in the Cleveland jumbo. That was good because there was nothing really to

Two-machine jumbo in a drift with bar and arms. Note the drill is mounted on the arms.

lift. We had five drills on it. We found out it went better if we took two of the bottom drills off to give us more room because we could always drop a drill to do the lower holes. With a three-man crew, we could drill off in about two hours. We were using that big steel with the bit on the steel, and we would use up to two hundred steel in a 24-hour period. That was for one round. Then they brought in the Crag bits. Once we got the Crag bits, we could usually cycle. This was a six-foot round and we were mucking forty to seventy cars, depending if we were slashing certain areas.

When we finished the portal [main mine entrance], we drove the incline up to where the 3800 Crusher is. And then the tail track for the five ore bins, and then the switchback where they left a train. Northern Construction was supposed to do all that but when they got in, they had lots of trouble with their equipment. Old Raynor, he kept us at it just to spite Northern. He

The Eimco
mucking machine
throws muck over
top to the car
behind.

didn't like them being there and he did us lots of favours.

Then I went with Hardrock Mac-Donald. Now that was a dangerous job. They would send us to get hang-ups down. We would look a way up a raise and there would be water coming down. Christ, we would be putting four or five 16-foot ladders up there to the bottom of the hang-up. I couldn't say that I was never scared working with him. I was scared all the time. He wasn't a bit scared. Could never convince myself that I wasn't scared. He would be a way up underneath the hang-up and I would be handing the shots to him and just shitting myself. I have never worked with a man more fearless than the Rock. It's almost like he dared the muck to get him, but in the end he drank himself to death.

Then I got my toes cut off. I was on transportation. I guess it was my own fault. We used to take turns taking the last train out. Each train had twenty big cars. There were four trains going out. I was coupling up a car to the next one and I was pushing the coupling with my foot to line it up to the next one as the train was backing up and, as it coupled, my foot slipped and went into the coupling and the couplings locked. The train bumped ahead and I was hopping along on my free foot when the train stopped again, and my foot got squished again.

I had a car block in my hand and I put it under a wheel. Gerald Atkinson came down to see what was happening and I told him to get the guy on the motor to move ahead a bit, real slow, and I'd pull up on the coupling. So when I got a little slack, I pulled the pin and got my foot out. My boot was stuck in the coupling, so I got a short steel to drive my foot out. The steel toes in the boot cut all five of my toes off. They were still in the boot. Just doing it wrong. I should have known better but we've all done it, right?

I went down a raise one time to blast a big rock that we put down. I was down about two hundred feet. We never told the chute-loaders that we were going down. It was a 40-degree raise. We just came to the end of the rope and were putting the shot on it when the muck started to move. The guys on the chute were pulling it. Christ, you want to see two guys move to get to the rope before the muck dropped too far and pulled us out of the chute. We would have been a hell of a mess but, there again, we were not doing what we were supposed to. I helped pull two guys out of the chutes and it wasn't very nice. They really got hammered up.

When I started, I was making $2.75 a day. My pay cheques were around $47 for two weeks. I had one pay cheque for $100. I was working doubles in the union office. I had worked seventeen straight shifts.

But, you know, in the old days the Company always turned their back on safety. I don't care what anybody says, production was first. When we were in the 3700 Portal, Raynor would come along. I was lead man on one shift. Coulter was lead hand on his shift and Bud on the other. We never saw a shifter. I'm sure Raynor told his shift bosses to keep out of the way. If we needed something, we just phoned and it got to us. They knew we were breaking all the rules in the book. That's the only way anything got done, and that applied to everything. Let them go and if somebody got hurt, raise hell about it, and if nobody got hurt, then it was all okay.

When we were sinking the pilot shaft for No. 1 Shaft, I was making $5 over day's pay. There were four of us down there, drilling with pluggers. There were two pumps in with us, pumping the water out. Our rounds were six by six and six feet deep. When we blasted, we would muck with shovels into a V-car. It was a continuous operation. We never stopped, changed crews right on the job. It was hotter than hell down in the hole but when you came up in the winter, it could be thirty below zero, and your clothes and slickers would just go stiff as boards. We were all young then.

We worked seven days a week for years during the war [World War II]. No overtime, no time and a half, nothing. Then they gave us a silver bonus, and a metal bonus, and then they gave us a bonus for tonnage. It was a couple extra bucks. It helped. But you could see the way we worked and didn't work. If that Company wanted to make money during the war, they could have, a hell of a lot more than they did.

Every time we blasted a bench in the stopes, they would have to have barmen go up in the stopes, but the two miners went too. The barmen had to put up ladders. The miners never helped them. That was the barman's job because it was a special job. So there was usually at least three to five days barring, with two miners sitting there waiting for them to finish, rather than letting the miners go work some other heading. There were hundreds of jobs to be done but, nope, we just sat there. That was the old family way of doing things.

Since there was no bonus during the war, nobody really gave a shit, pretty slack. Day shift would go into a raise, say a 40-degree raise, and they would bar down any loose from the previous blast, set up, drill the round off, and leave it. This was all bar and arm. They would be finished by lunchtime. We would come in on afternoon shift, sit around until eight, go load up the round, put the gear away, and blast going off shift. That was the job on afternoon shift. See, you didn't need a four-man crew for one round. Each shift could easily have taken a round but, since there was no contract, nobody was pushing us. But the Company still made money. I don't know how, but they did.

On graveyard, it was boring as hell. I learned how to run every mucking machine in that mine when I was on graveyard. I got so I could run them just as well as anybody in there. Just for something to do, I would go find a drift where the mucking machine was set up and practice.

The guys that were drifting would go in and set up the mucking machine, bar down and maybe muck out half the muck pile. Mind you, they didn't have the good mucking machines either. The next shift would come in and muck out the rest of the round, but they used all short rails [train track]. They never used long rails. The long rail idea was mine. When it was mucked out, they would set up the bars and arms, and drill off the back-holes. The next crew would come in and finish drilling, and sometimes they would blast and sometimes they wouldn't. It all depended on the drill steel they had. If they hadn't made a good batch of steel, they wouldn't have time to make the blast.

We were using 6-foot rails at the time and the mucking machine was off the track all the time because they were putting the ties too far ahead of the joints and you couldn't bolt the track nice and snug. Seems you always had a gap between rails, which would throw the mucking machine off the track. So I said to Raynor when we were working in the 3700 Portal, "How about letting us use two 30-foot rails and run them up to the face and leave them when we blast, rather than putting in 6-foot as we muck?" It worked really good. Hell, we didn't even need surveyors for line. We'd just follow the rails. It worked so good. They used that idea in other mines and I got $40 for that idea. Pretty good money them days.

I guess most miners would go back before they went home, if it was at all possible, to see what happened after they blasted. Christ, we would have one foot dragging along the rail as we went through the smoke and dust to keep us going straight, 'cause you couldn't see anything. You just hoped that there was a big muck pile there. I guess you could say it was an interest in your work. Lots of times you could tell if you drilled it right. If there was two or three feet of bootleg, you could tell the cross shift what you did and maybe they should change the drill pattern.

JOHN EKSKOG

Last of the old-time foremen...

Big John was one of the last of the old-time foremen. He was a big man with a big voice, and he was a stickler for doing everything by the book. Those who didn't know him were intimidated by his presence and he would use that to get results. Over time, John and those of us who worked with him achieved mutual respect, but he did not suffer fools.

Once when I was a shift boss for him, I blurted out in a moment of exasperation, "There's one thing about you, John. You treat us all equally." "And how is that?" he asked. "Just like goddamn dogs," I replied.

I stared at that large, bald head and those frosted blue eyes, thinking maybe I had gone too far. Nothing happened, just a hint of a smile emerged along that granite jaw. No explosion, nothing. He had heard me out and respected my opinion. John was like that. He backed his supervisors and men if they could explain their actions.

He took great pride in No. 1 and No. 2 Sections. This was his domain and woe to any strays that came into his section without his permission, whether they were mine superintendents, engineers or lost packrats. The Shaft was his life.

I started in 1936. I got on with the plumbing gang. At that time, the Company used to look after all the water in Kimberley. There was no City at that time. We put in all the water lines that went down Rotary Drive, and we dug it all by hand. We had this foreman that didn't have a hand on his arm. That's the way he was born. There was five of us on his crew and he was the boss and let you know it. And if he didn't like what you were doing, he would come up behind you and hit you in the ribs with his stump. It was like being hit with a broom handle.

What he would do, and this is no baloney, he would mark up what we were expected to do. It would be ten feet long, three feet wide and seven feet deep, and that is what you dug in all day. You dug that out by hand. You had to manhandle the larger boulders out of the hole and then we had to install this galvanized pipe. I believe it was all 12-inch pipe.

The only break we got was at noon. At that time, the Company had a dairy so when the milk truck went by, it would stop and we would buy a pint of milk, which was five cents, and have that with our lunch. We were making $3.36 a day and then we had another bonus, which was forty cents. It was called a metal bonus. They said they wanted to give us something extra for the family because we were all a family. Everybody got it, the guys underground and us guys on surface.

I got sent underground in 1938, after I dug up Rotary Drive, and worked in the outside shops. I started to work for Jimmy Riddell on the 3900 Level transportation, doing clean-up. You had to muck two 6-ton cars by yourself in a shift. That takes a lot of shovels, muck that was in the ditch or under a chute. That's where I learned a few tricks on how to make the car look full, such as getting old powder boxes and putting them in the bottom of the car and then piling rock on top to make them look full. By the time I got to be foreman, I knew all the tricks.

From there, I went up to 4250 and was working for Garnet Coulter's dad. He was a real gentleman, a real gentleman. I remember one time, Al Laface, Robbie Robertson and Al Lawley and I were all working up there on transportation and when it got to the end of the month, we were scratching for muck so we could make our quota. We would go up in these slusher stopes and just about sweep them clean to get muck into the raises. We worked damn hard to make that $1.90 a car.

This one time we had no muck to pull, so old Coulter said to us to take up four cars and go up this drift and clean up this wide ditch. It must have been three feet wide. It was all this loonshit caused by the run-off from the surface. Everything was going fine until after lunch, when Al Laface and Robbie got in an argument. Things were getting pretty hot. The first thing you know, they got into a punching deal and they both ended up in the ditch. When they come out of there, they were solid muck.

It was just at the end of the shift. We had to check out at the end of the shift at the doghouse. Coulter was a real quiet man. He looked at these two guys and he said in a real quiet voice, "If there's any black eyes under all that muck or any injuries whatsoever..." He stopped and didn't say no more, but the boys knew they wouldn't have a job tomorrow. They took it pretty good and had a beer after shift. All was forgotten.

Around 1940, I got on to the mining. I started with an old Swede fellow, Anton Swanson was his name. I didn't know too much about mining so I guess he thought he would take advantage of me. We were just going to start benching in this raise to start a stope. Heck, we were up around the 4200

Level and the muck that we benched went down to the 3900 Level. So we got all set up, got the drill and tripod all hooked up, and tied ourselves to the footwall steel so we wouldn't fall down the raise. We were going to take a 12- to 15-foot high slash.

Well, I don't know, but I'm sure he could have stopped the drill steel from falling down the raise, but away it went all the way down to the 3900 Level. He told me to go to the drill shop and get another one. You've got to remember the steel and bit were all one, not like today where you bring up a bag of bits and just screw them on your steel. So away I go, down the raise on ropes and footwall steel, for a new one. So I bring a new steel up and it wasn't too long before he dropped another one. He tells me to get another one, so I did. Now you're looking at a good five hundred feet up and down. I was pissed off.

The following day, we were just starting to get going and things straightened out, and Jesus Christ if he didn't drop another steel and said I better go get a new one. This is where I said, "No way. You've got to stop that. If you want a new steel, you go get it." And you know, after that, we got to be the best of friends.

My dad told me a story about old Anton when he and Anton were working together in the Top Mine, way before my time, probably in the twenties. One day they missed him; he didn't come to work. Everybody figured that he probably just went on a drunk and probably wouldn't show up for two or three days. Nobody knew where the hell he'd gone. Jesus Christ, he shows up three months later. He'd gone to the Old Country. He just came back to Kimberley, picked up his bucket and came to work, just like that. Didn't tell anybody where he was going, when he'd be back, nothing. He just showed

Making and sharpening steel in the underground steel shop.

up and went back to work. Nobody said nothing. He never got hell but there he was, ready for work. Those oldtimers. They were something all right, bless them all.

We drove a raise from 18 Drift on 3900 Level up to 4250 Level, just behind the old blacksmith ship. At that time, we had the old B-35 liners. Those goddamn things weighed 225 pounds and we put them up on the bar. It was nothing to use between two hundred and three hundred pieces of steel to drill a round. You would get in about two feet, maybe

three feet if you were lucky. It was special steel that was tempered in the blacksmith shop. You would crank the steel up to the face and you would see a streak of fire and then you would back it off and put in a new steel. There was no ground as hard anywhere in the mine as there was there.

I went on the bar gang in 1944 until 1948 and was working down in the lower levels, which was called the West Section, which is now called No. 2 Shaft. Then I went on staff in 1949, working for Howard Raynor at the time. I stayed at that until 1961 when

Underground blacksmith shop.

I got to be spare foreman and afternoon foreman. In 1963 old Jimmy Riddell started to get sick. He had been looking after No. 2 shaft, so I was down there replacing him. On Christmas Eve of '63, Robin Porter, mine manager, phoned down underground and told me that I was now the foreman because Jimmy wouldn't be back because of his illness.

When Howard was killed, I was made foreman of all the lower levels, No. 2 Shaft and No. 1 Shaft, which I held until I retired. You look at all the foremen that were ahead of me, like Raynor, Riddell and McQuarrie. They were all good men. They did a lot of barking but they knew what they were talking about and they expected the work to be done.

John Ekskog, left; unknown; unknown; Dick Shannon, far right.

A lot of people didn't like Raynor. I thought he was a hundred per cent because I got along with him real good. The one thing I admired about him was that whatever he said, he backed it up. It didn't make any difference. He told me right from the start when I started shifting, he said, "When you make a decision, you back it up, because that's the worst mistake you'll ever make is when you tell someone to do something and something goes wrong and then you try and back out of it. They'll never respect you for it." And he was right and I stayed with that rule. I guess a lot of the guys thought I was a miserable, stubborn old bastard but that's the way it was.

All in all, the Company was a pretty good outfit to work for. I got no complaints. We were like a big family. Like in the forties, when guys were starting to build houses, you could borrow a Company truck to haul stuff. The only thing that was specified was that you paid for the driver. They wouldn't let you borrow the truck and you drive it. You didn't have to pay for the gas or oil or anything, and usually the driver was a guy you knew so he would be helping you load and unload. And you could borrow all the tools and stuff you needed. I kind of think it was a "borrow and keep" policy. Yeah, it was a good outfit.

When we got into the war years, the wages went up. But even at that, the contract was never too high until about 1944. It got better when they took the limit off what you could make because prior to that, you could only make so much money. Say you were getting four cents a ton for breaking and scraping the muck. The company would not pay you over $1.90 a day. That's all you could make until the union got in there. Then the limit was off because they were crying for the muck. The guys could really pour it on then. It gave them incentive to really give it hell. The first place where the limit was taken off was in this stope in No. 2 Shaft. This was a place the Company really wanted because of what was in the orebody, and it was a bad one to work in because the back was always caving. There was no way you could scale the back because of its height. We were using four 20-foot wooden ladders to get up there to bar.

These ladders we used were especially made. There were no knots in them, all straight grain. They were all 20-foot ladders, just for barring. When you got four ladders up, one on top of the other, you didn't want anything that would split. These ladders would have two clamps on each side, about four feet from the end, where you would slide the next ladder in. Then you would raise them with ropes. You would have ropes for every ladder in the middle and on the sides that you could tie on to eyebolts that you had drilled holes for on the sides of the stope. You would climb up there and put your legs through the rungs and you would sit up there and bar. The one thing you had to be careful of was that when you barred, the rock wouldn't hit the rope. There was a lot of barmen that died because a slab hit the rope and knocked them off the ladder. The barmen made top wages then, I think it was about $7 a day. That was big money and steady day shift.

Well, getting back to that stope, at this time Percy Bloomer was the big wheel. He came in one day and took a look around and went out. Pat McDonald and I were working for Jack Carney at the time and we were reporting off at the end of the shift. He told us Raynor wanted to see us when we got outside. We figured we were going to get shit for something. When we got outside, Raynor took us to see Bloomer. Pat and I thought, Christ, this is going from bad to worse.

When we went into Bloomer's office, he said he had a proposition for us. He said that he wanted two more barmen beside Pat and me. He wanted Frank Heistad and his partner. He said, "You know that stope you've been barring in. I figure that there's roughly a month, probably two, of work to be done in there. There's nobody that wants to work in there because they're scared, and I don't blame them one bit. There's always rock falling off the back, but we gotta get that ore out." I asked, "What's the proposition?" "Well," he said, "I would like you four barmen to take over the job and I'll set the price. You'll get your barman's pay plus whatever you can make on contract. In fact, I'll guarantee you eleven cents a ton." I turned to Pat and said, "What do you think?" He said, "What's the difference? We're in there anyhow. Let's see how much we can make." At that time, the limit had just been taken off. We talked it over with Frank Heistad and his partner and they said, "Sure, let's go for it."

Bloomer told us the price that he gave us would be there until we were finished. So we went in there and worked the first month and we made $19 over day's pay. Now, I'll tell you, that was big money. Bloomer went on holidays and this other guy took over and he cut our price in half. Well, that didn't go over too good so we started bitching to Raynor about it right off the bat. Raynor said, "Do what you have to do but don't slacken off because if I know Bloomer, whatever he said before, he'll back it up. So you're gonna be in there anyway so you might as well make some money till it's finished."

When Bloomer came back, Raynor told him that he's got four real unhappy barmen in the stope. When we came out from underground, Pat and I were talking to the cross shift about what was going on, when Raynor told all four of us that Bloomer wanted to see us. So we all followed into Bloomer's office. Bloomer said, "What's all this bitching going on?" I looked around and nobody was saying anything. I said, "In plain English, Percy, I don't like to be screwed like this. When you made a promise, I thought you would be man enough to back it up, but soon as we made a dollar, the price was cut. Yeah, we're pissed off." You could see that Percy was mad. He said, "I set the price and I didn't cut it. It was the guy that took my place and that doesn't mean one goddamn thing. The price that I told you stays until you're finished. Now get the hell out of my office."

And that's all there was to it. He was a man of his word. We finished that stope in two months and nobody got hurt.

I had a queer thing happen to me, three times it happened actually, and why I wasn't killed, I don't know. I was working as a shift boss for Raynor and we were sinking 503 Shaft. First you would get the crew down on the skip and then you would start hoisting muck that the previous shift had blasted. This was on graveyard, and Peter Reed was the hoistman. I got on the empty skip to go check on the crews. It was about three in the morning. I gave the three bells and Peter gave them back, acknowledging that a man was on the skip. I belled for 3350 when I got on and I had my lamp hanging around my neck. I hadn't bothered to put it on my hat. All of a sudden, I'm going past the 3350 Station at a good clip and right up into the goddamn dump. And you know, I knew what I had to do but I couldn't see because I had my goddamn lamp hanging down around my neck. I just reached up and grabbed the bail on the block and got my feet up as tight as I could and the skip went right through. The doors opened as if to dump muck, and then it went back down about fifteen feet. I guess he realized what he'd done. So Peter left the hoist, ran out of the hoist room and hollered up, "John, you all right? Are you there?" "Yes, I'm here. Let me down," I said. He brought the skip down to the level and I got off. He said, "I never thought. It never entered my mind." He was overwrought. These hoistmen were under a lot of pressure to keep the muck moving and it's just one of those things. I let it go and never told Raynor about it. Pete and I kept it a secret.

The second time, Walter Galt was the hoistman but this time I had my cap light on my hat so I was ready. Kept that a secret too.

Then the third time, it was a little short fart, I forget his name, never reported it again. But I was getting nervous. I didn't know if I was going to make the fourth time. We were just about at the end of sinking the shaft, and Raynor and I were sitting talking and I mentioned it to him. I told him that I didn't want it taken any further than here, between him and I. I didn't want to cause trouble because these were all good guys and it wasn't done intentionally. We didn't need mine inspectors or Company officials all involved. Maybe if I got hurt, sure, but I wasn't, so let it go.

You know, if I hadn't had my legs in the right spot, they would have been chopped off. That was the closest I ever came to meeting my maker.

All during the war, we were on six and two. You would work six shifts and you got two days off. You would work right through, short change and all. You got your two days off after six shifts but, say there was a short change, say you worked Friday night afternoon shift, you came out Saturday morning on day shift until you completed your six shifts.

Jimmy Ross and Phil Olsen were on my shift, so we had worked Friday night afternoons then went day shift on Saturday. So I got in there to check on them fairly early. Jimmy had finished barring down and old Phil was madder than hell, cussing and swearing, throwing stuff around. I said, "What the hell's wrong with your partner, Jimmy?" "Oh, he's mad at the cross shift." "What the hell have they done now?" I asked. "I'll tell you what they done," said Phil. "They put the water hoses under the machines. The first goddamn things we need and we gotta move everything just to get to them. They don't have a goddamn brain in their heads." I asked, "When was this done?" "Last night," he said. I said, "It figures. You know who was here last night?" He thought for a moment. "Well, Jesus Christ," he said. "It was us. What a goddamn cross shift we are." We were all laughing at that for awhile. It always had been the cross shift's fault and always will be, I guess. It doesn't matter who they are.

I wasn't on shift at the time when the cable broke in the pilot shaft, but I was on that run on the opposite shift. That was a fluke deal where nobody got hurt. We were driving No. 1 Shaft, extending it. The raise was going into the pilot shaft where all the muck went and then we would hoist it up above 3350.

No. 1 Shaft and Skip, capable of hauling 24 normal-sized people.

My brother Walter was down below and he rang for the skip. He took it up to the shifters' shack on 3350 and sent it back down so it could resume hauling muck. Joe Garneau was the skiptender. His job was to fill the skip and send it up to dump. He loaded the skip and sent it on its way to 3350. Then he sat and waited, and waited. The skip never came back. So he phoned the hoistman. "Where's the skip?" he asked. The hoistman said, "You should know where it is." Joe said, "I sent it up." The hoistman said, "Well, it's at the bottom of the shaft." I guess that skip went by Joe so fast he neither saw it nor heard it. All that was left was a chunk of metal at the bottom. They never figured out why it broke. It was almost at the dump. Must have been a flaw in the cable. But I almost lost my brother that day. Just fate.

One incident I remember was when Carl Hansen and Jackpine were barmen and they were working for me in the lower section. Howard Raynor came to me one day and told me about this place where there was this sub with a short raise at the end. He told me he wanted to set up a diamond drill in the raise to take core samples. He said that the raise had been idle for quite awhile and there was probably low oxygen in there. He told me to send in the barmen and for them to take hoses in there and hook them up to the pipe and blow air up there so we can get in there the following day. I said I would do this, but there again, oldtimers, these old guys probably didn't think too much of a young guy telling them what to do. But I really emphasized what was to be done. "Yep, yep, we know what to do," they told me. So the next morning, I asked, "Did you get the hoses over there?" They said, "Yep, it's all done." I told them to take a ladder in so Howard and I could get up the raise.

I was to meet Howard on the 3350. When I got there, transportation was sitting there loaded, with no motor. As I was walking down the drift, I see the motor coming back. I asked the transportation, "Where have you guys been?" They told me, "We just took Carl out. He got hurt." Just then Howard came along. He said, "I want to go in and see where Carl got hurt." I told him I was just going in, so we walked in and Jackpine was still sitting up there. It was like a sub-level going across, with this raise going up at the end, maybe about thirty feet. So when we got there, here's the hoses coiled up at the top of the man-way. They had never taken a hose up there, never blown it out and, of course, the little oxygen that was there was just enough for Carl to get up and lay the ladder in the raise, but not enough to stay as long as he did. So down the raise he came, unconscious, and he buggered up his shoulder. It was never the same after that.

Howard and I got a safety ladder and a safety lamp, and I went up ahead of Howard. He was right behind me. Everything was fine and dandy until we got another six inches or so. Then the lamp went out. No oxygen. Just like that. So there it is, just foolishness. He was as much to blame as Jackpine. It almost cost them, just like it did Lloyd McLellan and Trevor Evans. A silent killer.

The first train that used to go out was at two on Monday and, of course, the track would be pretty greasy and slippery after sitting idle over the weekend. And at that time, all the big wheels and the shift bosses would ride the motor coming out. We had no coaches to take people out back then so riding the motor was quite legal. But this motorman, Fragella, was driving that day. He was quite a guy and a great motorman. Well, anyway, Bill Lindsay and a bunch of other outside guys got on for a ride outside. At one time, you used to stop about three hundred feet from the portal and store your carbide lamp and then walk out.

This one day, Lindsay wanted to go out early. Fragella and his partner had a train hauling thirty-seven loaded cars ready to go out. Lindsay was the mine superintendent at the time so he did what he wanted, so he and his crew got on. As the train broke over at the 5000 mark, there was no way Fragella could hold it and stop at the carbide station. The train kept on picking up speed. I guess they were going like a son of a bitch. They called Lindsay "Roaring Bill" because he was famous for his screaming. I guess he was sitting on the front of the motor and turned to Fragella, who was in the cockpit, and yelled, "Slow this son of a bitch down." Fragella just put his hands up. Bill yelled at him,

Ore train coming out from undeground through the main portal for the mine on the 3900 Level.

"You're fired, you bastard." Fragella yelled back at him, "You take it, you son of a bitch. There's nothing I can do." "You're fired, you bastard," Bill yelled again. The train shot outside like a bullet, around that corner at the entrance and halfway through the dump before it got stopped. And that dump was a good five hundred feet away. When it stopped, Bill yelled, "You're hired again, you bastard." That's the way Roaring Bill was, loud but honest. The greatest superintendent ever.

Here's another story about Roaring Bill. We were going on afternoon shift and we were standing around on the platform outside, waiting for the train and cross shift to come out. Everybody stole a little bit; you know, nails, stuff like that, 'cause a lot of us were still building houses. Big Bill Richardson, he was a timberman. I guess this day, Big Bill was a little hoggish and had filled his bucket right full of two and a quarter-inch nails. At that time, Bill Lindsay's office was right where he could look out at where the coaches stopped. Bill had a habit of having his window open so he could yell at the guys not to jump off the coaches until they stopped. Anyhow, the coaches came out and Big Bill Richardson jumped off and his bucket opened up. There were nails flying in every direction, all over the place, and Lindsay came out of his office like a big bull moose.

"You son of a bitch, Bill," he said. "You wanted nails, you pick every goddamn nail up." And Bill Richardson was down on his hands and knees picking up all these bloody nails with the crew change going on around him, laughing at him. Oh, Bill was mad, but he picked up all the nails and Lindsay let him keep them.

Bill Lindsay and his wife went to Montreal for a holiday this one year and he ran short of money. Being a big Company official, he thought he would just go into the Montreal office and get some money. So he goes into this office to talk to this girl. He tells her that he's Bill Lindsay from Kimberley, the Sullivan Mine, and he would like to get some money. "No," she says, "I couldn't possibly give you some money just on that." Well, I guess Bill's voice started to get louder and louder and he shouted, "I'm Bill Lindsay from Kimberley, goddamn it, and I want some money." She said, "You're not Roaring Bill by any chance?" He said, "You're damn right I am." He got the money. She'd heard of Roaring Bill but not Bill Lindsay.

My dad started in the Sullivan in 1923. He had been working in Cripple Creek, Colorado. He was only coming up here for two weeks. He and my mother were married in Cripple Creek in 1909. My brother Walter and my older sister were born in Cripple Creek. But before he came to Kimberley — I'm getting ahead of myself here — he took my mother, Walter and my sister back to Sweden. He thought they could live on what he had made on the sale of his part ownership in a gold mine he was in on in Cripple Creek. Well, that never panned out and by that time, my other sister was on the way.

This was in 1916 and back they came in 1923, this time to Canada. He thought he would make some money in Canada and then go back to Cripple Creek. He did some stooking on the prairies. This was in the fall and he made his way to Yahk, BC, which was all logging at the time. He wasn't a lumberman so he heard about Kimberley and the Sullivan. He showed up here looking for a job.

Jack Fortier was the mine foreman at the time. He went to the Company office, trying to get hired on. Montgomery was the super at the time and

he took him up to the Top Mine and introduced him to Jack Fortier. At that time, they were only hiring miners. They didn't want any more labourers. They had lots of those. So Jack Fortier said, "Well, I'll tell you what, if you're a miner, you got the job. If you're not, you haven't got a job. Get your tools and we'll find out if you're a miner or not."

Miners outside the Top Mine Portal. The lunch buckets had hot tea or coffee in the bottom section and sandwiches on top. Welsh miners called them "a letter from home."

Well, Dad thought he would just stay a couple of weeks and make a little grubstake to get him to Colorado. He ended up staying here for twenty-three years. While he was working here, my mother and brother and sisters were still in Sweden waiting to come over. Walter came out in 1927 and started to work in Kimberley. I was born in 1917 in Sweden and when my mother came over, she brought me. My two sisters stayed in Sweden. This was in 1932 and I was fifteen.

My dad was made a shift boss in the early thirties, a position he held until he retired. At the time we came out in 1932, the Top Mine was just about finished, with about a year to go. So when it finished, everybody was moved below. My dad built the house right beside the Catholic Church.

My dad told me when the first stopers came out, they were named "widow makers." There was no water and no ratchet to turn the steel. You had to ratchet the machine by hand, back and forth. He said you couldn't tell who anybody was. They were pure white from the dust. Then when you had the liner with the long steel, you had a chucktender who would suck up water with a squirt gun and squirt it in the hole alongside the steel, because there was nobody had figured how to put the water down the middle of the steel and out the bottom of the hole. God, just think of all the guys that died from silicosis from breathing that dust, because there wasn't any real ventilation at the time.

You know, when Bobby MacSporran started mining, he was with Bob Cameron. And there is no finer gentleman than Bob Cameron, or a better miner as far as I'm concerned. He was a perfect teacher and everything that Bob did came so easy. Young Bobby had been mining just a couple of months and they were working in a new cross cut on the 2800. It was just around dinnertime.

I came along and I could hear a machine running in there so I figured I would just go in to see what was going on. There was only one man. It was Bobby, and he was drilling with a jackleg and he had a sandwich in one hand and the machine in the other hand. When he saw me, he turned the machine off. I said, "What the hell are you doing?" He said, "Bob is a bunch of holes ahead of me and he's gone for lunch." I said, "It doesn't make any difference. A guy can find time to eat. You don't need all the cuttings and crap in your sandwich." He said, "I want to catch up with Bob so we can come out together." Bobby turned out to be a hell of a worker. He couldn't have had a better teacher.

Talking about Bob Cameron, Bob and Billy Masich were working together on the 3600. Well, they were just the opposite. Again, I come along to see my crews. It was about 9:30 in the morning and here comes Bob, walking out. I stopped and asked Bob if he was having trouble. "Ah, no," he said. "The little fellow — he meant Billy Masich — is throwing stuff around. I thought I would come out and have a bite to eat. Maybe he'll cool off by the time I get back. He's throwing wrenches and steel all over the place."

Some time after this, Bob said to me, "I've got the solution to stop Billy from losing his temper." I said, "What's that?" He said, "If I let Billy get ahead of me a half a hole, he's just a prince to work with. I watch him pretty close and when we start getting even, I slow down a little and let him get ahead. It works fine." That's all it was. He just couldn't stand Bob getting ahead of him. It didn't matter what Bob did. It was slow and deliberate, and he still beat everyone else.

When Kirkpatrick was the big wheel for the Company, I was in charge of No. 2 shaft at the time. He came in with Percy Bloomer for a walk-around inspection and I was introduced to him. It wasn't more than six months later when I went over for the 40-year banquet in Trail with a bunch of guys from Kimberley. They had a bar set up. I went up to the bar to get a drink and Kirkpatrick was up there with his back to me. While I thought it was no business for me to talk to a guy like that, doggone, if he didn't turn around and say, "Well, John, how's No. 2 Shaft? It's good to see you again."

Just like that, you know. There're very few people that can remember names. I guess they're trained to that. That's probably why they're big wheels and the rest of us are little ones.

BUD HART

Through this portal...

Mining, I believe, was number two on Bud's list of preferred ways to make a living. Being a cowboy would have been his first choice. Hell, he has a saddle on a sawhorse in his living room. I don't know if he sits on it to watch TV, or if he just looks at it, but if he wanted me to know, I'm sure he would have told me. Muscle and gristle make up Bud's 200-pound frame, and he's got fists like anvils that he didn't mind throwing when the occasion arose, especially if someone tried messing with his cowboy hat.

He is a courteous, intelligent man, able to converse with anyone on any subject. Good humour and a good joke are important to him.

Bud was a great miner with a lot of pride in his work. He was never fazed by conditions or circumstances; he always got the job done one way or another.

I started underground with the Company in 1937 when I was eighteen years old. I started at $3.75 a day, and we were getting a thing called an efficiency bonus that amounted to about $1.20 a day. It was later phased out.

I worked steady graveyard for over a year. There was no shift work for new starts, just graveyard. I finally got off graveyard working on the 3900 Level, working on the track gang, nipping, piping, transportation, a little bit of everything. This prepared me for mining, which I went into in 1940. I went with Garnet Coulter. He had been mining for a few months before me.

We went into a raise in 17 Drift on 3700 Level. There was a raise already driven but we drove a finger raise out of it that came out on 4250 Level. It was about four hundred feet at seventy degrees. This was for a muck raise. We used the old, common steel. We were putting in twenty-four holes to the round, which meant we had to pack twenty-four sets of steel up the raise at the start of every shift.

Old Joe Shaw was our shift boss. It got too far up for him to come up to the face to check on us so he would stand at the bottom of the raise and just bang on the pipe, and we would just shake our lights up and down if everything was okay, and that was fine. He was checking us steady.

I remember this day in December in 1940. We heard the banging on the pipe. We were almost at the top, close to breakthrough. There was old Joe signalling us by moving his light in a circle, which means "come to me." We just signalled back with the up and down motion with our lights that we were okay, but he persisted with the circular motion with his light to "come to him." We figured something had happened and he needed our help so down the raise we go on the ropes and footwall steel. When we got there, he said, "Garnet, you're a daddy." That was Jeannie, Garnet's first child, so it wasn't all that bad having to go down the raise. You don't mind that kinda reason.

After Garnet and I drove that raise, we got transferred to the Shaft to go drifting, using the old Armstrong mucking machine, which was a whole lot different mucking machine than they have today. These machines weren't self-propelled; they had to be pushed ahead and withdrawn with the motor. So what you had was the mucking machine at the face, a car, then the motor. They weren't bad mucking machines but they came off the track very easily because of the small wheels on them, and because they weren't self-propelled, they were very slow.

Garnet got a chance to go into a stope. That was a raise in earnings for him. I stayed in the No. 1 Shaft area from 1941 until 1967, over twenty-five years. Spent all that time drifting and raising. And in the later part, I was working as a barman, working ahead of the steel they were putting in as they were driving No. 1 Shaft from 3350 Level down. When they drove the pilot shaft down from 3350 Level, they sunk that raise down to

Head frame #1 Shaft. This is the head frame built above ground to house the pulley system for the hoist and skips. Surface is 4400 feet above sea level going down to a 2400 level loading pocket at 45 degrees. Top speed – 17 miles per hour. Built in early 1950s at a cost of $3,000,000.

the 2400 Level, and then they drove No. 1 Shaft up as a raise and all the muck went up the pilot shaft.

The main shaft was driven twenty-four feet wide by fifteen feet high. We hit bad ground up around the 2600 Level. We couldn't even cut out a station. The ground was breaking out too wide so we had to cut down the face to eight by eight until we got to better ground. We didn't bother timbering this part because there was going to be steel put in here, like the whole shaft. It was my job as a barman, and I had several partners, to go down ahead. It was usually done with a stoper or a plugger to widen this raise out to enable Ed Green and his crew to come down and put the steel in. Some of the guys were Nick Stuparyk, George Matheson and a lot of other guys, good workers all of them.

It was pretty hairy going through this bad ground because when you drive a raise you arch the back for ground support. We had to take out the arch and make it square for easy placement of the steel. In that eight by eight area, when we took it out to the proper size, we had to install the steel as fast as we could and block it tight. When you take these jobs, you take your chances. It was pretty scary at times and we were always on graveyard shift for part of the job.

At one time or another, I worked in every drift in the Shaft from the 3900 to the 2400 Level. I worked from start to finish in every crushing chamber. I worked from start to finish on the main haulage way on the 3700 Level, right down to and including the loading pockets just below the 3800 Level. That was a big job. There was some hairy ground in there.

I remember this one time when we were driving the main haulage, the 3700; it was all twelve feet by twelve feet. We had been in good ground at this time and we were breaking 8-foot rounds, which would give you thirty to thirty-five cars to muck out before we could set up and start drilling. We were hauling the muck about two thousand feet to the dump block. When we got mucked out, we didn't have to put track in yet, just put the ties in, then we would set up this jumbo.

It was a Cleveland jumbo. It wasn't a good jumbo. It was a big husky thing, took a lot of work to set up. The booms would swing side to side. It had three legs on it, something like stoper legs, to hold it in place. The back leg was right up against the crummy spot we had found when we were barring down. I had Les Carson with me. I was just breaking him in. And we had a young guy who was our chucktender, Bill Archibald.

We had a four-inch line coming in and a four-inch hose hooked up to that jumbo. We had just got going, collaring holes and all that, when all hell happened. Some loose came down and cut the hose that was hooked up to the jumbo behind us. We were right, tight up to the face. Our platform and everything else was thrown right on top of us. You can imagine what it was like with this big hose whipping about. It was throwing boulders and muck at us; steel, wood, anything that would move was coming at us. The roar of the air coming out of this hose was deafening. All we could do was lie down on the footwall and cover our heads.

Fog, oil fumes and roaring drills. It just doesn't get any better than this.

My first thought was something had caved in behind us and that Bill would be under it. He was always there, bringing steel up for us. But as it happened, he was back behind all this getting more steel when all this came down, and it missed him. He was there to turn the air off.

This all happened about 9:40 on afternoon shift. When the air cleared, we took a look. Jesus, what a mess. Track was turned, there was big holes in the ground where the hose was whipping about blowing, ties were rooted up, everything that could fly was up at the face where we were. It even sheared the legs off the jumbo. Yep, it was a hairy situation. They shut the place down for about a week. It was just one of those things that happens.

While we're on that subject of "hairy," I barred for years in the Shaft and have been so close to being killed in different situations or another. The worst thing we ever had to do was go into these old bar and arm stopes and scrape float day after day. The backs of these old stopes were so high that they couldn't be barred. The stopes were filled by gravity as far as they could and then we had to scrape the float according to the lay of the orebody, usually uphill because the orebody was higher.

We had to go under the back of these old stopes and drill eyebolt holes for our blocks to hook up our scraper cables. The shifter would come in and

The lunchroom was referred to as the "doghouse." You held your sandwich with a piece of wax paper to keep it clean. Note the electric heater on the floor.

mark where we could drill our holes, in between all these missed holes. Most of them were filled with inch and three-quarter stick powder, forcite powder. We were told to do this. The mine inspector said this was all right. The union safety committee all said it was okay. All the rules were forgotten. We were scared for our lives. We had to go there day after day. They all said we had to do it, so we did it. These things happen.

About two weeks after we'd finished, old Raynor told Jimmy Ross and me to go back to the stope and get the blocks we had left behind. We found out when we went there that the whole stope had come down and buried everything. When you look back at it, we shouldn't have done it, but that's the way it was then.

The raise that Garnet and I drove up from the 3900 Level broke through on the 4200 Level. There was a little timber yard cut-out just down from our breakthrough and off this timber yard was a little cut-out at the end of the drift. It went in about fifteen feet and was about nine by nine. And there was a brattice door over the opening. Yeah, that was our doghouse. It had two benches in it. We used to eat with our lunch buckets on our knees.

It was about 11:10. We were having our lunch when the wind started to blow. Just lightly at first. Then this brattice door started to come in more and more, and the wind got louder and louder and louder. And we all sat there and I can remember looking across at Jimmy McFarlane. He was pale as a ghost. I guess we all were.

They were backfilling with float at the time and I, for one, thought that the float had come in, that maybe a bulkhead had broke or something, and maybe the float was pushing the air ahead. It got so you couldn't hear. The brattice was straight out and there was rocks flying through the air and everything. Everybody rushed for the door. I can remember this one guy laying on his back, running. He thought he was running, but he was on his back. Three of us stayed in the doghouse. Bill Muir Sr., myself and another guy, we got up on the bench. I said later that if I could'a found a bootleg to crawl into, I would'a.

What had happened was that there was a big slough in this stope near us, and it sloughed all the way to the surface. The engineers, by displacement method, figured five million tons came into the mine creating a windstorm. On the 4200 Level, where we were, all the ventilation doors were gone, man-ways and slides, the water in the ditches, these were blown clean for hundreds of yards. It was one big bloody mess. Down below, all the shops were blown over. The shops were made of four by fours dowelled into the roof. They were all partitioned off into electric shop, mechanics' shops; these were all on the 3900 Level. These were all blown down. It was a hell of a mess.

There was some humour. One of the shift bosses was having his lunch when all this happened. I think his name was Thomas, but I guess he had a tomato in his hand and they ran outside of the shifters' shack into the drift, not knowing where to go with the wind and dust blowing. I guess when they finally got stopped running, one of the guys noticed Thomas' hand and said, "Look at your goddamn hand; you're hurt." He had hung on to this tomato and squeezed all the juice all over his hand. Yep, that was another hairy deal. That's what they called "the big slough."

In the hard rock raises — these were all timbered raises — we were using these drills called liners on vertical bars, no arms. We would just put the drill on the bar and clamp it on. We would set up close to the face. These liners had a 4-inch piston and weighed about two hundred pounds. Right today, I don't know how we hauled them up the raise.

What we used to do is build our platform and then get the bar set up. Your partner would be down in the hole on the bulkhead down below. He would tie

Miner's bar and arm in 1930. Collaring a raise off a track drift.

a rope around the machine, and the guy on the drill platform would straddle a plank and pull the machine up hand over hand. That was all right — it was only two hundred pounds — especially when you're young and strong. But to get the drill on to the platform, you would have to get it in the air and get it swinging so it would clear your planks and sprags. Then the two of you would push and pull to get it up on the platform and get it onto the bar.

They used to use a special drill steel. It was a light steel, about one and a quarter inches round. For hard rock, the gauge changed. There were no bits on them and the steel was sharpened in the steel shop. We usually had to change steel every six inches. The secret to drilling hard rock is to keep your gauge [sharpness].

These were crank machines. If you found you couldn't crank them, you stopped and backed out before you took the gauge off and put another one in. You used to shank them in. You would put a little chuck in so the steel wouldn't turn. It would just drive right into the bottom. You would give it a shot of air and if you were good enough, you could catch the crank in your hand. Then you would crank the steel into the chuck. It would catch the lug and you were drilling again.

I remember the steel shop was right near us once. It was in No. 18 Drift. We would get a whole truckload of steel from the shop. We used to test them before we took them up the raise by banging them on the track. If they broke, we put them aside. The rock was harder than the steel. They couldn't temper them enough. I just counted one day. I used forty-four starters and got in two inches. You can imagine how nice it was when the Carsted bit came out and all we had to do was take just the bits up the raise.

The Carsted bits enabled us to go to a 2-foot steel change. That was the big change in the Sullivan. Now we could take a round a shift, which wasn't possible before. This made drilling in the hard rock so that we could handle it a hell of a lot better.

When the Eimco 21 mucking machine came in, it was a big improvement over the Armstrong mucking machine. As time went by, we got very efficient on them. We learned a few things that the manufacturer didn't know, and a lot of miners also didn't know.

During and after the war, we had a lot of gold mines closed down because they were classed as non-essential mines and a lot of tramp miners from all over the country came in. The Sullivan miners knew what they knew and a hell of a lot more. The Sullivan miner was the best miner in the world, as far as I was concerned, in those times because he had to be versatile. We had to do it all, be it tramming, raises, drifts, drawholes or timbering.

Miners driving a drift, drilling a V-cut pattern. Slide rails on the footwall will be left when blasting so the mucking machine can go right to work after the blast.

We invented the slide rails when you're driving a track drift by pushing the rails with the mucking machine. The representatives from Eimco saw us doing this when they came around to see how their machines were working, because that was a big contract for them with the Company. They came to our headings and saw us pushing the slide rails ahead with the mucking machine. They had been all over Canada and never saw this before. It was probably an accident how it evolved, but it was probably some guy operating the machine bumped into the rail and it moved ahead. Just a fluke, but it worked, and so there it was. The representatives went out across Canada and showed everybody.

It was about 1968 when this guy showed up. He was called a rock doctor. I guess they're still called that. It's not much of a name for what these guys know. Below the 3900 Level, we were barring after a diamond drill blast. We found out that the whole footwall was sliding. You would bar it tight one day, and the next day it would be all opened up again. They knew something was going on. They brought this rock doctor in. He was there for about six months doing tests. I think his name was Ready. He looked to be about eighteen years old, wasn't a big man, slim, girlish. Well, he just scar't the pants off the Company. He told them if they didn't stop taking out the lower part of that orebody, which is down on the 2500 Level — there were diamond drill blasts going on all over down there — he said that they would lose the Sullivan. He said what they were doing was taking out the bottom of the orebody and the whole orebody was slipping in. They shut down the lower levels right away until they got more information on this.

We as barmen drilled lots of holes with extension steel, horizontal holes. We put light cables in them with instruments on the end to tell if there was any movement. Well, hell, the ground was moving all over the place. When they saw how bad it was moving, they shut it down. We pulled all the pipe and stuff out. It was shut down for over ten years.

When they shut down the Shaft, I was moved back up to the upper levels as a slusher miner.

We were on graveyard this one time. We had a three-man crew on transportation. Two men were chute-loaders and one guy was on the motor. Well, the guy on the motor had smokes but no lighter. You could get an arc off the trolley if you put the motor on one notch with the brakes on. This guy thought he could get a light off the arc so he pulled the pole down just enough to get an arc, put his smoke in his mouth for the arc, and the arc got him in the face. Burnt the shit out of him. We always had tannic acid in our first aid boxes so we smeared him up with it and got him out. This was for electric burns. His whole face peeled later on but he was real lucky he never lost his eyes. He was scarred forever over that. Dumb, real dumb.

One eighty-one Raise was the main muck raise for the South End. These two guys went up to pull it. I forget their names. Well, the chute was hung up and they had to blast. In those days, this was before primacord, you would light your fuse, you would have your stick powder tied onto your bulldoze stick, and then shove it up the raise. Well, anyhow, this guy had let the door down so he could shove the shot up and the powder came off the stick and rolled back down and into the car under the chute, right past him. He jumped off the chute and yelled, "I lost the powder. Get the hell out of here." The motorman started moving the train. The chuteman was running alongside the train, yelling at the motorman, "It's in the car, it's in the car." The motorman stopped the train and jumped off, and boom! Blew the hell outta the car. There was some shit raised over that, I can tell you, but that was funny, Jesus Christ.

Bruce Ritchie, mine superintendent, he got killed underground. He got hit by a shot up in a stope and got knocked down the raise that we pulled. I was on transportation then. The only way you could get him out was by pulling the chute. There were guys all over the place. We were told to pull just a little bit at a time. So here come these rubber boots, so okay, he's coming soon, and he did. So I guess it goes to show you, it doesn't matter who you are, when your time's up, it's up.

We had a kid that worked with us in the summer, like a lot of kids them days did. Getting enough money to go back to university. His dad was a shift boss at the time. He worked on graveyard on transportation. He was a timid boy. He liked to drink with us but he was a timid boy. He wasn't belligerent at all. He would just laugh and get along with the guys and that. But, anyways, old Jock, the shifter, sent him a way up this drift to muck under this chute, spillage and cuttings that build up under a chute that get washed down the raise. We took him up there and spotted a car for him to muck into.

There was this pump, an old air pump. You know the type, they just keep going. And as the pressure got too much, the air would just blow by the piston, making this "phtew phtew" noise. Every time it pushed into the pipe, the pipe would turn. The pipeline went a way up this man-way and every time the pipe would turn, it would make this tapping noise.

When the kid heard this, he asked us, "What the hell is that?" I said, "Maybe you don't want to know." He said, "Tell me." I said, "Well, there was a miner up there and it was a timbered raise and he went up and lit the round. He had pulled the muck so that he would have room in the raise for the fresh blast and he was coming down the raise on ropes after he had lit it, but he missed the hole in the bulkhead and couldn't get back up to the bulkhead before the shots went off and that's him scratching and tapping. That's his ghost." Well, away my partner and me went. Left him all alone by himself on graveyard. He must have been crapping himself all shift.

There was a character up there, underground. A great guy. His name was Brother and he was working by us. At lunchtime, I mentioned that I had heard a friend of his had died and I was talking to him, telling him how sorry I was that his friend had died. He said, "Yep, it could be worse." And I said, "What could be worse than dying?" He said, "It could'a been me."

Another time, when we were on strike and I was on the picket line, old Brother showed up and we were just standing around BSing and I mentioned to him that another friend of his had died and asked him if he was going to the funeral. He said, "Nope" and when I asked why, he said, "The son of a bitch won't be coming to mine." Just good humour. That's all it was.

When I first started, there was no union, just something called a craft committee. There was a limit on the miners. I believe it was $2 a day that you could make over day's pay. The miners were the only ones that could make it. Transportation, drillers, they got nothing.

The stope miners, it was quite easy for them to keep control of what they made. You would never want to go over the limit because the office'd cut you. There was just no way they were going to pay you more than $2, so you would just hold back. The Company used to watch the chute-loader's tally pretty carefully. If a crew of miners were putting in a good effort and this was quite apparent, the shift boss would tell the superintendent that this crew was really trying, and if they were lazy, they wouldn't get a raise. But if they were trying and weren't making anything, the shifter would go to the superintendent and tell him that this crew should get a raise. So we would get the raise up to $2. That limit stayed in effect until I was called up to go in the army. It was all up to the shifter. If he liked you, you would make money. If he didn't, tough.

I was working with Big Alf Ingebrigtsen in this raise and, oh God, it was hard. We worked like dogs, using them big bloody liners at the time. This is the place where I used fourty-four starters and got in two inches. I was drilling about three shifts, and some holes you got in would be a foot long and some two. If you hit a little iron, your steel would go crooked, and we worked hard. I worked in there for three months and couldn't make the limit.

Old Callahan was our shift boss. I hadn't been mining that long, but I had been there long enough to know that I wasn't going to take that all through my life. So I told Callahan that if I don't make the limit next month, I wouldn't be staying in there. I think he was telling them outside that we didn't deserve a raise. I think he had it in for me because my dad used to poke him. Callahan was a yappy guy and so I think my dad used to poke him a lot. My dad didn't like yappy guys, so I think this is why Callahan had it in for me.

So at the end of the month, I didn't get the limit, $2. When we came underground after payday, I got off the coach and just stood there. All the other guys took off to work and I just stood there. Old Callahan comes to me and says that I had better get going. I told him we didn't make the limit last month and I wasn't going back in there. I fully expected to get fired right there on the spot. I said the hell with it. I'm not going to work like that anymore. Christ, there were guys doing as much as me and guys doing less and they got the limit. I just said the hell with it.

Old Cal took off to see what he could do with me. When he came back, he sent me nipping, the lowest paid job in the mine. He told me to take a whole bunch of gear down to 3910 Drift. It was gear for drillers. I asked where could I get a motor and a flatcar to transport it. He said to pack it. I used to think those days that I'd show those guys that I could do it. So I put a 9-foot column bar that weighed about two hundred pounds on my shoulder and walked down there. It was halfway to the South End. I packed everything down there just to show them. There were some real pricks around at that time.

Callahan was still mad at me so they had me doing all these little jobs here and there. I got sent to the office after about three days, after they figured out what they were going to do with me. Well, this day they told me that I was going outside to work. I figured I was going on the bull gang but they put me on the backfill. I was on the backfill for six months, driving a Euclid dump truck. They finally brought me back underground. All was forgiven. I guess they needed my skills. I wouldn't suckhole to that guy. No sir. It's a good thing because I was almost ready to give in because the doctor told me if I didn't get off heavy equipment, I would be a cripple for life. My lower back was killing me. I was that close to giving in.

There was another foreman just after that where I took him a doctor's slip saying I was only fit for light-duty work. Well, he didn't like that at all and he tried to put me in several places but I wouldn't go. So he says, "Okay, you got a light-duty slip, I'll put you in a place that just suits a light-duty guy." So he put me on graveyard, mucking, for a year and a half. He thought I would give in. I wouldn't. I stuck it out.

Ted Holt was one of my partners and Ernie Pinchback. We had to muck on graveyard because there was no transportation. We were cleaning the drifts and he wouldn't allow us contract that went over $3. I went into the office to see about a better contract and I was told that this was all the foreman said we were worth.

It was about November, when my wife was a flag bearer for the Legion on November 11. She belonged to the Women's Auxiliary. This was on a Saturday and I just came off graveyard. Those days we worked Friday night graveyard. She told me there was a supper at six and that I should come down. I said, "Sure, that sounds good. I'll get a couple of hours' sleep and then come down." She said to come down early enough so we can have a few drinks before supper. I slept until noon, got up and headed down to the Legion about two. I stopped at a bar where a friend of mine was bartending, had three or four beer. You feel owly when you get up off graveyard so I thought a couple of beer would lighten me up a bit.

So over to the Legion I go and as I came through the door, standing at the bar was this goddamn foreman. And when he heard the door open, he looked. He said, "Hey Bud! Come over and I'll buy you a drink." I went over to him and said, "You get the hell out of here or I'm going to punch you right in the goddamn nose." I was so damn mad at this guy. Here's this guy that put me in a ditch mucking for a year and a half trying to make me suckhole and then he greets me like a long-lost friend. He beat it. I had to go to the bathroom and, in the meantime, he went over to my wife. I guess she knew how I felt about him. He said, "Your husband just came in." 'Yeah, I know," she said. "I saw him come in." He said, "He sure is owlly." She said, "If he is, you'd better get out of here." And he took off like the devil was after him. Just about tripped trying to get out the door. I often wished he had never left. I would'a loved to punch the shit out of that asshole. He ended up getting shot by a guy he pissed off more than me, I guess.

As far as the shift-bossing career, I had lots of chances to go shifting, which I did in the Sullivan. But then they wanted to ship me out to Tulsequa

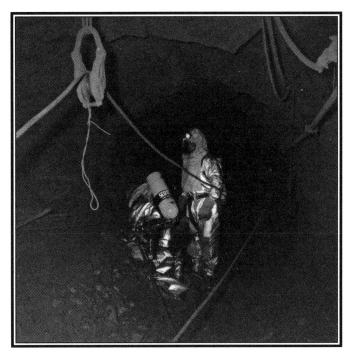

or Benson Lake. In those days there were no schools there and I had a growing family, so it wasn't very attractive. So they took me off shifting. I took the job three times and quit it three times. And so I said no, it wasn't for me. It was always a loss of money and to me there wasn't any future in it, and there still isn't. I guess it just depends on how you look at it. I was just a miner at heart and would just as soon be mining to earn my bucks than going around checking on guys. I found that you couldn't operate as yourself. You had to operate on somebody else's say-so the way you handled men.

The way they wanted me to handle men, I wouldn't do it. I absolutely refused. I was working for McQuarrie and he told me to "give that man a reprimand" and I told him to give it to him himself. He said, "That's your job." And I said "Nope." He had come along and found this guy not doing what he was supposed to and he had come into the office and told me about it. I said,

Hot-muck miners wearing asbestos suits and using "Scott" air packs for breathing. They are working in a sub where severe heat and SO_2 gas are prevalent.

"You found him, you give him a reprimand." And as a result, McQuarrie didn't give him a reprimand. It was this sort of deal that I didn't like.

I spent the last three years in the hot muck, with a good many hairy situations, too many to mention. So there's no point in going into that, but that was a bad deal.

I was down in the T-9 Block, with Hap Elliot, where one side of the manway was hot muck and the other side had cooled off. So they shut down the hot-muck side and opened up the other side. We were to put in the new type of powder magazine for your 24-hour powder storage. What we did here was take out a small room by mining it out of the rock, then put in a shotcrete seal to fireproof it. Then we built shotcrete seals in front of the hoists, with a peephole so you could see into the sub as you were scraping. The seal had a metal door on the side so you could travel in and out of the sub. We did all this work on graveyard. So I had run the whole circle. There I was on graveyard, working on day's pay, just like when I had started.

So you know, when your time has come when you're eligible for pension, it don't take much to stir you. And so here I was. I thought this is it, so I pulled the pin. I was fifty-seven years old and I had thirty-nine years in with the Company. That wasn't the only reason. I figured I'd better save a few years for myself because the statistics prove that if you hang in there too long, you're gonna suffer for it in your later years. So that's what I did. She was deep enough.

I would like to see a plaque put up commemorating all the miners. I would like to see it put up at the old 3900 Portal where it has the date "1915" up above the portal. I would like to see a plaque installed saying, "Through this portal have passed the best miners in the world."

BILLY MASICH

Could pick a fight in an empty room...

Billy was very dear to me and to the many others who were recipients of his generosity and that of his wife Maggie, who was my second mother.

"Crusty" would describe Billy, a small man, maybe five feet five inches and 140 pounds (with rocks in his pockets). It was his crustiness, though, that allowed him to mine using machines that weighed the same as he did.

As a small man with a lot of pride, he was always on the offensive, hence his nickname, "Billy the Bitch." He was always bitching about something. I'm glad I had a long association with him, even though he could be a miserable little bastard at times.

I started May 1, 1937, at the Company barns. There was about fifteen of us straining gravel. I was eighteen. Toss Hagen and Bud Brenton were part of the crew and a bunch of guys from Saskatchewan. We were making about seventy-five cents an hour. This gravel was for the [mine] road, from the top parking lot down to the dry, and they hard-topped it.

I went from this job to the rockhouse, loading CPR rail cars to go to the concentrator, Billy Richardson and me. I spent the winter and part of the summer doing this. Joe Giegerich called me into the office and told me that I had spent enough time doing this and that. It was time for me to go underground.

I went underground and spent fourteen months mucking under the chutes in 181. It was tough work shovelling the spillage into cars. That ore was darn heavy. I then got on as motorman and made two bits an hour more. Did that for six months and got on as chute-loader. This was fourteen months' steady graveyard. We all started underground on graveyard shift.

They put about twenty of us mining. I guess there was a big push. There was no such thing as mining school in them days. They just put us with experienced guys. I went with Rick Mitchell. That was fifty years ago. The average guy didn't mind teaching you but some were mean, like Charlie Parkhouse and Black Dan. They didn't like having rookies. I guess they had forgotten that they had to learn like the rest of us. But I was lucky. All those guys are dead and gone now.

Miner's bar & arm. Setting up arm to drill right-hand lifters.

All we used in the raises was those bars and arms with liners on them. Those bloody liners weighed over two hundred pounds. First thing you did was put in the bar at right angles to the raise. That bar weighed a good hundred pounds. It had one end that screwed out and you used blocking to snug it up. Then you put the arm onto the bar by clamping it. Then you would put the liner on. You could swing the arm around from one side to the other without taking the liner off, but not all the time. Sometimes you might have to take the liner off. You had to make sure that it never got away on you and dropped down the raise. It was damn hard pulling it back up the raise and getting it back on the platform with nothing but ropes. Some of the raises were eighty degrees. It was hard work. Nobody would realize how hard it was unless they had done it. Little guy like me worked like crazy.

We used this steel, special steel it was called. The steel and the bit were all one piece. You might get one turn of the steel before you had to change it, especially in chert. It seems like that's all we did was pack steel. We would usually try to get a 5-foot round and that usually took three or four days, going three shifts, before we could blast. We didn't have ear protection like they do now. We just stuck a rag or some cotton in. A lot of guys didn't wear nothing. Most guys my age are pretty deaf now, ears are always ringing and stuff.

Down on 3600 Level, when I worked with Red Mitchell, there was six stopes going at the same time. There used to be big air blasts in these stopes. You know the cold and the hot air in the rock didn't mix and so boom! Big pieces of ore would just fly off the walls and back. You could hear and feel it when it happened, even in the other stopes. When this happened, the guys in all six stopes would stop what they were doing and go check on each other. It always amazed me that a lot of us never got caught. Just horseshit luck.

One morning about three o'clock when I was working in the hot muck for George Cassavant, we had a power bump. We were working in T-24 Block, right down at the bottom. As soon as the juice went off, I took off up the ladder. It was a good two hundred feet to the top of the man-way. The whole crew took off behind me.

I got up to the top first. Hap Elliot was behind me, and then John McCollough. The SO_2 got John and he was coughing and losing consciousness and was just rolling down the man-way. Hap just caught him and I came back down to give Hap a hand with John and we dragged him up the man-way the last twenty feet on the ladders and got him into the fresh air. We got him going again.

We went and saw Cassavant in the doghouse and Hap and I went back to have a look. At the top of the raise, we had a 36-inch fan blowing air down the raise but the power bump had knocked it off. The auxiliary power had come on by then. So George and I turned the fan off to see what would happen. The SO_2 came up that raise just like a train. We couldn't believe it. I think that's the closest I came to death. That night we were pretty lucky we got out of there.

If I had to live my life over again with what I know now, I'd go back underground. But with what I know, you'd never get me back in the hot muck. All I have to do is look at the stupid oxygen bottle I drag around behind me. No way. There's somewhere around seven guys that I used to work with in the hot muck that are dead now. It's not very pleasant for me to think about it 'cause I know my turn is coming pretty soon.

I guess about the only good thing I could say about hot muck is that it made me quit smoking. There was no way you could light up a smoke without coughing, with all the SO_2 in everything on you. So I took up chewing tobacco, about fourteen years now. I used to come home even when I had a real long shower at work and have a long bath every day. I done it for six years, all the time I was in the hot muck. Even with all this washing, you could see the sheets on the bed getting stained with all this stuff coming out of your skin.

That hot muck was unbelievable. It would run down the sub just like water. It looked just like flour, only it was over a thousand degrees in temperature.

That's what got Carl Olsen. Don Roche was on the hoist when Carl came in to have a look at what was going on. He was the shifter. Don had told him that it was pretty dangerous to go in the sub and to be careful. Carl went in a ways just as a drawhole let go and he turned to run but tripped or stumbled and he went down in this red hot dust, about six inches deep. It went down his gloves, into his shirt, all over his face. His chinstrap and respirator were stuck right to his face. He managed to get up, though, and got to first aid and hospital, but he was burned terrible.

When I went to see Carl after he came back from the burn unit in Calgary, he was taking these big pills, something to do for his body, I guess they were antibiotics, and he had to cover his body with Noxzema cream to try to get his skin back to normal. But his whole face was black. All the nerves in his skin were dead. They had him wrapped up in a burn blanket for months and months before he came home.

He used to drop by the house after he could get around a bit and have a cup of coffee and a smoke with Marg and me. I always remember this one day when I was out in the carport and he came by in a car and he yelled out the window at me, "Hi, Bill." I was on afternoon shift and shortly after three o'clock, when we had gone underground and we were having a bite to eat before we went to work, the shifter came in and told us Carl had just passed away. I thought I was going to fall in a hole, the way I felt. I knew Carl all my life. Good guy.

Doug Keiver and his partner, Murray McLeod, got caught in the hot muck when they were barring a hung-up drawhole. Murray died about a month after it happened. I guess it screwed up his insides and he was burned over forty per cent of his body, from what I heard. Doug got out of the hospital two weeks after he got burned, and I've got to give him a lot of credit. He hung right in there until he passed away. Always was good natured and cheerful. He went through hell, boy. It had to be terrible to be burned like that.

Just before I retired, I was working with Dean Roe. We were drilling off a breakthrough round which we were going to blast at the end of the shift. We had finished loading the holes and had the round tied in and were sitting around waiting to blast, BSing you know, when I mentioned that I was gathering miners' stories and was going to make a book out of them. "Bill," Dean says, "I've got one for you. You're gonna love it."

At the time of this episode, Dean had purchased an old house on McKenzie Street and was in the process of restoring it. At one time, McKenzie Street was the main thoroughfare to the centre of Kimberley. The street is located where the footbridge is now, just below the Blarchmont hill, and extends past the College of the Rockies continuing education building. At one time there was a larger bridge able to handle heavy traffic.

When the house went on the market, the price was $22,000 and that included all the original furnishings, chandeliers, plumbing, the works. But best of all was the reputation that came with the house. It was an old whorehouse, built around 1920, and the added character and mystique was a bonus.

As Dean got into the restoration, some great characteristics started presenting themselves. In the kitchen were the original metal-lined bins for kitchen staples such as sugar and flour. The cupboards still had the framed-glass doors and there was also a large walk-in pantry, a great place to start for a guy with imagination.

Dean decided the kitchen needed a centrepiece so he installed a state-of-the-art natural gas six-burner Heartland stove at a cost of $5,000. He redid the cupboards and floor, and the whole works looked fantastic. He was now ready to move on. "Let's just see what other little treasures are to be found," he was thinking.

Upstairs, he found the wear and tear of the trade that took place there, which exemplified the true purpose of this grand old structure. As all the floors were made of hardwood, he first had to strip off the battleship linoleum and layers of paint that had been added over the years.

Stripping the floor in one bedroom, he came across a metal sheet that had been bolted down on the floor. Dean's first inclination was, "Hey, this is where they hid their gold and jewels." He feverishly pulled up the sheet metal only to find grooves in the hardwood, made from casters on a bed, so he surmised that the madam must have had some handyman come in and make it more user friendly. But, alas, no hidden treasure, just a lot of speculation about the comings and goings in this room. Talk about travel worn.

In the front bedroom, which overlooked the road, were two windows with two-foot windowsills. Each windowsill had the smoothest grooves in the wood. Dean was stymied. After a lot of thought as to what could have formed these perfectly formed indentations, it dawned on him. This is where the ladies sat waving greetings to the traveller going by. To confirm this, Dean stuck his own derriere in one of the spots and put his feet up on the sill across from him. Behold, a perfect match. The mystery was solved and so the work went on. He sanded the sills and refinished the wood, leaving the grooves, as he should have. You've got to preserve history, no matter how trivial it may seem to some.

One day during the restoration, Dean was taking a break outside, sitting on a pile of wood and mulling over his next move, when he noticed an old gent coming along the road toward him. It was an unusual procession. The old fellow was being pulled along by a small scruffy dog of questionable parentage on a leash. Behind the old gent trailed an oxygen bottle on wheels, which fed oxygen to the mask that covered his face.

When Dean started telling me this story, I knew exactly who he was talking about. This small apparition was none other than Billy the Bitch. Now, the name pretty much explains itself. Here was a man who could pick a fight in an empty room. If you had ever worked around the little fellow, you would have found the name well deserved.

The oxygen he hauled behind him was necessary to help his tortured lungs, as it was with so many of the older miners. This was the consequence of old-time mining methods and working in the hot muck.

As this unique procession laboriously made it up to where he was sitting, Dean, knowing this was an old miner, yelled, "How's it look, partner?" Billy seated himself alongside Dean while the little dog jumped up and found a seat on the other side of Billy. Pulling the oxygen mask off his face, Billy announced vehemently, "I hate that goddamn house."

Startled, Dean inquired, "Why don't you like it, Billy? It's a beautiful old house." Once again Billy stated, "I hate that goddamn house and I'm going to tell you why.

"My old man had a delivery service in town and I had to help him. We delivered groceries, coal, all that kind of stuff. We didn't have a truck or anything like that. All we had was a horse and wagon for the summer and a sleigh in the winter."

Between hacking and wheezing spells, Billy went on. "Every time we pulled up to this goddamn house, my old man would give me a smack alongside the head and tell me, 'Don't tell your mother we stopped here.' And in he would go, leaving me sitting on the wagon seat staring at a horse's ass. When the old man came out, it was always another smack on the side of the head and, 'Don't tell your mother we stopped here.'

"It was the same thing at home. After I got the horse fed and put away, I'd go into the house where my mother was waiting for me. And, Jesus Christ, came another smack alongside the head, this time from my mother. She would ask me, 'Did your dad stop at the whorehouse today?' This went on longer than I care to remember. I was bloody glad when my job helping the old man with deliveries came to an end. And that's why I hate that goddamn house."

Billy the Bitch was a dear friend of mine.

TUNNY PHENUFF

Built like a whippet and on the dead run...

If you filled Tunny up with tomato juice, you could use his body as a thermometer. He does everything fast. He walks fast, talks fast and when he's thinking, he thinks fast too.

He's one of those who disprove the myth that you have to be a big bugger to be a miner. That is just not true. All you had to do was watch him work. Everything was quick and with a purpose.

He is another one of those underground people with a great sense of humour and as a great storyteller, he was very easy to interview.

I started with the Company in 1937. I was seventeen. I was night watchman at the Company offices and the dry at the mine. They took me off this job because of a fire that burned down a bunch of buildings in the Crowsnest. They felt that my age made me not responsible enough for insurance purposes. So then I worked steady graveyard, making sure the furnace was fed and that there was hot water for the showers. I was only on this job a couple of months. I was making pretty good money for a kid, $1.67 a day.

Bill Lindsay called me in and told me to report to the bull gang, where I did various jobs until they sent me to the cookhouse in Chapman Camp as a dishwasher. Everybody else, all the young guys like me, turned it down, but I was the junior man so away I went.

We were feeding roughly about a hundred people. In the summer months, we fed about a hundred and twenty because of the summer students getting on. I was on staff now so I was getting sixty dollars a month and room and board, which was thirty dollars.

I was in there about a year and hated it. So every time I got an hour off, I would be up in the Company office trying to get out of there. It didn't work. So what I did the following summer was I took a month off, told them I was sick. I went and worked on a ranch up in Sheep Creek. When I came back and they were going to put me back in the cookhouse, I told them to just strike me off because I was finished. So I took the month off and when I came back,

I went up to the Company office and they told me to report up at the mine for the bull gang.

In 1938 the Company had just started pumping out the old Stemwinder Mine, just below the [Mark Creek] dam. I got on that job. We had to pack everything up to the mine, ladders, planks, everything we needed. We packed everything along the creek on this trail called the Burma Trail.

They started off with a siphon system. We had an air line going down to force the water up a 4-inch line that ran into the creek. That only worked so far because of the law of gravity. Then we had to start using pumps. So that winter, old Len Eckford and I worked graveyard just to run the pumps. We would pretty much have the mine dry for day shift when there was some diamond drills running. They were trying to find out if it was worthwhile going into that side of the mountain. We worked up there until the spring when they abandoned it and let it fill up with water again. I guess they couldn't find nothing.

Well, I'm talking about the Stemwinder. They had started a drift across the creek from the Stemwinder shaft. It was to come in like a circular tunnel. It was to come in from the 3900 Level in the Sullivan and come out here, and the plans were to have a trestle built along the creek down to the rockhouse. Big plans. This was the idea of the general manager at the time. His name was Ritchie. He got caught in a blast and died and so did his idea.

So anyway, we had our doghouse in this drift about fifteen feet in from the entrance. We planked it off, made a table and benches, made it as comfortable as we could. We had a coal heater in there with the pipe running outside. It was pretty good, except for the bloody packrats. It seemed to me there was thousands of them, especially when you turned your lamps out to have a nap.

This one night, Len and I built a trap to catch one. So I got an old powderbox and propped it up with a stick, put some bread in it, and I caught one. I was wearing leather mitts. I grabbed it and killed it with my crescent wrench. In the morning, as we were leaving to walk down to the mine to report off, I got a piece of string tied to the rat and hung it about face level in the doorway of the doghouse. Old Ed McMahon was on day shift and he used to walk up earlier than the other guys so he could get a spot by the coal stove. I guess from what the other guys said he almost bowled them over trying to get out of the tunnel. He was shouting and hollering. Scared the dickens out of him, we did.

We used to have to report off to the master mechanic when we got off shift. The next morning, he asked us how everything was going, then he said Joe Geigerich wanted to see us. Joe was second in command at the mine. So poor old Len says, "We're in for it now." So in we went.

In those days, even the second in command was like God. You would go in, take off your hat and stand there saying things like "good morning," "how are you?", all that stuff. He was sitting behind his desk. He let us stand there for awhile before saying anything. Then he asked, "How's the packrats up there?" I said, "Oh, we got lots of packrats." I knew where this was going. "Well," he said, "Tunny, you and Len were the only two guys up there the other night and old Ed McMahon happened to walk right into a rat. He came all the way down here to tell me about it. He wanted me to fire both of you. It's all right to catch packrats, but don't hang them anymore. Now, you're both doing a good job so get out of here." I think he was doing all he could not to laugh, but we never hung no more rats. It took awhile before old Ed would talk to us.

After I left the Stemwinder, they put me in the rockhouse just below the mine building, where we loaded CPR cars to take the ore to the concentrator. This one day, John Popovich and I were working together loading. Each car had four chutes to load it. John was on the top end and I was on the bottom end of the train. Actually, it was never really a rush to get the cars loaded but we liked to highball. We were young guys so we really flew.

So this particular morning, I had these four chutes running into a car and I had the next chute open in the next car up. The way you did this was there was a check wheel and you had a little wedge to hold the gate open.

From the left, machine shop, 3900 Level portal, mine office and dry. Bottom right, rockhouse and CPR train, loading.

The rockhouse just below 3900 Level. The ore was hauled out on the main line (3900) level by train and dumped into bins in the rockhouse. The CPR loaded cars from chutes at the bottom of the building and took the ore to the concentrator. This was the procedure before the 3700 Portal was driven. Thereafter, Cominco was able to haul their own ore.

Soon as you got your last chute open, you would run down the line and just put your foot on the wheel so that the wedge would drop out and the gate would drop.

Well, I just turned around to run to the next car and I knocked somebody over. I never stopped to look who it was because I didn't want a runaway and have muck all over the ground. I ran like a son of a bitch to get to the next car when I heard this hollering. It was this Roaring Bill Lindsay, the mine manager, that I had knocked over. My partner, John, was at the other end of the rockhouse, and it was pretty noisy in there, but he could hear Bill hollering. Bill said, "You French son of a bitch. I should fire you right now but I'm not going to. But if you ever have a spill, I'll shut this place down and you'll muck every piece of muck up into those big CPR cars, and then I'll fire you." I did kind of learn a lesson because we did slow down.

I was taken out of the rockhouse because I had a spot on the lung that they found on one of the check-ups that we had every year. I was out for three weeks and then they put me back in again. There used to be a fellow come in from the TB [Tuberculosis] Foundation. I guess they worked in conjunction with the [Workers'] Compensation Board. He had to cover the whole area. Anyway, I was out for three weeks on the bull gang, out in the fresh air, and then back in the rockhouse. I was there about a week on day shift when our shift boss, Henry Chambers, came to me and told me I had to go back on the bull gang again, right now. So out I go. I grabbed my bucket, took it to the bull gang lunchroom, spent the day doing nothing.

At the end of the shift, Henry came to me and told me to go to the rockhouse tomorrow morning. I asked, "What's going on?" He said, "You know that health inspector? Well, he dropped back in to spot check on you fellows who were sent outside. He wanted to check where you were working." We were sent out to work on the bull gang in the fresh air because we were dusted. So I guess the word had got out that he was coming and they wanted to be able to tell him that all us dusted guys were out in the fresh air and working on the bull gang so everything was fine. So that's the way that worked.

I was finally taken out of the rockhouse and went swamping on a truck. The Company had two of those old 1928 White trucks. One was a flatbed and the other was a dump truck. I was working with a guy by the name of Fontaine. We used to haul in a lot of gravel and sand for the mine. Then we hauled in a million loads of black soil from Marysville to the Cominco Gardens and to the [Kimberley] golf course, when they were expanding. It was the good old days when the Company did everything. I stayed on the truck until I joined the army in 1941.

It was a Company town and the Company built the water line that went up the main street. It was an old wooden-stave pipe being replaced with a steel pipe. There was a crew of about twenty guys digging it by hand. It was supposed to be eight feet deep, but with all the building going on, I'm sure in some places it was twelve feet deep. Some of the rocks in the ditch looked like houses. In those days you didn't have backhoes, so we used to get a chain around the rock and use the lift on the truck to move them. Some of the rocks couldn't be moved like this so we dragged them, and we dumped a lot of them up by the bridge going up to the ski hill. I think a lot of them are still there.

In the spring of 1941, there were three of us coming off the hill from work: Bill Graham, Lloyd McLellan and myself. We decided to join up, spur of the moment thing. There was a Colonel Philpot, a veteran from the First War, who was signing guys up. He had an office up above where Centre 64 is. So we went in and signed up. We told him we would like to stay together when we joined up. He said there was no problem with that. We never saw each other for five years, until we come back from the war.

Well, anyhow, we went up to the Company office the next morning to tell them that we had joined up and were finished. Old Bill Lindsay was there. He tore a strip off us for awhile. He told us we didn't have to go because we were part of the essential service to the war effort. But at the end of his tirade, he wished us the best of luck and said our jobs would still be here when we came back. And they were, five years later.

When I came back from the war in February 1946, I had a month's leave coming and when that was over, I went up to the Company office and told them I was ready to go to work. I thought I wouldn't mind staying outside, but that was not to be. It was all filled up out there, so I was told to report for underground. For the first three weeks they had me doing whatever needed done, mucking, packing, cleaning up, stuff like that.

Then they put me on the pipe gang. I think we were making about $7.50. The Centre Section and the North End were combined at the time and my partner on the pipe gang was young Billy Muir. Quite often we never had time to take a coffee break when we got underground because, on afternoon shift, they would take the pipe off to blast and it was up to Bill and I to get it back together before the miners got there. This was in the stopes, and these stopes weren't side by side. Oh no, they were all over the place.

So we were on a dead gallop because you would get shit from the foreman if the miners couldn't get drilling right away. Christ, we had other places to do like raises and subs, fix hoses. We never even had time to think. On top of that, we were supposed to be nipping. That's when they had all the common steel. We had to pack it out to all these places, down to the drift and get it to the blacksmith shop. So some days, we didn't get enough piping done or enough nipping done. The foreman got screaming about us not getting this place nipped out.

So this one day we said, "This has got to come to a head," and all we did one day was nip and no pipe got put in. So right off the bat, you got all the miners screaming about no pipe. So the next morning the foreman was going to fire us and so we got into it. This is when the shift bosses stepped in and said, 'Look, this can't go on. Two men can only do so much." So in the wisdom of this foreman, he decided to put another crew on. Christ, it wasn't like there weren't enough men. Jeeze, they were hiding men because they didn't have enough work for them.

At the same time, we tried to get a raise. Didn't get that. Hell, they brought in time-method guys and all that stuff. It was so comical that the only guys that got a raise were the pipemen sitting down at the shop. They were just better bullshit artists than we were.

I spent about a year on the pipe gang and there were miners that were really going after the money, like Joe Moore and Nick Seredick, and most often were running two faces at one time. So anyway, with this other crew to help out, we had a bit more time to spare. So Joe and Nick would take us aside and show us how to drill. Sometimes we would get a couple of hours' drilling, so we were getting into this mining business. So finally, I asked to get off the pipe gang.

Billy went mining before I did, then finally I got to go mining in a stope. There was no mining school. You just went with an experienced miner. He took you under his wing. Bob Varley, the Silver Fox, was my partner.

The place I went on my first real mining job was in this stope in the North End, past the blacksmith shop. This stope broke to the surface and in the wintertime, there was this downdraft from the surface so your water lines would freeze up and the footwall was covered in ice. Even though I had no real seniority, nobody bumped me out of there. It had to be the coldest place in the world. Our clothes and slickers were frozen stiff. We spent a long time in the shower trying to thaw out at the end of the shift. Christ, it was cold.

We finished that cold stope and in the spring, we were to start a new one, right beside it. So when it warmed up, some of these old stope miners thought, "Well, here's a new stope going to go and it should be pretty good money to be made with the muck nice and close to the raise, easy packing stuff, short scrape and stuff," so they thought maybe it would be a good time to start bumping guys and get it for themselves.

Bob and I went to our shift boss, Hamish Scott. I said, "Good God, Hamish, we spent all winter up in that stope freezing our asses off, and we didn't make hardly any money, when nobody else would go in there. Jesus, we were only making three or four dollars over day's pay. So now that we're starting this new stope, guys want to bump us out of there. I'm telling you, Hamish, this is bullshit and I'm going right out to the office and raise shit. It's not fair. If I'm getting bumped out of there, I'm quitting." So Hamish said, with that old Scotch accent of his, "I don't blame you." As it was, they left the Fox and I in there and we spent two and a half years in there.

This was a moneymaker for the Company. At the back of this stope was a band of galena. It was almost pure. It ran from ten feet to twenty-five feet deep, just glistened at you. This was a scraper stope so we breasted it down, taking benches. The drill we had was one of those old tripod liners that you hand cranked, but we did graduate to a lighter drill called a light automatic. The hoist we had was called a Windjammer. It went "clankity-clank" when you engaged the lever for either the haul-down cable or the haul-back. It made all these weird sounds until it engaged.

I found out you could smoke two cigarettes while the scraper was going to the face and one smoke while you were pulling the muck to you to go down the raise. These stopes were a good hundred feet long and with all the siwashes, it took time. You've got to remember these hoists ran on air, not electricity. We didn't do too bad in there. It usually took us two shifts to drill off and about four shifts to scrape it out.

We were using sixty per cent forcite for powder. We had to buy our own powder and fuse. The chute-loaders didn't have to pay for their powder so lots of times they would give us whatever they had left over. Old Hardrock, when he was barring, would often find powder that hadn't gone off in the diamond drill blasts and told me where he had it stashed and to go get it. It all helped.

One day, Hamish came to me and said, "Tunny, you've not gone to the mining school, have ye?" I said, "Well, no, I haven't but I've been mining for three years." He told me if I went to mining school, I would get miner's pay no matter what I was doing and that my rate couldn't be cut no matter what I was doing, mucking, piping, whatever. Sounded good to me, so what have I got to lose? I went to mining school.

So away I went with about ten other guys up to the South End. They had a little raise for us to work on. We would each take turns on a stoper, drilling a hole. It was a real soft touch. It was a 6-week course. We would learn how to put a splice in the cable. You know, if it's done right, you can't even tell the cable has a splice in it. Not like them loop splices, which caused you more problems than enough going through idlers and on the hoist drum.

Splicing school was just great. The weather was warm so old Pop Dietz had us take some cable outside the portal and work on our splicing. It took about four days. The sun was shining and old Pop would tell us to take five so we would stretch out. Like I say, it was a soft touch and till this day, I still can't put in a proper running splice. Couldn't get it right unless there was two of us and the other guy knew what he was doing.

Red Foster came up and showed us how to run a mucking machine. That old fart could do everything. Since we were up in the South End, it was like working in a miniature mine with the narrow gauge track, little tiny cars, motors and this tiny little mucking machine. I think Red must have laughed himself sick teaching us guys how to run this tiny mucking machine. We had it off the track more than we had it on.

I was working with Swede Dellert and we were driving a backfill raise at thirty-nine degrees, just enough so that the muck would run. It was to go up to the Top Mine so they could dump backfill down into the stope beside us. The first part of the raise went up four hundred feet and then we had a turn-over at ninety degrees to the left that went another four hundred or so feet. This was called a light timbered raise using sprags and the planks that were three by eight, muck compartment on one side and our slide and ladders on the other. The planks were three high on the sprags, just enough to keep the man-way clear of muck. At the turn-over, we had a platform with our tugger on it to pull the skip up the next part of the raise. We had the tugger set up right at the bottom staring up the slide, with a partial bulkhead to stop muck and that kind of stuff from hitting the tugger operator.

This one day, we had put some drill steel, our lunch buckets, bits and drill oil in the skip to pull it up to where we were working. I was running the tugger and Swede was standing over in one corner, out of the way because there wasn't all that much room. We had a marker on the cable to tell us when we were near the top. Just as the marker came to me and I was about to put the brake on, the cable went slack. I yelled at Swede, "She's gone."

I jumped from behind the tugger to where Swede was. He grabbed me around the waist and pulled me in. That skip came down and went through that little bulkhead right over the tugger, just nicked it, and it was gone down four hundred feet and then another two hundred feet into the stope.

I guess we stood there about five minutes before Swede let go of me and when he did, the back of his hands were covered in blood from all these splinters of wood that were stuck in them from the bulkhead. We sat around for awhile trying to settle down while we pulled splinters out of his hands. That skip probably weighed about four hundred pounds and dropped down about three hundred feet to where we were. If it would have hit us, I don't think anybody would have known for awhile where we were. More than likely, we'd be down six hundred feet in the stope and not much left of us to pick up. Just missed us by inches.

Walter Ekskog was our shifter when this happened. He came up, looked around, and told us how lucky we were. We kind of figured that ourselves. He sent out for a couple of bag lunches for us 'cause our buckets were long gone and we still had most of the shift to finish. At the end of the shift, Walter told us to go to first aid outside and pick up a couple of requisitions for new lunch buckets.

Swede and I went upstairs to first aid when we finished with our showers. I forget who the first aid guy was, but he was a jerk. I said that we came up for the requisitions for new buckets and this pompous ass says, "Heard all about that and I bet I know what happened. In fact, I know what happened. You were running that tugger way too fast and pulled that skip into the tail block and pulled the eyebolt out." I said, "Where were you about eight this morning?" He said, "I was right here." "Well," I said, "I was right there and I doubt that you can see through the mountain to where we were. You're just lucky that you're not buying two coffins instead of two lousy buckets." And guess who was standing just outside the door listening to this exchange? None other than old Walter, our shift boss. Well, I'm going to tell you, he tore a strip off that asshole like I never heard before, not even after five years in the army. It was tremendous. That's one of the reasons why Walter was so well respected.

Just after that incident with the skip, Swede and I were just setting up and starting to bar down the loose. We had two vertical rounds to break through to the surface. The raise was seven feet high by sixteen feet wide. All of a sudden, we heard this rumble. There was nothing falling off the face but we thought we'd just sit off to the side to let it settle down. So anyway, everything quieted down and we got set up and were drilling and along comes Walter. So we shut off the drills so we could talk and we told Walter about the rumbling.

Walter says, "What day is this?" I told him it was Wednesday. "I know what that is," he says. "It's Nels Nordby up there with a Cat. He's cleaning off the overburden for the break-through." So, it's funny. That day I ran into Nels downtown. I said, "You were up on top today cleaning the top off for us, eh?" He says, "How did you know that?" "Well," I says, "Swede and I are coming up there." And I was telling him about the noise. "Christ," he says, "you guys are that close? If I would have known that, I would never have come over there." We were only about twenty feet below him. He was told we were a hundred feet below him, not twenty.

Swede and I had to bar down this backfill raise so we could put in a bulkhead to divert the backfill into another stope. He called me over to where he was barring and showed me a bunch of bits he had found, tungsten bits. I guess somebody from the bit shop thought this would be a good place to get rid of all the old bits, just throw them down this backfill raise and dispose of them. So I guess whoever was responsible for getting rid of those bits just dumped them down this raise we were in.

Remember, in them days, we had to pay for bits that we lost. Heck, now we had thousands. We had bags of them that we picked up and stashed. A lot of miners never had to pay for lost bits for quite awhile after that. It finally got out though. Walter Ekskog came in this one day and he was looking around and, Jesus, if he didn't start finding bits. So what he did was tell the foreman. So the foreman called us in and said, "Now, look, I'm going to ask a stupid question. Nope, I'm not even going to bother to ask a stupid question. I know in my heart that you guys have been turning in these old bits, along with all my other miners, and enough is enough."

I don't know whatever happened on that. Somebody should have got it in the neck but nobody ever did. They didn't jump on our back because, after all, we're old hard rock miners. Hell, you've got to use every method you can to make a dollar.

Kurt Erlitz and I were in R-11 Raise from the bottom to the top. It had around five turn-overs in it. It went four hundred and some feet. Both Kurt and I were scrawny little bastards. A big dog weighed more than both of us put together.

We had Nick Seredick working with us one time when we were timbering a turn-over. These planks that we were using, three by twelve, had just come out of Fabro's timber yard. They were covered in snow and stuck together with ice. Old Nick, he tied on seven or eight of these planks. Kurt and I were at the top and we would take them off the tugger cable. Nick, well, he didn't like to climb very much and we were up around eighty feet. Well, he came up because, like he said, "I wanted to see two skinny son of a bitches try to lift those planks." He gave us a hand. He was an oldtimer.

But I can remember how sick you were when you came out. Your stomach muscles just pulled all to hell. It was tough. Kurt was one hell of a raise miner. No fear at all and a real highballer.

When I finally got off mining and got into slushing, hell, I was in my fifties and getting a little long in the tooth to be climbing up and down raises. Things got a lot easier on this old body of mine. I slushed in the cold muck for awhile then the hot muck came along. Conditions in the hot muck were bad. The SO_2 was as bad as it could possibly be. It was really difficult. Our mouths were blistered because the moisture coming from our mouth and nose would form sulphuric acid from the dust that got around our face. Billy Muir and I were partners. He was quite a hairy person. Under his arms he had big welts and down around your privates, that was all raw and welted. It was rough. They gave us this lotion to put on but it didn't work all that well.

The whole bloody block was on fire. We were using one and a quarter-inch cable on the hoists, the same kind of cable that was used on the incline shafts. It used to get burned right through. I remember we put on new cable on a Friday afternoon shift and when the cross shift came on Monday morning to start scraping and just tightened up the cables, they were gone. That's what the acid had done.

I was in the hot muck for six years. I've seen it so hot in the subs that it would go *bang!*, just like an explosion, and it would be the back of the sub breaking off from the extreme heat. If any moisture got on the muck down the ore pass, especially the waste rock, you could hear all these little explosions going on in the raise. It was all these rocks breaking apart.

There was this one drawhole, talk about temperature. The lead would pour down like a blast furnace. The lead would pour down and start building up as it cooled off a little and it formed a solid lead bulkhead that covered the whole

Hot-muck miners suiting up.

drawhole, and this was a big drawhole, probably ten feet by ten feet. Just kept damming and building up, and it's still there. How are you supposed to get something like that out? It's going to be there forever and then some.

When Bobo — Carl Olsen — got burned up in the North End, a slough had come down. Carl was with two other fellows in this sub. They all started to run out and Carl stumbled and went down and got caught in this red-hot dust. They were wearing MSAs. They didn't have asbestos suits on at the time. He was severely burned. The dust went down inside his cuffs, around his neck and onto his chest. His face was sort of protected by the mask. The mask melted right to his face. He walked out and asked that nobody touch him because of the pain he was in and got to first aid and then the hospital.

He was my neighbour. I can remember him sitting outside. He would be sitting in the shade. His skin on his chest was all cracked, just a real mess. I was over visiting him this one day when the Compensation Board person came to his place and was trying to get him to go back to work, up in the office doing those Mickey Mouse jobs they want you to do. I told the Compensation guy to get the hell out of here or he'll be the guy going on compensation. I was so mad. I knew Carl all my life. He didn't need to be treated like this. I was ready to punch this guy out.

When I got burned, there were four of us working together: Percy Sims, Ted Oliynyk, Joe Berard and me. We were on graveyard. I was working Sub A and Percy was in Sub B. When you blast, you shut down the whole area. Percy wanted to go into his sub and look at a drawhole that was hung up. It was No. 11 on the left side. We took a look up the drawhole and we could see the fire. It was up quite a ways. So we made up a small shot. We were using NCN. We put the powder in a plastic bag, put the B-line down in it, and then wrapped the shot with asbestos wrap, about three wraps. Then we ran the B-line down through asbestos tubing so the line wouldn't burn or melt before it got to the shot.

So we got the shot up and it was just a small one, enough for concussion. We went over to my sub to let it off. We might have trimmed the fuse a bit. The shot went off. It was just a small thump. So we were sitting there, just taking five. We had taken our leather gloves off because it was hot and our hands were all sweaty. All of a sudden, there was an outdraft from the sub and a big rumble. In a few seconds you couldn't see and you could feel the heat.

We took off for the man-way but you couldn't see. All we had on were those little pig snouts for masks. So down the man-way we went. I bumped into somebody at the top of the man-way and I moved over to the side to let this person go down ahead of me. I was about thirty feet down to Joe's sub. Percy had stumbled and finally got to us. My hardhat got hung up on something and I lost that, but I had my lamp in my hand and I put it around my neck and got to the bottom. I had to feel my way along the pipeline to the door where there was fresh air on the other side. I had a hell of a time trying to get the door open because of the air pressure.

I was the first one out. I stumbled right into our shifter, Ed Walsh, who was coming in to see us. Joe stumbled out, then Ted and Percy. I was in a daze standing there. When I looked at my palm of one hand, the skin was just hanging there. And Percy's one hand was hanging in shreds. So there we were. You're never prepared for things like this. We didn't even have a stretcher on top. There was a first aid kit so what I did was put some gauze on my hand and put it in a plastic bag and tied it on. That was my left hand but my right hand was really stinging but you couldn't see anything wrong with it.

We were really concerned about Percy. We got him into the doghouse, made him as comfortable as we could and phoned first aid, telling them to be at the bottom of the raise when we got Percy down. Since there was no stretcher around, what we eventually did was put Percy in this big skip, tied him in. We were up about eighty feet from the drift and this was an 80-degree raise. I went down first because I wasn't going to be no help to anybody with my hand the way it was. So I climbed down to help at the bottom. What they did was, Joe was on the tugger and the other guys would have safety ropes tied on the skip and they would just overlap each other all the way down, just lowering the skip easy.

Roy Carlson was the first aider and he was there with the transportation boys with the ambulance. Every bump on the way out put poor old Percy into agony from his burns. So we end up in the hospital. They had to cut Percy's coveralls off. Dr. Johnston was the doctor on call that night. He was going to start working on Percy but found out he couldn't. They had to put Percy under because of his pain.

Dr. Finch showed up to start working on me. He cut away all this loose skin on my hand and I was telling him my other hand was stinging like hell so he put it under hot water to wash it off. Well, I'll tell you, I hit the roof. "Oops," he says. Then he put it under cold water. You still couldn't see much. They decided to keep me in overnight.

Mac McArthur, the safetyman from the mine, came up to see us and because my hands were all buggered up, he gave me a shower and got me into bed. It must have been a good couple of hours when they brought Percy into the room. He was still out. I must have woken up just before he came in and I looked at my hand that had been under the water and it was covered in blisters. I guess when the water went on my hand it made sulphuric acid. Dr. Johnston was with Percy so he fixed up my hand with cream and bandaged it up.

Poor old Perce. When we woke up, he had his hands all bandaged up just like mine. It looked like we had boxing gloves on. A nurse came in and said, "Mr. Sims, we have to get a urine sample." Well, Perce, he started to laugh, even in the pain he was in, and we both started to laugh. So, anyway, we went into the bathroom together. I told him I would hold the bottle but nothing else. So there we are, all hunkered over, our asses hanging out of those stupid gowns they gave us to wear. So I held the bottle and I finally had to tell him to "shut that thing off. We got enough." We started to laugh again, really hard. Even the nurse out in the room was killing herself laughing. It was a good thing it happened, even in the pain we were in. It just broke the ice.

I retired when I was fifty-eight but I was going to go until I was sixty. This was during the transition period of the mine going mechanized and not much money was being spent in the conventional part of the mine. I was getting fed up at the time and I always said that it was Rolly Trenaman that gave me the nudge to get out of there. I was really getting fed up and I guess he was in a bind himself putting all the money into mechanized.

This one morning, Rolly and Brian Buckley came into where we were working with the foreman, Nick Kostiuk, just doing the tour thing. Rolly said, "How's it going?" "Not too good," I said. "The ventilation is all haywire." We had found where a small seal had got blown out and my partner, Carl Shonsta, being an old timberman, thought we could fix it up and help the ventilation into the subs we were slushing in. Rolly told us that it wasn't our job to fix it and they would look into it. This came from the superintendent, not the foreman, and he told us to get back to our own jobs.

Well, my back went up. I put in a couple of words. I got a little hostile and Rolly got a little hostile. Rolly says to me, "When are you retiring?" I said, "Maybe in about five minutes from now." So I looked at my watch and he took off. Brian Buckley stayed behind and asked me if I was serious and I told him I was serious. Brian was a good guy.

This was about April and a couple more things like that happened, and about June I remember telling my wife, Bert, "Maybe you better hang tough on the bucket. Maybe I won't be needing one." I hung tough to the end of June, but you know yourself that when you go to work underground and you're in that frame of mind, it's not a good place to be.

So deep enough is deep enough. I pulled the pin. I put in forty-one years counting the five years in the army. But I had enough. A guy knows when that's enough.

BOB VARLEY

The Silver Fox...

Bob was a slight man with a big sense of humour. There was a slyness about him that, along with his silver hair, earned him the nickname "The Silver Fox." Bob was also one of those small men who had to prove to everybody that he could do it, and do it he did. No, sir, Bob didn't take the backseat to anyone. He always got to the mine early so he could sit around with some of his cronies and swap anecdotes for a chuckle. Bob and his wife, Nellie, were always welcome company.

I came here in the fall of 1938 and I hung around until I got hired on in 1940. The Company put me on graveyard shift for seventeen months, seven days a week, working on transportation. I would get off shift at seven in the morning and be at home having breakfast at eight. I'd be going to sleep at the table so I would go to bed. I would be wide awake at ten. This went on for seventeen bloody months. There was just no way I could sleep so I spent most of my time playing poker. That's the way it was then.

When they first put me underground, I couldn't believe it, ya know. I was bored. There was nothing to do. Heck, there was four crews of four on transportation and you only used three guys on each train. So we used to take turns sitting in the doghouse at night. Jack McCormick was the mucker boss at the time. He was a real good guy. I went to him and asked if he could find me something to do. Jeeze, I sat in that doghouse on graveyard with these other guys for two weeks. There was nothing to do.

I used to haul around ten or twelve trains a night outside. There was two crews hauling at the time, one from the North End and one from the South End. Each crew would haul twelve trains outside to the rockhouse. I was doing that for a year and a half until I went mining. We used to have three men on a train. The job was soft enough. One guy was a switchman and one guy was a rover. The switchman ran the chute loading the cars. One guy had mucker's pay and one guy had motorman's pay and then there was loaderman's pay. I think we were making around $10 a day. I believe we had pretty full pay cheques because we were working seven days a week. There

Trammer dumping muck down an ore pass.

was no shift differential for the three shifts. It was all straight pay, no bonus. We cleared $78 every two weeks.

There was a couple dozen guys on the spare-board on graveyard, and on day shift there was over four hundred. These guys were told to go hide somewhere and keep out of sight. I kind of figure the Company was getting money from the government for the amount of guys they had on the payroll, being this was wartime. It was the easiest money I ever made. I was getting $6 a day for just sitting in the doghouse. I couldn't believe this kind of money after having worked on the farms on the Prairies where I came from, but it was just too goddamn boring.

In 1940, there was guys from all over working here, from Tennessee, the southern states, because the States weren't at war at this time. These guys just come up here and got a job. The Company would just take anybody on because they were that short of guys. All the local guys were in the war. If you didn't work, you went in the army. It was compulsory. Wartime laws were in effect at the time. A lot of guys come to the mine that didn't want to work but the Company couldn't fire them. These guys just got a job so they wouldn't have to go in the army.

The biggest train wreck I ever saw was when I was working with the Ingebrigtsen boys, Nels and Alf. We were a three-man crew. We were loading in 4 Drift just where the main drift goes into the South End. The dispatcher radioed us that the North End train was coming in from outside. Our train was out on the main line where we were loading the cars. So we backed off into where we could throw the switch and let them go by.

These trains come in at a pretty good clip, backwards, just flying. We got back in about ten feet past the switch but we had a bunch of empty cars at the end of the train. Well, they hit a rock under the chute. We didn't know how it happened but there was cars flying all over the place. We ran like hell into a branch track. Talk about a pile-up. They were piled up to the top of the drift, cars on top of each other, crisscrossed, air and water pipes blowing all over the place. The electric trolley was down. Sparks and smoke were everywhere. What a bloody mess. Must have been about twenty cars all over the place.

The shift boss, Dougie Smith, showed up and he says, "How did this happen? You guys forget to throw the switch?" It all happened so fast, we couldn't remember if we did or not. I was on the chute loading and I said to Nels, "Did you throw the switch?" He said, "I can't remember if I did or not." There was a car on top of the switch, sideways, about a foot off the track, and I got down on my knees and I could see that the switch had been thrown so that left us in the clear. They got it all cleaned up the next day because we only had a skeleton crew on graveyard, only one electrician, but that was probably the best I ever saw.

I was glad to get off transportation. I found it awfully dusty. A guy's lungs were always full of crap. I asked Ted Nagle if I could get off transportation after about a year and a half. He told me that there was some guys ahead of me but he would see what he could do.

When I did get off, I went mining. There was no such thing as mining school. They just put you with an experienced miner and he taught you. Some of the experienced guys were real bastards with new guys but most of them were real good because they knew what it was like to be green.

Some of those hard rock raises, ya know, had the hardest rock in the world. Christ, those guys had to put up crossbars and then hall up them big bloody liners and set them up on the bar. Hell, they were over two hundred pounds. I was just too small for that so I went into the stopes. It was a lot easier on a little guy like me. There's no way I could'a done it.

Some of those stopes we went in were four hundred feet high and a hundred and fifty feet wide, big bastards. We would bench them up and the barmen would come in and bar the loose off for us. They would be up there three, four ladders. They did a good job. They had to inspect it pretty close because they couldn't miss anything because it would just take a small rock to hurt somebody.

I had that happen to my partner, Charlie Parkhouse. We were setting up on the muck in this stope. It was a small one, maybe fifty feet wide. He got everything set up, one of these tripods. I went up to turn the air and water on in this little sub off to the side when I heard a crash. I could see Charlie laying on the muck. A rock that the barmen had missed fell from the back onto Charlie's head and he was out colder than a cucumber.

I knew transportation was going to pull this muck where he had fallen. It was too steep for me to get to him and pull him up. I hustled down to the drift to stop transportation and I just got there as they were going to start pulling. Well, he come out of that all right. He had a lump on his head about the size of a tomato. They come up with a stretcher and hauled him out.

Les Carson and I were working together in a slusher sub. This sub was just about finished and we were going to move the scraper and slusher down to the sub below this one. Les said maybe I should go down and have a look-see and see what we got while he kept slushing. So I went down and walked in about twenty feet to the first muck pile. I started looking around. I got dizzy in the head. I thought to myself, "Jeeze, there's gas in here." I stepped backwards and I was out cold as a cucumber. I must have stepped back one step and when I fell and came to, I didn't know if I had been there for an hour or a second. Just that one step backwards put me in the fresh air again. When I got back to Les, I asked how long I was gone. He said about five minutes.

I was with Bud Hart on the fourth level when that stope caved in. Boy, was that something. There was about a dozen of us in this little cut-out at the end of the drift that we used for a lunchroom. There was just a piece of brattice over the door to make it a little warmer. It was all open stope around us. We heard this rumble. Christ, we heard this big roar. It sounded like the whole mine was caving in.

The lunchroom/ doghouse underground with all the comforts of home.

Guys jumped up, grabbed their buckets and headed out the door, ya know. I can remember Bud standing up on the bench in the corner. All the other guys were just running through the brattice door and up the drift. I was out the door when I could see rocks flying up the raise and past the door, so I stepped back in and said to Bud that we'd be better off in here. So I jumped up on the bench too. Those rocks were coming up the raise from concussion. Bud was as white as a ghost and I probably was too. We were better off in the cut-out, I thought, because it was all open stopes around us and we didn't know where the cave-in was. So we stayed there for a few minutes until everything quieted down. Then we went down to the North End station. There was lunches and buckets scattered all the way down the drift. Panic, ya know.

When we got down to the station, you could see the corrugated walls for the shops and shifters' shack had all been blown out. There was stuff all over the place. Nobody got hurt. Lucky, just real lucky. I heard that about five million tons came down. That's a lot of muck, and not a soul got hurt.

ALF OLSEN

Always kept two fingers up...

Alf was a quiet man, not one to keep talking when there was nothing left to say. A product of the Depression and from the Prairies, he was used to hard work and making do. He was an old-time miner who got the job done, one way or another. He passed on his stubborn streak to his two sons, who followed him into the mine. They also shared his appreciation for the taste of the golden ale.

Alf enjoyed quaffing a few beers after shift, and he kept the bartender busy. The waiter would set two beers down on Alf's table and before he got back to the bar, Alf would have two fingers up, requesting another round. His philosophy was: "You work hard, you drink fast." There was none faster in Kimberley.

I started working for the Consolidated Mining and Smelting Company in 1928 at the Company farm in Marysville. I was looking after the cattle and pigs that they had there. I guess they figured that being a farm boy from Saskatchewan, I could handle this type of work. I worked here for a couple of years then went back to Saskatchewan.

The Depression was on at the time and most of the topsoil on the farm was heading to Manitoba. There was just no way that the farm was going to support our large family, so I headed back to Kimberley in 1934. I got hired on again by the Company and was darn lucky to get a job, what with all the guys out there looking for one. I worked on the surface crew for about a year and was transferred underground in 1935.

I got married to a girl from Invermere in 1940. Her maiden name was Olsen, same as mine, so as far as name changing, not too much went on there. In 1941 I started building a house in Marysville.

Well, I needed a wheelbarrow to use while I dug out my foundations so I went over to the Company farm where I had worked before and the same boss was still there. I asked if I could borrow a wheelbarrow from them. The old boss said, "Sure, go ahead and take one. Just be sure you bring it back when you're done with it."

In 1951 I replaced the steel wheel on the wheelbarrow with a rubber one so I could dig out my basement. In those days, you always dug the basement after you had built the house. I don't know why. It's just the way it was done then. Probably it was because there just wasn't enough time to do both if you wanted a roof over your family's head before winter, and you could take your time doing it whenever you had some spare time.

I was about ninety years old and living on my son's farm with my wife when I noticed that old wheelbarrow sitting off to the side. I mentioned to my son Gordie, "I guess I'm not finished with that barrow yet. I'll have to get it back to the Company one of these days. They're probably looking for it."

Just before I started at the mine, I had some brothers working there. My brother Oscar was working underground on the track gang and had only been there a few days when along came Bill Lindsay, the mine superintendent, who told him he was fired. So Oscar started heading down the drift to go outside when ol' Bill hollered at him, "Where in the bloody hell are you going?" "I'm heading home." "How come?" "You just fired me." "Well, I just hired you back again," yells ol' Roaring Bill. "Nope, I only get fired once," hollered Oscar, and he walked out of the mine. That was Oscar's career with CM&S and he never came back. You know, us Swedes can be stubborn bastards at times.

My two brothers, Lloyd and Roy, were working in the mine just before I got hired on and then my brother Phil joined us. I lost my brother Roy in 1951. He drowned. Lloyd and I worked until 1971, then we retired at the same time, and our younger brother Phil retired in 1974. In all, with all the time between my brothers and me, two sons and one grandson, our family has put in pretty close to two hundred years' service with the Company.

I was a barman up in the South End section of the mine for a number of years. In fact, there's a picture of me up on the third ladder doing some barring. I must have been a good forty feet up in the air and you can see the ropes that held the ladders in place. I think there were five ropes. It seemed like I was up there forever while they took pictures. Couldn't see a thing with all those damn lights shining in my eyes but it turned out to be a pretty good picture. I've got one at home. Going to get it blown up someday.

I like telling people about the time I fell off a 100-foot ladder. They all say, "You fell off a 100-foot ladder! How bad did you get hurt?" I tell them, "Hell, I never got hurt at all. I only fell off the bottom step." I can usually get a good chuckle out of that.

I did most of my mining up in the South End. I thought that I would rather freeze up there in the fresh air than breathe all that dust and smoke that was down in the lower levels. I didn't think those guys working in the lower levels would live very long breathing all that shit and I guess I was right. I've been retired for over thirty years. I'll be ninety-six this year.

I guess you could say I'm screwing Cominco out of that crappy little pension that they gave me. You know, after all the years I put in, I got a lousy $280 a month. When they gave us pensioners a $50 raise about ten years ago, they had the nerve to make a big issue out of it by saying they didn't have to give it to us but it was just out of the goodness of their heart. Big bloody deal. The blood-sucking bastards. I'm glad I kept that goddamn wheelbarrow now.

I never worked in the hot muck. They tried to tell me that I had to work in there. This was the first time that the hot muck showed up, in the fifties. I told them there was no way I was going to work in there. They told me I didn't have any choice. I told them that I had two good legs that would take me out of there. Anyway, I never did get into the hot muck. I look now at all the guys that did work in there. They're all dead, so I figure I made a pretty good choice.

Alf Olsen barring the back in a stope. He was a fearless barman.

I was sent into this stope with Andy Mellor. We were benching with those big bloody tripods and liners. Andy had been in there from the start. I came in quite a bit later to be his partner. I shone my light up to have a look at the back but couldn't see anything because it was so far up. I said to Andy, "You been in here from the start. What's the back like?" "Well," says Andy, "It wasn't too good at the start, but we're getting further away from it all the time." So it was a good eighty feet up and we had no idea what was up above our heads. So you just go in and hope nothing decides to fall on you. That's the way it was. We all took our chances. It was part of the job.

I was walking past the Credit Union this one day and here's old Hardrock MacDonald shovelling snow off the sidewalk. This is just shortly after he retired. He says to me, "That's a terrible back up there, Alf. It just keeps sloughing." That's when I knew he would always be a barman, when he refers to the falling snow as falling muck in a stope.

Boy, I had the shit scared out me this one time when I was on transportation. I was up on the chute loading cars this one day. When I dropped the gate so the muck would flow into the car, a bloody hardhat came out and went into the car.

I pulled the gate up as fast as I could 'cause I figured a guy would be coming next. Next thing I know, here comes a guy walking down the drift holding his light in his hand and waving it at me. When he got up to me he says, "Did you happen to see a hardhat come through?" "I sure did," I said. "I was afraid to drop the chute again in case the owner of it was coming through, all mixed up in the muck." "Well, don't worry about it. I'm the guy it belongs to." I can tell you I was darn happy to return that fellow's hat.

ED PENDRY

Combative as a pit bull...

"Pit bull" surely is the name that best describes Ed. He would go to the wall and fight in the trenches for his workmates. I never heard of anyone not wanting Ed for a partner or a cross shift. He was just a damn hard-working and reliable partner who enjoyed a beer and camaraderie with other miners.

Ed was one of the better storytellers, even though he had to haul his oxygen bottle around in his later years. He developed silicosis, and the hot muck also did damage to him.

I started in 1940, mucking, then I went mining and stoping. Them days, it was the old crank machine with tripods and crossbar. The Company made their own steel and when you hit that chert, you would need a flatcar of steel. You were lucky to get three or four holes, two or four feet long, with a flatcar of steel. You would just burp the machine and the steel was gone. We had nippers hauling new steel in and taking the old steel out. Then we went to those Crag bits, big old bits. We would bring in a bit rack that looked like a big safety pin. Then the Company got stopers.

I remember working with old Johnson. He would never work with a stoper. He would set up that goddamn crank machine and tripod and never use any water. Always drilled dry. And when we blasted, old Johnson would count the shots and when the last shot was gone, he was back in the stope. You couldn't see your hand in front of your face. I was working with him at the South End. Old Joe Shaw was the foreman then.

Joe came in one day and told Johnson and me, "You better get out of there 'cause your stope is sloughing." Well, Freddie Meister and his partner, I think it was Joe Pratt, had just put up a ladder and had it tied to a stump of a pillar they had taken out. Freddie said, "I'll just go up and take the rope off." He went up the ladder and undid the ladder. Well, because of the slough that damn ladder flipped and Freddie Meister came down head first, right onto the stump of the pillar. He had a big hole in his head. We packed him out. He didn't live very long. Well, that's where I was working in the spring of '42.

In the fall of '41, I had two weeks' holiday. I went down to Alberta. They couldn't find anyone to work. This fellow wanted me to harvest and, of course, he had a nice-looking daughter. Well, I stayed a month. She was a damn good-looking girl. That's as far as I'll go on that.

When I came back, Bobby Parkinson was working in my spot. Joe Shaw was mad at me and he said to hell with Pendry. He said if I couldn't be bothered to tell him when I was coming back, Bobby was to stay working in my place. It was probably the best thing that happened to me. I got away from old Johnson and all that dust. I'd be dead today if I had stayed with him.

Then I ended up working with Carl Kavanagh and we were stoping with tripods and stuff. Then I went with Benny Redisky. We would take a stoper and be all drilled off in half a shift. All finished.

Old Johnson would still be drilling a whole shift because he wouldn't change his ways. He didn't like a stoper. He had no use for a stoper. I seen him throw a stoper down the raise. He went and got a tripod and a crank machine. He just hated a stoper, and they were a way simpler, you know. He'd drill dry because he figured it was just a waste of time to hook up the water. Dust, holy Christ, no wonder he died. He died from silicosis, stupid bugger.

I got fired here. Yeah, old Ted Nagle fired Carl Kavanagh and me. Yep, it was a simple little thing, you know. We knew we were shorted a little money on our pay at that time. We got so much a ton. It only amounted to a few cents a day. We said before we go to work, we wanted it straightened out. Old Ted said you either take your bucket and go to work or take your bucket and get the hell out of here. So we went out. Old Chic Chisholm was there.

Well, anyhow, we went downtown and got drunk. Beer was only ten cents a glass. Back then you had to go up to the office at the mine to get your time. We got good and drunk, headed to the office to get our time. Joe Giegerich was the super. Well, anyway, he made Ted Nagle apologize to us, told us to go back to work the next day. You know, old Ted Nagle never talked to me for years. I forget the guy that walked into the creek here. He used to work in the butcher shop. He was the brother-in-law of one of the butchers. We were looking for him and found him dead in that sump behind Melody Motors. That's when old Ted finally spoke to me.

We used to come out on the early trains at night when the muck came out. I asked Johnny MacDonald, the foreman, who was standing there, if I could go out early. He said "nope," and he turned around. There was a bunch of guys there, you know, doing nothing. We was all finished. He said to them, "You guys are finished. You might as well jump on the motor and go out." I said, "You little son of a beehive." I jumped on the back of the motor. Johnny was on the front and you had to get off at the Hole in the Wall before you hit the portal. Well, he didn't say anything. That was afternoon shift.

The next day, Benny and I came out on day shift on our own. I wanted to change shifts so I just came out. Old John Olsen was my shift boss. He said Johnny MacDonald wanted to see me. I said "yeah," and I just went and sat down on the bench. Everybody went to work and, of course, Johnny had to come over to see me. I didn't go see him. That didn't go over very big, you know.

Well, he came over and said, "You know, I got a good notion to put you on the spare-board." I said, "You have, have you? MacDonald, as far as I'm concerned, you nor nobody else can put me on the spare-board. You can shove the whole mine up your ass because I'm not going on the spare-board." "Well, don't feel that way," he said. "You put me into a hell of a fix." "Yeah," I said, "goddamn you, I asked to go out. You wouldn't let me. You said no, but you let the other guys go and now you're bitching because I changed shifts." "Well," he said, "you go back down to your stope and get to work."

Old John Olsen was standing listening to this. He came over to me and said, "I told that stupid little bugger that there's no sense trying to bawl out that stubborn Englishman. He'll just chew the ass out of you. So what did you go and say anything to him for?" Oh, we used to have some great times in there, you know.

Another time, I was working with Doug McKee. That was after the war. I forget where it was now. I think it was up in Q Block. We had one of the big hoists. There was a big grizzly. I forget how big but it was flat, you know, and the big slabs would lie on there and you would have to go out and bar them down. 'Course Doug had to go to the bathroom, all the way down past the old pipe bench on 3900. It was a good hour or so, you know, and he was never in a hurry. Anyhow, I told him to go ahead and I'll just go ahead and bar the slabs down.

Well, instead of putting a safety rope on like I should have, like a damn fool I went out on the grizzly with a drill steel and not a scaling bar like I should have had. When I flipped one of those slabs, it hit the steel and the steel caught me on the jaw and slid down my neck and broke my collarbone. As luck had it, the steel threw me right across the grizzly onto the trail that went around the millhole. If I had fell, I would have gone down the raise a good hundred feet as the raise was almost empty. Really don't matter. I would'a looked like shit when they pulled me out.

I was on my hands and knees when Doug showed up. I was pretty woozy, I had no goddamn idea where the hell I was, just that I was hurting real bad. We had a vertical raise to go down, somewhere around a hundred and fifty feet. Well, old Dougie, he got below me and supported me all the way down. Hell,

I was out on my goddamn feet all the way down. Don't remember a bloody thing until we got me on a motor and over to the safety office.

Joe Shaw was in the safety office at the time. I told him that I was all right. Joe told me that I wasn't and that I looked like crap and sent me to the hospital. Well, they got wrestling with me on that goddamn table and that's where they found out that my collarbone was broken, my teeth were loose, and my neck was black and blue. Now that was a close one. I could'a gone down that raise. As it was, my bloody hat went down. You know, I could'a been down that raise and old Doug could'a started scraping, thinking that I had gone for something. Just horseshit luck in one sense, I guess.

Miners on active military duty were recognized on a board at the mine.

In 1942, a bunch of us went down to Vancouver to sign up for the army. You know, when you're young, you want some kind of change. If you come back, you got that time back with the Company plus your past Company time. The trick was that you had to come back.

A lot of guys didn't come back. The guys that come back got to laugh about it. They got to see a lot of country but, like I say, a lot of guys didn't. Hell, this guy I signed up with didn't. His name was Jimmy and he was from Creston, a good friend of mine. He got killed right off the bat.

I was only over there three years. Being a miner, they figured that I would have no trouble going into destroyed houses, small spaces, to get the snipers hiding in them. That was my job, all through France, Belgium and into Holland. It kept you on your toes.

I must have been pretty good at it 'cause I made it back and some of those guys on the other side didn't. When I got back, I went mining for the Company again, just took up where I left off. I'm damned if I can remember who the hell I went with. Getting old I guess, but I was damned glad to be back.

Yeah, I can remember when I just came back out of the war, ya know. I'd be down mucking a bit, just before I went back mining, and I was mucking in this sloppy old drift, when somebody let off a shot in a sub or something. Christ, I was flat on my face right in that slop in the ditch without thinking, ya know. Just instinct from the war, 'cause over there you didn't stand up and look around and see where it was coming from. I guess I was still gun shy. The guys working around me used to get a big laugh out of it until it finally went away.

When we first went mining, there was no contract. The most you could make was $2 over day's pay, which I think was about $1.30 an hour. It didn't matter how much muck you took out or how much footage you got, so you really never busted your ass. They used to pay us a metal bonus, like for silver, lead, and other bonuses, then they cut that out, but we still made our $2 over day's pay. But I still got this goddamn cough. Silicosis, ya know. They gave me that for nothing.

I worked with old Tom Lewis. Well, Tommy and I were the first guys to hit the hot muck. Christ, what year was that? Nineteen fifty-something. It was just after the war. I remember I was scraping, and you know that B-line that was orange? Well, I see this B-line coming down the sub in the scraper. At that time, we used to leave B-line and made-up shots in a empty drawhole at the back of the sub rather than going all the way back to the powder magazine — totally against the rules.

I thought that a roll of B-line had rolled out of the drawhole where we had our stash. So I stopped the hoist and told Tom to go in and pick up that roll of B-line. What I thought was a roll of B-line wasn't. It was a big rock on top of the muck in the scraper that was as red as could be, and red hot to boot, with a hell of a lot of sulphur dioxide gas present.

We was on day shift and when we got outside at the end of the shift, we went right to the safety office and told them that they got hot muck. Nobody believed us. Not a damned soul would believe us. I told them to get their asses in there and see for yourselves. They did. They didn't expect it, but there it was. Just wouldn't believe us. Thought we were bullshitting them I guess.

Old McQuarrie and I used to fight like cats and dogs. He was the foreman and we just never seemed to see things the same way, but this one time he stuck up for me. I was working in this hot-muck sub and was blasting a drawhole on the left side, and right across from it on the right was a drawhole that they didn't want pulled. It was timbered off so no muck would come down. It was a big drawhole but every time I blasted, a lot of muck would slough through the timber. I forget who the hell the shifter was but he accused me of blasting it down. I told him he was full of shit.

So in comes old McQuarrie to get this straightened out. I gotta give him credit though. He said there was no powder marks on the timbers, nothing to indicate that I was blasting improperly. He agreed with what I thought was happening, which was that every time I blasted, the concussion was picking up the timbers and the muck just ran around it. It was like I said. It was one big goddamn hole.

Old Doug [McKee] and I came into the same sub one morning and all I can say is, thank Christ nobody was working in there on graveyard. You know that whole sub, right from the bullwheel about a hundred feet, was right full of ash. It looked like the hot muck had just boiled out of the drawholes and flooded the sub. All you could see was a channel right down the middle of the sub, about a foot from the back of the sub and the muck pile. So we had to put in a block at the front of this slough and start scraping our way in.

When we finally got this cleaned out, we never saw a piece of the original cable. It had all burned up. The only piece we found was around the bullwheel. It must have been around two thousand degrees when she come down. You just never knew when it was going to slough. It would have been bad if some guys were in there working at the time. That's the way it was.

Miner in a manway, the usual passage between levels at 45 degrees.

Tom Lewis was working with me when he got hurt. How that happened was, we were moving to a new place and we were lowering all our gear out of a place we had just finished. We were using a skip and I was running the hoist. The skip was full of stopers and steel. Well, old Tom put his foot out too soon into the slide and the skip with three hundred pounds of gear in it, landed on it and crushed his foot pretty damn good. So I lost Tommy for awhile. They gave me another guy but he didn't last long. He screwed up his back.

They sent this other guy with me; I won't mention his name because he still got family around. Well, he and I were driving a raise and we were up about a hundred feet. It was a vertical timbered raise with a man-way divided with planks so that we would have a muck compartment on the other side. We were using 9-foot fuse all the time and you had to pull enough muck out of the muck compartment to allow room for the round that you were blasting.

Well, the goddamn muck was frozen at the mouth of the drawhole. I told my partner to get a big hammer and see if he can break it loose while I go up and light the fuse on the round that we were going to blast. He hammered away and I could hear the muck running, so I lit the round and threw the planks that we stand on down onto the muck. Well, when the muck stopped running, it drove all the planks into the man-way.

My way out was blocked and there I was with the round lit and no way to get back up to cut the fuses. I couldn't get out. So I hollered out to my partner, "Is that other drawhole full?" He yelled back, "No. I think you can get through." I was just going to get into the other drawhole and ride out the blast. I wrapped my shirt around my head and then thought, "That's stupid, the gas or the concussions will get me anyhow," as I was sitting right under it. Anyway, I yelled out to him that there was an axe just down below, that he should bring it up and bash out the planks so I can get out.

He never brung the axe. I guess he was more scar't than I was. I got over being scar't real quick 'cause I knew I had to get moving. I grabbed a steel and started prying the rungs off the ladder that had got jammed against the air and water lines, then I started crawling down the sides of the ladder. But, Jesus Christ, wouldn't you know it? I got stuck.

I took off my belt with my lamp on it and away goes my goddamn hat and light down the goddamn raise. So there I was, in the dark, stuck, and the shot is going to go anytime. Hell, I'm only fifteen feet away. So I hollered down to my partner to come up and pull on my legs and that I thought I could make it if he gave me a pull. I know he heard me, but he took off. He was scared. No doubt about it. I really couldn't blame him. He had just started mining.

So I wiggled and squeezed and finally got through. Pitch black it was. As I was saying before about clearing houses in Holland and Germany, them places, I was used to feeling my way around just like now. I got down to the bottom of the ladder, just slid out the hole, when *boom!* went the first shot. Ya know what saved my ass that day was the fact that I had decided to use 12-foot fuse for some reason, and that's the only thing that saved me, I would'a been stuck right in that bloody hole. Yeah, she was close all right, goddamn close.

When I went in to tell the shifter what happened at the end of the shift, I found out my partner had already been there ahead of me. He told everybody that he had gone back and pulled me out, the lying little bugger. I wouldn't tell anybody he was lying. I kept my mouth shut. I never said anything to him till years after.

I just lost it when I went into a beer parlour and he and his wife were sitting there. His wife sees me and yells out, "You wouldn't be here today if it wasn't for my husband pulling you through that hole." I stopped at their table and leaned over and said, "I've heard this and heard it many times and I'm getting fed up with that goddamn lie. When I was stuck in that hole, I hollered for him to come and pull, and he took off." Well, you should have heard his wife tear a strip off his ass. She started yelling, "You been telling a goddamn lie for all these years. You never helped your partner a bit." Boy, did she ever tie into him.

I never did tell the Company that he lied and, you know, he never did apologize. As I say, I never blamed him, it was just one of those things, ya know, a fella that's new, not used to handling powder and that, he was scared and that's it. Hell, I never thought about it till a couple days later. It dawned on me how close it really was, ya know, what could'a happened if I had panicked. All they would'a had to pull out was my legs and bits and pieces. Now, hell, if that had happened, all my troubles would'a been over and other people would'a had the worry and not me. Heh, heh.

This one time I was up a drawhole in the turn-over, I had to go over the muck to get to the raise to climb up. While I was up there, somebody had pulled the muck, so when I came down, I was screwed. So here I am at the edge of the raise with nothing but air for a hundred feet. I'm sitting there thinking, "Christ, I'm going to have to take a chance. If I fall down the raise, I fall down the raise." Hell, I'm looking at a good 12-foot jump to the footwall in the raise. So I jumped, hoping to catch a footwall steel or something to stop me from going down the raise.

I was lucky. I managed to grab a rope that was on a footwall steel. I guess it was stupid to do what I did but it sure as hell beat sitting there all bloody day hoping that somebody would come along and put up a ladder. It come out all right but, Jesus, I was lucky.

One time I was working with Bill Muir on the main line just past where the coaches turned to go into No. 2 Shaft. I was up this bloody drawhole doing a turn-back round and below me, about forty feet down, was a plank on two footwall pins. This raise was at forty-five degrees, so the plank was around six feet long, one that we used for a drill plank. Well anyhow, I don't know what the hell happened, but I guess one of my extensions kicked out and I went ass over teakettle down the raise over that turn-over.

I landed right on my back on that plank. Shit, I fell a good forty feet. I hit the back of my head but my back was the sorest. My partner, I forget who the hell that was, he went and got some guys to help out and they had to haul me out in a goddamn stretcher. My back was so bloody sore and was bothering me so much that I never mentioned my head. Ya know, I should'a mentioned it and had them have a look at it 'cause it caused me so much pain ever since. But at the time, my back was the worst. Christ, I was in the hospital a couple of weeks with that. I guess I could'a had a concussion or something. I know that it still aches and pains, especially when I lay with the back of my head on a pillow.

In all, I worked thirty-nine years as a miner. So many of us got dusted in the gold mines, ya know, because of the silica dust in the quartz rock. It was a real fine dust and ya couldn't see it. It was damn bad stuff. But, then again, ya gotta look at what this hot muck that we had here did to the guys. It was just as deadly as that silica dust.

It killed that Murray McLeod, ya know. I guess where he was working the muck was all clinkered up and then let go, and he got caught in it and sucked in a lot of that hot-muck dust. There was no protection them days for the guys, just those little respirators. They didn't do much. This was in the fifties. A lot of guys got burnt. It was awful stuff.

We used to use those MSA canisters for protection. They were only good for a certain percentage of gas. I forget what it was, but on the bottom of them was this piece of tape that you took off so that the air would get in when you were about to put them in use.

I was working with Hamish Scott. We used to take turns running the hoist while we were scraping because you would be in that hot-muck dust after you put a scraper down the millhole. You couldn't see a damn thing. It just engulfed you. You didn't stay too long without taking a break. Well, old Hamish was laying there taking a break on a bench so when he wasn't looking, I put the tape back over the hole on the bottom of his canister where the air goes in. I tell Hamish that it's his turn to scrape, so up he goes and starts scraping.

Well, when he dumped his first load down the millhole, the dust billowed up, engulfing him like usual. All of a sudden, there's old Hamish's hands flying away. His eyes are bulging out. He couldn't get no air. God, that was funny. He should'a known what had happened, being a shift boss and all. He just panicked. Just goes to show that you got to remember what you're taught. Oh, he gave me shit for that. You gotta have pranks so I kept my eyes on him, waiting for some kind'a retaliation.

Hamish was my shifter this time and we were on a slow-down strike and old Bonus John was my partner. We were scraping with a tandem scraper. The blade came off one of them and I didn't report it to Hamish at the end of the shift.

The next day, the foreman, old McQuarrie, comes to me and asks, "How's those scrapers doing up there?" I said, "They're doing good." You know what he said? "You little lying bastard. We just pulled the blade out of the chute you were scraping to so they can't be doing good." Now wasn't that a hell of a way for a foreman to speak to one of his men? So me and old Bonus John ended up hauling that goddamn blade back up and putting it back on.

On the same slow-down strike, old Hamish comes up to where we were scraping with an air hoist. He says, "How come we're not getting any muck down below?" I tell him that every time I get to the muck pile, the hoist powers out. He tells me to get out of the way and that he'll try. So he gets on the seat and hauls the scraper to the muck pile. It just so happens that where Bonus John and I were sitting, the air hose for the hoist ran between my legs, so I just pinched the hose and he wasn't getting no air on the hoist. He screwed around for awhile trying to get it to work then just threw his arms up in disgust and said he was going to get a mechanic to look at it. I never told him to this day what I was doing. Always wanted to though, just never did. Maybe at the right time.

Old McQuarrie and I would fight like cats and dogs; we just never could get along. Christ, one time we went at it right out in the office with old Andy Sterling, the super, sitting in his office just down the hallway.

I said to McQuarrie, "I'm not talking to you no more. I'm going right over your goddamn head, you goddamn stubborn bastard." "What the hell do you mean, over my head?" "I'm going to see Andy. Now get the hell out of my way."

I went around him, and through the door into Andy's office I go, and there's Andy sitting there, just killing himself laughing, with that little moustache of his twitching away like leaves in a tree. I liked Andy. Hell, everybody liked Andy. He was a guy that you could talk to, not like some of them guys we had.

Old Andy was sitting at his desk. He says, "You two don't hit it off too well, do you?" I said, "Jesus Christ, Andy, that son of a bitch, he starts bellowing and yelling and then gets me mad. I'm the goddamn shop steward and I asked him to get two things fixed. There's a ladder to be fixed and a sidewalk along the track so when guys are packing powder around the train, they're not slipping in the ditch and breaking their goddamn leg."

I've got a pretty good head of steam going now so I go on by saying, "We got a union here and the union is here to stay and he might as well get it through that thing he calls a head that he's got to listen." Andy leaned across the desk and says, "Ed, I would hate to see you guys without a union." That's the exact words he used. Yep, Andy was a hell of a good man, real honest man. I go up and see him once in awhile. He's in the special care home. Yep, you could talk to him.

A couple days later, I don't know what happened, if maybe somebody ate the ass out of him or what, but old McQuarrie comes in to my workplace and says, "Ed, you come with me." I left with him. He took me to the man-way in the vertical and pointed to the ladder I had complained about. "How's that?" "Looks good to me," I tell him. He takes me to the sidewalk that was on the list. "How's that?" he asks. I told him everything looks in good shape. Now a man won't be breaking his fool leg anymore. Jesus Christ, all that for a couple little jobs. He said, "From now on, when anything is wrong and needs fixing, you come and see me." I guess somebody must have tore a strip off him. I kind'a think it was old Andy.

When I was up seeing Andy at the special care home, just sitting around BSing with him, talking about the old days, I mentioned to him about this incident, and he says, "You know, Ed, that's the way he was with me, all his hollering and yelling. He spoke to me the same way at times. I just let him rant until he finished, then got on with business." So I guess it wasn't just me McQuarrie did this with, it didn't matter to him. He was a bull of the woods, just an old-time foreman.

Yeah, McQuarrie and I never got on. I got him one time, though. I was working with Bill Jones and Harry Wilkinson. We were driving a drift. McQuarrie come in and Harry and I started tearing a strip off him over something. I guess we were having a bad day or something, I can't remember, but anyhow, he could see the mood we were in so he took off to go see Doug McKee and Jack Smith down in their heading. Doug told me old McQuarrie came into the heading just shaking his head. "Son of a bitch," he says. "I had to get out of there. Those two bastards got on to me before I even had a chance to open my mouth. I had to leave, just not worth it."

Well anyhow, we drove the round. It was in a watercourse and it was a son of a bitch to drill. We had to use spacers between the solid ground so when one shot went off, it wouldn't set the others off out of sequence. Bill Jones was our shifter and he was there when we finished drilling and could see what we went through.

Well, the next morning when we come in, we could see a lot of miss-holes from our blast. That goddamn McQuarrie come in to have a look and says, "You call yourselves bloody miners? Jesus Christ, you didn't know enough to put in enough holes. What the hell's the matter with you guys?" So here we go again. Of course, I blew my top right then and now. I said, "What the hell do you mean, not enough holes? If you had a ounce of brains, you can see there's a watercourse there and that one of the shots set the others off, you dumb bastard."

Bill Jones, our shifter, who was there when we drilled off the round and loaded it, was sitting there on a sprag. I turned to him and roared, "What the hell's the matter with you? Aren't you man enough to stand up to that dumb bastard and tell him that you was there when we drilled off the round and that I had plenty enough holes in it?" I turned around and walked off and, of course, old McQuarrie yelled, "Ed, you get your ass back here." Of course, I just kept on walking. See, he just liked to get the last word in so, of course, I just kept on walking. That's the way it was between him and me.

On the whole, most of the bosses were easy to get along with and pretty damn good miners at one time, but every once and awhile someone like McQuarrie would come along. Maybe it was just me, I don't know. I can be a bit of an ass too, you know.

It used to be a pretty good place to work, you know, 'cause years ago if you needed a shovel or an axe or something, they would just give it to you. I went and asked for a shovel one day to take home. It was Turnbull I asked. He said, "You mean to tell me you don't have a shovel yet? You have to be the only son of a bitch here that doesn't have one." Nobody said anything them days. If you could pack it, it was yours.

The spare-board was a board that had all the names of the miners that didn't have a regular place or heading to go to. So if a miner's partner didn't come out and your name was on the board, and you had enough seniority, you would go work with that miner. If not, then you would be sent nipping or mucking.

When I first came here, I was on the spare-board when they sent me mucking. They had those 6-ton cars. Well, Christ, when I was working at the Bralorne mine, we would put down steel plates on the footwall so that when we were mucking, it was easier to hand muck. We were using 1-ton cars there. When the car was full, we would push it all the way outside, dump it and push it back in. This was all by hand. It was a good quarter mile one way. Jeeze, you got to thinking that you were nothing but a goddamn mule.

Hell, I was used to loading quite a few cars at the Bralorne, but here it was a different story with these bloody 6-ton cars. They sent me into a drift to muck out a ditch. Hell, I went in there and I was going to fill a car in no time, a 6-ton car, ya know. I caught on pretty fast to what the guys here were doing. We used to have those old wooden powderboxes and what we would do is get a whole bunch of them, put them upside down in the car, and put muck on top of them. Hell, that helped us fill a car in no time, way faster. We was on day's pay anyhow.

There was this fellow. I never worked with him, big guy. He was a pretty good boxer in the army. Well, him and I fought all night one time. We'd stop, have a beer, and go at it again, and every time I licked him. He must have nailed me a good one 'cause the next morning my jaw was sore as hell and all swollen and black and blue. Yeah, we fought all night. It was a good one, kind'a enjoyed it. It was just after the war and I was still young and stupid.

This big fellow and I got barred from the Legion for six months for fighting. I'll tell you how that fight started. I'm going to call the big fellow Fred. It's not his real name but that's what I'll call him. He's still got family around. He passed on a few years back.

Well anyhow, I just drove up to the Legion and here's Fred and Bob, I forget Bob's name. Now they had been fighting. Fred had knocked Bob down and was going to put the boots to him. I said, "Fred, don't you kick him." He said, "You stay the hell out of this." "You let that man up. You're supposed to be a boxer so let him up. You're not going to kick him," I tell him. He tells me, "You stay out of it or you're in it with me." I say, "Let's get it on."

So away we go. He's a dirty fighter, ya know. I didn't stand up to box with him. That would have been a mistake. I was a rough and tumble street fighter, stuff that I learned overseas. He tried to kick me in the nuts and legs, but he was boxer, not a street fighter like me. I took him out pretty good and I thought it was over, but he had other plans. That big son of a gun followed me inside the Legion. I guess this is where we got banned for six months.

Away we go. There was tables flying, beer spilling, women screaming, and guys hollering. It was a real mess. So a lot of people got upset and we got barred, even though Fred was a war hero. I gotta give him credit for what he did during the war. He was something. I don't know why I was barred. I guess people saw it different than I did.

Ever since that fight, he was determined to lick me. Sometime after that, I heard that he was looking for me. That was before the old Globe Hotel had burned down. I used to go into the bar and if Fred was sitting there at a table, I would sit at a table where he could see me. I wasn't running. If he wanted to go, I'd oblige him. I weren't scar't of him. One time in the bar, Fred came over to the table and put his hand on my shoulder and said, "I'll be seeing you around." "Anytime you want," I said. And, you know, that was the end of it. We even had a beer with each other after that. Funny how it goes.

Fred was a little different. To me, he was born a hundred years too late. When I first come back from the army, the wife had moved to Creston while I was away and so I was staying in one of the Company bunkhouses up on Townsite until I could arrange for a house for us. Big Fred was laying on his bunk in his room and that stupid bugger was shooting flies on the ceiling with that big six-shooter of his, and the bullets were going right through the floor where a little bookkeeper stayed. You should'a seen his face when he come flying out, little tiny guy with big thick glasses. I bet that little fella almost had a heart attack. Kind'a makes a bookkeeper's life a little more interesting, don't ya think?

Bunkhouses at McDougal Townsite for single miners.

Yeah, Fred was a tough old bastard. You heard about that fight he had with that big guy the Dynamiters brought in to protect the goal-scorers on the hockey team? I guess this guy was a boxer in the navy and not a bad hockey player. I guess he and Fred had been drinking all night upstairs in the Canadian Hotel and got to fighting. Ya know how guys will get when they got a belly full of beer, they can lick the world.

Well, I guess they headed out to the parking lot to get it on. From what I heard, they took turns knocking each other down, let the guy get up, and go at it again. They were big fellas, at least two-thirty apiece. And you gotta remember Fred was getting a little long in the tooth, had almost twenty years on the guy.

Well anyhow, this Mountie shows up. I guess he knew better than to get in the middle of this. Now this was getting to be later in the morning when cars and people are starting to move about. So what does the Mountie do? He stops traffic and lets these two guys fight, which they did.

They slugged it out all the way past City Hall right down to the Sullivan Hotel, a good two blocks from where they started. I guess by the time they got to the Sully, they were worn out. So you know what they did? They went into the bar and started drinking beer together, sitting there all bloody, dirty, with ripped clothes on, best of buddies. That's just the way it was with some guys. You know that they respected each other by not using the boots. Just wanted to know who was tougher.

Harry Wilkinson and I were partners for quite awhile. He was a good miner. I really enjoyed working with him. He was one of those guys you wanted to stay with. I broke in Pete Huppie. He turned out to be one hell of a miner.

Then they gave me a guy that was totally useless. All he wanted to do was be a shift boss. Jesus Christ, when his gear broke down, he would grab a water hose and wash down drawholes, or else get a scaling bar and fart around barring, rather than go get another stoper or go phone for a drill doctor. He had no intention of taking a round. Many times I would finish my round and then drag my outfit into his place and finish his round. He was nothing but a low-life contract rider.

The way I used to work was one guy would go up a drawhole and start drilling and the other guy would scrape until he had a place to set up and start drilling. This stupid son of a bitch would tell me, "Sit down and take five." I'd say, "Jesus Christ, I'm going to set up and get drilling. This is bullshit. The bloody cross shift are busting their asses and you want me to sit here and watch you scrape and keep you company? That's bullshit." So I just went ahead and did what had to be done.

He was doing his hose thing this one time when I lost it. When you start a drawhole, you never take all the muck out when you're at the third round. You leave enough muck on the footwall to put your drill plank on. This is usually at forty degrees. You're up out of the sub maybe ten feet. Here's my partner washing all the muck out, right down to the damn footwall. This was about the tenth time he had done this. That was it for me. I turned off his hose and yelled up at him. "What and the hell are you doing? Goddamn it anyways, I told you we use that muck to set up on." "Well," he says, "it makes the muck come out easier." I told him, "When we take that muck out, that will be on day's pay. We're not worrying about that now. We'll get it on final clean-up, and those guys that we're cross shifting are busting their balls and we're not holding our end up. If you want to go day's pay, we'll go day's pay. But I'm not going to sit on my ass while those guys are busting their nuts to carry me. You either put that goddamn hose down and take a round or that's it." I got rid of him. He got his dream. They made him a shift boss. Just as well 'cause he was no miner.

Talk about yelling at the cross shift for doing nothing. Christ, this one time I chased these two guys right off the platform outside where we used to stand when we come on shift to talk to the cross shift when they come out from underground. Hell, there was usually a good hundred guys milling around.

I chased these two guys right on to the coaches, right in front of the whole damn crew out in the yard. These two useless bastards, I get mad even today when I think about it, and this was years ago.

Well anyhow, I had these two guys set up so they could take four rounds off the same set-up. There was the two connections, the slot raise and the turn-over raise. I had the lubricators full, all the steel up on the drill platform, all they had to do was turn on the machines and give her hell. Would'a made all four rounds easy.

I was afternoon shift and these two wonderful miners were day shift, so I go in and find that my stoper hadn't even been picked up. I had big Sven with me because my regular partner, that little guy Lars Paulson, he had a big son of a bitchin' scar on his cheek, missed the next shift. Lars had taken a round in the drawhole across from me and the cross shift scraped it out and got set up for us, big bloody deal. I guess one of the cross shift had gone on a drunk the night before and just come in and went to sleep.

So Sven had three rounds to drill off and I had the four that cross shift didn't take. All I did was drill one round and slash all the way around using the one burn. It was a snap. When I had finished drilling, I went over and told Sven that I was going to get the powder. He told me he had just a couple holes to go and that he wanted to blast his side. It didn't make any difference to me because we could only blast three rounds because time was short. You gotta remember that we was using stick powder them days so it took awhile to load.

So I went and got the powder and by the time I got back, Sven had finished drilling and had all the gear torn down and put away. So we loaded and blasted, and left my four rounds for the cross shift to blast. So you can understand why I was chasing the cross shift across the platform. Jeeze, I was mad at them. I said to them, "You guys don't do bugger all" and the one guy says, "If we don't do bugger all, how come we make good money?" I said, "How come? It's because your goddamn cross shift is carrying you guys. You guys ain't doing bugger all. Now get off your asses or you're going to find your asses out of there." And that was the end of that. They got the message.

Then there was these two guys; they were the worst that I ever had to cross shift. One time, Gus and I came into the raise we were driving and they hadn't finished drilling off and blasted, so Gus and I had to go in and finish drilling and we blasted their round. So once we blasted, we had to blow out the gases with an air hose, go up and set up and, you know, that's dirty work with all that gas still in there. Hell, you know the headaches that you get from that stuff, especially with stick powder, with all that nitroglycerine in it. Christ, that stuff would bring tears to your eyes with the headaches you got from it.

Finally we went to the foreman, I think his name was Ed something. I forget his name. It's hard enough remembering mine now sometimes. Gus and I didn't say anything about the cross shift. We just told him we wanted out of here and wanted a new place to work. The hell with it, it just wasn't worth it. It was like this every day, hell, it gets too much. You don't mind if the guys are trying, but these were experienced miners not putting anything into it and making the same money as us, that's bullshit. Well, they told Gus and I to stay in there and those guys were moved out and we got a new cross shift. There was no need for all this in the first place. No, I didn't need that.

One time, I was working with Putt Pearson, great little guy. We were just nipping, clean-up, ya know. When we got into the mine and off the coaches, Putt noticed that he had forgot his wallet. It wasn't in his lunch bucket where he usually had it, and as it was payday, he had his money in it. We were afternoon shift. So he asked Dingy Bell, who was on transportation and would be taking a train outside soon, would he mind going up to his locker and getting it out of his pants pocket. Dingy said, "What's your locker number?" And old Putt, he had a hell of a stutter, ya know, says "Two-ffff, two-ffff, two and a fuckin' half." There was no way he could say two fifty. Jesus Christ, I never forgot that.

Walter Ekskog. Here was a guy I liked working for when he was the foreman. A real decent man, he was. There was this time I was in my working place with my partner, Hungry Jack Smith, and in comes the shifter, Jim Byrne. This was a time when they were really pushing the guys to wear safety glasses, and Jim asks why I'm not wearing my glasses. I said, "I'm not wearing them." "You just get them on and keep them on," he tells me, so now my hackles are up. I said, "Jim, I would hate to turn you guys in if you don't get off these goddamn glasses bullshit. I'll be in that outside office at the end of the shift to turn you in."

Just then Walter Ekskog came into the heading and asked, "Who's going to turn in who?" I said, "I'm going to turn him in if he doesn't get off this goddamn glasses bullshit. You can't see your goddamn hand in front of your face. These glasses ain't going to save me if I go down that raise." There was this little trail going around the millhole and this sub was dusty and foggier than hell, couldn't see nothing. You had to sneak around it. I told Walter, "Hell, if I have glasses on and I go down the raise because I can't see nothing, them bloody glasses aren't going to do me much good when I hit the bottom, are they?"

Well, old Walter took my side on that. He took Jim around the corner and must have chewed the hell out of him. Yeah, I liked old Walter. He was a hell of a nice guy. I did a lot of special jobs for him that were real shitty, dangerous, dirty, you know the kind, and he never once told me to put my glasses on.

Ear protection, hell, when I started, nobody wore it. Most guys wore nothing or maybe at the most just a piece of cotton waste jammed in your ears. I started wearing those little goddamn earplugs just before I quit and went off to war. Now, being the stupid bastard that I am, I have a hearing aid, silicosis, and a sore head.

I was there when different guys got killed. Those barmen used to take a real beating. I used to do a lot of barring. We'd have to go up there, four ladders, ya know. These were 15-footers, tied together. You would have guy wires, which was rope, and have these tied to eyebolts. There was usually five of them to hold the ladder up. You had to watch where you barred the slabs off the back so they wouldn't land on you or the ropes. You gotta remember that we're up there thirty or so feet. Yep, the hair on your neck stood up at times and there was a lotta nervous sweat.

Lenny Cond, he drilled into powder and got killed. How that happened was that the cross shift had drilled off and they stuck a stick of powder in each hole. They were just going to start loading, but didn't have enough time to finish it. They probably thought they would leave it for Lenny and his partner to finish loading, but they never told their shift boss. This was a big mistake; in fact, fatal. Lenny and his partner come in and figure they got lots of time to extend the holes, take a bigger round, you know. Lenny starts drilling and boom!, drills right into a stick of powder, and that was that. Oh, there was a big investigation over that. The two guys who didn't give the information to their shifter lost their tickets over that. Can you imagine how they felt? Just not thinking, that's all it takes.

I drilled into a miss-hole when I was working with Tom Lewis. We were drilling in a raise and had two stopers going. Tom says, "Let's shut her down and go have our lunch." I said, "I'm going to finish this hole." So he said that he was going anyway. So I said, "Goddamn it to hell, I'll go with you. It can wait." I had just started the hole so I just turned the machine off, and away we went, down the raise to where we had left our buckets, and had our lunch. When we came back, I got to looking and cleaning off around the hole that I was drilling on. That bloody hole was full of powder, blasting cap and all.

That was a close one. Ya see, in soft ground, you could drill right through the powder, but in hard ground, it would spark and set it off, unless it had a cap in it, which would set it off anyhow. Yep, more than once Tom and I had powder come out wrapped around the goddamn steel. Just shithouse luck that we never had our heads blown off.

I remember this time when Tom and I had to go up a muck raise through a chute for loading trains, and take out a bulkhead. We weren't in any hurry 'cause we were on day's pay, so we sat down and had a coffee. We finished our coffee and decided to get at it. The bulkhead was about a hundred feet up at forty-five degrees. I just put my foot over the chute gate to climb in, and I hear a racket, you know, and jumped back. A whole pile of muck comes down. Son of a bitchin' shifters hadn't told the guys up above not to scrape. Well, Jesus Christ, if we had been five, ten minutes earlier, they would'a scraped right on top of us. It was so goddamn stupid, with the bosses not telling anybody. Christ, so many close calls, it's incredible.

Gus Eliuk and I was working together this time. We were driving a raise, I think it was a 45-degree one that we had to timber. It had stulls, 3- by 12-inch planking, with a man-way and a muck compartment. We were using a little air tugger to help us and Gus was on the tugger. I had to step off the platform to put the bottom of the stull in the ditch I had dug, and I slipped and down I went. I went down the raise with the stull, about fifty feet, and the goddamn stull landed right on my arm.

When Gus got there and got the stull off my arm, I said to him that my arm was broken in two places. His reply was, "Bullshit," and mine was, "No bullshit." First aid took a look at it and told me that I had to get to the hospital right now. I wanted to take a shower before I went to the hospital but the first aid people said not to bother, that the X-ray technician was already there waiting for me. But she wasn't. Goddamn it to hell, I could'a had a shower. Instead I go in looking like an old bum. Well, the doctor comes in and takes a look at it and says there's nothing broke anyhow. I blew my cork.

"What the hell you talking about, it ain't broke? I'll eat that dirty old mine shirt I had on when I came in if it ain't broke." The next day I had to go up and have it X-rayed again, different doctor this time, and he found that both bones were broke. I saw that first doctor again and I told him, "You doctors. If the bones ain't sticking out, you don't know nothing." Jesus H. Christ, I guess there's good doctors and bad ones, just like miners.

Red Patterson and Rudy Esker were on Garnet Coulter's shit list for some reason. Garnet was the foreman. He had them mucking in the ditch, down on the 2800 Level, real windy and cold. It was a main ventilation source, bringing forced ventilation into the mine down a large raise right from surface, almost two thousand feet. The place where they were working, it was hard to even stand because of the force of the wind. They had big coats on and had rags tied around their necks, anything to keep warm.

So in comes Coulter. They're mucking away and he starts talking to them. They both turn their backs on him so he goes around the other side and starts talking. Same thing. They turn their backs to him. So off he goes in a big huff.

He goes a little way and all of a sudden he turns and comes back and says, "Fuck you guys. You can stay here for another week and freeze your balls off." Yeah, old Coulter could play the game, and he always won.

When I was a shop steward, I had this case this guy wanted me to take up. You see at that time, if a shifter or a foreman liked you, he would pay you a higher rate than what the job called for. So this guy comes to me, complaining that some guys working in the ditch were getting barman's pay and he wasn't. See old Raynor, the foreman, would pay some guys barman's pay but wouldn't put down what they were doing. He could be a good guy at times, if he liked you.

This guy who was doing the complaining says to me, "Jesus Christ, Ed, these guys are getting barman's pay. Why don't I get it?" I said, "Forget it. You're working in the ditch. If I go out there in the office and say Raynor is paying these guys barman's pay and why the hell you don't get it, you won't get it. The other poor buggers will be cut out and it's not going to help you, so just forget it. It would be just stupid. I won't even take it up. Just bite the bullet." I never warmed up to this guy from the first time I met him, always whining about something.

I remember the time I put in a suggestion to have phones put in the slusher subs. The reason was that when the muck raise was full, you could phone the mucker boss and he could have the trammer come over and pull your chute. Raynor said, "Nope, we'll just put up a red light." I argued, "That's all right if the train happens to go by, but this way it would be so much easier to just phone the mucker boss and he could get ahold of the trammers, instead of us sitting around on our asses hoping a train goes by and sees the goddamn red light." He didn't listen, the son of a bitch.

As it so happened, I had Carl Shonsta working with me. He and I put the phone in anyway. The tail block pulled out at the back of the sub and Carl was back there working on it when the drawhole came down and nailed him with muck and boulders. I ran to him as fast as I could and dragged him in between two drawholes so if the drawholes come down, he wouldn't get buried. Then I ran over to the phone and got the mucker boss. We had help before we knew it. All of a sudden, phones were a good thing. I got a whole $10 for that suggestion.

Before the contract system we have now, they used to pay you on the bonus system. If they liked you, you might make $2 over your day's pay, and if they didn't, you got bugger all. Then it changed so you got so much a ton if you were working in a stope, but you were only allowed to make so much. They didn't want to see anybody get rich, that's for sure. You had to watch that you only gave them so much. What we used to do is that if another crew was having problems getting their quota out, we would have the trammers come to our chute and take some of our muck, that's if we had some to spare. We always helped each other out when we could.

Old Putt Pearson and I were working in a raise; it wasn't a very long raise. It was full of muck, just around forty feet, and at the bottom was a big platform. Our job was to take the muck out, and all we had to use was a wheelbarrow. This is where the now-famous "jenny" came into being. It is used in mines all over the world.

I got the brainy idea to take an ordinary shovel down to the blacksmith shop that we had underground — we had a couple them days — and have a blacksmith heat and bend the blade over. Well, hell, this worked out slicker than shit. All I had to do was just pull the muck into the wheelbarrow. We had an 8- by 8-inch stull that we used for a stop block and just ran the wheelbarrow up to it and dumped in the car below us on the track.

Old Putt said, "We can't make any money at this." I had negotiated a contract for us for $120 with old Bill Muir. He wanted to give us $80 but I got $120 for us. Bill was fair. I forget what we was making but I believe it was about ten bucks over day's pay, which was pretty good money them days. "Holy Jeeze," says old Bill, "I'll never get away with paying that kind'a money. I'm going to get shit for that." That old bugger, you know what he did? He put two guys in there after we had it cleaner than a baby's butt, doing nothing, and charged their time against the contract to cut it down to about $7 or $8 so he wouldn't get shit.

There was some guys in the mine that always got the cream. If you got in the foreman's bad books, and he didn't like you, you could stay on the spare-board forever. There was this one guy who used to really get under my skin, an Italian guy, there was a bunch of them. These guys would get those subs that had twenty drawholes in them, a sub that you dreamed of getting. These guys would have them almost finished, with all the gravy gone, and then me and my partner would be sent in to take the last couple of rounds and then do the final clean-up. These guys would get a new place and contract. It was bullshit.

That's the way it was. These guys would be buying the shifters and foremen beer in the beer parlours, telling them to put their money away. It was BS. I've been right there and seen it, goddamn phony bastards. Jeeze, I'd be sitting there having a beer with these guys, and a shifter or a foreman would come in and here's these guys falling all over each other telling them to put their money away and buying them beer. Christ, I'm telling them, "They buy their round like everybody else, same as we do." I might as well been talking to my dog. I just couldn't do that. I guess that's why I was cleaning drawholes.

The Company brought in this special oil in the fifties to put in the lubricators for the drills. It devastated a lot of guys. It got right into the lungs and ate the hell out of them. A lot of those guys are hauling around those little oxygen bottles behind them to this day. Between the dust that gave you silicosis and that damn oil, you didn't have a chance. The poor buggers.

When I was in the hospital with my breathing problem, silicosis, I used to look after my roommate, Frank Malone, who was in there with similar problems. I used to crank up his bed and put his feet down and get his slippers on for him. I couldn't sleep. Hell, I was up during most of the night. Get up at four or five in the morning, just wandering around. When my roommate woke up, I would get him to the bathroom, then help him sit down, get his shaving gear out, put water in the basin, and help him shave. By the time we was finished, it was breakfast.

There was an old miner in the next room that I used to work with. I'd go over there and visit him ya know, play crib and shoot the breeze, that sort of thing. Well, after breakfast this one morning, I headed over to play a game of crib with him. There was a nurse in there cleaning up and she told me he had passed away during the night. His lungs finally gave in. I guess it's going to get all of us. It's just a matter of time. There was another miner in the room where the guy died and he got out the day before. His wife came and got him and took him home. He was dusted like the rest of us.

Frank Malone was a short little fart, a great guy. I remember, Frank and I were up the St. Mary's valley, picking huckleberries, and we had this damn bottle of goof with us. We was working it pretty good. There was this big log going across the creek that we were going to use as a bridge to get to the other side. Well, Frank gets on and starts over and into the creek he goes. Ya know what he does? Instead of keeping going, he comes back to where he started out, climbs up on that damn log, and starts over again. Same thing, into the creek he goes again. The little bugger was drunker than hell. I guess I was, too, because I fell into the creek laughing so hard.

So every time his wife came to visit him, I used to say to her, "You can't pick any huckleberries in here," and she would say, "Go to hell, Ed." She made one hell of a huckleberry pie, though. She always brought a piece for Frank and me when she came to visit.

Those little guys — like Frank, Shorty Bilyk, Gabe Cooke — mining was hard on them. Christ, they had to work like hell to keep up, especially on them bar and arm drills. Most of that stuff weighed as much as they did. I'll tell you, those goddamn drills burned out a lot of guys, but those little guys did it. You gotta give them a lot of credit, no whining or crying from them guys. They had one hell of a lot of grit, damn good men.

Right after the war there was about sixteen hundred guys working at the mine, and each section of the mine had a spare-board. This spare-board had the names of the miners that didn't have a regular working place. Most of these boards had the names of at least ten to twenty guys on it. There was this foreman who would stand there at the start of the shift, waving that stupid little geologist hammer, telling guys, "You go here, you go there." He was a regular little dictator. The shifters had no say. It was all him and, boy, was he a prick. I always hated those little hammers and those guys who used them to show their authority.

This foreman — if you had some sort of controversy or had given him some lip when he was standing at the spare-board giving out jobs — would pass you over and made sure that you didn't go mining and have a chance to make some good contract. Seniority didn't mean nothing to him. This was before we had a good strong union. Not too many guys spoke to him when he retired. They all had bad memories about him. Like they say, "What goes around, comes around."

There was guys that were against the union. These guys just didn't have any balls. They was scar't as old hell. That's what the Company could do to you them days. A lot of these guys remembered the Depression [in the 1930s] and how you hung on to the job you had. I kind'a think that the Company and a lot of the bosses played on that fear. If you didn't have a union, the bosses could put you mucking or some other bullshit job if he didn't like you. As it was, before our union got strong, the relatives and good friends of the bosses got the good jobs, and there wasn't a goddamn thing you could say. The favourites made $60 a day and the other guys would make maybe $14 for the same goddamn work. It was bloody criminal. No wonder we had to get a strong union in to help us.

I had this shift boss that would walk a mile or two to see me just to get a chew, chewing tobacco, ya know. He and I got along pretty good. He was a decent guy. One day he comes into where I was slushing and tells me that he has to put me on the loading crew. I told him that I wasn't going loading and that they could shove the loading up their ass. I went and got my bucket out of the lunchroom and was heading out of the mine. Ya gotta stand up to the bastards.

I went and saw the afternoon transportation boss and asked if he would take me out. He said he couldn't do that, but there was a motor that had to be taken outside and I could use that. So when I got outside, there was the superintendent, a couple of assistant supers, and my foreman all waiting for me. The super says, "You told your shifter to shove the loading job up his ass." I said, "I did not. I told him to tell you to shove it up your ass. There's a lot of guys in there that have got a lot less seniority than me. Put them sons a bitches loading."

So we argued and argued. My foreman, who was always in a bind, came to me and said, "Ed, I would really appreciate if you would go back in the mine and finish the shift." I told them that I would, just so long as it never happens again. By now it was about seven, so I went back in. My foreman was a pretty good guy. He could be an old woman at times, but I liked him. And my shifter, him telling them that I told him to shove it up his and not theirs, well, I think that calls for a pinch out'a my can, don't you? They all knew that I would do it again if it happened again. Ya know, I was just lucky they never fired me.

When I was the shop steward I used to have to go and see old Andy Sterling. He was the mine superintendent at the time. His office was downstairs, then he moved upstairs, and if I had any grievances I had to go see this new engineer. This new engineer's office was upstairs also. Old Andy saw me going by his office this one day on my way to see the new guy and calls me into his office. "Ed," he says, "how come you're up here all the time? We used to settle all our problems downstairs and we never had any problem."

I told him, "You know what it's like, Andy. We get these new engineers right out of university and they gotta get noticed, make a name for themselves. They're nothing but a pain in the ass until we get them settled down. They just love to make a big issue out of nothing." "Yes, I know. I got the same problem with them out here," he tells me, shaking his head. I never had a problem with Andy. He understood, ya know. He was honest and easy to deal with, not like some of those lunkheads that showed up around here.

While I'm talking about old Andy, there was this miner. His name was Donny and he took some time off, drinking ya know. I went and saw Andy to go to bat for him. I argued that he had a big family, trying to get sympathy, ya know. Andy says, "I know all that but, damn it, get him to work tomorrow or I'm going to take some action. This is unacceptable."

I had a talk with Donny, after I tracked him down in a beer parlour. I told him to get his ass back to work tomorrow or I'd be taking his case up with the Company. Donny assured me that he'll be there but I should'a known better. I had to go see Andy on some other matter the next morning and while we were sitting there in his office, he casually asks, "Do you know where Donny is today?" I say, "Yeah, he's at work, isn't he?" "No, he isn't," I hear and old Andy is just killing himself laughing. He thought it was a big joke. He said, "I don't want you to worry about it, Ed. I'll just put him back on the payroll when he decides to come back to work." You see what a great guy he was, a real decent man.

Andy kept old Hardrock on. He covered for him many times. Yep, Hardrock put his life on the line for the Company, and Andy knew it. There was no way Hardrock was going out of that mine without a pension as far as Andy was concerned. When I worked with old Hardrock, he'd have me on the go steady. He was a hard-working old bastard, never sat down, always on the move.

When I used to pick him up at the Canadian Hotel, where he had a room upstairs, he'd get in the car just reeking with booze after being on a bender. In his bucket, all he would have in it would be a can of that condensed Carnation milk and some digestive cookies. That's all he could keep down, coming off a bender.

After work, I would drive him home. He would go to his room and sleep off all that booze. He would wake up after a couple hours, go downstairs to the bar and order two beer and — this was a real particular thing that he did — he would only drink half a beer out of each glass, then go back upstairs and go to bed until the next morning. But this is the only way he drank beer, just half the glass, nobody ever saw him drink a whole glass. Nobody ever said anything to him about it, 'cause all he would do is glare at you from under his hat that was always pulled down to just above his eyes.

I took up a lot of cases for Hardrock, grievances, ya know. I tried to tell the Company, "You're stupid. He comes back to work after being on a bender then you turn around and give him a couple more days off, and he gets on a drunk again. It doesn't work. Just leave him be. You know Andy will never let him go."

I'd go on by telling them, "The worst thing you can do is put old Hardrock in the ditch, hand mucking, as punishment. Jesus Christ, that breaks his heart, ya know. It's downright insulting to him. You might just as well put him back on the bar, where he's the best there is and he's the happiest, rather than giving him more time off, 'cause you know as well as I do he'll just go on a drunk again."

That goddamn old Hardrock, he would never cash his pay cheques. That old bugger would save them all up for awhile then head down to Spokane, go on a big drunk and get all tangled up with a bunch of hookers until his money ran out. When he was broke and without any more credit, he would show up at the Sullivan ready to go to work and build up a new stake. There was always a job here for him because Andy respected him. He was probably the best barman the Sullivan ever had, and the strangest, and we had a lot of strange people.

As the story goes, old Hardrock came up from the States. He came here 'way before I started, sometime in the early thirties, I guess. He was part of that Western Federation of Miners. This was a large union the miners down there put together to go up against the mine owners, part of the Wobblies, and they were treated bad, not just by the mine owners but by the government. Hell, they were all in the same bed. I guess he was blackballed, couldn't get a job anywhere in the mines. Them days, the companies had a list of all the guys that had anything to do with unions.

He told me there was always a guy at the gate trying to get hired on, and a guy coming out just fired. That's the way the companies would keep the work force on edge. Safety wasn't even heard of. If a guy got killed, they didn't give a damn. There was always another guy at the gate. There was no such thing as compensation for an injured worker. There was nothing for the wives or families of injured or killed workers. People meant nothing. I figure that's how Hardrock got here. He couldn't get a job down there because of his union activities. I think there was a lot more behind old Hardrock than he told us, but you would never hear him talk about his personal life, and you knew better than to ask.

Old Otto Buterman came into my slusher sub one day. He was a shift boss, and this was the first time I had ever met him. He waved his light for me to shut down the hoist. I had the scraper under a drawhole, which was hung up at the time. Well, that goofy old bugger come up behind me and shut the hoist off, right under the drawhole. I pushed the button back on and brought the scraper down to the millhole and then shut the hoist off.

I turned around to him and told him, "Don't you ever lay a son of a bitchin' hand on my hoist again." "Well," he said, "I've been in this mine for many years and I like to protect myself." I'm pretty hot under the collar by now. I said, "You stay the hell back and wave your light, and stay there until I wave you in. If that scraper was under the drawhole, and she come down, who the hell is going to dig it out? It wouldn't be you. It would be me. Don't you ever touch that son of a bitchin' hoist again."

He ran right out to the office and told McQuarrie, the foreman. Old McQuarrie said, "For Christ sake, you leave that stubborn, son of a bitchin' English bastard alone. Don't you bother him at all, ever again, 'cause I'm the guy that has to talk to him and that would wreck my day." And that's the first time I ever met old Buterman and the first time McQuarrie ever stuck up for me.

Another time, my partner and I were driving a raise away up in that 3800 Drift. We had finished drilling the round off and had loaded the holes, tore down, and put our gear in the tool cache. So we were just sitting up in the raise, waiting for the time to light our fuse to blast, when we heard this crash, bang! I said to my partner, "Goddamn it, there's something wrong. Let's light this goddamn round and get out of here."

We had to go down the raise and out the chute at the bottom and onto the track drift. And sure as hell, we just got off the chute platform when here comes planks, stulls, water and mud down the drift. A bulkhead had broke loose somewhere and all this stuff was just about upon us. We ran like hell. If you stumbled and went down, it would be the end of you. We just made it to an intersection and all this shit went by us.

The next morning that drift was plugged tight, right up to the trolley wire. If we hadn't lit and got the hell out of there, we wouldn't have got out of there. We would'a just had to sit there until somebody mucked out the drift, and we were in there a hell of a long way. The worst thing about having to wait to get mucked out was that we didn't have our buckets with us, and that's where my can of snuff was.

When we worked outside, up in the open pit in the winter, it was so goddamn cold that you had to build a fire under the water line to keep it thawed. It was a cold and windy place to work. We used to spend a lotta time in the doghouse around the stove, where there was benches for us. There was a lot of packrats around. Old Dave Nelson used to go to sleep, ya know. I don't know who it was put a live packrat in Dave's lunch bucket, and when he opened it, the damned thing jumped right on him. Over he went, backwards. You should'a seen him scrambling. We all had a good laugh. Oh God, another time somebody put a dead one over his neck when he was sleeping. When he woke up and put his hand on his throat, that packrat went flying. I'm sure if he had ever found out who did that he would'a killed him. This time nobody was laughing.

Old Dave was kind'a accident prone. We figured that with all the fingers that man lost, at a thousand bucks' compensation a finger, he could'a bought beer all weekend for every man that worked in the mine. He was the only man in Kimberley that had to hold up two hands to order three beer.

DORY ARNFINNSON

The gentle giant...

Dory was a big man with a big smile and an even bigger heart. He was one of the nicest people you could hope to meet. It's hard to say whether Dory liked going to work because he enjoyed his job or because he liked to be with the guys. He was a good miner and shift boss, and he loved getting together with his family and friends on weekends for a few drinks and laughs.

I started mining in 1942. I had just got married in Lac La Biche and had to leave my wife there to start this job. I flew out of Fort McMurray and got into Yellowknife about two in the afternoon. I got a ride to Ptarmigan Lake, where the mine was, and got into camp about four o'clock.

The mine captain told me, "Dory, you've got to go to work tonight." I said, "How am I gonna go to work tonight? I got no hard-toe boots, hardhat or slickers. I got nothing." So he says not to worry about it, he'll go find some gear for me. He pointed to a guy and told me that he's my partner tonight. I looked at the guy and could tell that he was half snooted up. I figured I was in for a rough shift with this guy. The guy's name was Bob something. I said to the guy that he's going to have to show me around and what to do 'cause I never mined before. I was just a greenhorn.

So anyway, we went to work at eight o'clock. We worked from eight to four. Four hours was needed in between each shift to ventilate the mine from the blasting. It was mostly natural ventilation. Well, anyway, we got underground and it was all hand tramming, 1-ton cars, hand dumps. The chutes were all hand chutes. We each had about forty cars. You know, load the car, push it by hand down to the dump and empty it, and push it back. When the raise went empty, Bob told me that we have to clean up and for me to go get the muck sticks. I had no idea what a muck stick was. I told him I didn't know what a muck stick was or where to find them. He just laughed at me and went down the drift and came back with two shovels. That's how I learned what a muck stick was.

Bob gave me a lot of good advice because in them days there was no safety talks or anything like that. Hell, your partner told you anything you wanted to know about blasting or what to do and when to do it. It was all on-the-job training and if it wasn't for them telling you, you wouldn't know nothing. But there was a lot of guys here in Kimberley that wouldn't tell or show you nothing.

I was working with this old Norwegian guy. He pretty much showed me how to mine. I was collaring this bloody hole and a big chunk of rock come down and caught me on the knee and my knee just blew up like a balloon. Sore as hell it was. I could hardly stand on it. The old Norwegian took a look at it. He said, "Never mind, Dory. I'll come and fix it up after I get off shift. Just go down to the commissary and get a bottle of Absorbine Junior." He come up to the bunkhouse with a great bottle of horse liniment. He poured it on my knee and wrapped it with a cloth and poured on more. Christ, my sock was soaked.

There was a great big puddle on the floor but, you know, it worked. I was back to work in a couple of days.

Before I went mining I was pulling muck, then I went nipping. I was nipping for this old Norwegian named Gunnar and three or four other miners, you know, getting powder and fuse for them, hauling out old dull steel

Hand-tramming ore cars on narrow gauge track.

and bringing in new steel. I got put with this old Gunnar. He talked broken English and if I would have just stopped and thought, Norwegian is close to the Icelandic language, which I understood, 'cause a lot of the words are the same.

So we were drilling away with a liner, drilling some breast holes, and I was running the crank on the drill and he started saying something to me in this language that I had no idea about. Then he says it again. Christ, there he is talking away at me and I'm staring at him with a dumb look on my face. I say, "I don't know, Gunnar." He says, "Jesus Christ, you've been working with me for three days and you still don't know nothing. You absolutely don't know nothing. Jesus, Jesus." I guessed that he wanted to put on a 7-foot steel but once I started paying more attention to what he was saying in his broken English, we got it figured out. He was a real good partner, showed me lots.

There was this old guy, Chris. He was drunk all the time. A good guy, but always drunk. We'd give him whiskey and if there was a bottle around, he'd just help himself. He was cagey. He knew nobody would say anything if he just took a drink or two.

This one time, we were having a party and we didn't invite old Chris because we knew he would just show up. We were sitting in a room getting going. Everybody would bring whiskey, rye, gin, rum, and we would empty out a water pail and just dump all this booze into it. So old Chris comes staggering in and he was all snooted up and says, "Do you guys want some water?" Just an excuse to come into the room, you know. We told him, no, we didn't want any bloody water. And just to top off his excuse, he says, "Is it all right if I have a drink of water?" We told him to go ahead. This dipper was in the pail of booze. He was mad because he couldn't see any booze lying out in the open. So he took this dipper full of booze and took three gulps. Christ, it shot out of his nose and everything. It just about choked him. He was sitting on the floor. "Goddamn you guys, you're trying to kill me," he says. He probably thought that was the best water he ever tasted.

There was a guy up at Ptarmigan Lake. His name was Shuteye. The first time I come there, we had lockers to put our shaving gear and other stuff in. I had just bought a great big bottle of aftershave lotion, maybe eight ounces. Them days, you got a hell of a big bottle for a buck and a quarter. After a couple of shaves, I noticed my aftershave was gone. I thought maybe somebody had borrowed it and just forgot to put it back or put it in the wrong locker. After a couple of more days, when it never come back, I said to this guy, "Jesus Christ, I had this bottle of aftershave and it's gone. I don't know where it's gone." "Oh,' he says. "That goddamn Shuteye must have drunk it."

Sure enough, he used to get the new guys to buy him a bottle at the commissary when they first come in. He comes to me and says, "Hey, Dory, go and get a bottle of aftershave for me and put it on your bill and I'll pay you back on payday." I said that I would. The commissary guy wouldn't give him any. It didn't matter to me if he drank himself to death on this stuff. I went to the commissary and I guess the guy who ran the commissary saw me talking to old Shuteye. He says, "You're not going to buy aftershave for that old bastard, are you? 'Cause if you are, you'll not get it here." And so I never got it. I guess old Shuteye must have found somebody else.

When I started mining, I was making sixty cents an hour for an 8-hour day. Hell, if I wanted to go to a movie in Yellowknife, it would cost me three days' wages. It was expensive to go see a movie. One time, I worked twenty-three and a half shifts on one payday, no overtime. When I got my cheques, holy smokes, I thought I had really made some money. I made $117.50. Isn't that something? And out of that I had to pay, to top it all off, I had to pay $1.20 for room and board a day. That came off the $4.80 I was making a day.

I thought we were really cutting the mustard and, I'll tell you, we really put in our full eight hours. They expected, when you went underground, that you and your partner would pull at least a hundred cars. That was your set goal. And, boy, I'll tell you, to pull a hundred cars, you had to really go. Some days you got a few more; some days you got a few less. My partner and I were expected to each push a 1-ton car down to the dump by hand and back to the chute a hundred times. The dump was about a thousand feet. Some were closer, but not many. It used to be dangerous for the guy pushing the front car if the guy in the back was coming a bit faster. You would run right into the back of your partner's legs. Not too many guys got hurt this way but a few did.

When the Ptarmigan mine shut down and we were heading to Kimberley for work, the party was going for three days and it was still going when we left. We had all this money left in the recreation fund so we had a quick meeting and decided to throw a party. Hell, a quart of whiskey was four bucks, a day's wages almost, so we had lots of whiskey.

My old partner, Gunnar, told me not to leave Yellowknife without seeing him. He was staying in a hotel called The Old Stope in Yellowknife. I went the next day to see him. Poor old Gunnar.

He says, "Dory, I don't have much to drink." I say, "What have you got?" He says, "I got some rubbing alcohol." I didn't want to hurt his feelings. There was a washbowl in the room and the water hadn't been changed in months and months. I think, "What should I do? Take a drink of that water or a drink of this goddamn rubbing alcohol?" I thought the worst thing I could do is take a drink of that rubbing alcohol so I snuck a little of this dirty water into a cup and pretended I was drinking that alcohol. I said, "Skol, Gunnar," and he said, "Skol, Dory. You'd better have another." I told him that was enough. I had to get on the road.

I came to Kimberley with my family on September 17, 1942. My wages were less than what I made in Yellowknife but with all the bonuses we got, I made about two dollars more a day. So we were way ahead and stuff was a lot cheaper. All the time I worked in the north, I never had any fresh food until I got here, fresh food like oranges, apples, pears and plums. So when I got here, I was always eating fresh fruit. I ate so much that I couldn't look at it after awhile.

With the big crew working in the Sullivan, we were putting out about twelve thousand tons a day and there was no pillar blasting at that time. When I first come here, it was all open stopes, dangerous, a lot of rock falls. Pillar blasting and slushers never came in until the mid-fifties. I know that different guys — it never happened to me — but say these guys had gone for lunch or something and they had set up a tripod and liner in the stope on the footwall, which was usually forty-five degrees, and had come back from lunch and found their set-up was wiped right out. No machine, nothing left, just shithouse luck. Christ, some of these stopes were so big that you couldn't see the back. Surveyors would come in and have a balloon on a string and let it go up so they could get a reading. When the balloon hit the top, they would measure. There was no bolts or screen to protect you. It was just open ground.

We hadn't been in Kimberley very long. We had just moved here from the north in September. I went downtown to get a haircut at Joe the barber's. I was on afternoon shift. It was Friday, March 13. This guy come in and said to Joe, the barber, "Harold Swan just got killed underground this morning." I was just new. I didn't know him. Before I got out of the chair, this guy comes in and says, "Did you hear about the guy that got killed underground this morning?" We all said that we had. He said not that guy, but another guy by the name of Pete Buzan. Jesus Christ, two guys got killed and I haven't even finished getting my haircut. I didn't go to work that day. I didn't know what I was going to get myself into.

I guess Pete Buzan was working with Joe Beran, and Pete was up a 30-foot ladder in a stope drilling a hole with a plugger, and the steel got stuck. He was trying to get it out and the ground in front of him came loose and hit one of the guy ropes holding the ladder up and cut it. It flipped him off the ladder and he landed on his head and was killed instantly.

Harold Swan was working in a stope in a little trail, running a pipeline up it, and I guess he just stepped backward and down he went in the muck raise to the chute, and that's where they found him. He had a fractured skull. But there you are, eh. Friday the thirteenth. Can you believe it?

Quite a few barmen got hurt in the stopes. Some even lost their lives trying to make it safe for the miners. The barmen would put up ladders and have them hooked together and tied by ropes to eyebolts in the walls. After we blasted a bench, say fifty feet across and ten feet deep, they would set their ladders up on the next bench to be taken and bar out over where we would stand to mine. With the slope under them and the ground taken out, they could be a hundred feet to the lower footwall. The big problem was when they barred a slab and it came down and hit a rope. They were gone. It would just flip them.

I put in a few shifts on top a ladder and sure didn't like it. In fact, it scared the hell out of me. The only time a miner would do this is when a barman's partner was off. Usually, you just helped him and he went up the ladder. The barmen made a dollar a day more than we did. We made six bucks a day and he made seven.

There was a $2 limit that we could make over day's pay. That was the most you could make. Some guys would only make a dollar and would they be pissed off. Say if you were building a chute and the Company gave you forty man-shifts to build it. If my partner and me could build it in twenty shifts and other guys took thirty shifts, we got that much more than the guys that took thirty. The Company set the contracts: so

Miners with jacklegs drilling on a round in a stope. The third person is probably a shift boss checking on his crew.

much for a chute, timber raises, verticals, cement work, stuff like that. But it didn't matter if you got it done in record time; the most they would pay you was two bucks over day's pay.

Say if a stope was fifty feet wide, we would take a 50-foot bench and put in two rows of holes: 12-foot back-holes and 10-foot lifters. The bench was usually twelve feet high. We would put in the holes, maybe six or seven feet apart, and about six feet of burden on the lifters. We would put in around sixteen holes altogether. Day shift would get it all barred down and get set up and get in four or six holes. Afternoon shift would finish drilling and blast. The hardest part was moving that bloody tripod and liner on the sloping footwall.

We used stick powder to load. They figured it took half a stick of powder to a ton of muck. That's how they figured how much powder to use. We had to buy our own powder and fuse. Say we were getting about twenty-five cents a ton. That's where they used to get the money out for the powder and fuse, and the $2 limit would come out of that also. Say we made $3 over day's pay. They would charge us a dollar for the fuse and powder, and more if we broke more ground. They had us by the short and hairies, I'll tell you.

The best money I ever made in the Sullivan was when I was working with Freddie Wilkinson. This was when they started paying a decent bonus: by how much footage you broke. Gosh, we made $36 over day's pay. Jeeze, we were taking five rounds in two shifts, all drawholes, and no cross shift.

Superintendent Brian Buckley came in to see what we were doing to make this kind of money. He said there was no way anybody can make this kind of money. You know what he done? He sent in a couple of surveyors to measure up our goddamn footage. These surveyors weren't the ones we always had and these guys came up with the same footage. But I'll tell you, the contract engineers argued and cried about it. We still got paid. At that time, that was the most money anybody made in the mine. Now that's just peanuts compared to what guys make now. Christ, miners make more in a day now than what I made in a month, and they deserve it.

Raise miner collaring a raise with a stoper.

We had to do some real goofy mining that the Company came up with. We had to take the back out of some of those old stopes up on the 4600. There was bands of ore left behind from the early days. We had to stage up to thirty-some feet. We put up 16-foot sprags, nailed them solid, then on top of that we had to build another staging before we could reach the back. You had to drill vertical because if you drilled even a bit horizontal, the staging would shift. We had to drill vertical raises up there so you can imagine how tough it was for the first two rounds because you had to stage the same way twice, until you got enough muck to work off. Old Dick Shannon would be after us 'cause we couldn't set up in one shift. Crazy old bastard. It was a lot of work.

Talking about setting up, these guys were driving a raise in chert, and you know how hard chert is. Well, these guys come out from underground and met their cross shift outside. The cross shift asked them if they got set up. They said, "No, we never got set up. We're still putting in the hitches but we did mark them for you where we were working to put them." I guess they dulled their picks trying to get a hitch. Worked all day on them damn hitches.

There was this guy from the mine that wanted to do his dog in. It was an old dog. Some guy at the mine said, "Why shoot it? Get a stick of powder and a fuse and blast him." So I guess he thought this was a good idea and he took his dog up where the ski hill is now to blast him away. He tied this stick of powder on the dog and lit the fuse and took off, but he forgot to tie the dog up to a tree. And so here comes the poor old dog following along behind him so he climbed a tree. The shot went off and there he was, up this tree covered in dog meat. He was some dumb bastard, boy.

I'll tell you a little story about old Dick Shannon. Oscar and I were driving this sub. It went in about two hundred and forty feet. Old Dick told us to keep that place up to snuff 'cause the big brass was coming in to have a look. We were in iron ore and there's no way you could wet it down properly. The water would only go down about an inch and it stunk with blasting smoke and was dustier than hell when you stirred it up.

In come Colthorpe, Giegerich and old Dick. These were the Company big shots. We just wet down and had just scraped out and in they come. It was still gassy and dusty 'cause we had churned it up enough to be crappy for breathing. They come in and they didn't say too much but I could see old Dick wasn't happy. Old Dick come back right after dinner and started giving us hell. He says, "I got a good enough notion to give you a reprimand." I says, "Go ahead. What the hell is stopping ya?" He says, "Well, I don't like to but you know Colthorpe and Giegerich got headaches coming into your place." I say, "Too goddamn bad about them assholes. What about us? We gotta work in this goddamn place. You don't think we don't get a headache from this bloody gas?" He never said anything and took off.

I said to Oscar, "That stupid old bastard. We won't talk to him no more." Old Dick would come into our workplace and ask, "How's she going?" and we wouldn't say nothing to him. And that's the worst thing you could do to him, not talk to him. This went on for about two weeks. We would only talk to him about what we were doing but no BS like we always did. After awhile, I told Oscar that old Dick has had enough of this. We better start talking to him again. The old guy was broken hearted but he got the message. You know it's the worst thing that can happen to you when your crew don't talk to you.

Talk about different foremen, there was this guy that was a spare foreman at the time we were on day's pay. So we were on a slow down trying to get a better bonus. He was a good friend of mine. Anyway, he comes into where we were mining and we had the round drilled off. He grabbed ahold of a loading stick and was going to measure the holes. I said, "Jack, if you want to measure these goddamn holes, you come when we're out to lunch and I'm not here watching you. But God help you if you push that goddamn loading stick up a hole 'cause I don't know what I'm going to do." He says, "Do you mean that?" I said, "Goddamn right, I mean it."

We stood there and stared at each other for a bit and he put the loading stick down. I suppose he didn't want to put our friendship to the test. And to tell you the truth, I don't know what I would have done if he had shoved that loading stick up the hole, I really don't. They either trust you or they don't.

I was working down in the shaft part of the mine and Carl Kavanagh never come out this one day so they put me with his partner, Hardrock MacDonald. Well, here's a guy who didn't give a shit about nothing, and I'm going barring with the Rock. I'll never forget. I had just bought this brand-new type of smock that went over your bib overalls. We had to go down this 45-degree raise to scale it down. It got so warm down there that I had to take it off.

I asked old Hardrock, "How come you got no ropes down here?" He says, "You wanna get hurt?" Yeah, he had no ropes down there. There wasn't even footwall steel. I think I spent the whole shift spread-eagled on the footwall so I wouldn't go down. I was so scared I wouldn't even go back down to get my new jacket. That goddamn raise went down two hundred or three hundred feet. He was crazy, you know. No hat liner in his hardhat and a can of Carnation milk for lunch. But no doubt he was the best barman ever.

You know where Aikman's Café was? Well, that used to be called the Kootenay Rooms. There was rooms upstairs that you could rent. Well, there was this guy that worked in the mine and he was staying at the Savoy across the street. This girl — she was his girlfriend and I guess she was stepping out on him — was in charge of cleaning the rooms in the Kootenay. He was all snooted up and decided to take two or three shots at her with a rifle while she was cleaning the rooms. He had a straight shot at her right across the street but it's a good thing he was drunk 'cause he didn't hit her. I don't know what happened to him. Those bullet holes were still in the wall when Gertie and I stayed there when we first moved here from the north.

I was there when Murph Wells got blasted. What happened was there was some guys blasting up in the stope and their muck went into the chute Murph was pulling. I guess Murph had to blast a big rock in the chute and had his shot lit. He heard a shot go and thought it was his but it was the blast came from the stope above him. So he come back and was climbing up on the chute and his went off. That's how come he lost his eyes. He could have got killed. He was a remarkable man. Christ, you see him today shingling roofs and stuff. Doesn't matter if it's night or day. Quite a guy.

The big flood of 1948 in Kimberley, that was something. They hauled a lot of us guys out of the mine to do some blasting along the creek, like roots and logjams, the odd house that had slid into the creek. Tommy Young and I were working together and we would go out in the creek and put a shot in the jam and, Christ, it would lift them up a hundred feet or so. We were using primacord and tape fuse with forcite powder. The worst thing was all the people standing around watching. We didn't know where all this stuff was going to land. We would light and yell, "Fire." People would be running all over the place trying to hide from the stuff falling from the air. It was kind of funny.

You know where BJ's Restaurant is? Well, there used to be a house there. It used to belong to Mrs. Levesque. That house was three-quarters down in the creek. Tommy and I come along. I had a case of powder under my arm. She says, "What are you going to do?" I said, "I'm going to blast that house, that's what I'm going to do." She says, "No, no, no. There's a Cat coming and it's going to pull my house out for me." I told her she had ten minutes before I blasted it because it was starting to jam up the creek.

Sure enough, this goddamn bulldozer comes along. The way they used to hook up that big bloody cable was right through the house, and not around the outside, and what usually happened was the cable would just cut the house in half. It would be easier for me to blast. That house must have been really well built. That Cat pulled the whole house out and parked it where that Togs & Toys store is now. The Company paid our wages all the time we were out working on the creek. They did a lot for the City with men and equipment and everything that was needed.

I guess the longest raise I ever worked in was a ventilation raise that went from 3800 to surface. It was forty-five degrees and probably a thousand feet long. We drove the pilot raise seven by seven all the way to surface and then turned around and came back down, slashing it out to ten feet high to twenty feet wide. There was this bad spot near the top that we had to timber. It was a good five hundred feet of real crappy ground. All the timbers were ten by ten, legs and caps with 4-foot centres and then lagged with three by twelve planks.

They wouldn't give us a contract for this job. We wanted $125 a foot. They thought we were greedy so we said the hell with you; we'll do it on day's pay. What we were asking wasn't that far out of line. Christ, there was four of us on a crew. There was Ken Farran, big John Johnson, Charlie Hallgren and me. So we slowed it down. It could have been done a lot faster. All they had to do was pay what it was worth. It didn't take us that long. Every two shifts we got in about five feet, sometimes we got ten. All the timber was lowered from surface. We worked a hundred straight shifts, no time off, no weekends, nothing. It was a real important job but they wouldn't pay us a bonus so it took longer than what they could have had it. But that's the way it was.

One time, I took a couple of Oxford [University] professors from England underground for a tour on the Top Mine. We come down to the 4500 Level and there was Norman Moore doing some blacksmith work and he had a burning torch going. I was telling these professors that we had some really dedicated men here and one guy says, "How come?" I said, "Look at that guy there doing that welding. He's doing that welding and his coveralls are on fire and he won't quit welding." He says, "Well, I'll be goddamned."

Old Norm couldn't see anything with his burning glasses on and wasn't aware that a spark had lit his pants on fire. I'll never forget the look on these two guys' faces. I bet they never saw anything like that at Oxford. I got a letter from these guys thanking me for the tour. I guess it would be the only letter I'll ever get from Oxford.

There was this guy who blew himself up and this girl that didn't want to have anything to do with him. He had brought some powder and a fuse from the mine, and this girl was working in the police station, right where AG Foods is now. I guess he caught her walking up the path right where City Hall is now. He grabbed her and lit a short fuse that he had in the powder in his pocket and blew them both up. I don't know how true this is but I heard that the girl's head came right through the window in the Soderholm house and landed in the kitchen. Could be just BS.

I heard this story before I come here. I guess in the old dry they had here, there was a lot of mice so they brought in a bunch of cats to control the situation. These guys were in the dry changing clothes and I guess there was plank seats. This old guy was sitting there and his dinger was hanging down and, of course, when he was putting on his clothes his dinger would move and a goddamn cat jumped up and bit down and clawed him. Now that was a hell of a way to start a shift.

KEN DIETRICH

Always BS with the truth...

If you've read this far, you'll have learned that getting paid a fair return for the difficult and dangerous work they do is pretty important to miners. For that reason, I've included Ken's behind-the-scenes recollections of his experiences negotiating the contracts that paid bonuses to the miners. Ken was a miner himself...

There was always a bonus system in place at the Sullivan Mine. In the early years, it was paid at Company discretion, very much like throwing darts at a dartboard, a "system" that was used in many, many mines throughout North America. This method of paying miners' bonuses was in place at the Sullivan until 1951.

The union in the early days was called The One Big Union. The Mine Mill Union took over in the late forties, early fifties. When Mine Mill took over, the mine went into a seventeen-month day's pay situation. The union told Cominco they were no longer interested in their system of bonus pay and that they wanted union participation. The union fought hammer and claw and finally, after seventeen months, the Company relented and said they could have representation on a negotiated contract for the bonus system.

The first contract representatives for the union were Gabe Cooke and Frank Malone. In 1954 Ken Wocknitz was elected and worked with Gabe Cooke until Jack Glennie took Gabe's place. During this whole period of time, there were no records kept. Everything was kept in the head of the representative, which made it very difficult for the reps in future years to refer back to that time for data.

The contract system allowed the union to have control over the distribution of the contract dollars that Cominco was to pay. There was always a tiered system. The miners were the most valued contractors and then it decreased from there: drillers, timbermen, muckers and so on. There was always a hierarchy maintained. In the early sixties, the men voted to join the United Steelworkers of America and this union represented them until the mine closed.

STATISTICS

Labour (Cont'd.)

The division of mine labour per working day, based on average crews for the month of December, 1954, is as follows:

Open Pit

Drillers and helpers	4
Blast-hole loaders	4
Euclid drivers	3
Shovel operator	1
Miscellaneous	7
Operating staff	2
TOTAL OPEN PIT	**21**

Underground

Development miners	47
Production miners	83
Barmen	20
Core-hole drillers	7
Blast-hole drillers	38
Blast-hole loaders	12
Transportation	57
Timbermen	64
Mechanics	29
Electricians	12
Trackmen	7
Pipemen	15
Sanitation and first aid	7
Miscellaneous	84
Operating staff	64
TOTAL UNDERGROUND	**546**

Wage Rates Per Hour - June 1, 1954

Muckers	1.55	Blast-hole D.D.	1.75
Motormen	1.60	Core-hole D.D.	1.80
D.D. helpers	1.60	Timbermen	1.85
Trackmen	1.65	Miners, (stope, drift	1.85
Pipemen	1.65	and raise)	
Cage tenders	1.65	Miners (shaft)	1.85
Nippers	1.65	Blast-hole loaders	1.90
Conveyor operators	1.65	Traffic control boss	1.90
Crushermen	1.70	Barmen	2.05
Chutemen	1.70		

Plus $0.05 for afternoon shift and $0.10 for graveyard shift.

Incentive pay is given for most work.

1954 wage statistics.

Ken Wocknitz stayed on as contract rep with Jack Howlett until 1974. That was when he ran into the Cominco rep by the name of John Rokosh. Ken resigned. That was it for him. I took his place and worked with Jack Howlett. Jack retired after about three months with me so there I was, sitting there with no records to go by and no past knowledge, so everything that happened from that time on, I recorded. Everything from 1974 to the mine closure was complete. That made everything that happened from that point on during negotiations with Cominco that much easier.

The contract system was a very big part of Kimberley. We averaged around $4 million dollars a year on contract, and we have been at just over six million. You have to remember that involved around two hundred to two hundred and fifty individuals. That's a lot of money in a small community. So you can see that it's been a very important part of Kimberley. I still have all the hard copy from 1974 on, but before that there is nothing.

Initially, when I was involved, the contract system was paid on man-shifts saved. We and the Company reps agreed to a man-shift value. For example, say we agreed that a raise miner would get one hundred per cent pay, over and above his day's pay, in a man-shift value. That would be the maximum. A development miner in a sub and drawholes would earn seventy-five per cent over day's pay, and slusher miners, timbermen and transportation would earn fifty per cent over their day's pay. So everything was based on a man-shift value. We would look at a job and attach shifts to it.

The easiest example would be in development mining. Say we agreed that a 6-foot round was attainable in so many man-shifts. We knew it would take two men one shift, which was two man-shifts for them, but we would allot four man-shifts to the job. If they could do it in two man-shifts, they would make one hundred per cent of their day's pay plus one hundred per cent of their contract.

But say it took them three man-shifts, then they would end up with only fifty per cent of their man-shifts each because they used three instead of two. They would make one hundred per cent of their day's pay but only fifty per cent of their contract. It was pretty much the same with all the contracts, with some variations for slushing and timbering.

In 1987 we went to a new system where there were no man-shifts involved. There was just a direct relationship to foot advance per ton to ore extracted per feet drilled. This new system was a lot easier to understand for everyone involved.

If a miner knew that for every foot he advanced, he would receive $22, there was incentive for him to go eight or ten feet. His ability to work more quickly and be more productive on each shift translated into proportional savings for Cominco. All parties involved — including the contractors, the union reps and Cominco reps — found this new system a lot easier to administer and understand.

In 1981 I got off the contract committee and went back underground. I'd had enough of John Rokosh, too, a very difficult man to negotiate with. I was back mining for a short time when Cominco wanted to negotiate a contract for the mechanized part of the mine. They could see that their dream of having miners work without a contract system just wasn't going to happen. The two new guys on the contract committee had no experience in how to negotiate a mechanized contract so I was allowed to go out and give them a hand. It took about six months to get the contract in place.

In 1982 I was able to talk Ken Wocknitz out of retirement and come back on the contract committee with me. John Rokosh had taken another position with Cominco so it was harmonious around there and the job was fun again. A fellow by the name of Bob Wyka represented Cominco and he was a prince of a man to do business with.

Around 1983, we were threatened with day's pay when Merlyn Royea was mine manager. We were downtown at the union hall this day and in pops Merlyn with an airline ticket in his pocket. He threw down an agreement and said, "This is it. You either sign this or you're on day's pay forever. You can see I have my airline ticket for Toronto in my pocket." Kenny and I looked at each other and said, "Well, I guess day's pay is what it's going to be." So out the door goes Merlyn on his way to Toronto. We went home figuring that this was going to be a long one.

That evening I got a call from Keith Meyer, who was the Kimberley Operations superintendent for Cominco at the time, saying he would like to meet with us in the morning. The next morning, Keith says, "What's it going to take to solve this?" So we told him, but we were worried about Merlyn and his airline ticket. Keith said, "Don't worry about Merlyn and his ticket. He won't be back." And he wasn't.

The next confrontation we had with Cominco was when Jim Greenhaugh was mine manager. We had a six-month day's pay situation. They threatened us. They did everything. It was almost violent. There were flare-ups in committee, all that kind of stuff was happening, but along came this comical situation.

Remember that yappy know-it-all English engineer, Kevin Wright? Well, he was in a bar one night after a day of negotiations and trying to be a wise-ass. He could never hold his booze so he thought it would be smart to antagonize Mel Olsen, who was on the union bargaining committee. Kevin was stupid, too. He kept calling Mel a Norwegian. Mel's not a Norwegian. He's a Swede. Mel, who was not known for his cool demeanour, gave him a slap that knocked him right across the bar, so that was that.

At the next bargaining meeting, Wright was sitting on the Cominco side of the table and it was getting late, about three in the morning. It was really starting to drag and little things were happening. Jim Greenhaugh wanted to continue but the union side had just about had enough and wanted to go home. Big Mel Olsen had had enough. All of a sudden, he slammed that big fist down on the table. It was thunderous, and poor old Kevin Wright, who was sitting across from Mel, jumped up out of his chair, turned and ran right into the wall. I guess he had a good memory about the day before with Mel. It was the funniest thing you ever saw. The only guy not laughing was that English guy but, regardless of Mel and England's Kevin the Lionhearted, the contract was settled.

The toughest negotiations we ever came up against took place in 1990. We were dealing with Dave McMurdo and Bruce Donald. In our very first meeting, McMurdo said to us that this was going to be completely different, that he had the corporate backing to take us on.

The proposal that Bruce Donald threw down gave the Company the unfettered right to run the contract as they saw fit. The proposal had all these blank spaces, no numbers or dollar figures, just the wording and all these blanks. So I said, "That's fine. We'll accept it."

McMurdo and Donald almost fell out of their chairs. Then they said, "Fine. We'll fill in the numbers later." I said, "No you won't. We'll accept what you put on the table." "But you can't do that," they said. "There's nothing there." "Precisely," I said, "and that's what we're accepting, nothing. We'll accept it as it is with no numbers so our guys will just stay on day's pay. We'll have a contract in place but there will be no money. Just look at the cost savings to Cominco." McMurdo got real angry so he picked up his proposal and he and Donald stormed out.

McMurdo called me back and said they had put some numbers down, whereupon I told him that I didn't want to talk to him because I knew what kind of numbers he would have. We had the meeting and his numbers were ridiculous. Cominco, however, was real serious. They shut us down, the whole Cominco operation in Kimberley, not just the contractors but everyone.

It was pretty obvious what the Company was trying to do. They wanted to get all the other workers pissed off at the "greedy" contractors. So everybody was on EI, unemployment insurance.

The main negotiations to get a collective agreement in place for Trail and Kimberley operations were going on in Trail at the time. The contractors' contract at the mine was a separate issue. We got a call from Cominco asking Norm Walters and myself if we would go to Trail and work on the contractors' contract. We said sure and away we went. We went back and forth from Kimberley to Trail for about three months. We made no headway at all. It was a totally useless effort.

Dave McMurdo was trying his damnedest to cut the heart and soul of the contract system and Bruce Donald was a very big part of that. We knew what we needed and we maintained that position.

So the main collective agreement was put on hold because of our negotiations. A couple hundred contractors were holding up a couple thousand workers. At one point, the collective agreement was set to be ratified by all the locals in Trail and Kimberley. The union was taking it back to the workers to vote on.

In the Steelworkers' constitution, two locals are needed to veto any decision made in caucus. Trail locals were very busy trying to push the contractors into a settlement. They were the people that were on strike. We were on EI because we were shut out. The Trail locals were really upset with us guys from Kimberley but I told them there was no way we would sell out the contractors. This is what we had to have or there's no way we're going back to work.

Trail called for a veto vote. Kimberley Local 651 was very quiet at this time but Dale Craig, who was the president of Local 9672, the shifters' union, stood up and said they were in support of the contractors one hundred per cent and so then Mike Park, president of Local 651, stood up and said they supported the contractors too, so we had our two local vetos. The main bargaining committee had to go back to Cominco and tell them nothing was going to happen until the contractors' agreement was done.

It seemed like every time we had an agreement on something, McMurdo or Donald would change their mind. This came to the notice of the people on the sidelines.

Giovanetto, Henningson, Tommy Orr — all the big boys from Cominco who had been negotiating the main contract — came to meet with us and ask us what the hell was happening, so we told them. Tommy Orr, the personnel superintendent, asked if we would mind if he sat at the table to see what was going on. We told him we would have no problem with that. It didn't take Tommy very long to figure out what the problem was. Stuff that Cominco had agreed to and then taken away was given back so things were starting to move now, thanks to Tommy's intervention.

By this time it was getting late in the day. There was this question of cost to us and we were looking for $50,000 to cover our costs: food and lodging, transportation, all that kind of stuff. This was all part and parcel of the negotiations. This was going on until the wee hours of every morning, going at it hammer and tong. We got to a point where there was maybe six or eight items left. Things were getting really difficult now.

Dave McMurdo asked for a caucus this one morning and left the room. We were negotiating downstairs in the Terra Nova Hotel. We could see he was upset. Sometime later, Tommy Orr came back into the room and said, "Ken, I think we can come to some understanding. Dave is really in an awful state. How about laying off him a bit? I think we can resolve all our items." I said,

"Sure, we'll accommodate. No problem." So they came back in and we agreed to the items that were on the paper. The last item was the $50,000 that we felt was very important, and it was. It was costing us money to be there. Cominco relented and did cut a cheque for the fifty grand so the deal was done. It was about 2:30 in the morning.

Mick Henningson, who was the current general manager in Kimberley, ran upstairs to their room in the Terra Nova, broke into the liquor cabinet, stole all the liquor and left a note saying: "Please charge all this liquor to Dave McMurdo." All the Cominco representatives — Giovanetto and the other big shots — got together with us and we drank all the liquor. Shortly after that, all the contracts were ratified and we were back to work.

It's easy to see how important it was to have union representation when it came to bonus pay in the mine. In the old days, it was abused terribly. If you were liked and kept your mouth shut, you would make extra. If not, too bad. If it had worked, they wouldn't have had that seventeen-month strike. So, over the years, the whole system got to where it was generally accepted and respected by all involved parties. Today, favouritism is still a way of life in mines all around the world. In Kimberley, we were unique.

I was lucky when I got involved with contracts. There was a superintendent by the name of Andy Sterling in charge of the mine. He knew the value of a miner. He was fair to the Company and the men. He understood the value of a day's work, which was very strange for a lot of mine engineers in those days, and I guess even now. Andy Sterling, without a doubt, was a gentleman first and a good mine manager second. There is no doubt he was head and shoulders above any man we ever had.

Keith Meyer was a good one. He stuck to his word. Don Boyle, same way, a man of his word. Another gentleman we dealt with was Bob Wyka. A true man of his word and honourable, and there were plenty that weren't.

I like what Kenny Wocknitz told me: "If you're going to try and BS Cominco, you make sure that you're BSing with the truth. Don't ever get caught at lying because that is the worst thing that can ever happen to you."

That's not to say that we didn't skirt the truth, but we never lied. That's the one thing I can say until the day I die, and also that I did the best I could for our people.

PETE PAGURA

Mom's cooking was too good to ever leave home...

Pete is a pudding of a man, always ready to swap stories with you. He is a first-generation Canadian who grew up in Kimberley and followed his dad and uncle into the Sullivan Mine. He used to drive his foreman, John Ekskog, nuts because he and his partner, Pete Balonyk, would never work a Friday night graveyard shift. They just would not work Friday nights. They had some discipline problems over this but won in the end.

I'll always remember a hockey game with several hundred people in attendance, including women and children. An amplified voice announced: "Ladies and gentlemen, will you please rise for the singing of God Save the Queen?" In the lull between the announcement and the opening bars of the music, Pete's voice rose above the crowd: "Put your f . . . . . g money up." That was Pete, in his cups, making a bet on the hockey game.

Yup, that's Pete.

When I first went underground, it was 1945. I can always remember what my dad said. He said, "Pete, you can always tell when a guy is going to die, just look in his eyes. If you see them glassy, you know he's going to die."
And it just so happened after that, in 1947, I was on transportation on steady graveyard. We were told to go get the ambulance and go to No. 2 Shaft because there was a guy badly injured there. We were waiting a bit when they brought this guy up. As we were loading him into the ambulance, I looked into his eyes and they were glassy. Vic Dick said, "Let's get going and get him out." We were really dangling, just about outside, when Vic signalled us to slow down. He told us that the guy had died.

He was just a young kid from the Prairies. His name was Gillis. He had got caught between a moving ore car and the drift. It just crushed him. I guess my dad knew what he was talking about. He had been in the First World War. He saw a lot of action and was wounded himself. He had seen a lot of glassy eyes over there.

I'm sure other guys have told you about Hardrock MacDonald, but he was tremendous, probably the best there ever was, completely fearless. It's

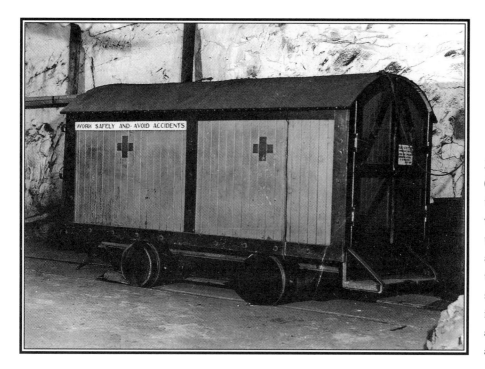

Main line (3900 Level) transportation would take the undergound ambulance to whatever section required it. A first aid attendant would accompany it.

probably the reason the Company never fired him. He would go into places no other guy would go. He had no fear, never panicked. He took on any job that was given him. He would climb up raises and go in amongst the boulders to place his shots. You never knew when it would let go.

My best friend, Skip McFarlane, was working with Rock and they were up a raise about sixty feet, working on a hang-up, and it came down with them in the raise. Hardrock just froze once he heard a noise. He just hung to the side of the raise and didn't move. I guess Skip got a little excited from what I hear and the muck took him down into the chute. But old Hardrock just clung to the side until everything went by. Skip got banged up pretty bad. The side of his face was paralyzed and he lost the use of his arm. I guess you could say he was worse off than me, even with the stroke I had.

That goddamn old Hardrock, he was something though. He only worked about six months a year and then he'd go on a bat. This one time when Hardrock was on a bat, there was this dirty job to do. Bill Cairns was the foreman. He got hold of Tommy Lewis. He said, "Hey, Tommy. Will you do me a favour? How about going down and getting Hardrock? We need him." I guess he was on a drunk for about three weeks. Tommy said, "Fine, but there's only one problem." Cairns says, "What's that?" Old Tommy says, "Who's coming down to get me?"

It's just stories like that that makes you laugh. When Rock was working, he wouldn't pick up his pay cheques for months at a time and when the Company got on him about it, I guess because the office was getting flak about this guy not cashing his cheques, he would get them all and go on a drunk for weeks at a time until he ran out.

I remember this one time when he came back from a big drunk. He was dressed to go to work and he got on the coaches. He was sitting on the coach beside me waiting to go underground. He was shaking so bad his hardhat wouldn't stay on his head. When they got him underground, you know what they did? His partner got a rope and tied him up to a big bloody timber and left him there for the whole shift. I guess they did this for about three days until he got straightened around, you know, until he quit shaking and stuff.

Gus Masi, who owned the Grill Restaurant, used to make his bucket for him: a couple of sandwiches and a can of condensed milk. He would come into the doghouse, take the can of milk out of the bucket, get an old rusty spike, bang two holes in it, and that would be his lunch. But he was the best. His whole life was barring and boozing.

During the last year of the war, I was on transportation. No experience at all when it came to blasting. I was working with this tramp miner by the name of Fontaine. We were blasting in this chute, some big muck, so that we could load it in the cars. He said for me to get down the ladder. I was watching him, and you know what he did? The son of a gun cut the fuse down to about three inches and lit it, and before he even got to the bottom of the ladder, boom! It pretty near blew your head off — and this went on. Hell, we never even had time to guard or anything. He was fearless or crazy, depends how you looked at it, I guess. And that's no bullshit, eh.

Then during the war, I worked with this Swede from out of town. This is good, eh. I had just started. The first job you got was they put you on steady graveyard or the supply gang. You brought supplies in and put them all around the mine where it was called for. It was usually a big train we brought in with timber, pipe, steel, cement and all that kind of stuff. Every night he would come to work drunk, and this was during the war when you couldn't get liquor. Christ, he would come to work just reeking with this aftershave lotion and just hammered and a mouth full of snoose.

We would be coming out of the portal with this big bloody long empty train of flatcars and V-cars. And no protection from the wind on the front of that bloody motor, and he would just put his head down, throttle wide open, and I would hang on to that trolley pole, just terrified. We would come out through the portal doors around that corner just outside like a rocket. Why we never went over and down the bank, I'll never know.

I asked him how the hell he could keep doing this night after night. He said, "Oh shit, that's nothing. Soon as I get real sick, I just go to the hospital and get my stomach pumped out."

This Pie Russell that ran the McDougal Hall, he used to buy I don't know how many cases of shaving lotion every month just because of these tramp miners. He made his living just selling shaving lotion because these guys were buying it for the alcohol. This Swede would drink twelve to fourteen bottles a day and come to work every night just hammered. Nothing to it. Christ, just go get the stomach pumped out. These were the kind of guys that were showing up around here.

I remember another time; I was just eighteen. I was working with this young guy from the Prairies and he had a terrible stutter. This Bertoia used to ride him steady, never letting up on this poor guy. I turned around this one day and here he had this Bertoia down on the ground under a chute and had a 2-foot steel in his hand and was going to crucify the bugger. A bunch of us jumped in and broke it up, but I'll tell you one thing. Bertoia never teased the kid again. He just had enough and that was the end of that. This was the kind of stuff that went on in there during the war, eh.

Pete Balonyk and I worked together for quite awhile and he told me this story about when he was tramping in northern Manitoba and he was working in this gold mine. I guess he was working with these Finlanders and these guys were real tough, mean guys. There was this foreman that used to really ride these guys and one day the foreman was found at the bottom of this muck

Trammer operates a train to transport ore from the chute to bins on 3900 Level.

raise, a couple of hundred feet down. It was well known that these Finlanders had thrown him down the raise but nobody could prove it. But they got him. It was a small mine so it would be easy to do. Pete swore to me it was the truth but you would have to ask him about it. But you know Pete, he would just look at you and laugh. Pete never had much use for supervisors.

I'll give you a real tragic story that I was involved in. It was August 1947. I was on transportation and was working with two guys. One was Swede Wallin and the other was Lloyd Searle.

TRAMMER
OPERATES TRAIN TO
TRANSPORT ORE FROM
CHUTE TO BINS

I was on the motor and the other two guys were pulling the chute up on the platform. I think it was about a 14-car train. Right behind me and the motor was a raise that went up about a hundred and fifty feet, and there was a little sub that went in maybe about fifty feet at the top. I saw these two guys going up the raise.

So anyway, I was sitting on the motor waiting for my partners to signal me when to spot the next car under the chute, and I hear this rumbling. I just jumped out of the motor and took off and ran towards the chute. I got up on the chute and told my partners that something was wrong. I was just a kid but they had heard it too. Then we heard a guy crying for help.

Swede told me to go get the ambulance while he went to find this guy. So anyway, I took off and I was about twenty feet past the motor and here was this guy's head sticking out of the mud. I didn't even stop. I knew he was dead. All you could see was this head. I went down and got hold of Johnny MacDonald and we got the ambulance and he came up with me. By the time we got there, Swede and Lloyd had got the other guy down into the drift.

There was a guy who was still alive — it was Hap Richardson — and the kid they picked up in the drift was a kid named David Brown. He was a kid I graduated with in grade twelve. Johnny MacDonald said to me, "Pete, you better not look at this. You better get out right now." I told John I wanted to stay and help. When we picked this kid up, all he had left on him was his belt. All his clothes had been torn off. It was just like picking up a rag doll, every bone in his body was just smashed.

I guess I started to grow up then. It took me years to get over it, especially when you know the guy. I was only a kid myself.

What saved Hap was his belt got caught on footwall steel and he just hung there as everything went over him. I guess what had happened was that at the end of the sub was a wall of muck blocking the breakthrough into the stope from where we were pulling. As we pulled the muck, it moved this blockage and behind this was thousands of gallons of water. So into this small sub went all this water, right onto these two guys. I guess it was just bad timing and being in the wrong place at the wrong time.

JACK TUCK

A man with a hundred songs and a guitar...

A proud Newfie, Jack can tell so many funny stories about Newfoundland that your ribs ache from the laughter. He loves having a few pints then bringing out his guitar and keeping those around him well entertained.

Jack worked underground for years in different aspects of mining until he went permanently on the hoist. As a hoistman, he had the very important job of lowering and bringing up the skips that transported men up and down the two shafts in the mine. He often had the lives of dozens of men in his hands, although he couldn't see them and had to rely on bell signals from the skiptender who was several hundred, or even a thousand, feet away.

I came to Kimberley from Newfoundland in 1946. My brother-in-law and his brother came west first. My brother-in-law got drowned with that bunch of guys on Kootenay Lake, by Sirdar. Well, he was a driller in the Sullivan when this happened. Four of them got drowned and one young guy survived. He had written us about what beautiful country this was and said we should come out and get work. I had been working in a mine down home on the Rock. Been working there for about eight years. It was a lead and zinc mine. I got tired of working there. Hell, we were wet all day, even though we had slickers on, 10-hour days at fifty-nine cents an hour. We used to have to push those little end dump cars into the stopes on 18-inch track to fill the stopes for support. We got no holiday pay or bonus. We had to buy our own gear — slickers, khaki clothes, gloves, shirts, everything — from the company store.

We lived in a fourplex. We only paid another $3 a month for coal for heat and cooking, which I guess wasn't bad. This was before the war, but we were treated as slaves. It was real hard. By the time they took everything off your pay cheque — rent, heat, food — there wasn't much left. But we could always make our own moonshine. We always had parties, music. Seemed like every second guy could play something. We had our good times.

What made my mind up to pack it in was the day I almost got drowned. My job was to run the pumps, at the end of the shift make sure they were on. This one day I was the only guy left in the mine, for the pumps, ya know.

The water was afoaming, ladder and pipe was coming down like crazy. I grabbed a couple of big electric train motors and moved them as far back down a drift as I could. When I got off the motors, I was up to my armpits in water. The water was up in some places to the trolley wire. I had to climb twelve hundred feet straight up this winze to get out, plus go through all the blasting smoke. All they had was natural ventilation. I had to get out of there before I got killed. You had to be hard, and we were, but there is a point when you know that's enough.

When I quit the mine in Newfie, the wife and I decided to take a chance and go out to Kimberley, so we sold all our stuff and headed west. We had never had a holiday.

My last shift was November 10, 1945. We went to Grand Falls on December 19, 1945, stayed for Christmas, and left to go on Boxing Day by train. Got to Cranbrook January 7, 1946.

The train we come on was packed with guys coming back from overseas. Now there's something I can't do is let elderly or women stand, so I spent most of my time on the train sitting on the floor or in the toilet. I had to get out when somebody needed to use it but that's how full the train was: standing room only. Everyone got on well, shared what we had. It wasn't bad.

I went to the Company office to see about getting hired on. Bob Ford was doing the hiring. I figured I was going to get hired on by the CM&S, but it was Northern Construction I was going to work for. They were just putting the steel in No. 1 Shaft. I was the second guy hired on that day.

Ol' Cy, the foreman, said to me one day, "Jack, what we're really stuck for is hoistmen. We could probably get one from CM&S. We got Peter Wiebe, but we need a couple of our own guys." I said, "I've run some hoists with a 3-foot drum, some electric ones and even steam hoists." He said, "Where the hell they still using steam hoist?" I said, "Back where I come from in Newfie. That's how we got rid of all the scrap lumber from the mine."

He got back to me in a couple of weeks and told me they were setting up a hoist just below the 3900, a double drum on a bench just below the collar. There was ol' Duke Downing and a bunch of us that set it up. I said, "Sure, I'll give it a try once we got it set up." So I just run it up and down for awhile till I got the hang of it. This was before the hoist at No. 1 Shaft was even there. They were still mining it. So they said, "You're the hoistman now." I didn't mind.

The skip was always a high-back car. You'd take chances by hauling men on it but we did it. We hauled everything on it: supplies, cement and, when nobody was around, the guys could ride on it. Those high-backs were great for pouring the footings for the steel in the shaft.

I worked for Northern for about a year then the whole crew got hired on with CM&S. There was Bud Jack, Sev Olmstead, Stan Lloyd, Eric Larsen, and Pete Corneilson. These guys were probably the best team I ever worked on. You know what it's like when you get a crew and everybody knows what the next guy is doing and what the next move is, can't be beat. Great way to work. Anyway, that's how I got on as a spare hoistman for CM&S.

Ol' Cy asked me if I wanted to go mining. I said, "Sure! If I'm going to be underground, that's what I would prefer." They were looking for miners then. I told him I had worked in Newfie square setting, moving hoists and pumps, stepped in when they needed miners. Yeah, I can do it.

So Ray Ulmer and myself worked on one side and Russ Evert and Steve McCoy worked on the other side. We slashed all the way from 3900 right up to the surface. There was just a small hole there, just big enough for a small skip. We just slashed to it. We set up on sprags or sometimes the steel square sets 'cause we were putting steel in as we went. At times, we buggered up a lot of steel when we blasted, especially around the stations.

Ol' Cy come to me one day and said, "Jack, you got the most work of the whole bloody works. Christ, you got to go up and down six, seven hundred feet five, six times a shift, so I'm going to give you a dollar a day more than the miners." 'Cause I ran the skip too. So I would ask the boys what gear they needed — steel and stuff — and sometimes I would go down to the hoist and forget something and back up I would go. I soon learned to write things down. I was making seventy-nine cents an hour plus that extra dollar a day for climbing up and down the raise. Jesus Christ.

So when we had finished drilling off and while the guys were putting the gear away, I would climb up four hundred or five hundred feet to the surface, make up the fuse and powder, and lower it down to them. They would spit the fuses and they were supposed to walk all the way up in the smoke. So what are you gonna do? They would jump in the skip, three guys, and I would hoist them up to just below where the collar is today.

One year, it was the coldest winter I had ever seen. For six weeks it was thirty to thirty-five below. You couldn't walk down the man-way. It was just like a glacier. We used to have a big toboggan we used to lower our steel down on. We put all that steel in below the collar and did all the mining around there while the ground was froze. It was a big area, a big hole.

Then we had to timber and block it up all around, all creosote wood, eight by eights, twelve by twelves. We used to bring up two truckloads a day. We'd be cutting the timber to fit with crosscut saws. It was a good way to keep warm. One night it snowed twenty-eight inches but we carried on. Some of these areas of timber are eight and ten feet high, plus all the cribbing. Lotta work. Ol' Cy came up during the shift and said, "You guys are doing a hell of a job here. You guys get the rest of this blocking in and I'll come up and pick you guys up and take you to the Elks. So at nine he came and got us and bought beer for us all night. Great guy, he was.

You know, those days you only had enough stuff to do the job. The Company didn't have much, so we worked with what we had. We had a mucking machine that mucked onto a belt and the belt put it right into the car. I don't know how old it was but it was a damned old piece of equipment. We made it work though.

I remember one night, we had this Henry, I forget his name. He was our boss on afternoon shift. We had this station, the whole bloody station full of muck. Day shift had slashed the back, big pieces of stuff that we couldn't muck with the mucking machine. And Henry wanted it cleaned up before the end of the shift.

When he came back at the end of the shift, we had it all loaded in cars, 12-ton cars. He said, "How the hell did you get all that loaded? I never expected you to get it all done. I was just kidding." We said that we drilled holes in the back, put in eyebolts, hooked up a block, strung out cable through the block and around the slabs, and lifted them up with a motor. We pushed a car under and then lowered the slab into the car. He said he couldn't believe what we did in one shift, but what the hell, you do whatever works, and it all worked because of the guys I was working with, good bunch.

Ol' Duke Downing was one of the best I ever worked for, one of the best. Billy Barn was part of that crew. They were called gang bosses. I worked most of the shaft, all the sumps and pockets, all the footing for the steel all the way down, poured all that cement, and that was with no bonus, but it was a job.

When we were done the collar, there was a guy by the name of Evans who had a truck and used to deliver sawdust and wood slabs around town for heating. He got the contract to fill these 45-gallon metal drums with gravel. I don't know how many hundred yards of gravel he did, but he would deliver them up to the collar.

You gotta remember this was winter, colder than hell, thirty below most of the time. We had to pour cement over the gravel in the drums to strengthen them but it was so cold, we mixed a quarter of a can of calcium chloride with two bags of cement so the water wouldn't freeze in the mixer. Those old mixers would take two or three sacks of cement. One day, we poured a hundred and eighty sacks of cement. There was five of us on a crew, but we kept warm by working so hard. These drums could act as support around the collar when placed together.

I never made no money with Cominco. I was never a big contractor like some of the guys. It was a good company, ya know, but some of the guys I worked for, the supervisors, I didn't care for and they didn't care much for me. But that's just human nature, I guess.

I sure would have liked to stay outside all the time. Once in a while I would get a break and I worked for ol' Abe Lilley in the Cominco Gardens when I was off with this rheumatism. I said "By God, this is going to be all right." I liked working for ol' Abe.

You worked hard. We had all the old bunkhouses. I used to walk miles and miles. I had to cut the lawns and do all the trimming around the cookhouse, bunkhouses, nurses' residence and hospital, and the Giegerich house — superintendent's house — and look after all the plants that we planted. But ol' Abe Lilley was a good guy to work for so long as you did your work. I know sometimes I would have to work half a day on Sunday. I had a Studebaker then. When I was ready to come home, he would tell me to sit down and have a beer with him. How many guys would do that now, ya know, sit down and have a beer with ya. And then he'd say, "Let's load up your truck with lawn cuttings out of the compost and take it home for your pigs to eat." Yep, he was a hell of a guy.

I worked outside in the car shop when guys went on holidays. Sometimes I would be sent underground when underground guys went on holidays, repairing cars at the repair area or hoists, wherever they needed me. I got after them one time because the boss wouldn't pay me any more for going underground, just a few cents more than what I was getting outside. They were tough to deal with those days. So one day I said, "If I'm good enough to fill in for those guys, I should get the rate."

I hadn't been here that long, only three or four years. I said, "Guess you're not going to pay me any more. I guess I'll have to quit." He said, "What are you going to do?" I said, "I guess I'll just go back to Newfoundland. I paid my way out here. I guess I can pay my way back." He called me in the next day and told me any time I went underground again, I would get the rate. He knew I wasn't just a goofy Newfie. I meant business.

The hoists I ran were mostly No. 2 Shaft and 27 Raise. We all had to take medicals every year, eyesight and especially hearing 'cause, you know, we never could see what we were doing. All we had to go on was the bell system given by the skiptenders. But, you know, it's like everything else. Ya never went by the book. Normally, you weren't supposed to hoist men without being in balance on a double drum. Sometimes the other skip would be buggered up and I would hoist guys on one single drum and they didn't even know something was very wrong with it.

In No. 1 Hoistroom, the hoistman on controls watches the arrows that tell him at what level the skip is on. The skip hauls men and material up and down. A bell system signals the hoistman where to stop the skip. The drum on the left is the main one used, the one on the right acts as a counter balance.

Like lowering V-cars up and down the shaft when you had a skiptender that knew what he was doing and you were on afternoon shift, you would lower two at a time. I'd get the skiptender to make sure nobody was around in the man-ways or on the stations. I knew exactly where to stop and the skiptender would lower the bridge onto the station and give me the signals. Went slick as hell. Saved him a lot of work up and down, up and down. When you're by yourself, it's a lot of work. So we lowered V-cars, timber cars, gravel cars, rail cars, and nobody ever knew. Shortcuts, ya know.

I don't know if I was the instigator or not but you know how it worked here was that the skiptender would give the signal for what station he wanted to go to and some hoistmen were pretty fast and the skip would go right now. So I told them that back in Newfie, when the skiptender gave the signal, the hoistman would repeat it and it gave just enough pause so's that guys were all sittin' down and gave the skippy enough time to get set. And, Jesus, you know, it only took them a couple of years to do what I suggested. It's a lot safer now than it was.

We were supposed to do all our checks before shift, like run the skip through the limit switches and stuff. Sometimes when there was three shifts on, I used to just get the boys on and take them to their levels so's they could have a snack or a cuppa tea before they went to their headings. And then I'd do all my tests and checks during the shift; lotsa times, I would do that. We had to check the limits in case, say, I passed out, the skip would only go so far instead of going up over the bullwheel or all the way down to the sump.

We had trouble for years with the skip at No. 2 Shaft, so's they brought this guy in. He was an East Indian or something, and our problem was that the skip wouldn't line up on the stations with a full load of men on it. This Indian gent, he said to load the skip up with bags of cement about the same weight as a load of men and then he came into the hoist room and told me to just let it freefall. So's I did and the limit switches stopped it. But, you know, he had it all figured out in a few days. Smart bugger he was.

He checked out the dogs on the skip that were a back-up to the limit switches. The dogs come out at a certain speed and grab the guides that were made out of Douglas fir. These guides couldn't have a knot in them. They ran all the way down all shafts on both sides. Eight by eight they were, pretty damn expensive but he got everything working good, him and ol' Harry Bryant.

This man-skip at 3927 Raise was used for taking men to upper levels from 3900 Level.

The worst accident I ever saw was down at the bottom of the incline on 3700 Haulage, you know, where that lunch station is. We were working in the new doghouse, putting in washbasins, tables, benches and counters; poured the floor; built the airtight seals; and installed the double doors. We were having lunch this day. We were expecting some gravel and cement to come in from the mill. Anyway, in comes this guy in a hell of a hurry. He grabs the stretcher and says, "There's a man under the car."

There was guys coming down from the crusher to give a hand. We had lots of guys. These are 40-ton cars and we needed jacks. The strange thing about it, the guy that was under the car had just come into where we were eating our buckets. The lunchroom was full and I had said to him to just wait a second and you can have my place. Well, he went out, I guess to find a place outside to sit and eat. I guess he didn't hear the train backing up or he slipped or got his foot stuck. Who knows, eh? When I got there, he was all balled up under the axle, just like an old gunnysack. We couldn't do anything.

They had to bring in the police and a doctor, and the doctor pronounced him dead. We had to go to the mill to get jacks. But the one thing I'll never forget is the guys that just vanished because they couldn't handle it. I didn't like it either. I don't even like killing a pig, but you do what you have to do.

3900 (main) Level. Man-car on the left. The ore train in the middle is capable of hauling 600 tons of ore. From this level all the ore in the mine goes to the concentrator four miles away.

We got a jack finally and Lenny says if I jack it up, he'll pull him out. That was the hardest thing I ever done.

We always had fun with each other, like ol' Band-Aid Charley. It seemed like he always had Band-Aids on every finger. We used to say he used them so he wouldn't have to buy gloves. He was the type of guy that when we were in the doghouse and the phone would ring, he would say, "That's for me, that's for me." He would jump up and run to answer the phone. Well, we used to put grease on the earpiece, never failed to get him. He would sit down to his bucket and he couldn't understand why all us guys were laughing at him. Great big gob of grease on his ear. Funnier than hell, it was.

Oh, Jesus, Jesus, he used to have that little side axe of his, one-sided axe for using when your left hand was putting your guides in. You couldn't stand near the bugger for fear he would cut your legs off. So we told him we were going to get a barrel for him or us to stand in. He was god-awful to work near. You didn't know where that axe was going to end up.

Another time, well, he took great pride in his toolbox and, oh Jesus, he had it nice. It was his pride and joy. Eric Larsen was always playing tricks on him. He found this guy, I didn't know who he was, but he was a real good artist. Well, he got that black paint and he painted Mickey Mouse and a whole bunch of characters on that toolbox. We thought it looked damn good, but ol' Charley felt quite bad about that and went right to the safety office. He figured the guys were going too far with it. He got over it, though.

This ol' mine foreman told me one time, he came into a stope, big ol' glory hole, some time in the winter. A lot of them had water in them and would be covered in ice. Well, anyhow, he heard this bloody music and he thought maybe it was just his imagination or something. He said he thought it was coming from an ol' chute that was below the stope. He said he got closer and closer and he looked down and here was ol' Freddie. Freddie was out step-dancin' and ol' Harry was playing the mouth organ for him. He said it was a sight to behold but he backed off so's they wouldn't even know he was there.

When I was in the blacksmith shop, we used to make eyebolts on afternoon shift in the summer. It was hotter than hell, but we'd make twenty thousand eyebolts. And once our work was done, our quota, we'd do government jobs for ourselves or other guys. The Company didn't care back then. Sometimes we'd play ball outside the shop, make a ball with rags and tie it up tight with tape. We had a lotta fun them days. Lotta shoutin' and hollerin' going on. Boy, it was great.

TERRY BLOOMER

A man with a presence...

Terry was foreman in the Centre Section for years. He was instrumental in developing the methods used to mine the hot muck and he worked to ensure there was a good safety program implemented throughout this complex and dangerous process. Terry spent most of his time in the administration end of the mine's operation, working as a foreman, shift boss, safety officer, trainer, surveyor, and in the ventilation department.

My father was born in 1900 in Nelson. He signed up to go to the First World War when he was fifteen and also fought in the Russian Revolution in 1917. He studied in England and became a mining engineer after the war. When he came back, he married my mother in Rossland.

He got hired on with Consolidated Mining and Smelting, which is now Cominco, in 1922. He ran several little mines around the West Kootenay for the Company for a few years and then was sent up north to run a small gold mine at Slave Creek. In 1932 I was six years old and so, along with my older sister, he hauled my mother and us up north. The only ways in were by plane or by foot. We went in on a Fokker AAF. This was a short-term job and a good thing it was, because my mother was alone except for us kids.

Then, in 1934, he was sent to the Box Properties, which was the gold fields in northern Saskatchewan on Lake Athabasca. Mother and us kids went along. My mother had taught me school up to this point. I was eight at the time and there was a little school going there and so when I entered school, they didn't know what grade to put me in. So I had to write a test and it all got straightened out in the end.

There were fifteen kids in this log schoolhouse of all ages and a real fine teacher. It was fun. In the winter, I would drive my dog team across Lake Athabasca about five miles with my sister in the sleigh. She was eleven and I was nine. It wasn't a big dog team, only two dogs. When I hooked up the dogs, I would throw a couple of frozen fish in the sleigh to feed the dogs when we got to the school. My sister and I would sit backwards to keep our faces out of the wind.

We spent two winters up there. I had my own little wall tent about ten by ten by ten with a stove in it, and my dad, mother and sister had a larger walled tent to live in.

When the gold fields petered out, my dad was sent to Pinchi Lake, a mercury mine, which was in northern British Columbia. I was sent to a boarding school in Edmonton where I finished my grade twelve, as there were no schools up at Pinchi Lake. After I graduated, I went up north and worked on logging trucks for awhile and then joined the navy when I was seventeen. While I was overseas, my dad was transferred to the Sullivan in Kimberley as a superintendent responsible for pillar extraction, which he had experience in.

After the war I went to university for awhile. Didn't like it so I packed it in and went to Kimberley to get hired on at the mine where my dad was the superintendent.

I started at the Sullivan in 1946 driving Euclids and Cats on the surface and then was transferred underground. There I went through all the jobs like trackman and piping, and then got on to mining. During this time, my dad won a gold medal for pillar extraction presented by the Canadian Mining Association.

I was made a temporary pipe boss and was making $450 a month and my wife, Marg, said if I could make this forever, we would be very happy. That was pretty darn good money then. After that, I worked in engineering, ventilation, supervision, foreman and then went outside into safety and training in the later years.

The first partner I had when I went mining was Carl Bruhaug. We worked for Garnet Coulter, who was our foreman. I thought Garnet was a top-notch guy. Carl and I drove vertical raises for Garnet for two years, just the two of us.

We used to be able to take 10-foot rounds. It was easy drilling because it was all in high-grade ore. We used to build these little houses for our tool cache. We would go up, say, forty or fifty feet and then build another out of sprags and planks, and these little houses would be connected with ladders so as we went up, we would move our gear up to the next house. Most of these raises were about a hundred and fifty feet long. We did this to all the little pillars that were left in the North End section of the mine.

When we finished the mining part of it, the long-hole drillers would move in and drill the walls, back and footwall, which would be blasted once they were finished drilling. Back then we were using the old Crag bits. They were a knock-off bit but by being in the ore, we were usually able to use the same bits from the start of the raise to the finish. Just like drilling in butter. We always had to put the cut off to the side, opposite the little house, so we wouldn't blow it down the raise.

One time, a shift boss sent a crew in there. I guess they didn't have a place to work that day. Well, anyway, they put the cut straight at the little house and so when they blasted, down the raise went the little house and all our gear. That's where we found it when we came on shift, right at the bottom of the muck pile. It took us about three days to get everything straightened out again. Put in ladders, rebuild the little houses, and dig the gear out of the muck pile, all that kind of stuff, you know.

Hot muck had to be the most dangerous situation that I ever experienced underground. Here we tried not to have close calls. We had six hot-muck pillars going at one time and with all the gases and fumes, concrete bulkheads had to be built to control the area. They were built wherever they were needed to control the flow of air. You had to have the airflow going into the subs just slightly less than what was going out the exhaust. It was critical that the airflow was balanced.

To do this, we had to build a concrete bulkhead about two feet thick between the hoist and the millhole, with small openings for the cable from the hoist and a small hole for the miner to look through. Alongside of the bulkhead was a steel door. At the top of the bulkhead was a hole for the fresh-air fan. At the back of the sub, where the exhaust went into circuit, was a regulator that could be adjusted to make sure that airflow going in was a little less than what was going out. The bulkhead at the back was also made of thick concrete and the regulator door was made of lead or steel. The purpose of this was to prevent feeding the fire in the ore with oxygen. When the air going to the fire wasn't controlled, you couldn't hear yourself think. It was incredibly noisy.

Gus Eliuk and myself went up a drawhole to find out why no more muck was coming down into the sub. What we found was that a large dome had developed. The muck had clinkered up. There was nothing but a large glow coming from this huge clinker. It was like being in an arena all lit up. It was about a

Miner in hot muck exiting from a sub. The hoist for scraping is behind a two-foot bulkhead with a steel door. Note the peephole for the miner to observe while working. Miner is wearing a Type N canister good only for very low concentrations of gas and dust.

hundred feet long and a hundred wide and I would say about a hundred feet high.

Ed Walsh was the shifter with us at the time. We climbed down out of the drawhole to discuss what to do about this and how we were going to get this thing down. I always thought that the best way to get a job done right is to ask the guys that are working there. Gus suggested that we haul 45-gallon barrels up onto the hogsback and fill them with NCN. So we got a crew together and did this. We put up about six barrels in the various subs and had it so they wouldn't go off at the same time because if they did, the damage done to the infrastructure wouldn't make the effort worth it.

When we set it off, it sounded like an atomic bomb going off. It didn't do very much damage but what it did do was put a hole in this dome of molten ore so that it started to come down, where we could get at it to scrape. We went to the hot-muck procedure where we shotcreted all the drawholes all the way to the back of the sub — there could be ten drawholes or more in each sub — and once this was done, we would open up a drawhole at the back of the sub and scrape it until it started running waste ore and then open up another, working our way to the front of the sub. It wasn't the best way to draw down the ore but it was the safest.

The hot muck got to a point where it was red- or white-hot. It was several thousand degrees, just running like water, dripping down to the chute-loaders down below on the trains. These guys were protected to the best of our ability with proper clothing, air masks and ventilation. We had water sprays to wet down the muck. This caused a lot of steam and the SO_2 gas was terrible. Usually by the time the trammers headed to the dump, the water on the muck had evaporated and there was a cloud of dust and SO_2 moving with the train. The train always went motor first into the ventilation.

All this molten muck caused lots of problems in the crusher. The crusher people had to contend with the hot muck gumming up the crushers, the dust and the ever-present SO_2 gas. All these people had to wear protective gear also.

People in Trail couldn't believe this hot muck thing so several of Cominco's big shots came over to investigate it for themselves. When they came to me, I told them they were going to have to take a course on how to wear hot-muck apparatus and go through the proper procedures if they wanted to look at this stuff. As we were going through the procedure, the top guy with them, I won't mention his name, he was a bit of an ass, said, "Enough of this. Get us in there." I told him that nobody was going in there until I said it was okay, and that it was like going to the moon. He was pretty defiant anyway, just an office guy who thought he knew it all.

So when I thought they would be all right, I took them into the hot muck with all the concrete bulkheads and miners there. In the doghouse, the place was so clean you could eat off the floor. The guys always kept it so clean, sweeping and stuff, the oxygen tanks hanging in racks on the wall. It was just damn neat. The big shot said, "You know, Terry, you didn't have to fix this place up for us." I said, "It's not fixed up for you. It's fixed up for these people. They look after it." And he didn't care for that statement. Christ, what a pain in the ass he was.

We left the doghouse and went to one of the subs where the miners were working. I told them they could only go to the steel door in the bulkhead in front of the hoist and look in. So they go in with their outfits on and here's the white-hot muck running on its own down the millhole on the other side of the bulkhead. They said, "We've seen enough. We believe you." And away they went back to Trail to their little office jobs.

There're a couple of stories I can tell you about some of the oldtimers. One was when Fred Turk thought he would like to get out early on day shift so he hopped on a waste train going out about one o'clock. So there he is riding out on the motor with the trammers and when they come out through the portal, here's a whole bunch of Cominco brass standing around outside. He told me this later. I was his boss at the time.

He says he had to make himself look like he was part of the train crew, pretending he was switching and checking the couplings and stuff. He could see that the brass weren't going back into the offices, so he had to jump on the train and come back in. It just didn't pay that day. He was quite a character. He was the unofficial spokesman of our section of the mine. He had all kinds of jokes. You couldn't keep up to him, he was just too funny.

I was working with this oldtimer and we were benching with those old tripod drills in a stope. Well, he came to work one day and you know how you look after your partners, well, he was a good four sheets to the wind. We were working up on the 4250 Level in this stope. It was a gravity bench but there was a spot where gravity wouldn't take the muck away so we had to scrape with this 30-horsepower hoist. I knew I shouldn't have let him come into the heading but there are things you do at times, so I told him to bed down behind the hoist and he promptly went to sleep until the end of the shift. He didn't get any drilling or blasting done that day but we did get it scraped out and set up for the cross shift. He was such a good oldtimer; I just couldn't turn him in.

Red Foster was probably one of the greatest oldtimers in the Sullivan. I was his foreman at the time of his last shift. He was sixty-five, although I kind of think he was older. He was the kind of guy that would mine until he died in there if you let him. Well, anyhow, he comes to me at the start of the shift and says, "Terry, it's my last shift and you've got to come up to where I'm working and I'm going to be on a stoper putting in a hole for an eyebolt and I want you to come up and see it." I said, "You bet, Red. I'll be up. What time do you want me there?" He said, "Come at eleven."

So I made sure I was there at eleven. Red was in the sub, stoper was all oiled up and ready to go, and I said, "Go to it, partner." Red grabs the stoper and starts to collar a hole. Well, where he was collaring, it was on a slip, running away from him. Well, the poor guy didn't get it collared and ended up on the footwall with the stoper. He looks up at me after I turned the air off and says, "Jeeze, Terry, I sure screwed up on my last hole." I told him that it didn't matter because he had drilled thousands of good holes in his life as a miner. Ol' Red had to be one of the most respected characters in the mine. They just don't make them like that any more.

I think the saddest person I ever saw was Nick Seredick when he came to work his last shift. Andy Sterling and I called him into the office to wish him well and shake his hand and the tears were just pouring out of his eyes the whole time he was standing there. He had such a connection to the mine and was really going to miss it. He was a good hard-working miner, a real miner. I think that had to be one of the saddest days I ever had at the mine.

I didn't believe in the old "bull of the woods" approach to discipline. A good example was when I first went shifting. There was this one individual who was a very strong person, a good boxer and a good leader of men, and later he became a shift boss. The crew was all standing around waiting to go up on the skip. I would say there were around thirty guys on hand. This fellow was a very good, strong speaker. He came over to me and said that he and the guys that worked with him were not going to work in this place today, this that and everything, I forget what the reason was. But here he is dressing me down in front of the crew.

So I said, "Where's your lunch bucket?" He said, "It's over there. Why?" I said, "Well, pick your bucket up and head out the portal — which was about two miles — and we'll have your cheques ready when you check out." All the guys were watching this exchange. He sniffed around, kind of not knowing what to do next. He was testing me, the new shifter. He did pick up his bucket but then backed off and went to work. He and I are good friends now, but you know how it is at times. I have a lot of respect for that man. When I told him to pick up his bucket, I said it very softly but meant it, and I have to admit, I was really happy when he picked up his bucket and went to work. So that was the approach I took to talking with the men. No shouting, no hollering, and it works a lot better than the old way.

What I found is that the person doing the job — miners, timbermen, transportation, whoever — that if we included them in planning what we were going to do, it was more likely to be done right because they knew more about the job than we did.

We had to do a lot of mining up in these pillars that were starting to crack and it was going to be some real tricky mining. We took the miners and the shifters and had a general meeting about how we were going to tackle it. This way the miners were to be included in the actual planning. We would all sit down with the blueprints, along with the planning engineer and the ventilation department, and have a good discussion.

Usually the prints would already be drawn up but were susceptible to change. The miners and shift bosses came up with suggestions on how to go about doing it, and the engineers would take notes and make changes on the prints. So by including the actual individuals that were going to be doing the hands-on work, it probably saved Cominco a lot of time and money. I really believe in this way of doing things because it works to everybody's benefit.

When we were extending the conveyor system from the 2800 Level down to the 2500, Ed Green had me shifting for him. I was kind of new at shifting at the time. The decline was at thirty degrees. The conveyor was over to the far side, then there was a railway that had a large skip for hauling supplies and material powered by a large hoist to move the skip up and down. Then there was a man-way for pedestrian movement. Riding on a material skip was strictly forbidden and warning signs were posted all around. I came around the corner and guess who's sitting on the skip, ready to ride down on it. There were Stinie Vander Maaten and Pete Huppie. There they were on this skip with oxygen bottles, acetylene bottles and all these tools, and my boss, Ed Green, was standing there and it looked to me like he was about to climb on as well. I couldn't stand it. It was totally wrong. You don't go riding down on a thing like that; you just don't do it. If it got away, you'd kill three guys, and then what?

I said, "Where do you think you guys are going?" Stinie says, "We're going to work." "Oh, no, you're not," I said. "You guys get off and walk down. Send the tanks down and then hoof it." So off the skip they got. My boss, Ed, didn't say anything. He just kind of stood there, not knowing what to say, but I bet he was riding that skip with those guys all the time.

I put in thirty-nine and a half years, counting my navy time, and I would do the same thing all over again, absolutely. I wouldn't have changed anything. With all the good people I worked with, it was an experience of a lifetime.

PETE HUPPIE

Always a new face at the table...

Pete was one of the top miners in the Sullivan. Along with his long-time partner, Nelson Todd, they set the pace for the other miners in the South End section of the mine. They always earned top bonus. What drove Pete to make top money was his large family. It seemed to Pete like there was always a new face at the table.

He always enjoyed getting together with his family: his brother Tommy, another great miner, and his sister Gertie and her husband, Dory Arnfinnson. They did enjoy a party.

I came to Kimberley in September of 1947. My sister and brother-in-law, Dory, were already here. So I had a place to stay until I got into the bunkhouse. I got here September 23 and was working at the mine on the twenty-fifth.

The first week, it was pretty much just indoctrination, showing you around the mine and showing you how things were done. Then they put me on transportation. I was running the motor on a three-man crew, two guys up on the chute loading cars. All I had to do was sit there and move the train whenever the guys on the chute signalled me. I wasn't doing nothing. I couldn't believe they were paying me eighty-seven cents an hour to do this. On payday, I couldn't believe I was making all this money for doing nothing eight hours a day, five days a week.

Then they went to six and two. I didn't like that 'cause here you're going to work on a Saturday afternoon shift and the bars are starting to get going and I was thirsty. I stayed on transportation for about three years, long years. I just got mining when they had a cutback so they took me off mining and put me on the belt. I hated that.

I ran into Doug McMillan downtown. He says that they are hiring at Kemano and how about we quit and go to Kemano. I thought that was a good idea and went home and talked to the wife about it. We got married in 1948 and had a young son at home.

Doug and I headed up and got hired on. They were driving a 15-mile tunnel. You had to put in sixty shifts before they would pay your expenses for coming and leaving. Talk about a haywire place. It was said that one guy per mile was going to get killed driving this tunnel. One guy had just got killed before we got there so we thought we'd be all right for awhile.

One day, I got hit on the head by a rock and my partner, Doug, took me out. He said, "You were breathing and then you'd stop, you were breathing, you'd stop. I thought you were dying and if you died, I'm taking your clothes and I'm outta here." I was all right after a couple days and they put me driving a loci. I made more money driving a motor than I did mining because this was part of the electrician's job. Anyhow, we stayed our sixty days and come out. It was pretty lonesome with my wife and new son so far away.

I didn't get hired back on with the Company for about a year. I spent some time working at the concentrator but I was always bugging them to send me to the mine. I finally got to the mine and worked outside, putting in that big water flume that ran from the dam down to the mine. And, of course, this had to be done in the winter. Christ, it was cold and windy. Just about froze my ass off. After a lot of bugging, they sent me underground to go mining. First guy I went with was Toss Hagen and then with a number of other guys. I spent six years down the Shaft working for Howard Raynor. I found he was okay with the miners. It was just everybody else he didn't like. Then I was sent to the South End in 1964.

When I got to the South End, they were just starting to drive that big ventilation tunnel. It was sixteen by sixteen on the 4600 Level. Johnny Barr and I started slashing the old drift just to get it collared. This is where I got hurt pretty bad.

What happened is that I had to take one of those little motors outside to get some rebar. I think the track was narrow-gauge track, only about two feet wide. Johnny stayed behind and I went outside and loaded up about forty 6-foot rebar, just threw them on the front of the motor. I didn't tie them or anything, you know, big hurry. I'm ripping along pretty good and the motor starts wobbling and, all of a sudden, the bolts started to fly right at me. I got hit in the face and chest and knocked right off the motor onto the track. My lamp cord got hooked on the back end of the motor and took my light. All I could see was the motor going down the track with my light bouncing along behind it.

I had a good idea I was hurt because I could feel the blood running down my face and I was having a hard time breathing. It was pitch black. I couldn't see anything. So I tried using my lighter to see but it was useless. I knew I had to get out for help so I put my heel against the track and dragged it along to keep me straight. I had about a thousand feet to go to get outside. When

I got outside, I let the portal doors slam to get the attention of two guys who were working outside.

The two guys came running 'cause they could see I was in bad shape. They wanted to lay me down but I told them no because I was having a tough time breathing. Chris Nesbitt was one of the guys and he ran down the hill to the portal at the 4500 Level to phone for first aid. He came back up with a small first aid pouch. He wanted to stick one of those ammonia stink bombs under my nose. I told him not to because I was having a hell of a time breathing. He said, "Good, 'cause I need it. I need it." He was up in age at that time. It was just too much excitement for him. It wasn't very long before the ambulance showed up and took me to the hospital.

I was kind of embarrassed about the dirty and bloody clothes they had to cut off me. They had to put a lot of stitches in me. I was a horrible mess. My brother, Tommy, came up to see me. I was in the bathroom when he came. I stepped out of the bathroom. Tommy just about fainted. "Jesus, Jesus. You're going to kill yourself," he yells. Oh God, I looked terrible, lip, nose, cheeks all sewed up. I had several broken ribs also. This all happened on a Thursday. On Friday, Frankie Lowe and his wife came up to see me in the hospital and asked me if I was ready to go for a beer. I told them I was so we went downtown to the bar. Should have seen the looks I got when I came in. I was back to work on light duty on Monday. I was lucky.

I bought my house in 1958 and I paid $6,700 for it. The house is now sixty-seven years old. When it was first built, it sold for $1,200. We used to help each other dig the basements and pour cement, all by hand. I dug so many basements for everybody else by the time I got to doing mine, I was sick of it, so mine is only a little better than half dug out, just enough to store sawdust for the furnace.

Sawdust gave a nice heat and was cleaner and smelled better than coal. But you had to have big storage 'cause you used so much of it. It took up a lot of room. I stuffed it everywhere I could in the basement. We had to go get sawdust at least twice a year. We used to get it from Fabro's sawmill. We got it for free. Bobby MacSporran had a truck so we would help each other. This one time, we were shovelling into the back of Bob's truck from this big pile when it collapsed and buried Bobby. He came out of there spitting sawdust. Wouldn't that have been something? You work as a miner and get killed in a sawdust slough.

When we moved into the house, there was a sawdust stove for cooking. We got rid of it within a month because when we were cooking Christmas dinner, the turkey was done fine, but the potatoes and other vegetables were cold. So that was it, out she went.

Miners with stopers drilling on a round in a stope. Note the cables and blocks from the scraper hoist.

The Company used to give us a turkey for Christmas. It had all the guts and stuff in it. The first turkey we got was twenty-seven pounds, for just the wife and I. We had no refrigeration or anything at that time. And years later, when I had six kids, they were giving out 10- and 12-pounders. Jeeze, we had to save up two of them by then to make a meal.

At one time, they used to give us a turkey and $75 bonus at Christmas and a bag of fertilizer in the summer. As they started making more money, they pretty soon cut all this off, bit by bit. I guess all those turkeys and fertilizer was cutting into the bottom line. They just got cheaper and cheaper over the years. Bean counters, you know.

I have to admit that I enjoyed mining and that's why I did it. I always tried to get started on another round after I got finished on my first. It kept it interesting. I never ever said just because I got one done, that was enough for the day. That's just the way I thought, and with a big family, it made you move. I always tried to move more than the cross shift, and if you got a cross shift that thought the same way, you had it made.

STINIE VANDER MAATEN

The best foreman I ever worked for...

Stinie was probably the best foreman I ever worked for underground. He didn't miss a thing when he walked into a heading, and he didn't like to tell you twice to correct something. Stinie had a good way with the men; he was a guy you could talk to. He was one of the most knowledgeable and honest of the supervisors. He was also one of the best in mine rescue and mine safety. He took these issues very personally. He was instrumental in getting the new mechanized mining operations up and running successfully.

I was working with my dad in Kelowna in 1948. He had a business putting on gyproc, plaster, lathing, shingles, stuff like that, in the construction of houses and packing plants. He heard there was a big project in Kimberley building houses, which is now Lois Creek subdivision. So he came over and put a bid on the job.

When he came back, he told me there was a lot of work over there. So I went over on Labour Day. Got hired on pouring cement, stuff like that, just a construction labourer. I was put on a truck as a swamper and got trained as a driver and got my class three license. I drove until Christmas and went home to Kelowna. I came back to Kimberley, worked for a few days, then quit. It was too cold here for me, compared to Kelowna. So I went logging for the winter over there.

I came back in the spring and started working for Northern Construction, driving truck when they were driving the 3700 Portal. I guess there were about forty guys working outside the portal at that time. When they broke through, meeting up with the guys coming from the other end, I got laid off.

I went over to Trail and I put my application in because CM&S Company in Kimberley wasn't hiring at the time. My dad, mother and brother had worked in the smelter at Trail during the war. I thought it over and told myself that a smelter is not where I wanted to work. So I came back to Kimberley and put my name in at the office and was lucky to have got hired on. This was all in a week's time. Just happened they needed a guy at the concentrator. This was December 22, 1949. I worked there until Christmas then I heard that they were taking people up at the mine.

So I transferred up to the mine where I worked for Bob Foulkes on the outside bull gang for about three months and then I got transferred underground. I worked on the conveyor for quite some time and then went on the track gang, and later on I went slushing. This was when there were two men on a slusher. All this was over a period of two years.

I was working for Jimmy McFarlane. One day, he came to me and asked me how would I like to go mining on development. I told him that I had never done anything like that. He told me not to worry about it and put me with Ralph Wismer working in a sub. When I first met Ralph, I told him that I had never done this work before. He told me not to worry about it. So I go in there and he starts working and I asked him, "What do you want me to do?" He says, "What do you mean?" I told him what I had told him before, that I didn't know anything about mining. He said, "I thought you were bullshitting." Hell, he got me going, showing me what to do, and I ended up working with him for quite awhile.

The place we were working at the time was an "old man's home," nice soft drilling and easy set-ups, stuff like that. Even with him helping me collar holes, we were easily finished by eight on afternoon shift. We were working at the South End for old Dick Shannon then. I worked with different guys after I left Ralph but he got me started.

In April 1952, I was working with Al Lawley. Gordon Edmonds was our shifter. At that time, we used this big white chalk to mark the bootlegs. The big drawback was that it would wash off. Gordon Edmonds marked all our bootlegs up and checked everything out and gave us a hand to collar our holes and left. We were almost drilled off when we drilled into some powder and got blasted. Al was hurt the most. He was unconscious. I was bleeding quite a bit with superficial cuts to my face and arms. I went and got help and got Al out of there. He never woke up until the next day. He had broken cheekbones, that kind of stuff. We were pretty lucky on that one, especially with the volatility of forcite powder.

After the investigation, white chalk was never used again. We went to yellow chalk that had a wax base in it so it wouldn't wash off the face anymore. After we came back, I was asked if I wanted to stay mining. I told them that I wouldn't mind getting off it for awhile to think things over. So they put me on transportation.

In 1953 there was a cutback and I was transferred back outside. I enlisted in the army in 1954 and was discharged three years later. I came back to Kimberley and got hired on as a miner again and went mining down the Shaft. I worked with Gord McKenzie, Pete Huppie, different guys, and worked different phases of mining. I eventually got into first aid, mine rescue, competitions, things like that. I was successful in writing my shift boss ticket and went spare shifting. In 1964 they asked me to go as underground safety inspector. I worked in the safety office for about two and a half years. In 1966 I told the Company I would really like to get back underground, working with the guys. I worked for awhile as a spare shifter then finally got a full-time shifter's job down No. 2 Shaft, working for John Ekskog.

Just after I came back to work after being blasted with Al Lawley, Dick Shannon called me into his office. He had this really weird way of talking. It was a stuttering English accent. You couldn't help but laugh when he talked to you. He says to me, "You, you know, know that three, three strikes you're out, you know, know." I'm killing myself laughing and answered that I had no intentions of two more strikes, but, boy, did I ever want to stutter back at him. It was all I could do not to.

Another one about old Dick. I was working with Ralph Wismer on the 4600 Level. We had to walk up an incline from the 4500. At the top was the doghouse. I was in there having my lunch one day. There was about six of us in there. I'm the rookie. I'm sitting by the door and a miner by the name of Ed Johnson said to me, "You know you're sitting beside the peep-hole?" "Peep-hole?" I say. He says, "Yeah, see that knot-hole right by your head? That's the peep-hole and you're supposed to be watching for any shift boss coming up the raise." I took one look out the peep-hole and said, "I guess we better go 'cause Dick Shannon is on the other side looking in." And here's Dick looking in, saying his favourite saying, "What the boogery hell, what the boogery hell." So out we go.

In 1975 they asked me if I would consider going over to mechanized, which was just starting up. I was made mechanized foreman. There was no contract mining going on at the time over there. There was a block system being used to train the miners. They all had to go through

This new trackless portal was put in when the office and dry complex was moved. Men and material entered this way, eliminating the need for the old track drift on 3900 Level.

each phase of it. Most of these guys had never mined before. This system never really panned out because of the time factor. The Company was pushing pretty hard to get it going so a lot of the guys never really got trained the way they were supposed to in all the aspects of mining.

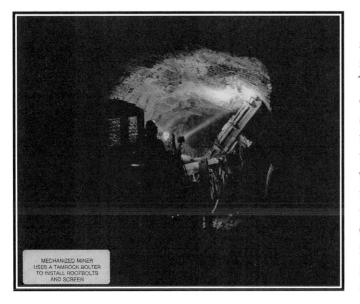

MECHANIZED MINER
USES A TAMROCK BOLTER
TO INSTALL ROOFBOLTS
AND SCREEN

This Tamrock bolter is used for bolting and screening.

The guys were getting an hourly rate a little higher than the conventional miners to offset not getting bonus. The guys could see the bonus the conventional miners were getting and so they slowed it right down until they got a bonus system. That's when they really turned it on because they were getting pretty damn good on the equipment by now and so away they went. This was a time when the Company was trying to get away from paying bonus. They thought the guys would just be happy working for an hourly rate.

Boy, were they wrong. The Company used all the old clichés like safety, easier on equipment, things like that. Miners don't want to hear that stuff. They'll look after themselves, just get out of their way. I personally think that a lot of engineers and staff just didn't like the fact that a good miner could make more than them. I was general mine foreman for awhile and then went on a special project outside. That's where I finished up my career at the Sullivan.

There was a vast difference in attitude between management and the men from when I started until I finished. There was the old-style foremen, bull of the woods type. They were all like that then. It switched around. Sure there were still arguments, but no screaming and yelling. Now if a guy was being disciplined, it was done in private, whereas before, the foreman would be yelling and screaming at a guy while the crew was standing around watching and laughing and talking.

The old foremen like McQuarrie, Raynor and Coulter, when they got mad, they were mad. It was the same with shifting. I'm not knocking any of the shifters or foremen 'cause I worked with all of them. I enjoyed working with them. I've done things wrong too and got dressed down but I never had anyone yelling and screaming at me. It was the same with the shifters. Instead of telling a guy what to do, you would ask him what he was going to do. It formed a better relationship. Sure some of them had their pets and let them get away with things, but, all in all, it went better.

In 1967 I was involved with the Balmer North Mine explosion in the Crowsnest Pass. From what information I got working in the safety office in Kimberley, a rock fall caused the explosion. Apparently, when the rock fall occurred, it stirred up a lot of dust and there was a dust explosion. That's where the methane gas would happen and go boom!

This explosion happened right at shift change and the thirteen guys going in entered the mine by the exhaust circuit. I guess it was a lot warmer than going in the fresh-air circuit. I could understand that, especially in the winter. They were killed within five hundred feet of the entrance.

PULLING ORE FROM A DRAWPOINT USING A SCOOPTRAM

Pulling ore from a drawpoint using a scoop tram.

You could see visible damage just outside the exhaust portal. There was a large fan blown completely over to a big dump area. There was a telephone pole approximately fifteen inches in diameter sheared right off at the bottom like it was cut with a chainsaw. There was a big reel of electrical cable, 2-inch cable. All the cable came off the reel and the reel was lying against the wall.

That was the force that shot out the exhaust. It was a nerve-wracking experience as there was the explosion itself, with the chance of another, and none of us had ever worked in a coal mine before so you can see what it must have been like for us.

I was the captain of the [mine rescue] team so it was up to me to take air samples with the safety lamp as we went along, keeping my eye on the flame inside the lamp. When we hit the first intersection, I raised the lamp up slowly to test for methane and got a reading of five per cent. That's when the flame will get up into the steel gauzes. So I turned and lowered it slowly and extinguished the lamp because if the flame gets through the gauzes in the lamp, you've got another explosion.

Bobby MacSporran was the vice-captain. He gave me shit after. He said he wanted to see that cap on the flame when it got up into the gauze. I told him I wasn't going to let him. That's why I put the lamp out. It was bad enough that it scared the shit out of me, never mind everyone else.

We made two trips in. The first trip, we were to divert the air by putting up a seal. The seal was made of brattice with a sort of plastic on it. We worked on that seal for the two hours we were underground. We were only allowed to be in the mine for two hours at a time, no more. I brought the team out three minutes over the two hours and was told never to do that again. "Come out early," they told me, "but never late." And they meant it.

There were fifteen guys killed in that explosion. Other crews went in after us to do rehab and exploratory work. Thirteen dead guys were brought out first, but there were two mechanics to be brought out. They were further back in the mine. One crew was sent in by a certain route. They couldn't get very far because of the rock fall that caused the explosion. It was very hazardous so they came out and reported what they found.

My team was asked to go in by a separate route. We took along a couple of local guys that worked in the mine as guides. We got in around a back way to where these two fellows were. We were told to find them and come right out and not to recover them. I asked specifically if they wanted us to bring the bodies out and was told no, just find them and come out, so we did. The other Kimberley team, led by Jack Walsh, went in and recovered the two mechanics' bodies.

I can't say enough about Gordon Edmonds, the way he looked after us when we got to the surface. As we were coming out of the darkness of the mine and you could see daylight at the portal, you could always see Gordie poking his head around the corner to see us coming out and if we were okay. He was a terrific guy to have on the team outside.

Another bad experience was at the Sunshine Mine in Kellogg, Idaho, where they had a bad fire. We spent ten shifts working on that one. There was ninety-one people killed in that one, only two survivors.

It was extremely hot working. There were two mines that joined. We would go in one mine and go down a man-way about fifty feet and then we would be in the other. For lunch, they would give us some sandwiches and stuff in a paper bag that we could carry in with us. By the time we got to where the gas and smoke was, the paper bags would be dissolved and falling apart because of the humidity that was around eighty per cent. We got in by the hoist room and built some seals and dealt with whatever came up.

The cause of this fire was spontaneous combustion. What they were doing was throwing all their old timber and material into the old stopes. So over the years there was quite a collection built up and this is probably where it started. You couldn't get away with this in Canada. Our laws are a lot stiffer than the States. In Canada, all old timber and wood has to be brought outside.

Our job was in recovery — bringing out bodies — which wasn't very nice, especially since they had been in there ten days in all that heat. It wasn't very pleasant. Putting them in the body bags was really miserable. I'm glad I'll never have to do something like that again. The thing that bothered me the most was that when we came up on the shaft station on the skip, there would be all these families and friends staring at you, looking for some good news as you went by them. Of course, there was none.

About two months after the fire, a committee came up from the States and interviewed Jack Glennie, Jack Walsh and I, and asked for recommendations. Jack Walsh later took a job down there as mine-rescue instructor. He held this position until he retired.

Those were two of the worst things that happened to me in mining. Probably the very worst is recovering somebody you knew, which I have done. The other was hard enough, but it's harder on you when you know the person. All in all, I enjoyed mine rescue, the companionship and that. Same thing as mining, the bullshit that goes on, the laughter. It really grows on you and you do miss it when it's over.

Billy Masich was a short little fart. He was cross shifting us at the time. Each heading, the miners got two sets of slickers. Hell, you would come in, put your slickers on and start drilling away. All of a sudden, you would feel water going down into your boots and you would look down and the legs would be cut off about knee high. What Billy had done was cut the legs off the slickers to fit him. He was happy.

Another time, I was working in the conveyor system and Billy and his partner were working in a timber yard right there. I was trying to get this block out of an eyebolt but couldn't reach it. So I went over and asked Billy if he would give me a hand. He said, "Sure, what do you want me to do?" I said, "Reach out and get me that block." He said, "Sure." So there he is, out there trying to get this block and says, "Christ, I can't reach the bloody thing." I'm a good six inches taller than Bill was and I said, "Neither can I." Well, you should have seen his face. He didn't know whether to throw something at me or laugh. He laughed.

Over the years, I noticed the attitudes in the men changed, and I'm not talking about the last few years. It seemed years ago the miners took a lot more pride and more care in their mining practices. I could see it deteriorating bit by bit. At one time, when you were mining, you never went to the doghouse when you were on contract. You could see the guys starting to go to the doghouse and taking more than the twenty minutes you were supposed to have. They just started staying longer and longer. Not all of them, but some, and these were the guys that weren't blasting at the end of the shift.

Most of the time when you were on contract, you would slip behind the hoist and have a sandwich and a half a cup of coffee and you were back to work. These were the guys that made the money. Hell, you never ate until you were drilled off, torn down and the round loaded. I can remember lots of times I never ate my lunch until I was on the coaches going outside. The doghouse miners were the guys out on the platform telling their cross shift that they couldn't make it, but it's drilled off and all you gotta do is tear down and load the round. And then on payday, they would bitch about the low contract they got. Just didn't get it.

I remember this one time there was Howard Raynor, Frank Goodwin and old Bill Muir. They were trying to figure out why all this backfill was coming out of this ore chute. The chute was empty at the time. This was down on the 3600 Level and they were dumping backfill from the surface.

Well, anyhow, I guess there was a bulkhead missing and the backfill would flow over to this other side. So they were standing around the chute when, all of a sudden, they could hear this big whoosh! and muck was coming down towards them. Well, they took off running. They thought the whole place was coming down. Frank was in the lead, and where the ditch crosses from one side of the track to the other, there is usually a plank, but I guess it had floated off. Frank stepped into the cross ditch and did a spread-eagle right into the loonshit between the track.

Old Bill stopped to pick Frank up and said, "What's the matter, Frank, think you can swim faster than you can run?" and they kept on running with Old Bill dragging Frank along behind him. This was when Frank was just a new engineer. He later became mine superintendent and then general manager of Cominco Kimberley Operations. Young engineers were always a great source of entertainment.

Mac McKenzie and I were walking along 3200 Level one time and we could see this light coming toward us. It was Jimmy Paterson and he was just a' gumbootin' it. He gets to us and I said, "Where the hell you going in such a hurry?" He said, "Get outta the way. I got the shits and I gotta get to that can fast." When he got alongside of us, Mac grabbed one arm and I grabbed the other and pinned him against the wall. He was hollering, "Let me go. Let me go." He couldn't fight or he would have shit himself. We let him go, anyway. It was just good fun.

Seahorse Johnson was notorious for bumming a pinch of snuff off the guys, and he didn't take just a little. He would dig two fingers into the can and pull out a great big wad. He was nailing Mike Petrosky every day, so this one day Mike figured he'd beat Seahorse to it and asked him for a chew. Old Seahorse said, "Sure" and passed the can to Mike and Mike dug in and popped a big wad in his mouth, and I'm laughing away at him. So the next day Mike and I were sitting in the doghouse having pie before we went to work and in comes

Seahorse and I started laughing. Mike says, "What the hell are you laughing at now?" I said, "Just watch."

Seahorse sat down and opened up his bucket, put his finger in his mouth and fished out this big wad of snoose and put it in his snoose can and put it back in his pocket. Mike never asked him for a chew again.

I've always said that I like working with wood and that if I wasn't going to be a carpenter, I would definitely be a miner. If I had to do it all over again, I would be a miner. I worked with a lot of good men and had a lot of fun and I had a big family and made good money here and raised them all, so it worked out excellent.

CARL HELLAND

A calm and quiet man...

Carl was another miner who could, and did, do it all. Tall and slender, he never got too excited. He had a calm about him that belied his productivity. I worked in the hot muck with him and he taught me a lot. He was very experienced in mine rescue and was a good man to have around during a bad time.

I was working with Mutt Ennis. We were working up over a turn-back in ore. I didn't like this slab that was right above the turn-back. I put a bar to it. There was a fair size crack in it and I couldn't budge it. So Mutt and I crowded ourselves tight into the far corner of the raise. We weren't too far up, maybe fifty or sixty feet. It was seven feet by ten in size. So we put two bars on it to try to get it to come. No way would it move.

The foreman came up with the shift boss to see how we were making out. We BSed for awhile. I told the foreman that I had a funny feeling about this slab and that if we couldn't pull it, I was going to blast it. He said to do whatever had to be done. He and the shifter left. They climbed down the turn-back on the rope and out the drawhole, right under it. The only place that this slab could go is right where these two guys went. So I looked at it again and I noticed that there was a little rock wedged under it at the far side.

I got Mutt to hang on to my belt while I reached out with my bar. I just tapped that little rock and that bloody slab took off. There was tons of it. It took my bar right out of my hands. It had to be four feet thick and seven feet long. Just minutes before there were four of us standing just below it, wondering what to do with it. I just had that funny feeling that this was bad. I've had those feelings before and it's kept me out of trouble. You have to go on your instincts.

In the mid-sixties, when there was that mine explosion in the Balmer Mine in the Crowsnest, there were two Kimberley mine-rescue teams that went down to help out and I went down as a spare. I went in with one of the Fernie teams. I made one trip into the mine. We were supposed to explore this one area where they thought some of the bodies were. On the way in, we ran into this other team and got waylaid. We had to go put in a seal that this other team was supposed to do.

Gordie Edmonds took one squeeze with the tester for CO and the tube was blacker than hell, right off the chart. Edmonds said all you need is one sniff of that and you're dead. We were using those old McKay breathing apparatus. They weighed about twenty pounds. There was no face mask. There was only a mouthpiece that you bit on, a nose clip, and those little eye goggles with water in them to stop them from steaming up. After what Gordie said, I'll tell you, I bit down on those two little tits on that mouthpiece until my teeth hurt. There was no way I was going to sneak a breath. The visibility was great but that's what could fool you.

We went in to build this seal for ventilation. What we were using for the seal was this plastic type of canvas. The drift was sloped. It was ten feet high on one side, down to six feet on the other side. Being hard rock miners, we didn't know anything about coal mines.

On the high side, we put up six by six posts and the [mine rescue] captain motioned to me to pick up the post. I thought, "How the hell am I supposed to pick up this post by myself." But that timber was lighter than hell. It must have been balsam because I had no problem putting it up. We nailed the seal to the posts and then stretched it over to the walls. I was looking for some little pieces of wood to run from the posts to the wall so we could nail the seal on. The captain came over with his copper hammer and hammers the nails right into the coal. I never saw that before and I've never forgotten it.

I didn't realize that once we put up the seal, we were in fresh air. The captain didn't say anything. He wasn't going to take a chance. We were in there for quite awhile. We worked the machines until we got to a fresh-air station. Gordie Edmonds was getting pretty worried because we were fifteen minutes late.

The mine rescue there was a hell of a lot different than what we did in mine-rescue competitions. Everything there was coordinated from outside. You were told exactly what you were to accomplish in a certain time period and out you come. Everything was on schedule. The McKays were good for about two hours. You would have to watch the gauge for oxygen on it.

One of the Kimberley teams went to get the last two bodies out. I guess these were two repairmen that were working overtime on a continuous miner machine. When we went in, we had to go around a big cave-in.

Most of the damage was done outside. The blast took a building right off this flat area and right into the creek just below it. The miners were going on shift when it hit them. There were thirteen guys walking in at the time. They walked in on the exhaust side. I guess on the intake side, there was a hell of a big fan pushing air on them. They would go in on the exhaust side where it was warmer. They were beat up pretty bad. The two repairmen were intact but dead. I guess the CO got them.

All I remember is how scared I was, along with everybody else.

ALEC "HUNGRY" HUGHES

The most frenetic of men...

There were times I wished I could have given Prozac to Hungry. He just never slowed down. It was enough to drive you nuts. Even when there was nothing to do, he would find something for us to do. He's skinny as a rail, just muscle and sinew, but has a powerful character. His nickname, "Hungry," describes his voracious appetite.

He is a great person, willing to help out anyone, anytime, and one of the best partners I had. I went with Alec when I lost my partner, Mike. Ol' Hungry kept an eye on me and taught me a lot, especially a good work ethic.

I n 1952 I got hired on as a summer student driving a Euclid up in the open pit, hauling backfill. I did this for two summers then I also got a few days' work around Christmas, handing out turkeys from a boxcar to the guys.

Ken Campbell came out to our farm and asked me if I could come to work just temporary, working on the track gang outside up at the mine. I did this for about six months. Them days, you had to put in ninety days before you got hired on steady so you would almost have your ninety days and, usually, they would lay you off with a couple of days to go. Then in about two weeks, they would call you up and you would start all over again. Finally, I got my ninety days in and went to the fertilizer plant loading boxcars with bags of fertilizer.

After awhile I was sent back to the mine and worked outside as a core drill helper. I was working out in Meadowbrook surface drilling with Albert Kahl and Arnold Hedquist. I did this for a couple of summers and then

Miner and diamond drill long-hole drilling in a large block of ore to be blasted.

I was broke in as a core driller. As the driller, I made fifty cents an hour more than the helper, which was all right considering the hourly rate was about two dollars. When the fall came, I was sent underground on the track gang. You worked your way up from the track gang to the pipe gang and then I went on the TNT drill, then the percussion drill.

The mine went on day's pay so I got a chance to go mining. I went with Dick Alessio, Bill McGregor and Dory Arnfinnson after about two weeks of mining school. Once the day's pay issue was over, I was sent back to the pipe gang because I had no seniority and had to work my way back up through the drills and stuff until I had enough seniority to go back on mining.

I had some close calls mining. This one time, I washed down the face and missed this one hole that had NCN and a fuse in it. The bit on my steel just took that live cap and twisted like a screw and it never went off. I told John Ekskog about it. He said that I was very lucky to be here telling him about it. That's after he tore a strip off me.

In 1975 I was working with Tommy Huppie. We were working as barmen at the time and a special job came up where we had to go up to the collar at No. 1 Shaft and drill a hole through a cement foundation for a new electric cable to go through. We were using a stoper to drill. Where they wanted us to drill, the hole was marked up, so I started to collar the hole using a two and a half-inch bit. I got the hole collared. I stopped for a sec and then turned the stoper on full. All of a sudden, there was a big flash. I was knocked backwards on to my ass. Tommy's face was singed and my eyebrows were gone.

We had drilled right into the centre of a 6,000-volt cable. I guess, over the years, they had never kept up the changes on the blueprint. Nobody was aware of it being right there. The only thing that saved me from being fried was that I was wearing rubber gloves and boots and was holding the rubber hose on the drill.

I would say it was less than two minutes until we had the whole world there. We had shut down all the power in the mine, hoist, fans, everything. The brand-new bit that I was using was just a blob of melted metal. This happened around lunchtime so everybody had to walk, no skips, no motors, nothing was running. John Ekskog sent Tommy and I to the hospital to get checked out. Everything checked out fine and we came back to work, whereupon John Ekskog told us to go home and take the rest of the day off.

Another close one was when I was working with Gordie Olsen. We were driving a raise. The main raise went up about a hundred feet at forty degrees, and at the top we had two finger raises. We each had one, which went another hundred feet. All we had in the raise to climb on were ropes and footwall steel.

We had just come back from lunch and had climbed back up the raise and I said to Gordie that I felt sick to my stomach. He said we'd better take five. We were standing on a plank that was on two footwall steel, holding on to a rope. I must have passed out 'cause the next thing I knew, Gordie was telling me to wake up. I was hanging upside down and, you know, the only thing that saved me was the strap on my bib overalls. All that stopped me from falling a hundred and seventy feet was the threaded end on the footwall steel catching my strap. That's one of my close calls.

January 3rd of 1986, I reported to go on shift and the shifter told me that I wasn't going on the slusher today because there was a special job to be done. I was told they needed a barman with experience to do this special job in the 3350 timber yard. They sent a guy with me that had no barring experience. Mike something. I guess he was there for safety. I didn't know that somebody else refused to go into that place.

It was real blocky ground and mechanized was mining just above it, so you can imagine what the ground was like. I checked it out, the whole area, and about 10:30 I came across this rock and it wouldn't drop by prying on it one way with my scaling bar. Just then two electricians came down out of a man-way. It was Guy Ambrosio and Rob Crooks. I told them, "Hold it a minute. I know it's almost lunchtime, but take five until I get this rock down." They said, "Okay, Hungry, give it shit." I went around to the other side and gave it a tap and then another and down she came. I must have seen it coming 'cause I turned, and that's when it got me. The rock was about two and a half tons, they tell me.

I woke up in the Cranbrook hospital. I'm lucky it never hit me higher up. The guys had to use a cable hooked up to a loci to lift it off my legs and feet. The heel on my left foot was smashed. I drifted in and out of consciousness as they took me out on a man-carrier or an ambulance. I can't remember. I do remember John Lyon, the first aider, telling me to keep awake. I tried my best. They got me to first aid outside first, then to the Kimberley hospital where Dr. Johnston gave me a shot, and then I was sent to Cranbrook hospital. They had to give me eleven pints of blood. I spent nine days in the Cranbrook hospital, where they put casts on my legs and pinned the worst one.

One ankle was going bad so they sent me to Calgary by air ambulance. They tried to save my ankle and heel by putting a flap on it. This is where they take skin and muscle from your back, and after a 16-hour operation that didn't take, they were going to do it again. That's when I called in another doctor. He said it wouldn't be worth it and that it would cause me trouble forever. He suggested that the best thing to do was to remove the leg below the knee. I told them to go ahead and do what they had to do. It was one of the hardest things I ever had to do, sign that paper to authorize them to take her off. My pelvis was broken in four places also.

After months of therapy, I came back to work with my new leg. I told the superintendent that I was ready to go back slushing underground but he said, "No, Hungry, we'll find a better job for you." They put me in the lamp room. It was all right, I guess. Lots of guys to bullshit with. I was there about five months.

The Compensation Board sent me down to Vancouver for assessment. The doctor there asked me how I was. I said I was fine, and that was it. Expo '86 was on at that time, so I phoned the wife to come on down. She did and we had a great time. This is all in the same year. Hell of a year.

I worked another four years then retired. The one thing I miss is the bullshit with the guys. Now I build birdhouses, hundreds of them, for the Mountain bluebird. I help out at the special care home, cross-country ski, and look for people to bullshit with.

BOB MacSPORRAN

Always hits the floor running...

When it comes to highballing in the mining game, Bobby MacSporran pretty well epitomized the meaning. Small in stature but big in heart, Bob was one of the best contractors in the mine. He could sniff out every dollar to be made. He loved every bit of mining, especially the jackleg and stoper part of the work. He was involved in a lot of mine-rescue work where life or death issues were very present. He was one of the top mine-rescue people in the province and he worked his teams very hard so they would be ready when needed.

I started in June 1954 as a mail boy at $125 a month, big bloody money, and I bought a car with my first pay cheque. I was a mail boy until 1955 when I turned eighteen. I then went in the warehouse for about six months and then to the open pit, where I drove Euclid trucks and helped on the air drills that were drilling down holes thirty feet deep.

I gotta tell you this one. Remember Rusty Glenn? Well, he was never very strong, skinny as a rake, but a real good guy. Well, here's old Rusty loading one of these 30-foot holes with powder, and he had a 30-foot pole to tamp the powder down the hole, when a gust of wind came up and blew Rusty off his feet. Instead of letting go of the pole, Rusty hung on.

Well, Jesus Christ, he looked like a flag on a pole. His legs were straight out and he was flopping around. There was a bunch of us watching this, totally fascinated by this spectacle. None of us wanted to laugh because Rusty always took everything to heart. When the wind quit, Rusty fell to the ground. So being a practical bunch of guys, we went over and helped Rusty up and filled his big coat pockets up with big rocks. And, you know, old Rusty thought this was the practical thing to do, but we did keep an eye on Rusty when the wind came up.

Ol' Percy Bloomer was a stern old guy. When I first started, I was a mail boy and, I'll tell you, I liked him. He was very down to earth. I used to have to go into his office to deliver his mail. He was the mine superintendent then. He would always ask how I was doing and tell me whatever I did, I should get back to school. So I tried it and went back to school for one fall but my heart wasn't in it. I wanted to get into the mine and start making some money. I'm not sorry about quitting school. It just wasn't the place for me.

I went underground after my time in the open pit. I was put on the TNT drill for awhile then there was a call for more miners so I went in and seen Howard Raynor, my foreman, and told him that I would like a chance to go mining. He told me that I was pretty little but I persisted and asked him to give me a chance and if I couldn't cut it, fine, but just give me a chance. So he put me on.

My first partner was Stinie Vander Maaten. We were in a raise down on 3050 where we used those big old RB stopers with an 18-inch change. After about three days on these heavy bastards, I was ready to go see Howard and tell him to get me off mining and put me on the skip as a skiptender. I toughed it out and then we got the little JR 38 stopers that made it a hell of a lot easier.

I mined pretty steady until I got married, then there was a big slowdown. A bunch of guys got laid off and I was bumped back to being a skiptender, then on the track gang. It seemed like forever before I got mining again. I guess it wasn't that long but to me it seemed like forever. For two or three years, I had to do all these other jobs. I was on the spare-board for a long time, no seniority.

I got mining again in 1965. I only worked in one section, the lower section, No. 1 and No. 2 Shafts combined, except for a brief time in the South Section. I worked mining in the Shaft until 1975 so I knew the Shaft as well as anybody. In 1968 I tried being a boss on the crushing and conveying section of the mine but I wasn't cut out for that. Hell, I was too young for that bullshit. I went in and told them to get me the hell off the belts so I went back mining.

John Ekskog was a foreman I really liked working for. When I was a young guy just starting to mine, he always made sure that I was with an experienced miner. He had me teamed up with Phil Olsen, who was a fantastic miner, and Bob Cameron, who I think was probably the best miner ever to work in the Sullivan.

When they did put me shifting, I hadn't done any spare shifting at all. One morning, Ekskog grabbed me coming on shift and said, "You're not going mining anymore." And I asked, "How come?" He said, "You're going on staff and you've been on staff for a week." I said, "You're not going to beat me out of the money I've been making all week, are you?" He told me I would get paid what I made mining but from now on, I wouldn't be making the big money. "Them days are over. You're on staff now."

I liked John Ekskog, except when he was cranky. Jesus, he could be a son of a bitch at times. One time, John came in to where we were working, driving a sub and drawholes. I forget who our cross shift was but, anyhow, we were drilling and installing 6-foot rebars, putting in nine holes and grouting them in each row, right around the sub, about four feet between rows. This was for ground support. Hell, we were getting a dollar a bolt. I couldn't believe we got paid for doing this.

Well, John came in with the superintendent at the time, Richardson was the guy's name, and he used to ride John quite a bit. I guess there was a personality conflict of some sort going on between them. Well, John reached up and grabbed a rebar and it came out in his hand and it was only about eighteen inches long. He started climbing my frame, yelling and carrying on. Christ, I couldn't even talk. Finally, he cooled down and I said to him, "I would never install a short rebar 'cause this is such an easy job that I'm quite happy with what I got. Just take that one off the contract." He said, "I want to find out who did it." I said, "Well, it wasn't me or my partner, that's for sure." I don't know if the cross shift owned up to it or not. I really couldn't see somebody cutting a piece off, just the bother of it all. Could have been a piece they found somewhere and shoved in the hole. It would have fallen out on its own or with the first blast. It was just a joke.

I really enjoyed mining, especially drifting. Tommy Huppie and I worked together, drifting down on the 3200 Level on steady day shift for quite awhile. I worked with Tom's brother, Pete, drifting on 3650 and on 3350 Levels. Bob Cameron was my first partner when I went drifting in 1958 when we had those old bar and arm drill set-ups. I should have been killed, I was so stupid. Old Bob, he looked after me pretty good. I worked with a lot of good guys, especially one of the greats, that was Jack Glennie.

Jack Glennie came to work with me this one time when he didn't want to work on development anymore. He was getting on in age and had enough highballing. He was a spare shifter and should have been a full-time shifter, if there ever was one. Well, anyhow, my partner never came out this day and we were driving a drift down on 3650 Level so the foreman, Big John Ekskog, told Jack to go up with me. Jack says to John, "I don't want to go with that little asshole. He don't stop for lunch." I said, "You can stop for lunch. It won't bother me." Jack said, "I'll go with you, but I'll hate your guts."

Jack and I had worked together about six or eight weeks when my wife got a new set of false teeth. Jack saw the wife downtown one day and came up to her and said, "Vonda, smile." So Vonda smiled. He said, "I guess it was worth it. I didn't think that little asshole would buy you your teeth, but it was worth it. You got a real nice smile."

Jack was one hell of a good guy. When he got sick, just before he passed away, I went down to see him at his house. His wife, Hilda, said that he was sleeping and could I come back. He was really sick at that time. I said I would come back tomorrow. I came back the next day. He told Hilda to wake him up when I came so she woke him up and George Cassavant, another miner, came over and we sat around and reminisced about the old days, had a hell of a good laugh, and that was the last time I saw him alive. He was a good man. I thought the world of him. Everybody did. It was guys like him that put a smile on people's faces. It's hard to replace someone like that.

My dad, Jack, came to Kimberley in 1933. He had been mining at other mines before he came here. He couldn't believe what an easy mine the Sullivan was to work in, compared to other places he'd worked. He couldn't believe that you only worked eight hours. He said he couldn't get over that you went to work at seven and came out at three. "Christ," he said, "You could party all night and still make it to work the next day." And he was quite a party guy.

Dad got ahead quite fast. He was a good miner. He went shifting when he was quite young and then got to be foreman and that's when he went around the bend. The Company pretty much screwed my dad like they did to several other foremen. They would tell him that they would back him up, and he was gullible enough to go in and raise shit with the men. Christ, at one time in the mine, several union guys had a petition going around to fire my dad and Garnet Coulter. Both of them were old-time foremen where being a prick was the norm. That's the way a lot of these supervisors thought was the best way to run the crews.

One day when I was working down in No. 1 Shaft, I came across Ed Pendry getting signatures. When he saw me coming along, he left. I knew what he was doing and I asked some of the guys if they signed it. "Oh, yeah," they said. I told them if my dad gets fired over this, there is something wrong with the system. My dad's best friend at the time was Roy Hummer and he signed it. He told my dad, "Jeeze, Jack, I had to sign it because I gotta work with these guys." I understood what Roy did because he would have got just as bad a time for being an ally of my dad as he would if he was his partner. He had to look after himself. As it was, my daughter ended up marrying the son of the guy that was trying to get her granddad fired. Funny world.

My dad liked to drink with the guys, then he would think he was better than them when he was half cut. Oh, he got the shit beat out of him a few times by going down to the bar and telling the guys they were assholes 'cause they couldn't do this or couldn't do that. When he was younger, he could hold his own with his fists but as he got older, he took a lot of beatings with booze talk. That was never my way. I just liked to laugh and have a good time.

He got sick about the same time in life as I did. We both came down with real severe arthritis. The Company sent him down to the fertilizer plant. I guess they thought it would be easier on him to get around. He really never accepted his new role. As far as he was concerned, the mine was the only place he belonged. Mentally, it really affected him. But by then, he could hardly function.

The sick leave was so different then, when he finally went on it. When he finally got Canada pension, he owed Cominco $6,000. My mother had a real rough time the last few years of her life. I don't know how she did it. She used to have family meals all the time. My wife and I tried to help her all we could but she had it really tough. She was one heck of a woman with all that she put up with.

My dad worked in the stopes when he first come here. The big liners were just going out and they were switching to the new stoper drills and they were big heavy bastards. They used to call him "Burn-cut Jack." That was his nickname. I guess he was one of the first guys to use a burn-cut, rather than the V-cut, in the stopes. When they went to the smaller faces, the smaller burn-cut made more sense. He and this guy, Dave Wells, were the first guys to start this.

I don't know if this Dave was smart or not, but when the war broke out and the government seized all the Japanese fishing boats down at the coast, he hit the big time. He went down and bought some of the boats and made a killing. He eventually retired in Nevada with a pocket full of money. It was an awful way to make money. Not something you want to talk about, but somebody was going to do it and I guess he thought it might as well be him. It's not something I would do because the Japanese fishermen earned it by working hard. No, I wouldn't have been proud to do something like that, but I guess he hated working in the mine. I couldn't have done that and, besides, I hate the smell of fish. I would rather smell blasting fumes than fish. I hate fish and boats. I get seasick too.

My dad worked with Mac McPherson cutting bulldoze sticks, sprags, stulls and ties for the track underground. They worked after shift and on weekends. This work was all done with crosscut saws and axes. They worked darn hard at this, just trying to make extra money. They got ten cents for bulldoze sticks, a dollar ten for sprags, three dollars for stulls, and two bucks for ties. All these would be sixteen to eighteen feet long.

The bulldoze sticks were nothing but saplings. The sprags would be from four inches to eight inches around, the stulls twelve to eighteen inches. Old Mac was something with a broad axe. I guess he would fall a 60-foot tree, square up all the sides with a broad axe, and then cut the ties up into 4-foot or 7-foot lengths, depending what was called for, and they would all be a perfect six inch by six inch. All this timber was hauled out by horses until he got a truck and a tractor. But this is what they did in the early days to make ends meet.

Mac supplied Cominco for years until he just got too old. He had his kid, Dougie, working with him for quite awhile. Dougie was quite a businessman at an early age. He was getting ten cents for bulldoze sticks so he would hire other kids to cut for him and he would pay them three cents. He had a car before any other kid in town. He knew what he was doing.

When mechanized mining started, it was all day's pay and it just didn't work, no matter what the engineers said. And there was no way that they would listen. George Crowe was the foreman, Harvey MacDonald and Swede Dellert were the trainers, and three of us were shifters. We all went over to Brilliant to the dam there to see how mechanized mining went, and the Sullivan was going to revolutionize mining.

Well, when we came back, we had this big meeting and what the engineers came up with — Christ, I heard it a hundred times before — is that no matter what you do, you get the top wage grade once you've been trained on all the jobs and equipment. So you can see what the Company was up to: get rid of the contract system. Hell, you would have thought they would know better after all these years, but here you have it again. The engineers couldn't stand to have a working stiff make as much, or in most cases, more than they did and this attitude screwed up mechanized until they smartened up. For educated people, some of these guys were pretty dumb.

I told them right from the start, you've got to pay the guy by the foot. The way they had it, even

A two-boom electric jumbo. Just plug it in and start drilling.

MINER OPERATES
A TWO BOOM JUMBO
TO DRILL HOLES
FOR EXPLOSIVES

if the guy was a janitor and had been trained, he would be making the same as the guy busting his ass, breathing diesel fumes, getting wet, and in harm's way for the whole shift.

Ed Kraft was the superintendent and he told us we were going to get electric jumbos and scoops and all this new mining technology. I was in seventh heaven when we came back from the Brilliant dam. I think it took us about three years before we got a new pump for pumping water, and we used to get all this shit equipment from the Pinchi Lake Mine, like the old air jumbo that would only drill lifters on one side of the face. Nothing but crap.

Scoop loading truck in a stope.

I remember one Friday night when we were on graveyard shift and I had a crew of about four guys. We were mucking with this old scoop that we had. It was the only one we had. Well, the goddamn thing stalled and none of us could get it started. We tried everything. There was no mechanic on our shift, just us guys who knew nothing about diesel engines or hydraulics and all that stuff. Hell, we were all green when it came to this new type of mining. So I phoned the head mechanic, Bill Harris, at home. He told me to do this, do that. I did all this stuff but still nothing.

On my last phone call, Bill said, "There's nothing I can do for you from here." I said, "That's fine, Bill. You stay at home and go back to bed." He said, "What are you going to do?" I said, "I'm going home and I'm sending the crew home too." "Oh," he said, "You can't do that. They'll fire you." "That's a chance I'm going to have to take," I said. So I went to the boys and told them I was sending them home and that they were guaranteed forty hours a week pay and that's what I did.

Haulage truck operator moves ore to an ore pass from an active mining site.

On Saturday morning at eight o'clock, the foreman, George Crowe, shows up at the mine and says to me, "Jesus, Bob. What did you do?" I said, "How can miners that don't know a bloody thing about fuel injection,

HAULAGE TRUCK OPERATOR MOVES ORE TO ORE PASS FROM ACTIVE MINING SITE

Atlas Copco electric jumbo drill. Just plug it in and you're ready to go. Note the reel for electrical cable on the back.

hydraulics or anything like that, be expected to keep all this junk running? For Christ sake, we've been asking for months to have a mechanic. Even if we had one on afternoon shift, it would help us."

I was getting pretty worked up by now. George says, "How am I going to tell them that?" I told him just to tell them what I had said. I showed up on Monday for day shift. I left my bucket in the dry and went into the offices in my street clothes. Kraft was in the hallway and said, "Aren't you going to work today?" I said, "First of all, do I still got a job?" He said, "Yes, you do and not only that, you got a mechanic."

So I guess it paid off, getting mad. I don't think I was irrational. I would try, and always have tried, to make a job go. I'm not the type of guy to just go sit in the doghouse when things go bad 'cause that would just make me madder. Crowe said he was surprised at how well they took my reaction and it was probably because I had never done anything like that before.

My thoughts on going mechanized were somewhat mixed. I was shifting down in the Shaft on conventional mining and I really enjoyed what I was doing at the time. I really didn't have much choice about going over to the mechanized part of mining. My foreman, John Ekskog, came to me and told me they picked the guys they thought could handle it the best to get it going. I really liked it until we just couldn't get any equipment or supplies. Just before mechanized went on contract, Christ, you couldn't ask the guys to work any harder because there just wasn't any incentive to bust your ass. But I would have liked to stay to be a mechanized miner because that is the way to mine. It's such an easy way to mine. Christ, I used to jump on a scoop when the guys went to lunch and run the scoop, mucking for them. It was fun.

I remember one time I was driving a track drift with Keith McBain and we had one round to go, and about thirty feet from the face, the whole back came down. At the time, Keith and I were at the dump with the train. When we came back, we could see what had happened. If it had been one little rock, it would have been nothing, just bar and check the area, but this was pretty big. I would have to say it was one and a half feet deep, thirty feet long and nine feet wide. If this had landed on you, it would have pretty much screwed up a guy's weekend. But it was just luck that we weren't there. That would have been it for us.

I was in on that big drift we drove in the South End. When we got to the end of the drift, the Company had an outside contractor come in and sink a shaft from the surface. When they had finished, they didn't leave a pump in so, for two weeks, water ran down the raise and built up because they hadn't broke through from the bottom yet. We had about forty feet to go. We set up a percussion drill on the muck pile. Christ, when we broke through into the shaft, the water pressure almost washed the muck pile away with our drill set-up. The goddamn water ran for about three days and we had to work there, drilling, to square up the raise. Jesus Christ, we were soaked all bloody day long. I don't know why they just didn't let it drain out and make it a little nicer for us guys, but, oh no, another big rush job. You know how they are. It's easy to make these great decisions when you're in a nice dry office.

The four-man crew I was with was Johnny Barr, Pete Huppie, Dickie Clarricoates and myself. Dickie didn't like mucking with the mucking machine. That was fine with me 'cause I liked mucking. Johnny, he liked to drill, so Dickie worked with Johnny on the drilling part. Pete and I would drill together every once in awhile.

One time we went up to the face and there was only one machine. I had a big grin on my face. He said, "What the hell you grinning at?" I said, "Look at that. Only one machine and two of us." He told me to go ahead and drill and he would spell me off. I got five back-holes in and Pete indicated that he would spell me off now. I said to him, "What the hell's the matter with you? Aren't I drilling fast enough?" He said, "It's not that. I'm freezing my ass off watching you." So we traded off and on, and between the two of us we got the round drilled off.

When we finally got the raise drilled off, we had to load it with forcite powder. We used safety fuse or tape fuse, along with I-cord, to tie it in. When we went to light the round, some of the fuses kept going out because of the water pouring down. We stood there trying to re-light the ones that had gone out while others were burning. Finally I said, "Come on, boys. We've got to get out of here." Pete said, "Hold on. Maybe I can get these others going." I said, "No. Get down here and get on the motor. We've got to get out of here before she goes. I'd sooner come back later and get them. We're cutting a fine edge right now."

We all got on the motor and took off like a bat out of hell. We got maybe six hundred feet down the drift when she went. The whole area lit up around us. We could see the shots going off and really feel the concussion. Maybe another few seconds and we could have gotten hurt. Our foreman, George Crowe, had gotten us this 30-foot aluminum ladder to work off and I had packed it about four hundred feet down the drift to a spot where I thought it would be safe from the blast. A rock flew down the drift and took out every rung in that ladder. It was like the cut was aimed right at the ladder. Old Crowe was impressed.

George Crowe came to my partner, Alec Hughes, and I one day and said for us to take this plastic rope with us and try it out in our raise. This was going to be another cost saver. We were up about a hundred and fifty feet at forty-five degrees. After setting up, I tied the rope to a sprag and was going to go down and get some gear. Jesus Christ, I took off down the raise like a son of a bitch, no grip whatsoever with greasy wet gloves. Hell, I was at the bottom before I could blink.

Crowe had come in just as I hit the bottom. He says to me, 'What do you think of the new rope?" I yelled back up the raise to Alec, "Cut that goddamn rope off, Alec. It's the shits." So that was the end of that idea.

I didn't mind going drilling because you could make six or eight dollars over day's pay. Stinie Vander Maaten and I were partners for awhile, long-hole drilling. Our cross shift was Don Barry and Killer Young. We made good money. Our drill was on an individual contract, not a blanket contract where you had some guys giving it shit and a bunch of guys just riding the contract. We used to leave each other in good shape for when our cross shift came on. We'd have drilled holes in the bank for slow days with machine problems or moving bad ground, stuff like that. We did pretty good.

The Company put Stinie shifting and he was told to go and check my holes. He was to make sure that I was drilling what I put down on my drill report. He came in and measured. Hell, if I wasn't two or three feet short on each hole. He said, "Jeeze, I can't believe you would do that," and he went and measured again. I think they were 80- or 90-foot holes. The loading sticks he was using with the threaded ends were supposed to be five feet long but the ones he had brought in with him were five foot, four inches. As he measured with the wrong sized sticks, it looked like I had lied about the length of the holes on my drill report. Boy, was he relieved to discover he had made a mistake. He would have had to tell them if I was cheating. That's what he was sent in to do. When I came out at the end of the shift, he told me that he thought he was going to have to turn me in. I would never have wanted for him to cover for me, but I asked him just jokingly if he would. I would never put him in that situation.

Stinie and I worked together for quite awhile, drilling, mining and shifting over in mechanized. Stinie and I were wingers over there. I think I could have been foreman in mechanized if I hadn't gotten sick with this bloody arthritis. I was striking out pretty bad in 1981. My whole goddamn body changed.

I went to see the doctor to see if there were pills or something that I could take. Within two weeks after seeing the doctor, I was in the hospital with double pneumonia. My mouth was weird; I had to get all new teeth. I thought I was dead. I was to the point where I was shopping for a new husband for my wife. I had never felt that tough in my life. I couldn't get up in the morning. I couldn't get to the bathroom. It was one hell of a hit I got. I was in the hospital for a month.

I really can't blame all of my arthritis on mining. Some of it probably, but most of it is hereditary. In 1992 my knees were bothering me so I went and saw a specialist and he told me that my knees were shot because of heavy lifting due to mining and I had to get them replaced. Then a few years later, the bones in my hips were completely gone so I got a hip replacement. Yeah, I'm pretty much rebuilt now. No guarantees though.

I started in mine rescue in 1961 and stayed with it for thirteen years. In that period of time, I was fortunate enough to have been on two provincial winning teams. On one team I was the captain. I won the East Kootenay championship a couple of times and the local three or four times. I really enjoyed competing.

We had four teams from the Sullivan so we had to compete against them at the local competitions, then the East Kootenay, and if you were good enough, move on to the provincials. When you got to compete against those guys from the Crowsnest, you had to be on your toes. I loved those coal miners. I thought those guys were a cut above everybody else in mine rescue. That was their life. They always had to be on the watch for methane gas. Not like us guys. Our big worry was low oxygen, which wasn't that prevalent. But, to me, they were the real mine-rescue people and the nicest bunch of guys you could meet, so when they beat you, you didn't feel too bad.

I would have kept on playing but it just got too tough on the family. My wife said that it seemed we just never had a summer. If you kept winning, you went right into June, so from April to June it was mine-rescue practice every night and on a lot of weekends. It really tied you up. But all that practice came into good use when it was called for. I quit mine rescue in 1974. They wanted me to coach but I couldn't do that. If I couldn't go with the team, I wouldn't do it. But I really enjoyed the people. You really build a good camaraderie with the guys. These are all people that you could trust with your life.

In 1967, when the Balmer Mine in the Crowsnest Pass had an explosion, I went down to that. Stinie Vander Maaten was the captain. We were designated to go in and find the two mechanics. We were told where they should be, and so into the mine we go. Jack Glennie and Curly Unruh were both on our team and Curly was driving Jack nuts.

Curly kept hitting his shovel on rocks as we were walking along. Ol' Jack figured this would cause a spark and we would all be blown to hell. We found the two mechanics by the continuous miner [coal mining equipment] that

Curly Unruh, team captain, in lead. Mine rescue team emerging from Balmer North after two-hour shift.

The Calgary Herald

Aftermath of disaster at Balmer North, April 1967
(Glenbow Archives NA-2864-4042-18)

they were working on and came right out once we confirmed that they were dead. It wasn't our job to bring them out. Two other teams were sent in to retrieve the bodies. It was a good mile in.

Our last trip in, we had to establish ventilation at this intersection. The air was "blue," well into the explosive range, around ten per cent. We had some coal miners with us. I guess they could tell that we were nervous. We had to hang some brattice up to direct the airflow and since I was the lightest, they hoisted me up on a 45-gallon drum to hang the brattice. "Just nail it into the rock," they told me. Hell, I never nailed into a rock before but you can do it in coal, I found out. Stuff like that showed us how different a hard rock mine and a coal mine really are.

I guess the most difficult part of a rescue operation is when you come out and the family and friends are on the sidehill, crying, watching for some word from you. The eyes killed you. It reminded me of what you see on TV from Kosovo. All the old people, Old Country people, women with bandanas on, old coats and rubber boots. You watch them go down the road with arms about each other, comforting one another. God, it was tough.

The people in Michel have to be about the finest people around, the way they treated us. When Bill Howe and I were called out of the Sullivan to go down to the Balmer, we were on afternoon shift. The rest of the crews were down there and they needed two more guys. So we never even changed into our street clothes. We just drove down in our diggers.

In the morning when we came out of the mine and went to a restaurant for breakfast, I still had my diggers on. I said to the lady, "Just put a wooden chair in the corner and I'll sit over there 'cause I don't want to mess up your floor or table." You know how you can stink. She said, "No, no. You sit here in the booth." She put down some towels for me to sit on and some on the floor for my boots that were covered in muddy coal dust. Them days, I could eat like a son of a gun. We had steak and eggs, the works. We were only there for that one night and were sent home. They paid us $150 for that one shift.

In 1972 I went to the Sunshine Mine disaster [in Kellogg, Idaho]. Ninety-one guys died there. That was a bad one. Brian Buckley picked the teams to go. He didn't pick me because my wife was in the hospital at the time but about four days later, word was sent back to Kimberley that they needed two more guys so Roy West and I were sent down in a rented car.

Jack Walsh and Stinie Vander Maaten were the captains from Kimberley. We had guys from Riondel on our teams also. Bill Steenson went with an American team. They scared the shit out of him. They didn't have the same discipline or training as us. I guess they were pretty haywire. Jack Walsh got hired on after this to train them properly. He stayed in the States for a few years after this.

The Americans were really appreciative, really great with us. We didn't save anybody, but they were just great. There was always a local miner that worked with us as a guide.

The first trip in that I went on, I was with Stinie. I had never ridden on a vertical skip. They go like a bullet and when the skip hit the level where it's supposed to stop for us to get off, the cable had about eight feet of play in it. So there we are, bouncing up and down in the skip until it stops, with all this gear on, our breathing apparatus, stretchers and tools. It was really weird. We would set up our fresh-air station at the shaft and proceed in from there down the drift. There was fresh air at the station and as we proceeded down the drift, we would hit the smoke. This is where we would set up a phone. The carbon monoxide here was lethal. If you took off your mask, you were dead.

The mine foreman told us to go a bit farther because there was another airway coming in. We went along a ways and I told Stinie that we needed to stop. I told him that we were getting beyond our point of limitations. Our machines were good for two hours but this isn't what I was worried about. What I was worried about was that we couldn't see, couldn't see nothing. We were roped together and just feeling our way along, using our feet against the rail tracks. If one guy had tripped, he would have pulled everyone else down with him. So we came back to where we could see but it was still deadly, blue air. We went into a place where the ground was very porous so we filled up the cracks with this foam that we would spray in. This enabled the air to go one way rather than losing it up in those cracks.

None of the miners at Sunshine had self-rescuers on their person. These were all stored in one place, not that they would have helped them. The gas was too strong for those to have been of any use. You could see that they were retreating. Most of them were found in between two ventilation doors. Didn't have a chance in hell. It took days to bring out the bodies. You had to bag them and carry them out. It was a terrible job, but it had to be done.

When your shift was over, you would go to the dry and strip off all your clothes, which were promptly burned. They were covered in body fluids from us handling the dead miners. It was hell, something a guy will never forget. Every day at the start of the shift, we put on new clothes.

When we arrived at the collar after putting in our shift, we would get off the skip. This was probably the hardest part of the shift. We had to walk through the crowd and everybody — family, friends — would be just staring at you, like give me a hint, anything. We had to find a different route. It was just too hard trying to avoid these people's eyes. So we found a different route through a machine shop just off to the side at the collar. It was a real eerie feeling, the quietness, but you could feel the expectation. It was hard on you.

A couple of years later, I went back to the Sunshine, when Jack Walsh was there as a safety instructor, and went on a tour with Merle Brown, who was a shifter there. He worked in the Sullivan a few years before the disaster. I wanted to see where the guys worked. I had never been in a cut and fill stope like they did in that mine. Merle worked with us on the rescue and I got to meet some of the miners that were involved.

It's so hot in the mine that all you wore was a tee-shirt and jeans. I ruined a belt that day. I wore just a pair of jeans and my belt stretched about three inches, just from the heat. When Merle took me up to the surface so he could do his own work, like do his run, Jack Walsh met me on the surface. He asked, "Where do you want to go now?" I said, "If you go by the first bar, I'm getting out." God, I was just dehydrated. I'd like to have met more people but I got a tour so I was happy, especially meeting some of the guys again that worked with us during the fire. They figure the fire was caused by spontaneous combustion from old timber stored in stopes.

Them Yanks had never seen people drink beer like us. At the end of our shift, we used to go to this tavern and we drank a lot of beer because we had never worked in a place that hot. This owner would always set out forty-eight Hamm's beer for us every night and the bartender would give us anything else we wanted. Just super. One particular night after a tough shift handling the bodies, we were all pretty down. The bartender says to me, "A beer, Bob?" "No, I need something better." So he gave me a double rye. It was all on the house. They wouldn't take our money.

When we were finished at Kellogg and got to Coeur d'Alene [Idaho], the Sunshine Mining Company put us up at that fancy hotel on the beach, "Twelve Nine," put us in real nice rooms, fed us steak and lobster, and a night on the town on them. Mac McArthur and Gordie Edmonds signed all the chits for whatever we had. It didn't matter. Anything we wanted at that hotel. We toured the town, not that we were in the mood for partying. We just wanted to have a few drinks and relax, for whatever it was worth, I guess. This disaster was definitely not one of my better memories of mine rescue but it was what we were trained for. It's just too bad that we couldn't have saved someone.

What I really liked about being on a mine-rescue team is when we went and had a beer after practice. You got to be pretty close with each other, got to know each other, about our families and stuff, sort of like being a partner in the mine. When you don't have to talk anymore, you know you're doing pretty good. You learn to trust each other. The camaraderie that you found with guys that worked in the mine is darn hard to beat.

Hell, if I could have mined until I was fifty-five or sixty, I would have but my health wouldn't let me. God, it was fun, like when we were driving that big tunnel up in the South End. We were on three shifts with a four-man crew.

We used to meet in the Globe Hotel every Saturday morning to see who did the most work during the week. It was absolutely pathetic. Christ, we just saw each other the day before but by the time you were on your fourth beer, stories got funnier and funnier. It was fun.

Mine rescue competition. Author is closest, Bruce Dudley and Bill McNeil in back.
Courtesy Bill Roberts

Team finishing mine rescue problem at competition. Hope we won. It's beer time now.
Courtesy Bill Roberts

JOHN CHERNOFF

Solid as a rock...

A stump of a man with a deep Russian voice, John is usually very serious, but his eyes twinkled when he told a good story. He was brought up tough and hard but he had no complaints. He worked with dogged resolve to get the job done. His chief enjoyments were his family, good homemade goof, and storytelling.

I started at the Riondel mine [the Bluebell on Kootenay Lake] in 1956 at eighty-four cents an hour on graveyard shift, working on transportation. In two weeks, Harold Shaw, who was the foreman, made me a lead hand. I felt so foolish that I didn't know the mine and that he had to take me through the mine and show me everything.

Being the lead hand, I had to check the pumps and tram at the same time. Any big rocks on the grizzly, I had to pound through with a big sledgehammer; any chute that was hung up, I had to bring it down. It was hard work.

When the Doukhobors [Sons of Freedom sect] bombed the power line, I was on afternoon shift with Larry Fiddler on Level Eight when the power went out. We were about four hundred feet below the bottom of the lake. Larry and I were putting in bulkheads with oakum in between to keep the water out. We would run out to get a breath of air, grab a four by four, chuck it in and run out again. You could see the gas with your lamp. It was just blue, CO_2, carbon dioxide. It seemed like your eyes were popping out, getting a big head. There was no air. It was near the end of the shift when Larry and I were on the loci and we were coming out to go up to the surface. The lights were green so all the doors were open. They should have been red and the flood doors automatically closed with a power outage, but they weren't.

We knew the pumps were down and we were in trouble. These pumps were pumping around nine million gallons of water out of the mine in a 24-hour period. Donny Muir and his partner had just come out of where they were working. They didn't know about the power outage. They were quite a ways from us so I took the loci down to get them because I knew they wouldn't make it by walking. Gas was building up with no ventilation fans running.

I couldn't make it because I was getting dizzy but this other guy who had joined us got to them and brought them back. There was an escape way for us. There was a borehole five feet in diameter that ran from Eight Level to Five Level. It was about three hundred feet. It had a cable ladder in it. The five of us started climbing for our lives. The gas was right on our tails. We honestly thought we were done for. It was hard climbing up that ladder. It was slippery with the water coming down the borehole; no place to really grab the ladder rungs. If one of us went down, we would all go. We crawled up to Five Level where there was ventilation from the auxiliary power. I really thought we were going to die.

The Company issued these boots to us. I don't know where they came from, but we all got allergic to them. The body's immune system just couldn't take it. You know, scratch and itch. While this was happening, they sent Joe Bower to Vancouver to have people look at him to see what was going on. Dr. Carpenter and myself took some of the boots and some of the slickers and experimented on our arms to see what would happen.

You can see on my feet today, right up to where the top of the boots went. They look terrible, still scarred. You might not believe me but you would take a wire brush and start scratching until it started to bleed, then you could start relaxing. They found out that it was some chemical that they put in the rubber when they made them.

Even now, I can't stand synthetic rubber or aftershave lotion. So at Christmas, when my family gives me aftershave lotion, I have to give it away to my boys.

BILL McCORMICK

Loved his fellow miners...

"Springhill Bill" was his nickname. He was a proud man who never forgot his roots. Like a true Nova Scotian, he loves a good story and a laugh. When I worked with him, he would drive me nuts by volunteering us to do lesser-paying jobs so they would be "done right.""I can't let the young guys do it because they might get hurt," he would say. His respect for the tradition of mining was unequalled.

I like to tell the boys why I left Springhill in the late fifties. I came home one day and there's the wife with my life insurance on the table, red shoes on, shortening her skirt. She had gone down to the post office and heard that I was killed. There was an accident and it was in my working place.

I had a partner whose name was Abe McFarlane. He was a powerful man, but he wasn't a leader. He didn't like to make the call or make decisions. Anyways, the miners used to go down early, and Abe wouldn't go to work until I showed up. I was late this day, so when I got to work, there was Abe sitting by my basket in the dry, waiting for me. So we got down late in a later skip. When we got to the bottom, the boss says to us they had put somebody else in our heading 'cause they didn't figure we were coming out.

It didn't make any difference to us because we were sinking a raise. It was down another skip ride from where we were, down at the bottom of the mine. There was a hell of a bump down there, and word got out that everyone was killed. So Janice is at the post office. There was about three hundred people gathered around, talking about who probably got killed and that I was probably one of them. So Janice went right home. So I tell everyone that when I got home there's Janice sitting at the table with my life insurance policy, a pair of red shoes on, shortening her skirt. She wasn't waiting.

The two guys that took our places that day were killed. Good friends of mine. If I had been on time, it would have been Abe and me. Just luck that I was late that day.

I remember I was working with five other fellows when the back and wall caved. This young guy about eighteen years old, a good friend of mine, got buried, and the guy working beside him got hit on the arm. Well, he just took off. We had an old guy there and he took over. We dug out the guy that was buried. I put my arm around that kid and we got him out, but he dies on the way to the hospital.

I went home in the morning after shift and I got out of bed in the afternoon and my old man told me this guy was coming down, the guy that ran. I told the old man that I don't care if he's coming or not, I'm leaving. I didn't want to be in his presence. The old man asked me what happened and I told him. He said, "Don't ever judge a man until you're in his shoes." Hell, I was just a kid. I was only seventeen when this happened. The old man told me to be polite and just sit here when this guy comes. Maybe I'd learn something.

The guy comes down with a bottle of gin. He and the old man started drinking it. He said to my old man, "George, I did something I never thought I would ever do. I ran. I didn't even know what happened until 9:30 this morning when I was sitting in the hospital on the bed." In other words, this guy just pushed the panic button. He said, "I can't go back in the mine and face the men." He quit that day and moved on.

That was something you never do, run when somebody is hurt. In hindsight, I suppose this is something that he will never get over. I think I was too darn scared to move. Christ, I had some of that rock in my boots, I was that close. Nobody knows how they are going to react, even this oldtimer who had probably seen this stuff many times before. But who's to say?

I'm glad the old man made me stay. It sure gave me a different look. It's a lot like when a guy gets killed underground. After something like that happens, the guys usually laugh and make jokes. It's not because the guy got killed, but because it wasn't them. The tension just flows out of the guys. Hell of a way for relief, but it works.

When I first came to Kimberley in 1961, I was working as a first aid attendant for old Joe Shaw. I was there for old Hardrock. That was comical as hell. The drawholes came down as he was placing a shot. When he never showed at the end of shift, we went looking for him. You know, he was laying there with a broken leg, happier than a pig in shit. You would think nothing had happened. There wasn't a bit of sweat on him or a bit of worry. His legs were buried. He was moving muck off his legs just as calm as could be, cool, not excited as you would expect, just laying there brushing the muck off. He was a fatalist. If he was going to go, that's the way it was. You would never know that man was in an accident.

When I first met Hardrock, it was in the old Globe Hotel. That's where I stayed and he was staying there at the time. It was two bucks a night. I was walking by his room one day and he hollered, "Hey, young fella. Come in the stope." That's what he called his room.

Dingy Bell and Hugo Mackie were in there, just sitting around having a drink, and he told Hugo to give the young fella a drink. Hugo had a case of five-star whiskey. He reached for a bottle, took the top off and threw it away. Old Hardrock grabbed that bottle and filled one of those ten-cent beer glasses right to the brim and passed it to me. Jesus Christ, I was there two hours trying to get that sucker down. There was no mix or water, no nothing. But he was so hoarse from all the drinking he had done he could hardly talk.

The first time I worked with Hardrock, hell, I wasn't a kid. I was used to work, hard work. I was thirty. McQuarrie, the foreman, called his shifter, Bill Cairns, over and told him to put me with Hardrock. I was on the spare-board at the time. Cairns comes to me and said, "You know where that sub is?" and I said, "Yeah, I know where it is." He said, "You go with Hardrock for the day" and away I went.

I walked in to where Hardrock was working. He was only up about three steps off the main level, just down the sub. And I walked in and introduced myself. He said, "Sit down, young fella." And that was the last thing said to me, that was it. I was freezing to death 'cause I wasn't dressed to sit on my ass. I was impatient, nervous to a certain extent 'cause I didn't know the rules or regulations. It was a new mine to me. I looked at the old bastard and I'm thinking what the stinking is going on. I'm getting wilder by the moment.

Finally, at eleven, I went out to the shifters' shack and called Bill Cairns out and asked, "What the hell's going on?" He says, "What's the matter?" I said, "I'm sitting in a corner with this old guy, freezing my ass off, and he doesn't even speak to me. All he does is sleep. I thought I was supposed to be working. What the hell is going on?" "Bill," he says, "that's just old Hardrock. Just stay with him until he gets sober. Don't worry about it. He'll be all right."

You know what? We went into the same place the next day. He sat there. He had a can of Carnation milk. He poked holes in it and drank it. I don't think that man said four words to me. I guess he had just come back off a two-week drunk in Spokane, where he drank and whored until his money ran out. Finally, about one, he got up and we walked back in the sub where there was a raise. He looked at it and that was it for the day.

The third day, I went back with the guy. We sat down for about two hours. I wasn't allowed to do anything once we got going except hand him the powder, and we got this hung-up raise down. There was no way he was going to let me go up there. He figured it was too dangerous. It was okay for him but not for me. He looked after me. That's probably why nobody ever bothered old Rock.

He did the jobs nobody else would. It's like he told me, "Bill, I got no wife or family so it's better if I get it than you."

The day he retired I was day shift, sitting on the coaches waiting to go underground, and here comes Hardrock just a'strutting. I yelled at him, "Where you going, Rock?" He says, "I'm going to see the guv'ner, young fella." That was the day he retired.

The last time I saw Hardrock, just before he died, he moved into the Canadian Hotel. They had some apartments upstairs. He had a deal made with Kavvy, the hotel owner, to do all the nipping around the hotel in order to get cheaper rent or beer or whatever he wanted. He was in his sixties at this time. He had two by fours out the window, two storeys up, and he was standing on them, barring the ice off the roof. He had the two by fours anchored under his bed. Just no bloody fear at all and there's Kavvy down below telling him to get in the room. There's old Hardrock standing out there, barring away, slicker coat and hardhat down over his eyes, just giving it shit. God, what a man. Somebody should have got a picture of that.

Another character was old Billy. He was set in his ways. He had a hat. We used to have a doghouse built up on an old chute over by the South End. Well, old Billy would come in and hang up his belt, hang up his hat, and put his bucket down. He had napkins. He would lay out his napkins. He always had toast and boiled eggs. He always took the boiled egg and clunked it against his forehead and peeled it and ate it.

The boys switched eggs in his bucket and my partner, Bert, and I had heard about this so we thought we best go up and see this 'cause we never went to the doghouse to have our lunch. We always ate after we blasted while the smoke cleared. So we had to see this. Well, old Billy took the first egg right down the side of his face. He didn't say nothin', just looked around. He grabbed the second one. Clunk, same thing. "Goddamn wife," he says. "I'm going to kill her." Then we all started laughing and old Billy caught on. You should'a saw him, egg running down all over his face and laughing like crazy. Good prank, it was.

I remember Barr and I worked together and we had this new engineer, real arrogant bastard. You know the type. Thought he knew it all. Well, he come in this day and told us what way we were supposed to drive this sub. We knew he was wrong but kept quiet. Coulter came into the heading after the engineer had and we told him what the engineer had said. We were Coulter's favourites. Every section had its favourites. South End, North End, Centre, Shaft.

Coulter knew the engineer was wrong but told us to do what he told us. So away we went. We took two rounds that day, scraped out, and had the cut and square up in for the next shift. By the time that engineer came back, we were going twenty-four feet the wrong way and, you know, he couldn't be nice enough to us after that, just takes respect.

You get engineers, new ones, that come underground with weird ideas and they want to change everything. Basically, they don't know, just no experience. The last few years, they basically didn't let you run your crews the way you should have handled your crews. They come in and want to change things the way you done things. You got a lot of guys with twenty years that were doing things right. Why change the system? I guess they had to qualify their jobs but why change what was working?

It was like you and Mike having powder at the face while you were drilling and you got called in over it. They wanted to make a big issue out of it. I managed to let them let me handle it. No big deal, but the point was made. Let the shifter handle his crew.

I still think if you're looking after a crew, you got responsibility, especially with everything involved. You have to do things your way and if they aren't satisfied the way you're doing things, replace you. Don't change the system that's working. That's kind'a dumb. I believe when you do try to change the system, you lose the closeness of the people. I think it's a lot different where you fly in and fly out [of mines], work ten or fourteen shifts; you're not close with those people.

In my case in this town, a lot of the kids I had in minor ball, boxing or bowling, are the guys you ended up working with. The stress, or whatever you want to call it, was different.

Like in my situation as a shifter, I had the son of a guy I had worked with come to work drunk one day. My crew looked after me. I had five phone calls about this kid from guys on my crew. The kid had come in late and I had missed him. I had already gone underground. I went and found him and told him he wasn't going in the raise, where he was working on a two-man remote drill. You could cut a man's hand off. I wouldn't put him in there, just too dangerous. The guy got real despondent and said, "You and my dad were partners and good friends. How can you do this to me?" I told him, "I still want to be a friend of your dad's but I probably wouldn't be if something happened." So I found something like that stressful because things look different to a younger person than an older one.

I never worried about guys drinking underground because it just wasn't done. Sure, some guys come to work smelling like a brewery but not often. I had this one guy named George Hedlund on my crew that was comical as hell. But this guy was hired and he was a drunk long before I became a supervisor. In fact, I was late becoming a supervisor.

I was called in the office one day, and I laugh like hell about it because the guy in charge of electricians was also there, and I was getting balled out about George and had to do something about this guy and his drinking. He wasn't drinking on the job but you could smell it on him. But what I would do is put him, isolate him, where there was no danger. Hell, they put up with him for twenty-five years. What could I do with him?

This electrical boss was there and saying yup, yup, something has to be done. He was agreeing with everything that was being said but he didn't have a clue who we were talking about.

Well, the reason they had called me in was that there was a big job to be done which required my timbermen and an electrician. So the next morning, we met in the doghouse at 3800 to discuss the job, the electrical boss, my timbermen, and the electrician. Every time we said something, the electrician would jump up and go yeah, yeah, yeah, and then sit down. When I got all my men placed, I looked at the electrical boss and said, "You know, you're right. We gotta do something about this goddamn drinking underground." You should'a seen the electrical boss's face. This was a Friday and all us guys that knew George knew he would get drunk on Wednesday, miss Thursday, and come out Friday. Just the way he was. He was still probably the best underground electrician we had. He always found a way to get you going. You never saw so many red faces and dead quiet in your life.

I had a lotta things happen to me after I came out here after that bump at Springhill. A lotta guys come out here looking for work and said they worked at Springhill. That's how they got jobs. I had this guy, Liddell. I come to work this one day and my shifter, Bill Carins, said, "Bill, I got this guy from Springhill and I'm going to put him to work with you." So I said, "What's his name?" He said, "Liddell, and he speaks mostly French." Jesus Christ, I looked at the man, and in the coalfields you knew everybody, and I knew this guy never worked there.

We were driving a raise. The raise was just off the sub. This Liddell says, "What are you doing?" I said, "I'm driving a raise and I guess you're my partner." I asked, "Where in the hell you from in Springhill?" He said, "I was never there. I just said that to get a job."

Well, I said we gotta set up so I went up the raise first. We were only up about twenty feet, put the extensions in and got the stoper over onto the drill platform. I told him to go turn on the air, just hook up the hoses and turn on the air. Jesus Christ, I sat there for twenty minutes, had a smoke. I went down and turned on the friggin' air, went back up and started drilling.

Jim Byrne, who was a Member of Parliament at the time [Kootenay East 1949-58, 1962-68], he was a boss back then, and he come in and shut me off. "Jesus Christ, McCormick, what the hell you doing?" he asks. I said, "What the hell do you mean, what am I doing?" "Well," he said, "that partner of yours says you're crazy and he left." I told him there was nothing wrong with the way I was set up. You see where he come from, he wanted that whole goddamn raise planked right to the top, eh. That was all forgiven.

So the next day, we had to go up another raise. It was over a hundred and fifty feet at fifty-two degrees. We had a breakthrough that had to be barred. So I grabbed some rope and started up the raise, using the footwall steel to climb on, and said, "Come on. Let's go." I turned around and I had no partner. Bill Cairns come in and said, "Bill, you got no partner." I said, "I know that. I've been here myself for about an hour and a half." I guess he went to the shifters' shack and said, "There's no way you're going to get me standing up there like a trapeze artist." And away he went. He quit and never came back.

One of the funniest things that happened to me, I was just astonished, amazed by it. I was working with Johnny McDonald this day. He was on the pipe gang. I was put with him. This was the first time I was on the pipe gang. So we had to go away up to 90 Block, I think it was. I drove it with Alf Jolie. We had to put in pipe for the drillers. We got up there at lunchtime so Johnny had to go to the doghouse to eat his bucket. I had mine with me so I told him I would stay here and have mine, rather than go all the way down. He had to pick up a small part anyways.

So when Johnny left, everything stopped. Everything was quiet but I could hear this talking just over from me. I said, hell, I'll go over and eat with the boys. I get over there and here's Jimmy Hume all by himself and he's going, "You're no goddamn better than that, Jimmy." "I know, goddamn well I do, but that's the way things are." I actually thought there was two people. I just backed off and let him carry on. He didn't need me for company. He had all he could handle.

Ed Peterson was foreman in the open pit and at that time, there was the main drift that went into the North End part of the mine and we were hauling the Pine Point ore in from outside and dumping. They had built this brand-new dump and we were told to start using it. So in comes Johnny Hume and me. I was by the dump, signalling Johnny with my lamp. We had to take it easy because this ore didn't slide out of the car when it hit the dump block. It was caked right in there. So, I'm signalling away. All the welders were still there, watching, when Peterson grabbed my light and said, "I'm the boss here. I'll do the signalling."

Well, you wouldn't believe it. The car went up on the dump block and came down the other side. The muck never came out of the car and that damn car went right over and into the dump. That whole goddamn dump was wiped out. Peterson never said a word, just turned and walked away.

They used to call him "Wrong Way Ed" because he was always lost. Every place he went, he carried yellow chalk and he put an arrow, so we'd go and put the arrow the opposite way. We were working drawholes the first time I met him. Jolie and I were working together. Naturally, when you went in the turn-back you were in another sub, so Ed was up talking to me. He went down the sub, crossed over and went down that sub, and was over talking to the drillers. Then he walked right over to where I was and said, "What the hell are you doing here?" I said, "I'm still at the same place I was when you last saw me. I got the same stoper and I'm drilling on the same face, you silly bugger." He had no idea where he was. I could see why he was called Wrong Way Ed.

Old Lawrence Somner had this young guy put with him mining and McQuarrie came in this one day. This kid couldn't carry a bucket of water he was so dumb. McQuarrie says, "Where's that young fella? I don't know what to do with this guy. I put him with you mining, and he's no good. I put him on transportation, and he's no good. I put him here and there, and he's just no good. I don't know what to do with the guy." Lawrence looked at McQuarrie and said, "Why don't you make him a shift boss? None of them are any good either." Guys up there always had an answer.

We had this Scotsman for a shifter. I forget what the hell his name was. We were on day's pay, Lawrence and me. It was a Wednesday and we only get barman's pay on Friday day shift. Ol' Lawrence says to me, "You know, Bill, we should get barman's pay today." I says, "How the hell we gonna get barman's pay today? Christ, it's only Wednesday." "Yeah, I know," he says, "but we'll get it. Let me work on it."

We had this sub that came into our stope and ol' Lawrence farted around with a bar in the sub for awhile, while I was doing something else. Pretty soon, in comes our shifter with Roy McMichael, the super, and the safety guy. Our shifter says, "Lawrence, it doesn't look like you barred this sub down." Ol' Lawrence says, "Oh hell, it's good enough, it's good enough, Jimmy, it's good enough."

Oh boy, old Jimmy just flew off the handle and he made us both stop what we were doing. "Jesus Christ, Lawrence," he says, "you got a young fellow with you. You're setting a great example." The big lecture went on. Anyway, away they went. Lawrence leaned on his bar and said to me, "You know, Bill, maybe I can't do anything else, but I'm a cagey old barman." What he had done was loosen up a bunch of rock on the walls and the back just before they got there so that they would have to notice all the loose. He was a cagey old bastard. He got us barman's pay for the day.

Big George Kalmakoff, big Doukhobor, one powerful bastard. Ol' Lawrence had a Volkswagen and Lawrence loved this car. It was probably the best thing Hitler did for the world. Well, one day George picked me up to go to work. When we got to the parking lot, there was Lawrence's Volkswagen parked. Ol' Lawrence always parked it so it wasn't close to another car. He didn't want anybody dinging it.

Big George went over to Lawrence's car, reached down, picked it up and turned it sideways so that it couldn't be driven until somebody came and moved their car. Old Lawrence just couldn't figure out what the hell happened. He figured somebody had a set of keys for his car. Big George did this all the time to Lawrence's car. It didn't matter where it was, at the mine parking lot or downtown.

As the war was coming to an end, CM&S started building houses in expectation of the boys returning. The whole area of Lois Creek was stripped of all trees and subdivided. Roads were put in, water and electricity. It looked like a moonscape.

The Company built one hundred and forty-one homes, all at 18- by 22-foot dimensions, very basic. The bottom floor consisted of kitchen, front room and bathroom. Upstairs had one or two bedrooms. One wall of the house was solid. It had no windows or such, in the event the owner chose to build on. The landscaping was up to the owner. He would have to level, haul in dirt for lawn and garden, plant trees and shrubs as he went. There were three designs of homes to choose from. A contractor who hired anybody who could swing a hammer, no experience needed, built the homes. All homes were void of any insulation. The owners usually stuffed the walls with sawdust. The going price for these homes at the time was $4,500. Payments were taken off your pay cheque.

When I bought this house, I paid $8,500 for it. They told me I could have this house for $62 a month that would be taken off my pay. Well, Jesus Christ, when the wife and I came up here, we bought a new stove, new chesterfield, took all the money I had and invested in all new stuff for the house.

I come home from work one day and the ol' lady says to me, "I got a call from McFarlane today, something about the house." Jim McFarlane was in charge of housing rentals and sales for CM&S down at the Company office. I had to come up with a down payment for the previous owner or I would have lost it. Nobody had told me this when I signed for the house.

I had no goddamn credit here so I had to go to Creston, where I had worked, to get the money. All I could get was $750 and I needed $1,000. They let me have the house for $750 down. If not, I would have lost the house. They didn't tell me that. They told me I could rent it for $62 a month at the start. Here I had put all the new furniture and stuff in. The bastards. I could have killed them at the time.

When I came to the mine, there was probably a thousand or more men working here at the time. There was a lot of development going on with miners, drillers, timbermen, riggers and track crews. Every section had its own bunch of people. But you look today, you don't have the working headings that we had then. We would go into a block and develop it. You would drive your man-way. You would drive your exhaust, your muck raise. Sometimes you would be the only crew in there, and drive two subs and two sets of drawholes. And that would be developed before you put your long-hole drillers in there. You would very rarely see a driller in the block until the block was finished being developed.

When we drove V-7 [pillar], it was shaped like a loaf of bread. We drilled off the top and blasted it and left your bench. You went so far ahead, then came back and benched it, where today you could take that all in one round. But you couldn't then. You couldn't go sixteen feet high and fourteen feet wide with stopers. All the top was done with jacklegs and then we would do the bottom. Then we would steel arch the bottom and do all the timbering.

When we started that V-7, we had a five-man crew on three shifts. Today, you would do it with a two-man crew, then you would put your timbermen to do the arching. We had to arch as we went. We never had the interference. We did all our own barring. What you had to do, you did. Little bit of difference than what you have today.

The mine has changed so much with mechanized mining coming in. You don't have the blocks of ore left now that we had in those days. Another thing, you were spread out more. You had the air and water, all you wanted. But now it's so congested there might be six percussion drills on the air and water lines ahead of you. I've seen where I could change steel on my stoper without turning it off because there was six percussion drills drawing off the same line.

You had a different system then. You had your older guys there. This was basically what we did in those days. It was necessary and it worked out with a blanket contract. They had so many young guys and so many old guys. The blanket contract gave you the same share of the money, no matter how much work you did. I've seen me help the old guys for a whole week, just move their drills around from one spot to another. The blanket contract worked so long as everybody worked. The guys that wrecked it were the contract riders. But it was necessary. We had so many older people then because they couldn't get a

pension until they were sixty-five. So what the hell could a guy do when you had that many guys between fifty-eight and sixty-five? What could they do underground for a living?

Those days, the only guys that got to be slusher miners had to be in development. The only way you could go slushing earlier was that you were a development miner and had got injured. Other than that you had to wait on seniority, which was about twenty-two years, before you got a slusher. This made a hell of a difference when you look at your crews today. Now, of course, seniority doesn't matter and it doesn't matter how old you are. If you are not in this trade group, you can't do the job. In those days, there was no such bullshit.

We had old Fitzpatrick, Carl Adams and old George Mawson. We had pretty old guys drilling. So when I was cross shifting old Mr. Adams, I would leave him sixty feet that he could turn in on his report sheet because us young guys were bored to tears. We didn't want to kill the contract and where the drilling was good, we would make up for it when it was bad drilling. You did have to babysit to a certain extent, but it worked both ways.

Slusher miner barring down a drawhole with dragline cables and scraper bucket. Broken ore would flow down the drawholes.

In the coalfields, without the older men, I wouldn't have survived. I might not have been dead but I would have been hurt goddamn bad. They didn't allow you to make a mistake. They were the kings. The boss wasn't the king in the coalfields. You paid attention to the guy you worked with when you were a rookie, not the bosses. They didn't interfere. Nobody came and told you what to do. When you had a bad area to work in, they put their top guns there, the guys with experience. If you were a good worker or a kid that looked a little mature, you went with him until you learned the racket.

I found out when I went shifting that the Company was making shift bosses out of guys that had no business being shift bosses. When you look at some of the ground we went through, like the South Ramp and everything we had down there, how the hell can you talk to a timber boss that never mined a day in his life? How can you talk to someone who never, never did any ground support? How can you talk mining to someone that has never drilled a burn in his life? You've got to have the experience. Basically, you relied on your older people.

I can't say that the Company trained me. I was trained by guys like Alf Jolie, Len Cinnamon and Bob Cameron. These are the guys that trained me. When I started here, you could not go by the book. Nobody drew something out for you and said you put fifty-four holes in. If you did, you wouldn't make any money. You wouldn't have made a goddamn nickel. What you did was take what you could, then experiment. This is where you got your slash V's, V-cut, your three-hole burn, [first holes of a blast pattern] and your five-hole burn. We went up to twelve-hole burns in some of that ground. Nowadays, nobody does that.

In some respects, I was probably the most disappointed man of anybody in that mine when I hit mechanized. As far as I was concerned, the biggest percentage of the miners knew bugger all about mining and, in particular, about powder. Of course, as you know, every hole was loaded right to the hilt. There were fires started underground because of mechanized blasting. When I went to mechanized, there was fuse boxes blasted almost every day. Doors blasted. They laid NCN on the footwall.

In those days before mechanized, you had a box of powder. You had to pack the sucker. You made it do what it would do. You'd drill the holes and when you saw bootlegs, you would put more holes in and if you didn't, you would cut down on holes. So you experimented. You were allowed to experiment them days, not like today where some blasting expert tells you how many holes to put in, some guy that never pulled a round in his life but got a goddamn certificate that proves he's an expert. Expert, my ass.

I remember this one shifter who came up to where Jolie and I were working and he put a loading stick into my back-holes to check them. Jolie went ape-shit. I thought he was going to crack. That's something you didn't do. That was the difference in mining those days. You had to know your ground and Alfie thought that with him being the senior miner, my holes would be all right and he didn't need some shifter coming along and checking out his rookie's holes. Your top miners, it wasn't that they worked any harder than your poorer miners; it's a fact that they knew ground better.

This shifter got killed later on by going up on a platform that some other miners used to put some shots up to blast down a hang-up. Just as he got up on the platform, the shots went. This shifter was a real hyper person. I'm not saying anything bad about the man, but he ran up to check it just as the shots went and that was the end of him. Very, very hyper. That's what probably got him.

There's a lot of difference that I could see. Of course, I worked in both eras. The old conventional and the new mechanized. I see a lot of differences, such as procedures and respect. I think that when the Company hired so many new people, they never had time or experience so they had to do it on a system. I think the system they went to at the start of mechanization was a lot more costly than it was in the old days. But now most of the mechanized miners are getting experience with the few experienced mechanized miners they brought in, and the guys are getting training. The guys that did come over from conventional mining are finally getting trained. But you've got to remember how all the conventional miners fought change. Then gradually they could see this was the future in mining.

Conventional face in the 1990s. From left: Arne Egge, shift boss; unknown; Willie Kronsteiner, miner; Billy Muir, miner; unknown.

Every time you get new management, you were retrained; you'd go through a change. I never understood the change because, like I say, if you do something one way or you handle men one way and if they're satisfied with you, I think they should leave you alone. But they always manage to come out with one bullshit deal or another.

I was called into the office because I didn't give out enough reprimands. I never gave out a reprimand in my life. The only reprimand I gave was this. I was called by the office downtown to give this driller a reprimand. They had found some marijuana and an old Company wrench in his house. They called me on graveyard and told me who he was and to give him a reprimand. This security guy, I think he was a cop at one time or something, said he would not let this guy or his girlfriend make a call to the mine, and so that's what I wrote for a reprimand. Well, the superintendent we had went ballistic. The next morning, when he saw this bullshit reprimand, I told him this is what I was told. He said, "Bullshit" and tore it up and threw it in the garbage.

To me, a reprimand is for a very, very serious offence. It took away pride in those days. You had pride in your ability. You had pride in your work. Miners them days took reprimands very serious but with this new management, it made a reprimand a joke. In fact, down the Shaft for awhile if you didn't have at least two, you weren't even part of the crew. For awhile, with the management we had just before the shut down, they were giving reprimands to guys that weren't even here. The bloody guys were on holidays, like old Black Dick. He got a reprimand for not doing enough work. He said, "I couldn't have done enough work because I was on holidays." Can you believe it? That's what we had for senior supervision at that time. The guys didn't know whether to be mad or just laugh. It ended up with a lot of laughter and shaking of heads.

I think with me, I've always felt that if I was going to make it as a shifter, I would have to be mature enough. I still say today that if I was a good shift boss, it was because I had a good crew. If I wasn't a good shift boss then I screwed up the crew. Basically, without the men, what good is the shift boss? Forget about it. I don't care how good you are, how smart you are, there's no one that can tell me they can go into that mine and know every phase of it.

This is what makes it really bad today. They come in here and they don't realize that we have done every type of mining there is. You're not showing me anything when you show me a V-cut or a three-hole burn. They are not about to show you anything about ground control. We've got some of the baddest ground you'll ever see and our men done it. Yet people will come in with wild ideas on how to do it. Christ, everything they come up with we already done.

Ol' Garnet Coulter, the foreman, was funny, talk about a funny thing happening. In this stope, we had a bulge in the back. In the coalfields we would call it the hogsback and they were dangerous as hell. It would run into a crack where one type of ground would run into a different type, and down it comes.

Well, up in that stope, we had one that was still hanging on the back, just up from the blacksmith shop, and I would say it was about eighty feet long. Coulter told Bert Frocklage and I that he wanted that rock bolted. So Bert and I, all we had was 6-foot Mark-D bolts, and I'll tell you, I started on one end and Bert on the other. When Bert was drilling, you could feel that son of a bitch going. I told Bert that when he was drilling, I could feel that bastard and he told me that when I was drilling, he could feel it moving also. So we made sure that when either one of us was drilling, for Christ sake don't get under it. So by the time Coulter got up there to see us, we each had about ten or twelve bolts in.

Coulter had a whole bunch of Orientals with him. I don't know if they were Chinese or Japanese but they were all dressed up in mine tourist clothes. There must have been about twenty of them, all standing around, shining their lights in our eyes, big shit-eating grins on their faces. I said, "Garnet, this is the shits." Well, Garnet grabbed a steel, putting on a big show, and taps the back and then gave us a big lecture for about ten minutes. When he finished, he said, "And that's my lecture for the day." Then he and the Orientals took off, leaving Bert and me wondering what the hell that was all about. This was on a Friday, eh.

When Bert and I came to work on Monday, the whole goddamn thing had fallen out all in one piece, just lying there. Here're all these stinking bolts sticking out. Looked like a friggin' porcupine. Christ, some of those bolts were only in about an inch to two inches and there it was, just lying there. So Bert and I started packing up our gear, stopers and hoses. No sense in leaving everything here. We might as well get it back to our face where we were working. We had everything moved back to our heading except for the steel. I told Bert to start setting up at the face and I'd go and get the steel. So when I got up to where the slab was lying, there was Garnet standing there. I grabbed the same 6-foot steel that Garnet had used to tap the rock and I tapped the rock and said, "And that's my lecture for the day." And away I went, just laughing.

Ol' Coulter just loved Barr. I suppose it was because he could see a lot of himself in Barr. We had these mine inspectors come in one day with him and that was the first time to my knowledge that we had to put anything up on our extensions so you couldn't fall backwards. Usually, all we ever did was put our extensions in and put two planks at the bottom of them to drill off. We were driving a 45-degree raise. Well, the mine inspector wanted something higher up on the extensions. We had a rope so we looped it twice around the top. So the mine inspector was happier than hell. But as soon as the inspector left, that was the last time we did it.

So I don't know how much later it was, a month or so, but along comes Coulter with the mine inspector. We were up the raise, drilling away, and had no friggin' ropes up. Coulter said, "How come you didn't put the ropes up, Barr?" "How come you never told me the goddamn mine inspector was coming in?" yells Barr, and that was it. Everybody laughed.

We had this new shifter, a real stinking arsehole, and he was going to get the work done. You know what some of these guys are like. Gonna make a name for himself, a real dickhead. Well, he had this oldtimer on his crew that was driving a drift and was using a mucking machine to muck out. The young shifter told his foreman that he would get it mucked out. He thought he was a pretty big wheel, so he tells this oldtimer, "I want this mucked out. I want this face clean. This is bullshit." There was no rush to get it mucked out at the time. He said, "When you come out of here in the morning, I want this mucked out clean." The old guy says, "No worry, when I come out in the morning, she'll be mucked, and mucked clean." This young shifter got on the skip and says to the skiptender, "You just got to know how to handle these old bastards."

So the old guy goes in to his heading and comes out to go up in the skip at about five in the morning and tells the skiptender to take him up. I guess when the skiptender came back down, the young boss was at the station and asked him if he saw the old guy. The skiptender said he just went out. "How's his heading?" the shifter asked. The skiptender replied, "Said it's as clean as a whistle." The young boss said, smug as hell, "I knew I could get it done." He put down in his report sheet that the heading was mucked out.

I guess he was in bed when he got a phone call from his boss. I guess the boss went down to have a look and what the oldtimer did was muck it out all right, but he never put a car behind the mucking machine to muck into. He just threw a couple of tons of muck over the machine onto the track behind. But the face was clean. The oldtimer just packed up his gear and quit. You gotta be careful how you speak to people on graveyard.

I believe that a lot of accidents are caused by stress, guys not having their mind on what they're doing. Remember how we went on day's pay that one time? Well, I went to a supervisors' meeting and I told them that the accident rate was going to go up and they wouldn't believe me. They said there was no difference between this time and the last time we went day's pay. They didn't realize that the last time we went day's pay, they let fifty or sixty men go.

There's enough stress when you go on the job. How often have you seen people go on bad jobs and then they go in the doghouse and laugh about it? You'd know how difficult it was or what a close call they had had. It breaks the tension. But when you get people worrying about other things, they're not working safe. I've seen guys mucking in a draw-point with just the ass of their scoop sticking out. His mind wasn't on the job. He's worrying about losing his job. It wasn't day's pay.

I think about humour in the mine. Our job underground is stressful. How many times a month are we in bad ground or whatever? That's enough goddamn stress. You don't need it twenty-four hours a day. We always used humour, jokes and what not, to eliminate that stress. There is nothing worse than going into the doghouse and there's no humour. You want to get it out of your system. I think it's a mistake when you take humour out of the workplace. The Company got rid of the nuts we used to have, the characters. The nuts or characters we had in the old days were very necessary. What they did was eliminate the stress. It took our minds off the bad things. We could always find something funny about a situation.

We all react different to different circumstances. I don't care who you are. Some guys get hurt and they laugh. Some guys get hurt and they go out of sight. Some guys will cry for three days, and some guys will get drunk for three days, when a partner or a friend gets killed. It doesn't mean that the guy that gets drunk doesn't feel what the guy that cries feels.

I've got a lot of memories over a thirty-year span. I went back to Nova Scotia on my holidays to say good-bye to some of my friends at the Miners' Hall. The last two years I worked there, twenty-three of my friends got killed. That wasn't just the big Springhill bump. That was several accidents. It's not pleasant thinking about these things. That's why we all react different. You have to look at your own responsibility.

A friend of my dad's caused an accident by being drunk on the job. He forgot to do his job and he always blamed himself. He said to me, "You know, Bill, when you kill yourself, it's quite simple, but when you kill someone else, you have to live with it for the rest of your life." I think this is what changed me. The difference between old Hardrock and me was that he was a fatalist. He thought if you're going to get killed underground, you were going to get killed.

When we first went in the hot muck, nobody really understood it. We worked all the drawholes at the same time. Sometimes, you couldn't see going back to the back drawholes to bar down or blast or whatever. And if your No.

5 drawhole was spewing dust and SO_2, you couldn't see dick all. If you were going back to say No. 18, you just stumbled, tripped and felt your way along. It was the shits and damned dangerous.

Finally, we learned just to work certain drawholes one at a time, leaving the ones not being worked but RDOed, to take when we needed them. In fact, I was working with Gerry Decosse and we had two RDOs to blast. I loaded one round myself. We were using forcite stick powder and safety fuse. I think we were loading No. 20 drawhole and No. 18. So when I come out, Gerry says to let him load the next one and for me to hand the powder up to him. We just about had it loaded and I told Gerry that I was going to go tie my round to the igniter cord.

I went up into my drawhole and I could smell the powder in the holes burning and I knew it was just a matter of time before the blasting caps would go, then the powder. I said to Gerry, "Let's get the hell out of here. I've got a live round here." We just got out of the sub when the shots started going off. Both drawholes went off. Me, like an idiot, had to go back and have a look. One round broke perfect. That was too close. It would have been a bastard if we both were up that second drawhole when the first one started going off.

We got a lot of sloughs in the hot muck at the start of it, before we got a system going. It was extremely dangerous for the guys working in the sub because you never knew when it was going to let go. What would happen is that when the clinker got too heavy, it would break up and just flood the sub, sometimes as high as the back of the damn sub.

We had a hundred feet, or at least eighty, in some of them. You could hardly see the back. All you would see is a red glow up there, with all this molten lead and other ore melted together forming this giant clinker, some eighty feet long. We would crawl up there and put asbestos down on the hogsback and pack up ten or fourteen bags of powder, 50-pound bags, and then go down below and let the sucker go, just a big concussion shot. Doing it this way was extremely dangerous. Say you were going to blast a drawhole at the back of the sub, you would go by all these hung-up drawholes. What we found out is that some of the shots we placed at the back of the sub would go off premature from the heat and guys could get trapped, as the drawholes behind them would come down from the concussion.

That's how Percy and Tunny got whacked, because the shots went premature while they were going down the man-way to blast. They just got out of the sub and were starting down the man-way when boom!, they got blown down the man-way. That was kind of funny. Percy got his hands burned and Tunny had his pecker burned from the hot dust.

As far as I was concerned, the understanding of hot muck wasn't there. Here's an amazing story. This is the truth, I swear to God. When I first came here in 1961, I was trained in industrial first aid. The guy they had as an industrial first aid man underground had a heart attack so I went in as his replacement. There was a lot of people that the SO_2 was bothering because of the ventilation at the time. We had a lot of visitors coming in every day to look at the situation. You know what it's like, people tripping over each other, getting in each other's way. We had the pig snouts and those canisters for the MSAs.

What I had to do when they came in was blow the pig snouts off with air, see how good they looked, and put the good ones back in the box to use again. When you came in to get a canister, I had to put the date and what time it went out and we had to re-use those canisters. I got pissed off about it and started raising hell. I took the canisters, put a pick to them, and threw the goddamn pig snouts away. I'll tell you, I was in severe shit over that. I think what saved my neck was a guy got killed.

He was working in the exhaust circuit. They drug him out of the circuit. He was suffocating because he was sucking sand through one of those old goddamn canisters. He was okay when they drug him out but he died later because of all that hot-muck dust he sucked in. This all happened when I was getting my ass chewed out by the guys above me. I quit right there. I would not go back in the first aid room. I was a stubborn old bastard.

So they shipped me outside to show me a lesson. They gave me all the dirty jobs. I swept the road from the guardhouse all the way down to the dry. Being a miner, I was belittled being on a broom with everybody watching. Then they put me down on the belts, mucking on clean-up. A supervisor said to me, "Now don't you wish you had stayed in the goddamn first aid room?" and I said, "Nope, I can do this job and you can't." Screw them all, was my way of thinking at the time.

We didn't understand the hot muck even when I was there, the SO_2 gas and dust. You can ask my wife. I would wake up in the morning and my sheets would be covered in blood from the rashes from under my arms and other parts of my body, my chest, between my legs. It was a living hell. See, what nobody understood at that time was that when you were sweating because of the bloody heat, all that fine dust was going through your clothes and turning into sulphuric acid. It collected where all your body hair was. It would hang up there and get activated. One guy went to the hospital for a bloody week with this.

There was one hot-muck slough that came on Rudy and I. We were in the Centre Section. I was working the top sub. When it went, we knew that something big had happened. Well, I crawled down to Rudy's sub because I could hear his hoist running. I figured he was dead. I crawled over to his hoist and turned it off. No sign of Rudy. When I got to the doghouse, Rudy was already there. He left so fast, he didn't even pause to turn the hoist off. Pretty damn fast for an old guy, I thought, but I think I could have beat him. When that happened, it was so fast you couldn't see your hand in front of your face.

That hot muck was bad. If you never saw it, you wouldn't believe it. The heat, the fire, the flames. Most people would never believe you if you told them. I remember this one time, we were supposed to leave a guy underground between shifts to watch our chute so it wouldn't burn. We figured it was fine and nothing was going to happen so we all went out. Wouldn't you know it, that's the time it burned to a crisp, all those twelve by twelves and all that other wood? All that was left was metal from the chute, all sitting in the middle of the track.

But the hot muck was an experience, though when you think about it, it was one of the things that being a miner required us to do. Those guys dynamiting oil wells to put them out when they're on fire got a million bucks a shot for it, but in hot muck we thought we were lucky when we got $20 over day's pay, and we had to negotiate for that. Christ, the Company had the sheriff deliver summonses to us at our houses to get us back to work when we were holding out for that lousy $20. It was just like back in the early days before we had a union.

I remember one time Fred Turk and I were driving this raise. It was about four hundred and fifty feet. There was a turn-back at about two hundred feet. Here's where we widened out so that we could put in a tugger station. This was a bullhorn raise at fifty degrees. Fred and I were at the top of the raise, timbering, putting in the stulls and planking. We had little Hardrock — Hardy — at the tugger, two hundred feet below us. What Hardy would do is get the measurements that we sent down in the skip and then put the measurements in the next skip and send them down to old Davey Jones down in the drift below.

Fred marked down on a wedge that we needed a stull seven feet long, put it in our skip and sent it to Hardy. We sat and waited for it to arrive and when it did, it was seven inches long. I guess Hardy had dropped our wedge with the measurements down the raise and made his own wedge, where he put two lines behind the seven instead of one. You know how Fred was. He took one look at this little timber and then at me and said, "You know, Bill, I think Hardy must have been smoking one of those Thinking Man's filters." This was a reference to a cigarette commercial popular at that time.

Johnny Barr was a stubborn bastard. Barr and I were working together driving a raise for exhaust at the end of this sub. We got split up. We each got a new guy so we were cross shifting each other. This raise was just a short one. It only went up about sixty-five feet but you had to scrape the muck out of it to get to it.

Well, this one day we were held up by the surveyors and didn't get going till late. Coming off shift, I told Johnny that he should change the cable on the hoist, as it was looking pretty ragged. I told him he would need about four hundred feet of haul-back. I went back the next day and there was no cable changed. I said to myself, "All right, you bastard, I'm not going to change it either." So I hand mucked just enough to get up to the collar of the raise, drilled and blasted. Before I left, I cut the cable, thinking he would have to change it now.

I came back the next morning. Guess what? Barr tied igniter cord to each end of the cable as a big joke. He must have mucked like hell, hand mucked, so he could crawl up the raise and take his round. Well, being the stubborn bastard that I am, I mucked like hell so that I could get my round. I worked my ass off. So when I blasted my round, I lit Barr's I-cord splice and when we came back the next day, we had new cable. Christ, we laughed over that for years. We were just trying to out-stubborn each other, but God, it took a lot of work.

When Barr and I went up to Pinchi Lake Mine to do some work for the Company, the first thing we did was go into the bar that Billy Yanosik was running. He was from Kimberley. We got drunk and ended up arm wrestling every Indian in the bar. We had a hell of a time. This one guy came up to us. He was an exceptional person. He was an Indian and his name was Pal. He came up to us and said, "Jesus, pal, when I knew you guys was coming, I went to the superintendent and said I sure would like to get a chance to work with these Kimberley miners." And he told me this I don't know how many times.

But the first time on the job, we went underground and took a look at the ground and they told us that we were going to need a nine-hole burn with a big hole in the middle. Barr said that we could probably pull it with a three-hole burn. So we put the three-hole burn in and it bootlegged and the miners laughed like hell at us.

But there you could blast any time you were ready. Besides that, you didn't have to wait to go underground. It took us five minutes to drive underground, so we re-blasted the bootlegs and then went in and took another one. The next day we took three rounds. We figured out that we could blast with a five-hole burn and that's all there was to it. I'll tell you, there was no more laughing at us after that. We were making a pisspot full of money because they promised us the Kimberley contract before we went up there.

They split us up so there was Barr on the opposite shift, cross shifting me. I had this young fellow, Pal, and I couldn't figure this guy out. I'd collar all the holes. He'd seem to be funny when he came to work and as the shift went on, he seemed to get funnier. I couldn't figure it out. The smell. We were going through this shit that was like clay, like blue clay. I thought it was the smell of the ground. Well, anyway, he offered me a cigarette and that's what the bloody smell was. It was marijuana. He sat up and smoked this shit all night and continued on during the shift. That was my first experience with marijuana. I'd never smelled it before in my life. No wonder he got acting funnier during the shift.

Well, anyway, I had to work the weekend. Barr, he was too drunk to come out. They wanted this job done. So I said, "Jesus, Pal, I got no partner tomorrow. How about working with me?" We were all sitting in the hotel room. He had a bottle of rye. "Jesus, pal," he says, "I always wanted an opportunity to work with you Kimberley miners." I said, "Great, Pal, you come to work with me tomorrow morning." He said, "Okay."

I took off, went home at nine o'clock, and went to bed. I got up, drove to the mine twenty miles up in the bush and went to work all by myself. I came out, went right back to the hotel room and there he was, sitting there. He had his finger stuck in the rye bottle, all swollen up in there. I said, "I thought you were supposed to come to work with me this morning, Pal." He said, "Jesus, pal, I always wanted the opportunity to work with you Kimberley miners but my finger got stuck." You couldn't get mad. All you could do was laugh.

This friend of ours, Billy, who ran the bar, was having a lot of trouble with this black guy, a real goon, and his friends. Well, I said, "The next time this sucker comes in, you go out with him and we'll tag along to back you up." Well, the guy shows up with a couple of buddies and away we go outside, Billy, Barr, myself and a couple of other miners. When we get outside the guy took off. There was no fight. So when we got up the next morning, there was no side window on the driver's side of Barr's new truck, just a big rock sitting on the seat. We went home with a beer box in the window. Barr never ever wanted to go back to Pinchi Lake. That was one comical place.

I got a phone call one day from Garnet Coulter saying he would like me to go to Greenland, saying he had a good deal for me, would I come down to his house and talk about it. I said sure. So I go down to the house and he says, "Look, I want you to come over there mining and I'll be putting native help with you and I'll make sure you'll make money. You'll get this and get that."

Redpath Contractors were in there, and I knew what they were making. They were making between $5,000 and $5,600 a month. I said okay, but what about my partners? They're all native help. Up there, all native help were Danes and what he wanted to do was get them used to the contract system of mining. I said, "Jesus Christ, these guys have never mined before. They're all tradespeople. How about a guarantee?" I told him I wanted $2,200 a month, which was day's pay over there. He said he'd see about it. Three weeks later, he called and said that he had a real good deal for me. I said, "What's the deal?" He said, "Twenty-two hundred a month, no contract." We argued back and forth but I said, "I don't care what you got. I'm not going without contract." He never spoke to me again for over a year. Can you imagine going to Greenland, dark and cold, just to lose money? He had to be nuts.

They came out with this new NCN mixed with aluminum dust. Coulter wanted all the back-holes in the sub drilled with jacklegs. It was okay to drill the rest of the round with stopers but the back-holes had to be flat so they had to be drilled with jacklegs. We said okay, if that's what you want. Coulter came up with us at the start of the shift to see how this new NCN worked. It didn't. The whole round was still sitting there, just like we had just finished drilling. Coulter took out a loading stick and shoved it into the back-holes. We were caught. He could see that we had used stopers for all the holes. He checked Rudy and his partner's round in the next sub. Same thing. We got shit for that. That goddamn new NCN gave us away. Them and their goddamn controlled blasts. We never used that crap again.

Coulter had it in for Rudy Swirsky. I remember I was in Rudy's sub, by his hoist, getting a block or something, and there's Coulter walking down Rudy's sub with a loading stick, eight foot six, holding it across his body. He got to this one spot and he said to Rudy, "You're kind of narrow here, aren't you?" Rudy says, "Hold your thumb there, Garnet, and I'll go get the sandpaper and I'll get it out to size for you."

Coulter made him slash the whole sub on day's pay. It makes you shake your head at some of the things that happened in there. Christ almighty, hold your thumb there and I'll get some sandpaper.

GORDIE OLSEN

Big man with a big laugh...

Interviewing Gordie was really enjoyable, just non-stop laughing. Gordie was one hell of a miner — when he came to work. He really enjoyed mining but enjoyed his time off more.

As a shop steward, he was a great one. He would stick up for a worker like nobody could, but if that worker was a malingerer and abusing the system, Gordie would come down hard on him. Big Gord was not somebody you wanted to piss off. He would get physical.

I found him to be a great partner. He made it fun to come to work.

I started in 1964 at the mine. My dad, Alf, told me I would be a lot better off working in the mine rather than down at the fertilizer plant or at the iron plant. He didn't like the gases and chemicals that were in them places. I remember going in the mine for the first time on the coaches. I figured I'd never see daylight again, but when I thought about my dad and a lot of other guys that had been going in and out of the mine on these same old coaches for a good fifty years, I guessed I'd make it.

I spent a couple of years on the belts and in the crushing chamber and then I finally got trained on the diamond and percussion drills. I ran these drills for about three or four years and then I got a chance to go mining.

I never went to mining school. All they said was, "Go with Don Barry. He needs a partner" and so away I went. He was the first of many to come over the years. I stayed with Don and learned quite a lot. At that time we were driving raises, then I went with Tommy Huppie for a few months. When I first got married, Tommy was telling everyone that he didn't want to work with some guy that just got married because the guy probably left his best work at home. Hell, all you had to do is look at the size of his family. Tom was a hell of a man to keep up with at work. He was always going full bore ahead. Even today, if you were walking down the street with the old bastard, a guy would have one heck of a time keeping up with the old fart. Even being such a scrawny bugger, he was one of the best.

I was pretty quiet and stuff in those days. I just kept my mouth shut and tried to learn as much as I could. I was sent to work with this old Swede named Carl. This one day we were working in this sub. I was drilling and placing 6-foot rock bolts and Carl was drilling on a round ahead of me in the sub. Well, anyway, in comes John Ekskog, our foreman, and he starts tearing a strip off me for not wearing safety glasses. My partner could hear me getting shit and so when Big John finally left, he came around the corner and proceeded to start giving me shit all over again for not standing up to the big son of a bitch. He says, "He's no better than you are. You're a Swede and he's a Swede and I'm a Swede. Don't you ever take no shit from him again. Just because he's the bloody foreman that doesn't mean nothing. The next time he gives you shit and you don't give it back to him, you're really going to get it from me."

I kind'a think I was more afraid of old Carl than I was of Big John. So after that, whenever John gave me hell about something, I gave it right back to him and after awhile he pretty much left me alone. I guess he wasn't going to get anywhere with two stubborn Swedes locking horns.

I was working with Hungry Hughes. I was up in a drawhole barring the loose muck before I set up and started to drill. As I was barring, a piece of ore broke the back and glanced off the footwall and struck me just above the steel toe and broke a small bone in my foot. I was off work for about a month. I really didn't want to lose Hungry for a partner so I came back probably before I should have. When you get a good partner, you like to hang on to him. I hadn't been back with Hungry very long when it was his turn.

Hungry went up a drawhole to set up. He was up about forty feet at forty-five degrees. My job down at the bottom in the sub was to tie sprags and planks to a rope which he would pull up. He had a pick with him and he hollered down for me to stand off to the side so that he could bar some loose down. The next thing I knew the drawhole was full of muck; I never heard nothing. I hollered up at him and got no answer. All I seen was the bottom of his feet in the muck. I started digging until I got a big enough hole where I could crawl through, and here's old Hungry lying there like he's sleeping.

He had got cold-cocked by a piece of loose. His chin was split wide open. When he got mobile, he said he better go up to the shifters' office and get a bandage for his chin and that he would be right back. I never saw him for the rest of the shift. They sent him to the hospital to get sewed up. I think he picked up about ten or so stitches.

Another time while I was working with Hungry, we were driving a raise. We were up only about thirty feet. The raise was six feet high by eleven feet wide at forty-five degrees. There was a turn-back raise going up to a backfill stope coming off the main raise. The surveyors figured that the last round should have broken through into it so we went up to have look. There was no breakthrough so we thought that we better set up and take another round. Hungry noticed that one corner of the face looked odd and that he best put a bar to it. There wasn't enough room for the two of us so I went down to the sub.

I could hear him tapping away with the scaling bar when all at once I could hear, "Holy shit," then I could hear the muck running and running. I'm thinking, "What the hell is going on?" Pretty soon, the muck stopped running. I figured that's it for Hungry. He's buried. Then I hear this voice, "Olsen, you all right?" I said, "Hell, yeah, I'm okay. What about you?" "Yeah, I'm okay, but you better come up and see this."

I guess when Hungry put the bar to that corner, it just started opening up and just started getting bigger and bigger. As soon as he could see what was happening, he grabbed a rope and started running headfirst down the raise and into a connection between the two drawholes, and the muck flowed right past him. He claims he made it to the bottom in one jump, and he probably did. You can do a lot of amazing things when you're scared.

I would have to say about the scariest time I had with Hungry was the time we were driving a 58-degree raise and we were up about seventy feet. This was before the regulation came in that you could only go fifty feet before you had to timber. That was after the degrees of the raise steepened up over forty-five degrees. Timbering meant that you had to install a compartment on one side of the raise for the muck to go down and the other side was where you put in your man-way, slide and services. This was divided by stulls and timber. Them days, all we used were ropes tied on to footwall steel. It was wide open them days, just the ropes and steel to stop you if you fell.

There was a raise going off to the side of the main one, in about thirty feet. We set up in this finger raise first and went for lunch, figuring that we would set up in the main one after we had our buckets. This other raise went up another forty feet higher. Old Hungry never ate anything. That was real unusual for him 'cause here's a guy that could eat a car. He said he wasn't feeling very well. I told him to stay in the doghouse and I'd go and do the set-up myself but he wouldn't hear of it. We pulled ourselves up to the first turn-over on the ropes, and again he mentioned he was feeling crappy. I told him to go and sit on a plank on the footwall so that he would be out of the way in the event of me knocking loose down on him, so up he went and sat down.

I was up in the other raise picking hitches for the sprags and getting measurements for the planks. All at once I heard something like a rock hitting his hardhat. I looked down the raise and I could see his light swinging close to the footwall. It looked like his hardhat was hanging there and it didn't look right. I couldn't make out Hungry's form and he wasn't sitting where he was supposed be. So I took off running down the raise and there he was, hanging upside down. He was caught on the footwall steel by half the strap on his bib overalls and he had passed out. Son of a bitch.

Well, I got my shoulder under him and held him there until he came to. Once he came to, I managed to get him back on the plank. If that strap on his overalls hadn't got caught on that footwall steel, he would have gone down two hundred feet and that would have been the end of Hungry. Just shithouse luck. He told me that he threw up while he was sitting there and passed out. Hell, he tells me he passes out every time he throws up. Go figure.

This one time I was on afternoon shift and when I got underground, the shift boss told me to take this guy with me. I really didn't have much use for this guy. I said to the shifter, "You gotta give me a different partner than that. I don't want that useless son of a bitch." The shifter said, "Look, I got nobody else to send with you. Just take him and I'll see what I can do." I said, "I'll see you tomorrow." And so I started walking out of the mine.

I never knew that the track on the main line was so slippery. When I was about halfway out, and I'm slipping and sliding all over the place, I started thinking that maybe this was one real dumb-ass decision that I had made. Hell, I still had a good three-quarter of a mile to go and here I'm just about killing myself to make a point. It was a real bad move, but I gotta live with it now. I always made the statement that if they put that useless bastard with me, and I was on afternoon shift, I would be out of the mine by four.

It was five after four when I hit daylight. I was up at my locker changing when the superintendent came up and was standing there, fiddling with his cigarette. I said, "How's she going?" "Not bad. How about you?" he replied. "I'm okay." He never said nothing more and I'm still taking my clothes off. I said, "By the look of you, my shifter must have got ahold of you." "As a matter of fact, he did. What's going on?" he asks. "I'm going home." "Well, maybe you better come and see me tomorrow when you come on shift before you change your clothes," he said. "No problem. I'll be there," I told him.

So I went home and my little girl, who was about three years old, met me at the door. She says, "You went to work. How come you're home so soon?" I said, "I got mad." I never thought anymore about it.

The next day I went in and saw the superintendent in his office when I got to work. "You went home without permission yesterday," he starts. I said that I had permission and that I told the shifter I was going home if he didn't give me another partner. "Well, he didn't realize that you actually meant it." "Well, when I say something, I usually mean it," I told him. "Well," he says, "I mean to give you three days off for walking off the job." I said, "You're going to give me three days off for saving a guy's life?" "How do you figure that?" he asks me.

"It's like this," I tell him. I told the shifter that if I had to go with that useless bastard on the job that only one of us would be coming out at the end of the shift, and there's one hell of a chance that it wouldn't be him, and that's how I figured I saved that guy's life. Even though I saved that guy's life, they still gave me three days off. So the super sent me home.

As this was a Wednesday, I kind'a felt like I lucked out. This would give me a nice long weekend. The three days off were worth it 'cause when I went home, my daughter met me at the door and asks, "Dad, are you still mad?" I started laughing and said, "No, honey, they're mad now." So we loaded up the car and headed across the line to the States and went skiing. It was like having an extra week's holiday, just because I saved a guy's life. It don't get any better than that.

I missed a Sunday night graveyard shift this one time. At the time I was working with this Nova Scotian by the name of Dan, and what a character he was. Well, I guess he went into the heading by himself and started cleaning a drawhole out and a rock come down and hit him on the knee, which split wide open and all the fluid started running out. Well, Dan started walking out to go to first aid, which was about a mile from the heading.

When he got to the main line, instead of going right where the first aid was, he turned left. Old Dan kept on walking. He walked into the South End shifters' shack figuring he could get some help there. Nobody is there so out to the main line he goes again. No one was working in this part of the mine on graveyard shift. Now we're talking about a lot of distance here. It's a good quarter-mile back out to the main line. After he walked, I would say, a good two miles to the portal, down that slippery old track, he finally got to the portal doors. It was about five in the morning. His boot is full of blood and knee fluid and he finds that he can't open the doors because they are electrically operated.

So here's old Dan standing inside the portal doors, pounding and yelling away. God, his knee must have been throbbing like hell. The night watchman, who just happened to be walking by outside at the time, hears all this commotion, goes over and opens the man-door that is right beside the double drift doors, and lets old Dan out. Dan told me he doesn't remember how long he stood there yelling and hollering, and here's this old guy that just comes over and opens the door and lets him out. Old Dan was pretty embarrassed about this but he could hardly wait to tell me. That gave us all a good laugh for quite awhile.

Dan used to phone me up when he was partying and sing all these Nova Scotian songs to me. He always said, "Graveyard is a killer shift," and you know something, he died when he was on graveyard shift.

I hadn't been off development mining for very long and was working as a slusher miner, when Mac McKenzie came to me and asked if I wouldn't mind going back on development for a couple of shifts. I said it all depends on the heading and who my partner is going to be. "Well," he says, "the heading is a good one but the partner is going to be a problem, but for two shifts you should be able to handle it." "Who the hell ya giving me?" I asked. "Your brother, Mel." He had a big smile on his face to go along with his answer. "I can handle two shifts but no more," was my reply. Two years later I went up to Mac one morning and said, "Hey, Mac." He says, "I know, I know. The two days are up." And that was that. Mel and I could never work well together. We were just too bone-headed.

Mel and I were on afternoon shift on a Friday this one time. I don't know what in the hell we were there for because we never worked Friday afternoon shift, but there we were. Everything that we touched turned to shit. We broke the cable on the hoist. We had the scraper upside down behind the muck pile. Just one big mess. We weren't even scraped out yet and we should have been set and ready to start drilling by then, so we said the hell with it and went for lunch. As we were eating our lunch, Mel says, "Phone the shifter." "What for?" I asked. "Tell him that we'll see him Monday. We're just wasting the Company money and our time the way things are going." So I did.

We walked out to the main line and caught a ride on the waste train heading outside and went home. On Monday morning we get into our heading and see that the cables are broke, the scraper is upside down, and Mel starts to rant, "What the hell are they doing putting a graveyard shift in here on Sunday night?" I said, "Hold 'er, hold 'er, boy. Don't you remember last Friday night? We were the last guys in here. This is the way we left it." I guess he just forgot who the hell he was cross shifting. Like they say, there's nothing worse than cross shifting yourself.

Our shifter, Stan Comfort, came around this one time to give Mel and me job performances to look over and sign. It had on there that we had missed an excessive amount of shifts the previous year. It didn't have Stan's signature on it. I asked, "Who's signature is on this?" He tells me, "It's your superintendent's. Don Boyle's." Me and Mel figured if he wrote these out, he should be the guy that gives them to us. We told the shifter to take them back out and give them back to Boyle and if he wants us to have them, to give them to us personally.

A couple days go by when our foreman comes to Mel and me just as we were coming on afternoon shift and tells us that the superintendent would like to have a meeting with us. So Mel and I wait until three and go into his office. We say, "We hear that you want to see us." He counters with, "I hear you guys see me." I say, "Let's get on with it." Boyle says, "I thought you guys would be in before three. I got a meeting to go to."

I mentioned to him that since it was Company business, we're not on the payroll until three and that our meeting shouldn't take very long. I told him he should have enough time to get to his meeting, and that he would probably have to arrange for a ride to get us into the mine because the mine coaches are just going into the mine. It was after four before we got out of his office.

You know what he was worried about? I had missed twenty-eight shifts and Mel had missed about forty shifts the year before. He was worried about that. I don't know why. We weren't. We asked him how far back the records went. He said about a year. "Why?" he asked. I said, "This is a pretty good year as far as we're concerned. This is the steadiest we've worked for a long time." "What do you mean?" he asked, showing concern. "Hell," I say, "I usually miss about forty-five shifts and Mel misses about sixty. This is about the steadiest we've worked in quite awhile and nobody has ever said anything to us before and now you're worried about it?" I was on a roll now.

"My kids have clothes on their backs and food on the table. What's the bloody problem? I never see you sitting at my table." We told him that if he looked at the shifts that we missed, it was usually on a Friday and that we had a good reason for it. "And what is that?" he asks. I could see he was getting into it by the little smile on his face and he wasn't going to be intimidated by the size of Mel and me. We're both over six feet and two hundred and fifty pounds.

I go on, "You know that we both come here to work." He says, "Christ, I can't take that away from you. You're dammed good workers." I go on by saying, "You know it's cold and damp on development and you know that you're just wet all the time, and sometimes, on a Thursday, you start getting run down, sort of like the flu is coming on. But by taking the Friday off, you got three days off to start feeling good again, and by Monday you can start giving it again, and if you worked that Friday you just end up by missing the whole week."

He's laughing by now. He can see where this meeting has gone. But we did say to him we could work every day if you wanted 'cause we know that there's guys that have been here thirty years that have never been sick or missed a shift. "Yeah, we do have a few guys like that," he says, "but, Jesus Christ, it would be nice if you two could become just a little like that." We're all starting to laugh by now. I give him one more to work on. "How about if we do just as much as those guys?" "What do you mean?" he inquires. "Well, those guys have been here thirty years and haven't done a day's work yet." Old Don let Mel and me get away with murder that day, he was an easy guy to talk to.

I always had fun mining. It was great to be paid to do something that you really liked doing. To me, it kind of went downhill when you didn't have to go to the pay office to pick up your cheque. When you got your cheques, you could see what you made for your efforts, but once they started direct depositing into your bank account, you had to go to the bank to see what the hell you made. I didn't like that.

It used to be fun standing in the line-up BSing with the guys. I remember standing behind an old miner and there was a new guy handing out the cheques and this new guy asks the old guy, "What's your man-number?" The old fellow says to him, "I don't know. Everybody just calls me Bob." And that's the way it was them days. If the regular payroll guy was there, old Bob wouldn't have had to answer all these tough questions to get his pay statement.

Once you got your statement, you would go to the bank or the credit union, stand in another line-up to cash it, then go to all the bars in town. Usually there would be another line-up to pay off your bar bills by buying back the cheques they were holding for you so that you wouldn't lose your credit rating.

Another thing that I think took a lot out of the comradeship that we had was when we stopped riding in on the man-coaches. The mine had switched to mechanized mining so the old way of riding, sitting beside each other in a row, was gone. There was usually about eight guys on a coach, but when we went to those bloody man-carriers, we were crammed in them, sometimes over thirty guys, with the fellow's knees across from you in your crotch. And you were always leaning against the guy beside you because of the degree going in or out of the mine, which was around twelve per cent. These goddamn man-carriers had four rows of seats. Christ, we were jammed in there like cattle.

Then there was the bloody diesel fumes, which would be with you all the way in or out of the mine. Your bloody eyes would be watering, guys would be hacking and coughing. It was damn-well dehumanizing. It was the shits and that was the end of it for me.

I got a job outside in the warehouse but I really missed the old days, especially the guys and all the bullshit. I always wanted one of those old coaches so I could put it out on my front lawn, you know, put down a few ties, a couple of track, fix it up nice, give it a fresh coat of paint, but a guy would have to leave the graffiti. Some of it was pretty damn good, the rhymes and the pictures. I thought it would be nice when somebody came to visit, we could sit in it and drink beer and wave at the vehicles going by on the highway. I guess I'd have to get that past the wife. I never got a coach. The historical society got the ones that were any good to rehabilitate. I do feel bad about it though. I should have jumped in earlier.

This one time there was four of us designated to sink this shaft down on the 3300 Level. There was Moose Bradley and me, and Carl Hallgren and Louis Gilmar as our cross shift. This little shaft went down about thirty feet and was eight feet by eight feet. As we got down about ten feet — this was all drilled with pluggers — we would put pins in the walls with planks laying on them. We would hand muck the blast muck up onto the planks then go up and muck it out into the drift, where we would clean it up with a mucking machine. We did this all the way down; it was real tough slugging, I'll tell you. I think we made about $8 over day's pay. Didn't like that job.

Right above us was this bore hole about four feet in diameter. It went up to around the 3900 Level. This was drilled with that bore-hole drill the Company brought over from Riondel since that mine had closed down and had no further use for it. It did a beautiful job. It used a 4-foot bit, and the ground where it had drilled was like looking up a 4-foot pipe, nice and smooth.

There were two old guys, I would say maybe a hundred feet above us, working in slusher subs. I believe it was Nels Persson and Nick Seredick. They would never let us know when they were blasting. We would hear the blasting whistle blowing, then boom! We never had a chance to get out of our hole. Christ, the shot would drive our hats down over our ears from the concussion.

One day we were going to blast so Moose and I are hollering up the raise to Nick and Nels to let them know that we were going to hit it. Both these old guys were deafer than hell. I guess they could hear something but they couldn't understand us. Then we could hear one of them say, "I think they're going to blast." Then the other, "What are they telling us that for? Why don't they go ahead and blast?" That's why most of the old guys didn't figure they were blasting heavy 'cause they were all deaf. Hell, everyone else in the area could hear or feel the shots going off. It was just a little poof to them. You got to remember that they didn't have the ear protection when they ran the drills in the old days, just some cotton waste or nothing at all.

I remember when I first started sitting on the coaches, waiting to come out from underground at the end of the shift, with all the old guys. These guys would be all crippled up with arthritis. They all had bottles of aspirin with two hundred or five hundred pills. They would borrow off each other if one guy was short. They had to when they were in so much pain.

Then you look at a guy like my old man. He never took an aspirin for a headache. The only time he got a headache was when he went loading. That's when a large block was all drilled off and was loaded with forcite powder, which had glycerine in it. The glycerine would get into your skin, especially if you're sweating. It would get on your hands and, if you wiped your forehead, it would get into your head and besides that, you were breathing it all the time. God, you would get fierce headaches, even with those ammonia bombs that we sniffed, trying to alleviate the bloody headaches. Well, the old man swore that the only cure for a powder headache was draft beer. So he would check in with mom when he came home from work and get the okay to go down to the bar for some draft beer. He used that excuse for a long time, even when he was retired. My brother and I used the same excuse when we saw how the old man BSed our mother and now we're still using it, just like the old man.

Getting off man-cars at the end of the shift and going into the lamp room to put lamps away.

– 245 –

The "Phantom Shitter" was an individual that had a unique way of leaving his mark with Cominco. The first stories I heard about him originated out of the mechanized section of the mine. Nobody knew who he was or where he came from. The first report of him coming into prominence was when he deposited one of his calling cards on the seat of a scoop tram, much to the dismay of the scoop operator. The next strike was in the North End shifters' shack. His deposit was right in the middle of the floor, concealed with a 5-gallon pail. He knew all the shifters would be out on their runs and felt it to be safe to do his dastardly deed.

I suppose he was getting quite confident in his stealth because his next move was to park one in the corner of one of the large showers that we had, and this was in the middle of the day when there is usually a lot of people moving about. He was definitely getting quite bold. The "Cookie Monster," who was a janitor in the lower section of the mine, reported that the filthy fellow had dropped one right beside the handle of the toilet on the 3300 Level. This would have required an athletic ability.

A massive investigation was in progress at the time but, alas, no perpetrator was ever found. There were rumours and suspicions, of course, but nothing substantial, all to no avail. There was just no way anybody could catch him with his pants down.

The best I heard about the Phantom was when I was in the shower one night, coming off shift. This guy showering beside me started cursing away that the Phantom was at it again. I said, "Oh, where did he strike this time?" "Well, Gord, there's no doubt about it. He's got to be the sneakiest bastard around. You know what he did?" This guy continues scrubbing away then stops and looks at me with a real serious look in his eyes, "That sneaky son of a bitch shit right in my pants when I was wearing them the other night, and if you don't think just wearing rubber slicker pants coming out on the coaches in the middle of winter isn't cold, you got another thought coming."

So you can see that the Phantom was getting the blame for things that he had no control of. Here's this guy trying to let a little fart out and it comes out wet, so who you gonna blame but the Phantom? He never got caught. He dropped the odd one every once in awhile just to keep the legend alive, but he pretty much slid off to obscurity, never to be heard of again. I don't know if anybody knew who he was, but he definitely had a problem. If anything, he had a real crappy outlook on things.

My wife's grandfather worked underground as a timberman. He started in the late twenties. His name was Jack Tams, or "Cactus Jack" or "Flapjack Jack." He got his name because he was a cook out in the bush for drilling crews and hunting parties, and especially when he had his chuckwagon in local parades. That's when he would cook up flapjacks for the hungry parade watchers.

In 1933 Jack went with the Company geologists to Burns Lake [BC], where he was to be the cook for the exploration crew. It was July when they landed on the lake in a floatplane and set up camp on the shore of the lake. There were five people altogether in the party. There was an early snow in September and the plane that was to pick them up couldn't land because of the ice on the lake. So they packed what they could and started walking to Edmonton.

One of the guys broke his arm. They splinted his arm using Jack's tea towels to wrap him up. They had no radios or any way of communicating. They got to a Hudson's Bay post, which was about ninety miles from where they started. They caught the odd ride from scattered homesteaders along the way and got into Dawson Creek. They finally got into Edmonton on Christmas Eve. The temperature averaged forty-five degrees below all the way. Jack retired in 1964. The Company certainly got their money's worth out of old Jack.

My dad told me a story about old Hardrock MacDonald. I guess they were sent into a place to do some barring in some bad ground. When they got there and were standing at the entrance ready to enter the heading, Hardrock tells my dad to stay at the entrance. My dad says, "Why?" and old Hardrock says, "It's not very safe in there." My dad says, "I thought that's why they sent us here."

"Yeah," replies Hardrock, "it's not a very good place. I was in there the other day and it's really bad and, hell, you got a young family to raise yet and I got no one, so you stay out here and if I don't come out at the end of the shift, don't you come looking for me by yourself because I won't be worth picking up. You just go out and tell everybody that there's no more Hardrock." That's the way he was.

One guy that really sticks out in my mind was Simon Fitzpatrick. He was a gem of a guy. When you think of what a leprechaun would be like, you would think of Simon. He changed right beside me. I was on the diamond drills at the time. Well, the little bugger was outside all summer running a core drill, so with winter coming on, he was sent back underground to go drilling on the diamond drills. We were changing in the dry to go on shift and I said to him, "I see you're coming back underground. The weather must be getting cold." "Yeah," he says, "it was a beautiful summer, it was. Are you still drilling, Gordie?"

I said that I was and that they had me on a diamond drill. "Ah," he says, "and what is the number of your drill?" I could see what he was up to. The little bugger was going to bump me off my drill using his seniority. I remembered seeing a drill motor laying in a drift and waiting to be set up once all the gear was rounded up. The hoses, steel, controls, tools, all that stuff you need to get set up, and then move it to where it was going. Its number was twenty-eight. I told him I was on No. 28.

When he got underground, he went to the foreman and asked if he could get back on a drill. The foreman told him, "No problem. What drill did you want?" Simon tells him that he would like to go on No. 28. "I really don't think you want to go on that one, Simon." "Yep, that's the one I want," he tells the foreman. The foreman went on to tell him the state of that drill and that he's going to have to round up all the gear and haul it away up into this godforsaken place. "But," says the foreman, "you can go on this drill number thirty-three." Guess what? That's the drill I was on, and I ended up rounding up all the gear and hauling No. 28 away up into that godforsaken place and setting it up.

That little Simon just gave it to me after that. "I didn't mean it, Gordie. It was unintentional, honest, Gordie." I heard him saying that any time he saw me and you could see the laughter in his eyes. He was a hell of a guy, always cheerful and laughing. It was hard to be down when he was around.

There was this driller by the name of Jim and he was running a long-hole drill just down a raise from me, maybe about twenty-five feet away. I was in a drill sub just off the raise. Whenever I would shut down my drill to change rods, I could hear Jimmy's drill going away and then I would hear it stall. Then I could hear his voice coming up the raise, "There, you went and did it again, didn't you? How come you did it again? The last time you did that you told me that you wouldn't do it again and now you've done it again. Oh, you're sorry, are you? Well, you told me that the last time. Oh, so you're really sorry this time, are you? Well, I'll give you another chance."

Then I would hear Jim get going again and I would hear the same conversation all over again. This went on all day long. I wonder if he talked to his old lady this much.

I guess, all in all, it was the characters that I worked with, and the fact that I really liked my work, that made me happy   have been a miner. I have few regrets. It was good work.

BILL ROBERTS

My story...

My career with Cominco started in 1961 when I was a student hired on for the summer. At that time, if your dad worked for the Company and you were a student, you were almost guaranteed summer employment. This helped a lot of young people to attend university and, as most of these jobs were on the end of a broom or shovel, I'm sure they served as an incentive to most to stay in school. But the world of academia was not for me. Like so many young guys, I had professional sports in my sights, but I was to be denied that.

After nearly four years attending Father Athol Murray's Notre Dame College in Wilcox, Saskatchewan, I was summoned home by my dad in the spring of '63. It had become obvious to him that my interests lay elsewhere. It was time to get real. After my less-than-stalwart year at school, my dad told me to go up to the Company office and see Kenny Campbell about a job. Ken and my dad were friends. I'm sure they had this set up.

When I told Ken I wasn't going back to school, that I was looking for a full-time job, he told me to come back at the end of the summer when the students had returned to school. So, in the fall of 1963, I was hired on full time, sort of. The Company had this thing with all the new starts; you had to work ninety consecutive shifts before you were hired on full time. But they also had this weird system where they would let you work eighty-five to eighty-nine shifts and then lay you off for two weeks. This happened to me twice before I got on full time.

For two and a half years I worked at various jobs at the fertilizer plant but the seven and two schedule, with only one weekend a month off, was hell for a young guy.

A Rookie Disguised as a Miner

In the spring of 1966 I heard that the mine was clamouring for guys. Miners worked a five and two schedule with every weekend off. My application for a transfer was on my foreman's desk on a Friday morning. By the end of the shift, I was told to show up at the mine on Monday morning.

I managed to borrow a miner's belt from an old miner by the name of George Rossick and a miner's hat from Curly Lord. I didn't want to go up to the mine looking like a complete rookie. After a brief introduction, all of us new guys were split up and sent to the various sections of the mine. There were about ten of us that came up from the fertilizer and four of us were sent to No. 2 Shaft where John Ekskog was foreman.

We were put on the track gang where a really great guy by the name of Bill Graham was boss. He took us down to a lower level to install track. None of us had ever done anything like this before but we were eager.

The new track was to be laid under about four inches of water. You had to pick and chip away to make a place for the ties. The drift we were working in was about the coldest place I had ever been in. It was a fresh-air drift with gale force winds blowing on us from the surface. Yeah, I might have had the old miner's hat and belt on but I neglected to buy miner's clothes. All I was wearing were a short-sleeved sweatshirt, blue jeans and leather boots. No long johns. I managed to tough it out till the end of the shift. I was still a rookie.

At the end of the shift I stood in the shower trying to get warm until my skin pruned up. God, that shower felt good. I headed downtown after the shower and bought some wool underwear, a doeskin shirt, bib overalls, wool socks and rubber boots. Now I looked like a rookie pretending he's not. I don't think I fooled anyone.

Author, 1995, heading out to work, bit bag over his shoulder and lunch bucket in hand.
Courtesy the Kimberley Daily Bulletin

The wool underwear never cut it. I hated wool against my bare skin so after an itchy shift, I was throwing them in the garbage when an oldtimer offered me a buck for them. I accepted. Then I bought some cotton underwear. I had solved the clothing issue. Now I was ready for whatever came next.

Before I actually went mining, I spent a number of years on the timber gang working for Dan Boone, the timber boss in No. 2 Shaft, and learning how to put in drift chutes, square sets, arches and man-way raises. Dan put me with George Matheson, probably one of the best timbermen around. He was in the same league as Nick Stuparyk and Carl Shonsta. Those guys were incredible. There wasn't an underground structure they couldn't build. They were the best there was.

I think it took about four months before George would have a conversation with me. I heard that he liked to sit out on the front steps of his house and drink rye. Not to be daunted, I showed up at his house with a bottle of rye one afternoon and joined him on the steps. George was a quiet man, but I think that bottle did it. After that I spent two years with George and learned something new from him almost every day.

He taught me how to use a cutting torch, weld and read blueprints. He was a great teacher once he took a liking to you. He got me on to Doublemint gum thirty-some years ago and I've been chewing it ever since. Old George was part of the crew that put the steel and cement in No. 1 Shaft, forty-five hundred feet of it. Those old-time timbermen were unbelievable.

After what you might call my apprenticeship on the timber gang, Dan Boone thought I could handle most jobs and started putting me to work with a variety of other guys. One time, I was with Lefty Lafortune working at the end of a deadend drift.

Timbermen building an ore chute on the left using a "Go to you, Come to me" saw.

We had a motor and a couple of flatcars on the track. Our job was to bring arches up a slide about sixty feet out of a sub to the drift, using a tugger near the top of the slide. We were to put the arches on a flatcar and transport them. I was running the tugger and Lefty was down below hooking on the arches for me to pull up.

The tugger was about ten feet from the top of the slide. Right beside the tugger was an I-beam about eight feet long and two feet wide, made of 1-inch steel and weighing about a thousand pounds. The I-beam, called a drawhole bumper, was part of the arched sub construction. The arches came in halves and were bolted together at the top. They were six feet high and big enough to get a scraper into. Every twenty-five feet there would be a drawhole where the broken muck would flow. The I-beam bumpers protected the arches from being badly bashed by big muck falling into the sub. The arches were used in bad ground and were installed every two feet, with connections between them. Everything was blocked tightly to the ground outside the arches. Blocking consisted of cedar logs or planking, whatever it took to fill the void.

Lefty had hooked a half arch onto the cable and signalled with his lamp for me to take it up. I had got the arch to the top of the slide when it hooked a bumper lying on its narrow side, flipping it over onto my instep, and knocking me down. I couldn't move. I was pinned. Lefty couldn't see me, or hear me because of a fan howling away, so I figured I needed to get his attention. I threw a rock down. A couple of minutes later, Lefty's face was staring at me. Blood was running down his forehead. I had nailed him with one of my attention-getting rocks as he stared up the man-way. He was somewhat pissed off.

Lefty and a couple of other fellows got the bumper off me, loaded me up and took me to the shaft station at No. 2 Shaft. The first aid man was at the station on 3500 Level. He put a new type of splint on me, one they had never used in the mine before. All you had to do was put this sock-type device over the injured limb and blow it up. By the time they got me up to the 3900 Level, where the trammers had their motor and the ambulance was waiting, the air had leaked out. So all the way outside, the first aid attendant had to keep blowing this damn splint up and my foot was just throbbing. That was the only time they used that type of splint.

A few days later I was to get out of the hospital with my badly bruised foot. Jack Glennie was coming to take me home. It was after supper, a cold winter evening, and I decided to go outside and meet Jack. It was too cold, though, so I went back inside to wait. When I went through the doors, my crutches, now encrusted with snow, hit the tile. My feet went out from under me and down I went. I guess the nurses must have heard me scream or swear, probably both, when I landed. Oh God, that hurt. They put me back in the bed I had just vacated for two more days, well medicated. With all the trauma my foot had gone through, it looked like a black and blue ball attached to my leg. It was huge and it was sore. But I was on the mend and eventually it got better.

"Cactus" Jack Rallenson and I worked together as partners on the timber gang for a couple of years. An old coal miner from the Crowsnest Pass, Cactus was fun to work with and kept me entertained with stories from the Pass.

One particular day, we were shovelling gravel and sand out of a V-car and mixing it with cement into a cement blower. The cement blower is exactly what it sounds like. The cement mixture is blown under compressed air through a 6-inch pipe for hundreds and hundreds of feet. We were blowing cement up into subs and filling up forms that were to support a huge pillar blast about to take place. We had been doing this for almost a month so the lustre was beginning to wane and, besides, we were on day's pay.

At the time, everyone was on a slow-down, and I mean really a slow-down, because the Sullivan's contract system, which included miners, drillers, timbermen and transportation, was being re-negotiated, as it was every two years. That meant everything was moving very slowly until a new agreement was reached between the contract committee, elected by the underground contractors, and the Company.

Well, anyhow, Cactus and I were standing in a gravel car, leaning on our shovels, when along comes "Precision" Pete Kotush. He asks us, "Do you guys want to go to mining school?" Cactus and I looked at each other and were about to jump out of that gravel car and plant a big kiss on Pete, but I believe Pete must have sensed our intentions and he put some room between us. "So I guess that's a yes, is it, boys?" And he marked our names down in his book and said, "I'll see you tomorrow coming on shift."

Cactus and I were darn excited. There was some apprehension but we could see ourselves being part of the elite, the kings of the hill, if you will. This was what it was all about, being miners, not lowly timbermen anymore. We were damned pumped up coming off shift, I can tell you.

Wrestling with a Jackleg

The name "Precision Pete" pretty much gives an indication of how Pete observed things around him. Along with all that he was responsible for, he was to be our mining instructor. Pete was an old-time miner. He was a shift boss but because there was a clamour for miners, he was designated to be in charge of several mining schools going on. He had a new sub all set up to be our schoolroom. All the drills and steel, everything that a regular crew of miners would need, was there. He even had X's marked on the face where he expected us to drill holes for him.

Pete says, "Get that jackleg off the tool cache and haul it up to the face." The face was about eighty feet from where we were, on the flat. No problem. A tool cache, built with two steel rods drilled into the side of a sub, is where you store your drills, steel and planks. It is up about four feet off the footwall so that a scraper is able to travel up and down the sub.

Man with a jackleg drill.

I went up to the tool cache and lifted the jackleg, all hundred and thirty pounds of it, whereupon it folded in the middle, pinching my hand and nailing me on the knee. I went down as if I were pole-axed, the drill on top of me. This was becoming a nightmare. I hadn't even turned it on yet. Jesus. What a start.

Cactus, with a great deal of superiority says, "Here, let me get that for you. You bring the hoses." My self-image was taking a beating along with my body but I readily agreed. Jack grabbed the drill under his arm and proceeded to drag it up to the face. Now, the leg on a jackleg when retracted is about four feet long with a claw on the bottom of it. This claw hooks onto a rock and pulls the periscope part of it out another four feet. I was stumbling along with the air and water hoses and drill steel when I stepped on the claw and stumbled forward, right into Jack. Down we went, our first pile of people and gear. At that point, I don't think Pete could see anything of value in Cactus or me.

Cactus and I finally got the jackleg to the face, hooked up the air and water, and surrounded it. Laying on the footwall, it didn't look all that imposing so we stood over it, trying to intimidate it, until Pete showed up and started explaining some of the finer points.

There are only two controls on the machine. One gives the drill rotation and impact, and the other supplies air for the leg that gives the drill push. The leg is about four feet long and has another four feet of extension inside it, a periscope effect. As it was explained to us, it all seemed pretty darn simple. Pete even picked up the drill and with no effort, drilled a hole on one of his X's. It looked so damn easy. Our education on the jackleg was about to begin.

"Who's first?" asked Pete. Cactus, showing some boldness, stepped forward, picked up the jackleg, turned the air on and was promptly pinned to the back. Just a little too much air on the leg. Pete said he would help Cactus collar the next hole, so he held the drill steel in his hands and put it on one of his X's. And again Cactus put too much air on the leg, only this time he was thrown into Pete and both of them ended up piled into the corner at the face, cowering before the screaming drill. I was mesmerized by what was happening. "Shocked" would be a good description. I managed to regain my senses, stumbled to the air header and shut off the source of life to the rogue drill.

Cactus had a couple more tries. It didn't get any easier for him. I could see the shade of defeat drawing across his eyes.

Okay, it was my turn now. After what I had been witnessing, I had more trepidation than confidence by a country mile. It just looked so damn easy when we watched the older miners. Cradling the drill, I approached the face with a 2-foot drill steel sticking out of the business end of the drill. With frantic eyes, I searched for a friendly X to drill my inaugural hole. Settling on one, I put the bit on it. So there I was, ready to go.

I was doing all right just standing there. When I looked back, I could see Pete behind me, wondering when I was going to turn it on, but I just stood there, frozen in time, trying to remember what it was he had said about applying the right amount of pressure to the leg. I believe I could have stood there all day, but at last I turned the drill on, all the way. The rotation and the impact were engaged but nothing was going to happen until I applied pressure to the leg that would push the drill steel and bit into the X. By this point my anxiety level had risen quite considerably as the roar of the drill reached the 90-decibel level, fog and oil spewed all over the place, and Precision Pete stood off at a safe range, shaking his head in wonderment.

Okay, here I go. Apply just enough air to the leg to get the steel to my desired X. At this point, the X and the drill had formed an alliance to conspire against me. The X was not nice and flat on the face but ran off on a slip to the right, which encouraged the rotating bit to roll off the X and pretty much go its own way. I wrestled the machine back to my X and applied more air to the leg in hopes of stabilizing the balance and getting control of the situation. Believing the demon jackleg had made up its mind to humiliate me, I strained every fibre in my body and held, or should I say cradled, the drill in my arms, got it on the X and applied full leg pressure. Big mistake.

The leg and the drill steel formed an A-shape with the drill at the top, pinning me up so my feet weren't touching anything. I couldn't believe how fast it happened.

I'm not convinced that Pete went to the air header as fast as he could but he did eventually turn the air off. I relaxed my death grip and the drill and I formed a new pile on the footwall.

I like to think that as the day went on I improved somewhat, but until you get used to a jackleg, you'll wrestle that son of a bitch all over the place.

(I've often thought that wrestling a jackleg would be a real crowd pleaser on World Wrestling Federation TV shows. First the machine would be on top of the human, then the human on top of the machine, and when the ref put an end to the bout by turning the air off, the human would find himself on his back with the machine on top, pinning him to the footwall — or in this case, the mat — and both competitors would be wrapped in a vice grip by the air and water hoses.)

When I finally re-gained my composure, old Precision Pete was standing behind me with a big shit-eating grin on his face, saying, "Let's pick it up and let's do it again."

Well, I never really did master the jackleg but as far as I was concerned, I could usually fight it to a draw. Cactus thought it would be prudent for him to stay on the timber gang since he was older than me. And, besides, with him being a family man and me being single, he felt that I could afford to sacrifice more blood and skin learning the skills of being a miner.

How much worse could it get? I was about to find out.

Memorial to Mike

Sunday, August 30, 1972, is a date I'll never forget. It definitely made me think about my career choice.

My partner at the time was a quiet, gentle person by the name of Mike Lysohirka. Mike was an experienced miner. In fact, he was a damn good miner, one of those who wasn't afraid to get his hat dirty, a guy you didn't mind doing a long raise with. Prior to coming to Kimberley and the Sullivan, Mike worked in mines around Yellowknife where he met and married his wife, Angie, a happy, bubbly soul. Together they had a son, Mike Junior, who was about four at the time Mike and I were partners.

I've relived this night so many times over the years, it's almost like it happened yesterday. I remember the subdued banter amongst the guys as

Man-coach in 1929, just starting to modernize. Coaches had end walls and a roof, but no doors yet.

they changed into their diggers in the dry then headed to the lamp room to pick up their lamps. It's always quiet the first shift back after the weekend, especially on graveyard.

It was warm and muggy as Mike and I climbed aboard the coaches and found a spot among the other miners waiting for the eleven o'clock whistle to blow. The trip from outside to No. 2 Shaft on the 3900 Level was about twenty minutes' long. When we arrived, our shifter, Bill Graham, told us what had been done by the last shift on Friday, then we picked up what we needed from the tool room and got on the skip.

The No. 2 Skip held about twelve men and ran from the 3900 Level down to the 3300 Level at forty-five degrees. Five of us got off at 3300, two sets of miners and a trammer. From there, we walked along the track drift to a man-way raise that took us down to the 3200 Level. The other two miners were working in a sub on that level and the trammer was pulling muck on the same level. The raise that Mike and I were driving came off the 3200 Level at forty-five degrees. It was eight feet by ten feet and we were up it about a hundred and fifty feet. All we had for climbing were ropes and footwall steel.

The first thing we did was have a cup of coffee and a sandwich. We knew we weren't going to see our buckets again until we had scraped out, drilled off and loaded the round. Only if there was time at the end of the shift would we finish our buckets. Mike always left a cookie or two for his son. I guess to a kid, these were the best cookies a guy could have. After our pie time, we stashed our buckets off to the side. It was time to start giving it hell.

We each grabbed a 50-pound bag of NCN, stuffed our bib overalls with safety fuse and I-cord, threw our bag of bits over our unoccupied shoulders, and headed up the raise.

We had flattened off for about twenty feet at the top of the raise and this was where we had our gear stowed, along with our powder storage. We had a 10-horsepower air hoist spragged down at the edge of the raise and two siwash blocks on the left wall, facing the sub that we were driving on the right side of the raise. The sub went in about forty feet and a fresh muck pile, blasted by the Friday afternoon shift, was sitting at the face.

I told Mike I would hook everything up so we could scrape out the sub. This meant that I would grab a couple of cable eyebolts and a 12-inch block and haul them over the muck pile to the face, where the eyebolts would be inserted into pre-drilled holes. Then I would hang the block from one of the bolts and string the cable from the hoist to the scraper, then through it. This would allow us to move the scraper to the face so we could pull the muck through the sub to the edge of the raise and down. When the muck had been scraped and the sub cleaned out, we could set up the drills and carry on with drilling the rest of the sub.

Bill Roberts barring loose from the back.
Courtesy Bill Roberts

But as I was crawling over the muck pile with the block and eyebolts, I noticed that the back of our sub had broken through to the sub above, the one we had expected to break through to. I hollered to Mike that I would crawl through the breakthrough to get our bearings. I got myself up into the sub above and could hear Mike barring down below in our sub. He had been barring on the right-hand wall and was working on a large pie-shaped wedge which was connected to other slabs or blocks above him. When he loosened the wedge, he inadvertently loosened what was above him. I had just told him where we were when I heard one hell of a crash.

When you hear that sound, you know something bad is happening. I yelled down to see if Mike was all right. There was no response. I jumped down through the breakthrough and onto the muck pile, not knowing what I would find. All I could see was an arm and a leg sticking out of the muck pile.

I started frantically digging with my bare hands, trying to find Mike's head so he wouldn't suffocate. He was moaning and still alive, but in bad shape. A large sharp rock was stuck in his face but as I tried to move it, his head came up with the rock. I had to use my knees to hold his head down while I removed the rock.

Mike was close to the edge of the raise and I was worried more loose would come down on him. As I was about to move him, some small muck fell off the back. I was trying to protect his head by shielding it with my body when a piece of muck hit the plastic clip that held the lamp to my hardhat and broke it off. Jesus H. Christ. What next?

My light was still working so I slung it around my neck and moved Mike closer to the edge of the raise. Then I went over to the sub where the air hoist was and grabbed a rope that was tied to one of the sprags holding the hoist down. I brought the rope over to Mike and, with a lot of effort, managed to get him over one of my shoulders. Then I grabbed the rope, swung out into the raise with Mike draped over me, and hand over hand, with my feet searching for any kind of toehold in the footwall of the raise, I lowered us down.

When we finally made it and I got Mike into the sub, I was violently ill for a moment. I don't think I had ever put such strain and physical effort into anything in my whole life.

Getting Mike into the sub and out of harm's way gave me time to go for help. I was just starting off down the raise on a rope when I heard Mike cough. I went back up. I was afraid he might come to, start thrashing about and go down the raise. When I got to him, it was obvious that he was choking on his own blood. The first of the ABC's of first aid are airway then breathing.

Cardio could wait. I sucked as much blood out of his mouth as I could. He started breathing.

I knew I couldn't leave him where there was a chance he could get to the edge of the raise and go down. So I dragged him into a sitting position, tied him to one of the sprags holding the hoist down, then, using the rope, headed down the raise again at a run. The rope was the only brake I had and I was hoping it wouldn't break. About halfway down I slipped and fell but managed to hold on. "This is no good," I told myself. "Slow down, relax. You won't be able to help Mike if you do a header down the raise." So I forced myself to use some caution. That was hard.

When I got to the bottom of the raise, I headed right over to where the other crew of miners was to tell them what had happened. They headed back up the raise to render what help they could to Mike while I got a rescue operation underway. I stopped the trammer, told him about the accident, and we set off for the lunchroom where there was a telephone, stretcher and first aid kit. It was about 12:30 by now, only ninety minutes into our shift.

The first person I phoned was our foreman, John Ekskog, who was at home in bed. John agreed with me that our best chance was to bring Mike up No. 1 Shaft, which, at the time, wasn't working on graveyard. John assured me he would get his neighbour Albert Almack, a hoist man for No. 1, up to the mine and would arrange for a first aid attendant, doctor and ambulance too.

No. 1 Shaft was our best bet to give Mike a fighting chance. It was going to be time consuming just to bring him down our raise off 3200 Level and then up a couple of hundred feet on ladders through a narrow man-way, where we could use only two men on the stretcher, to 3300.

If we then took him to No. 2 Shaft on the 3300 Level, we would have to carry him to the station, get on the skip to 3900 Level, take a train to the mine ambulance to get outside to a regular ambulance and, finally, to the hospital. Mike didn't have that much time. So taking him to No. 1 Shaft and direct to the surface was our best option, in fact, our only one.

With the phoning done, I grabbed a stretcher and crash bag, threw them on the motor, and the trammer and I headed back to the raise. I borrowed his hardhat so I could use my light and, dragging the stretcher, climbed up the raise. We got Mike bandaged up as best we could, strapped him in the stretcher, tied a rope to it, and started down the raise. Two guys at the top of the stretcher lowered it using the rope, while the one at the bottom guided and supported it to make sure it didn't flip over. Every so often we stopped, made sure Mike was breathing, changed positions, then went on again. It was painstaking work.

It seemed to take an eternity to get Mike to the bottom of the raise and loaded onto the motor. The four of us took him to the No. 1 Shaft station, about half a mile way, and waited about twenty minutes before the skip came down. On board were a first aid attendant, Dr. Rodger Stanton, Superintendent Brian Buckley and John Ekskog. An ambulance at the surface took Mike directly to hospital.

The four of us were back at the station rehashing everything when our shifter showed up. He was on his run and couldn't find any of us, but when he climbed up to our working place and saw the mess, he knew something bad had happened. When we told him about Mike, he was shaken. He sent the three other fellows back to work and took me to the No. 2 hoist room where the hoistman could keep me company for the rest of the shift.

The ride out on the coaches in the morning was probably the quietest one I've ever taken. I could sense the warmth and understanding from the other miners, the direct look into your eyes, the pat on the back. I think they all knew Mike hadn't made it. Somebody must have phoned from outside and told the shifters.

I guess I knew that Mike had passed away when I came out of the lamp room and a fellow coming on shift put out his hand, saying how sorry he was about my partner. Just then Brian Buckley came out of his office and called me in. He confirmed that Mike had died about five hours after reaching the hospital.

Mike was forty-four years old.

Never in my life had I experienced such an emotional and physical draining. I remember sitting by myself on a bench between two rows of lockers, half undressed and starting to break down. I felt I could finally let go because nobody was around to see me. The dry was almost empty, but I'll never forget the one guy that came and sat beside me, Bob James. Sometimes it's good to have company. I did appreciate that.

In those days there was no such thing as stress leave, counselling or therapy. About all that happened was some guys would take you out to the bar and you'd get drunk for a couple of days. Jack Glennie kept an eye on me and would come to my place and talk. He was a great guy, a real caring man.

For years, just about every day and night, I relived that shift and the feelings of regret and guilt that came with the memories. Now that more than thirty years have passed, it's not so bad. That old memory filter is working. Now I remember only every three or four days.

Struggle and Emerge
After Mike died I found myself at a crossroads, wondering whether I was going to stay at mining or get on with some other endeavour. I guess my

desire to be a miner overcame any inhibitions that I had. The Notre Dame motto *Luctor Et Emergo*, Struggle and Emerge, was enough to keep me at it. And I'm glad I did.

I was fortunate to be placed with two experienced miners in the years after Mike. First there was Hungry Hughes, who had a work ethic that was second to none and a good-natured way about him to boot. He was always laughing, no matter what was going on or how hard the job was. I learned a lot from Hungry.

The best miner I ever worked with was Ralph Blaney, my partner after Hungry. They were two totally different people with two different ways of doing things.

Ralph was very patient with me. He would just smile and chuckle as I went through my rookie tirade of swearing and throwing stuff when things weren't going right. With his calm persona, he would suggest that I go and retrieve whatever tool I had just thrown down the raise in a fit of anger, pointing out that we were probably going to need it shortly. I believe a certain amount of Ralph's calmness rubbed off on me and I think a couple more years with him would have completed it. He did teach me to laugh at my silly antics and myself.

I did finally learn not to throw things that I was going to need so when I was working in mechanized mining, operating a bolter, I had a little piece of ladder about three feet long that I kept nearby. I would throw it in moments of madness and it worked. You've got to do what you've got to do.

My gratitude to those two guys will always be there. Their patience and understanding kept me in mining, and I thank them. I couldn't have asked for two better "pards."

After I had gained some experience, Cominco decided I was ready to take a green partner on, and so an onslaught began. There were some that were just plain dumb and should never have had a chance to work underground, never mind being miners. They were quickly weeded out and put on other duties more in line with their capabilities.

But Bob Gyurkovits was a good one, a keeper if you will. Bob's a big bugger, six four and two hundred and forty pounds, a size that was good for hanging pipe but horrible when it came time to drill the second round in a drawhole "three by five." I remember fondly as I stood at the face in a sub, six by six, drilling on my round, the screaming and swearing coming from behind me down the sub as Bob, on his hands and knees, tried to collar the back holes three feet off the footwall. The stoper was throwing Bob all over the place but, hey, I was the senior guy.

I used to screw around with Bob when I got him right out of mining school. We'd be up a raise and I would tell him that the first guy finished drilling always got the powder and fuse. I would always be a way ahead of him most of the shift, but near the end of the shift, he would pass me and he would be laughing at me. Then away he would go, down the raise, to get the powder and fuse. I've got to give him credit. He would jam his bib overalls with rolls of fuse and I-cord then haul up two bags of powder, fifty pounds each, using nothing but rope to get up to the face.

I usually had the gear put away in the tool cache and was having a smoke while I watched Bob huffing and puffing up the raise. He would be just giving it shit, happier than hell that he beat me at getting drilled off. I let him beat me for some time before I told him that I cut my throttle back to half speed so he could win. That kind of took the thunder out of him. Looking back, he finds it kind of funny, but he was pretty disbelieving when I first told him. It's good to nail the rookies, keeps them humble.

While he was a rookie, I had Bob convinced that I was the most important person in his life, more important than his wife or God. He always brought me a Burnt Almond chocolate bar. He was a good partner and, under my tutelage, became a very competent miner.

I enjoyed all the time I worked with Bob but there came a time when I had to shove him out of the nest and he was on his own. He did okay. Bob became a shift boss and was the last foreman in the Sullivan Mine.

Behind the Shifters' Desk
The Company in its wisdom deemed that I would do well as a shift boss and so it was to be. I have to admit I was pretty darn excited and honoured to be asked to go on staff, but the lustre faded. It took three years. Big John Ekskog pretty much groomed me for the job. I guess he saw some leadership qualities in me, or else they were having a difficult time recruiting shift bosses, because there were a hell of a lot more qualified people out there than me.

Becoming a shift boss, you immediately take a huge cut in pay, no more contract money, just a monthly cheque. So if you are happy being able to call yourself a shift boss and you are willing to take a cut in pay of $20,000 to $40,000 a year, you go for it. Shifting is a good job for guys that are screwed up physically or getting on in age, but I saw too many young guys going shifting who were just plain lazy. It was a good way, though, to get them out of the way of the miners who wanted to work.

The Company would not pay to get good frontline supervisors in the last decade before the mine's closure, so they made frontline supervisors out of guys who had never mined. We were very lucky that nothing serious occurred as a result. Glorified bookkeepers was all they were, with little respect from the men or the Company. I would have found it unbearable to be on staff during that period. But enough of that.

I started shifting in 1977 at No. 2 Shaft section for Big John Ekskog. I have to admit that I liked working for him but you had to be on your toes. He would go with you on your run, where you visit all the headings and the guys working there. He wouldn't say anything about what he observed but when he got you in the shifters' lunchroom, he sure as hell would let you know in no uncertain terms about certain gaffes. It was darn hard to concentrate on your sandwich with that big bugger climbing all over your frame. But you got used to it and he didn't play favourites, he did it to everyone. One thing you could always count on was that Big John would back you up. Tell him the truth and he was there for you.

I was spare shifting just before I went on permanent staff. One Monday morning, while I was behind the shifters' desk dispersing my crew, Big John came up to me and asked me to pull Mel Olsen off the coaches which were parked in the yard waiting for the seven o'clock whistle to go underground. I was to send Mel home for missing Friday afternoon shift. Hell, Mel missed every Friday afternoon shift. To make it worse, Mel and his brother Gordie were my cross shift in the heading that I worked in when I wasn't shifting. The Olsens are not lightweights. They're both around six foot four and weigh at least two fifty. Plus, there were at least fifty guys on the coaches to bear witness to what was going to occur. Bloody wonderful.

So, with one look back at Big John hoping for a reprieve and all the other shifters and foremen watching, out the door I go. There was no give from Big John. He gave me a job to do and expected me to do it.

Bill Roberts, shift boss, underground in front of jeep. Surveyor, Murray Bray, in background.
Courtesy Bill Roberts

– 263 –

I felt like the loneliest person on the planet as I crossed the yard to summon Mel off the coaches. All conversation ceased as I approached. I'm pretty sure the boys knew what was up. "Mel," I said, hoping my voice didn't crack or I didn't show too much sweat, "I've got to send you home for missing last Friday." "No problem, Billy boy," he says and jumps off the coach with his bucket. "Just phone me when I should come back." I couldn't believe it because Big Mel didn't mind giving you a piece of his mind when the urge arose, which was rather frequently.

At another time and another encounter with Mel, Big John told me to give him a job performance for missing shifts. Just as before, I was spare shifting and Mel and Gordie were my cross shift. I had every expectation that when I presented Mel with his job performance, he would tear it up in front of me and tell me where I could shove it. So, thinking I would outsmart him, I made two identical job performances so when Mel ripped one up, I could wave the second one at him and enjoy a small victory, however small it might have been.

Into the sub I went, full of determination, until I stood before the Olsen boys. Those guys are big. The two of them had me surrounded and I didn't want to make any quick moves. I didn't want to startle them. Slowly I brought out Mel's job performance and handed it to him. I believe I blurted out, "This isn't my idea, Mel. It's Big John's," as I quickly tried to divert any blame from myself. Self-preservation was a factor. Mel glanced over it, then at Gordie. Mel asked, "Have you got a pen, Billy boy?" "I do. I do," I blurted. Mel signed and handed it back to me. "Will that be it? If so, could you just bugger off 'cause Gordie and I've got a round to blast." That's the way it was. You just never knew.

When I finally got on as a full-time shift boss, life got interesting at times. I was on my run, going around visiting my crew, which was usually made up of between fifteen and twenty-five guys. As I walked into this sub, I could hear two fellows, partners at the time, hollering at each other. Each one held a 12-inch crescent wrench in his hand and they were just about ready to go at it. I can't remember what the argument was about. One fellow was older and spoke broken English. I believe his name was Otto and the other fellow was Mike. Mike had some mental issues. I took them out to see John Ekskog and both were sent home.

I wrote in my report that I didn't believe Mike should be allowed underground again as I didn't think he was mentally capable of working in the underground element. I suggested that a job on the surface would be more appropriate. The Company put him on the loading crew where long-holes are loaded with powder to be blasted. Mike managed to squirrel some powder away and blew himself and his Cranbrook apartment up. I guess I was right in my observation.

One afternoon shift, Jack Jenkins and I were having lunch in the shifters' shack on 3350 Level when an urgent call came in to report that a man had possibly gone down the ore dump.

Stu Tiffin, a hot-muck miner from the Centre Section, had gone into the No. 2 Section to transfer hot muck on its way to the 2800 Crusher. The miner controls the bypass, or drop of the muck, from one level to another by operating an air tugger that lifts large chains that stop the muck from flowing. Stu had already bypassed the ore above him on the 3800 Level down to the 3500 Level, where it would be stopped by another set of large chains.

All these measures in the transfer of hot muck were necessary because of the heat, dust and sulphur dioxide that are freed each time the muck is moved. You try to mix cold muck with the hot so it would be easier to handle when it got to the crusher.

As events went, I guess Stu was in the middle of the track at the dump doors when in came an ore train to dump its load. Stu tried to flag the motorman down but when the dump doors opened, he was enveloped by hot-muck dust and steam. When the motorman last saw him, Stu was attempting to put on his respirator.

The motorman, who was also covered in hot dust and gas, stopped the train just before he got to the dump block and crawled to an old lunchroom, where he passed out for awhile. When he came to, he shut the dump doors and backed the train up. After an unsuccessful search to find Stu, he told his shifter what had happened and headed off to first aid. The shifter then phoned in the report to me.

Jack Jenkins, who was the afternoon blast-hole loader boss, and I immediately headed out to offer assistance. We took the No. 1 skip from the level we were on up to 3500. On each level is a box containing a 50-foot cable safety ladder weighing about two hundred pounds. There was no loci motor to transport the ladder so we got a 6-foot drill steel, strung it through the ladder, hoisted it up on our shoulders and headed off to No. 2 Shaft, about a half mile away.

Jack had a good thirty years on me but both of us were exhausted and literally on our knees when we got to the dump. I moved the motor from the train up to the dump doors and we hooked the cable ladder to the motor and dropped it into the dump. Then I climbed down to see what I could see. The muck was a long way down and I couldn't see the top of it or Stu. The sulphur dioxide, heat and fog were almost unbearable.

Climbing back up that free-swinging ladder was something else. I felt myself getting weaker. If it hadn't been for Jack pulling on my safety rope, there was a good chance there would have been two bodies to remove. With the adrenalin running and not thinking straight, I almost compounded the problem by not thinking about important things like breathing apparatus or getting more help. I just went for it. I was lucky.

After trying to explore the dump that Stu went down, I stopped all trains from dumping on all levels and put guards on all the dumps. Then I phoned Superintendent Brian Buckley and the section foreman, John Ekskog. By this time, approximately eighty cars of muck had been dumped down the ore pass where Stu was.

It wasn't until nine the next morning that we retrieved Stu's body from just above the 2800 Crusher. It was a very sombre group of miners that escorted him out to the No. 1 skip, where he left the Sullivan for the last time. A nicer man would be hard to find. Stu was forty years old.

My second year of shifting was spent at the North End section. Harvey McDonald was the foreman. Harvey was a nice man but he had his favourites, and we really got into it one time. Dickie Allesio and Sec Semenzin were working on my crew as slusher miners. One Friday afternoon shift, they didn't come out to work or call me with any kind of an excuse. The policy was that the shifter would write up a job performance on them and it would go on their record. No big deal, so I did it.

Monday morning, I showed the job performances to Harvey and he told me to rip them up, so I did. The next week, Rudy Swirsky missed a shift and Harvey wanted to know why there was no job performance on him. I told Harvey that if the other two guys didn't get them then neither did Rudy. Harvey didn't like that but it didn't matter. I wasn't going to give Rudy a job performance. It was little inequities like that that made me ask for a transfer to mechanized mining when it was just starting up. I felt I was at a deadend in the North End section.

Stinie Vander Maaten was the foreman in mechanized. Here was one guy I didn't mind working for. He knew his mining, his men, and he was honest with his crew. You just didn't want to cross him twice or you were going to hear about it.

At the time I was president of Local 8320, the supervisors' union that was just starting up. Now this was a job that nobody wanted and, as I went along, I could see why. We had all the frontline supervisors in Kimberley signed up. I believe there were about seventy-five of us. The Trail supervisors were another story. From what I could see, it was the pinnacle of life for an individual to become a frontline supervisor in Trail and, because of their concern about job repercussions, we couldn't get them to commit to joining us. They were scared. I was embarrassed for them. I think all the guys in Kimberley were. What an awful way to live your life — afraid.

So there I was, president of a union with bargaining coming up, shift boss in mechanized where I'm telling guys what to do when I don't even know how to turn on the equipment they run, and going home with an attitude that wasn't very welcome. I was getting ready to bail. My wife, Sandra, could see where all this was going. I wasn't a nice person to be around anymore. Sandra put it pretty bluntly. Get off shifting or live alone, so I bailed out.

Being a supervisor and a union leader just weren't for me. Other people are good at that kind of stuff but I wasn't. When I got back on a stoper driving a sub, it was like the weight of the world left my shoulders. I was back where I belonged.

From Hot Muck to Mechanized

I mined conventionally for awhile with Hunky Perih. Hunky was one of those guys who are on every committee going. He could miss work, go to a meeting and still get paid.

One time Hunky and I were setting up in a drawhole, building a platform to drill on. I guess we were in a hurry to get going so we didn't have any ventilation with us and we didn't blow the gas out with an air hose. We both came to in the sub about fifteen feet below. The carbon monoxide had knocked us out and down we went. It's a good thing we didn't fall through the collar of the drawhole at the same time because we would have got hung up. Hunky was a little bigger than a boxcar, fun to work with when he was there, but I got used to working alone.

One Friday on afternoon shift, I mentioned to Hunky that I wasn't feeling too good but I was going to tough it out. I was working up a drawhole drilling when Hunky waved his light at me to shut down. "What's the problem?" I asked. "I'm soaked. I fell into that deep puddle in the sub. I've got to go home." And away he went. I'm pretty sure he did a belly flop into the puddle just in case I went home before him. I stayed and Hunky went home. I should never have told the Hunk that I was ill.

A chance came up to go work in the hot muck, something that I wanted to do. I was sent to No. 2 Shaft in the 308 Block. This proved interesting. I saw things I never thought possible. I saw a rock so hot you could see the scraper bucket right through it. You could see the molecular structure moving in the rock. I saw lead running out of a drawhole and into the sub like water, just like lava from a volcano. It was really something to see.

Certainly the stage for disaster was always set but the crews sent into these areas were mostly experienced people. There were safety systems in place that were generally adhered to and the miners could improvise on a spot's notice. None of the guys in there were greenhorns.

The moon-suits we wore in the hot muck were made of asbestos. This enabled you to go into the sub and work in extreme heat. You also had an oxygen tank on your back that, together with the suit, became pretty damn cumbersome. Just after the moon-suits became the thing to wear, we found out that asbestos was bad for you and they were taken away. So between wearing asbestos suits and breathing SO_2 gas and dust, it's little wonder so many of the older miners, whose lungs were already damaged from years of mining, didn't last very long once they retired.

After the asbestos suits were withdrawn, the new clothing issued was a fire-resistant coverall in either green or gray, take your choice. It was pretty obvious who worked in the hot muck because we looked as if we were wearing some type of military outfit. In some ways, I guess we were an army of sorts.

The Company paid for all our clothing in the hot muck. You had to get all-wool clothing to wear under your overalls: wool shirt, underwear, socks, everything. If you got trapped and covered in hot-muck dust, supposedly none of these clothes would melt and stick to your skin. Well, as I have already said, I hate wool against my skin so I substituted a nice comfortable cotton-polyester outfit. The way I looked at it, I was going to lose my skin either by having this wonderful thermal underwear stuck to it as I turned into a crispy critter or I was going to peel it off with my fingernails, scratching because of that damn wool underwear. I took my chance. I won.

Our footwear was the best money could buy: top-name high-top leather boots costing well over the $100 range. Those boots might last three months once the hot-muck dust got on them. When you add a little bit of water, it's instant sulphuric acid. Good-bye boots. The Company was not cheap by any means when it came to safety in the hot muck. We just sent them the bill when it came to clothes and putting in safeguards. But I wonder if they ever really understood what the consequences were to a man's health. But, hey, we were miners. That's what we did.

The end of the hot muck came and I put my name in to go to mining school in mechanized mining. It wasn't hard to see that this was the future in mining. I finally got a chance to learn how to run a scoop and drill with a jumbo. When I was a shift boss that had never happened. Mechanized mining really eliminated the physical part of mining. It wasn't hard to tell who was a conventional miner and who was a mechanized miner. The conventional miners looked in good shape and the others started to look like Pillsbury doughboys. The mechanized mining devoured the ground. It was easy to see the demise of the old way of mining.

My first partner when I came out of school was Mike Boucher. Mike had been a mechanized miner his whole career. He was probably one of the best mechanized men at the time and probably the best man around on a jumbo. He taught me a lot. I went with various guys after Mike. The most enjoyable was Gordie Olsen. We had a lot of laughs.

One time, Gordie came into our heading late. He had been at a meeting while I had been drilling on the jumbo. He shook his light for me to shut down. "Get your safety glasses and chinstrap on. I think we're in for it now," he announced. I'm wondering what the hell he's done now. Gordie was a shop steward and on the grievance committee at the time so he had to be careful about his work habits, so naturally, as his partner, so did I.

What Gordie had done was give our shift boss, Dick Lofstrom, a reprimand. He told me he really wasn't mad at Dick but at this other guy, an inexperienced miner who came to the Sullivan with all these other inexperienced miners from Sudbury [Ontario] when the mine there was doing some culling. The people Cominco sent to hire the Sudbury miners had absolutely no idea what qualifications to look for. Christ, did we ever get some gems. They finally smartened up and sent miners down to hire miners.

Now, this guy that Gordie was after was also a shop steward at the time. He came to Gordie and said he wanted off the shop steward job so he could go on the union safety committee where he could help more people. Gordie okayed it and said go right ahead. The next day, when Gordie came to work, there was this guy standing behind the shifters' desk. He was made a spare shifter. All he wanted to do was show the Company he had no more union connections. Gordie had no problem with a guy wanting to go on staff. All he had to do was tell the real reason, not all this other bullshit. So when the opportunity came along to stick the guy, Gordie jumped on it.

A man-carrier from the lower levels had broken down so the carrier from the top levels went down to pick up the men at the end of the shift. When it got back to the upper level, it could hold only about half the crew there so the other half stayed underground until the man-carrier returned. Dick Lofstrom and the Sudbury guy, who were both shifting, went out in their Toyota jeep to report off to the incoming supervisors.

But there is a rule in the Ministry of Mines rulebook that says no people shall be underground without someone with a shift boss certificate being present. So there it was. No shifter underground. Gordie quickly leapt on this infraction of the Mines Act. When he got to the surface, he demanded some reprimand slips from Dick Lofstrom, explaining that he intended to use them to report the two shifters for contravening the Mines Act. The foreman,

Bob Gyurkovits, got the reprimand slips and was stuck with what to do about them. It never got beyond that stage.

Big Gord and I had one hell of a laugh about this but we had to watch out for a few days until it blew over. It was never dull working with Gordie. You just never knew what was around the corner.

After a couple of years, Gordie and I split up. I had the chance to go on a brand-new bolter that the Company had bought for almost half a million dollars and Gordie went on the timber gang to get off graveyard shift. Like he said, "Graveyard is only for hookers and bakers." I really liked the bolter. I worked on my own and at my own pace. The money was there if you went after it, and I did.

The bolter was a diesel-driven, four-wheel-drive piece of equipment capable of bolting and screening even the most severe ground. This unit, when used properly for what it was designed for, was one hell of a machine.

I would drill a 6-foot, one and a half-inch hole then use the bolt driver to install a split-set bolt, which expands as you drive it into the hole. The bolt driver, mounted on its own drill, can even pound bolts into holes that cave in as you drill. Both drills are fed by ninety pounds of air pressure.

On an average day, I could usually drive 120 to 150 bolts and install ten to twelve of the 7- by 10-foot screens that the bolts hold to the rock. I really loved this job and enjoyed going to work. But, like they say, don't get too comfortable. Change came with a demoralizing affect.

At the time, the Company was having a difficult job getting mining engineers of good quality to stay. I think they could see the approaching demise of the Sullivan and believed it wasn't in their own best interest to be on a sinking ship. So the Company decided to name the most senior engineer at the mine as the new mine manager. I don't know if Dave McMurdo pursued this position or if it was thrust upon him but as time would tell, he was unsuitable for the job. Dave was a nice enough guy but he was a geologist, not a mining engineer. He had no idea how to handle a couple hundred miners. He slowly lost the confidence of the men. Perhaps what did it was when he gave up too much of his control to a new engineer from the States. The new guy was the assistant mine manager and he probably did more harm to the Sullivan than any ten people put together.

This pretender wore a mantle of arrogance and pettiness, complemented by a pair of silly little high-heeled cowboy boots that shouted: "Yeah, I know how to handle you assholes." There wasn't a man at the Sullivan who had any respect for this fellow. He demanded it but it was not forthcoming, except from those few who kowtowed to him.

The bolter machine that I was operating was effectively shut down for a year because of management's decision to switch from a split-set bolt to a Swellex bolt. The split-set bolt could be hammered into a caved-in hole or cracked ground but the Swellex bolt, which expands with water pumped into it, would only go into a clean straight hole. Swellex bolts are pushed into the hole very gently, but being gentle is great only if you are a heart surgeon.

The Atlas Capco engineer and the mechanic who came to convert the bolter over to Swellex bolts said this was one of the dumbest ideas they had ever heard of, but it was $50,000 for their company, so on it went.

So the lay engineer from the "Show Me State" would come in and see how we were doing. We would show him. We showed him that on a good day we would get maybe ten or twelve bolts in and one screen on, compared to a hundred and fifty or more bolts and ten or twelve screens in a shift. I believe he figured we were conspiring against him. We weren't. For an entire year, because of his arrogance, good bolting and screening were not being done, and a lot of miners' headings were not being bolted and screened so they sat idle until one of the other two bolters could get to them.

The best thing that happened during this period of dismay was that Bob Jacko arrived to take over from Dave McMurdo. Bob was a miner and could speak "miner talk." We finally had a competent man at the helm when he was made mine manager. Dave McMurdo was transferred to a Cominco operation in Chile and the wannabe hung around for awhile but his input was quickly diminished. I can only hope he learned something by being around Bob Jacko. He needed to grow up a bit and change his attitude a whole lot.

After the year in purgatory, work became fun again. I had great cross shifts in Normie Beaton, Mac Thompson and Carl Johansen. We worked well together and we made damn good money.

It would be remiss of me not to recognize the great mechanics who looked after the bolter and the other mechanized equipment. John Strong and Gordie Mudie, the mechanics on my shift, kept that machine running. I knew how to operate it but these guys could fix it. They were fantastic. My cross shift had Danny Sivorot and Mel Ricketts, same thing. There was nothing better than to see those guys show up in their Toyota, drag out their box of tools and say, "So what did you screw up now?" We owe them a lot.

After thirty-eight years, it was time for me to pack it in. I started having physical problems from years of working underground. I needed surgery for a rotator cuff injury, and for a number of years I had the old miner's disease, carpal tendonitis and white hand. Along with all that, my health was deteriorating.

It became harder and harder to go to work and enjoy it. My wife, Sandra, could see it. Finally she said, "You've done enough. It's time for you to retire from this work," and so I did.

But, like all those guys before me said, "I'd do it again if I could" and, by God, I would. I do miss it. It was good work.

"If there is one thing better than the thrill of looking forward, it is the exhilaration that follows the finishing of a long and exacting piece of work."

From Alex Waugh's *On Doing What One Likes*

JOHN, NICK, JIMMY & ENZO

It could'a happened...

When I tell people that I believe in strange phenomena such as the little people, ghosts, wizards and such things, they look at me with leery, skeptical expressions that I choose to ignore. Maybe it's my Celtic roots coming to the fore but that's the way it is with me, and I wouldn't change it for a minute.

I t was a couple of hours into my shift and I was running a drilling machine called a Tamrock bolter. My job was to secure the ground for further mining once the development miners had drilled, blasted and mucked out. Before any more advancement could take place at a heading, I went in with the bolter to put up 7- by 10-foot screen mesh secured with 6-foot bolts that are impossible to pull out.

This bolter drills seven-foot 1½" holes and inserts split-set bolts. It is also used for screening.

The bolter is a unit about forty feet long that runs on large rubber tires and has a diesel engine. It has drills that run on air pressure and a water hook-up that washes out the drill cuttings and eliminates as much dust as possible. In the 1990s, it was just about the slickest piece of mining equipment underground.

I was standing on the deck of the bolter where I could operate the hydraulic controls while watching the drilling and

keeping an eye on the ground under the glare of the machine's halogen lights. I had my bucket open on the seat behind me and was having a sandwich and a cup of coffee. As I turned to refill my cup, I noticed what appeared to be lights sixty or seventy feet down the drift. Then they disappeared. I thought they must have been caused by my cap lamp shining on water dripping from the back and didn't think any more about it as I turned back to the controls.

I was immersed in what was going on and enjoying my cup of coffee when I felt the hair on the back of my neck rising. This is a warning to a miner that something is going on around him and it's time to take note.

As I turned to look behind me, I was startled, to say the least, to find four figures watching the machine and me.

"Jesus Christ! You scared the hell out of me," I bellowed. "Who the hell are you and where did you come from?" Although I thought I knew everyone in my vicinity, I didn't recognize any of the apparitions standing there.

I turned off the drill so I could speak to these strangers. From where I stood up on the deck of the machine, about four feet above these guys, I couldn't help but notice their dress. Cloth hats with carbide lamps, clothes that looked different from what most miners wore. I knew then I had a situation that was going to have to be addressed.

Once the initial shock had worn off, even though my neck hair was still at attention, I jumped down from the

Author at controls of abolter under a protective canopy.
Courtesy Bill Roberts

bolter and extended my hand. "Hiya, boys. My name's Bill."

The tallest of the group stuck out a large hand that engulfed mine. "My name is John Moran," he said in a strong English accent. "My partners are Nick Yavolski, the Pole. The little mick there is Jimmy Ward. He's Irish. And

Miners in 1913. This was probably one of the first pictures ever taken undergound at the Sullivan Mine.

the other guy is Enzo Cavalli. I kind'a think he might be Italian. He doesn't speak any English but he's a good worker. What are you?"

Shaking hands with the others, I managed to blurt out, "I'm Canadian."

After the introductions, I just had to ask the question. "Where did you guys come from?"

John the Englishman pointed his light back to where they had come from and said, "There's a hole back there with ladders coming down. That's where it is we came from."

I knew the hole he was speaking of because I was using it as a travel-way. At the top of the ladder was the 3900-foot level, the original drift into the mine. It was started in 1915 and at its completion was 11,500 feet long. The drift I was working in was about twenty feet below, running parallel with it. We were mining country that was first worked in the early part of the twentieth century.

The little Irish guy, Jimmy, said, "Yes, we're working just up above you. We're in about eight thousand feet from the portal."

That got me because I knew the drift went a lot further than that. "Just what year are you in right now?" I questioned.

"Why, 1917," says John. "What year are you in?"

"1998," I responded.

There was a long pause as the five of us, even Enzo who couldn't speak English, grasped that something was amiss.

"Well, boys," I said, "there seems to be a difference of eighty-one years here."

Having pointed this out, I could see it was of little concern to them. The fellows were much more interested in exploring the bolter. A couple were up on the deck looking at the controls, the steering wheel, instruments, even my bucket and Thermos. The guys on the ground were examining the engine, tires and drill, but when it came to my bag of bits lying on the ground, I could see big interest.

I told them about the tungsten bits and explained how long it took to drill a hole and how many holes one bit could drill in this ground. They must have thought I was BSing from the skeptical looks I was getting.

"It sometimes takes us sixty steel to drill one hole, depending on the ground," John said.

The steel they were using was just sharpened steel, whereas I had interchangeable bits and could use the same steel for an indefinite time. I let them take turns drilling. I could see their awe each time they drilled a hole — the open mouths and wide eyes, looking at each other, shaking their heads, grinning.

Finally, Big John stuck out his hand and said, "Thanks, Bill, but we've got a round to pull and we better get back to our heading."

The other fellows shook my hand and followed John back down the drift. I stood there for a second and then yelled, "Hold on! I want to see what you're doing."

I scurried after them and we all went up the ladder to 3900 Level. I couldn't believe it. Where I was used to walking was now solid ground.

At the face was a liner, also known as a drifter drill. These drifters weighed a hundred and fifty pounds plus, unmounted. The drill was mounted on a bar and arm arrangement. The column bar was tightened into place between the footwall and the back of the tunnel with a threaded screw. The drill itself was clamped to an arm on the bar and was fed forward by hand turning a feed screw and crank mechanism. The holes were drilled dry.

There was a stack of used steel on a flatcar behind the drill, and piles of sharpened steel lined the drift. The used steel would be taken to the blacksmith shop outside. I could see that the track was 18-inch gauge. The electric motor used for transportation was a two and a half-ton Jeffrey, a type still being used in my day. Off to the side was a cumbersome-looking machine called a Myers Whalley Shovelling Machine, one of the first mucking machines and a technological advance that eliminated hand mucking, a job every self-respecting miner hated.

The roar of the drill being fired up drew me back to the face. Enzo and Jimmy were running the drill. Being good miners, they didn't let something like running into me hold them up. The most important thing to real miners is pulling the round. Nick was bringing up new steel and taking the dull ones back to the flatcar.

From the way he just stood around and watched, it dawned on me that the English guy, John, was some kind of boss, maybe a shifter or a foreman. And he had one of those little hand-picks in his hand, sort of a status symbol that was present even at times during my career. Miners knew where the bosses could stick that.

I stood and watched for awhile. When they shut down to change steel, I asked how much an hour do guys get paid. (I had to ask again because these guys were really deaf. I noticed none of them wore any ear protection. In those days, miners took pride in the bare ear.)

Early Days Drilling Set-up

An early bar and arm set up.

Jimmy, the little mick, answered, "We get $3 a day and $1 metal bonus, but we have to pay fifty cents a day room and board to the bunkhouse at the portal. Now if you're finished asking questions, will you let us get back to work?" And with that, he threw on the throttle. My type of guy, not here to socialize.

Reluctantly, I started back to the hole with the ladders. I turned once to wave good-bye with my lamp. They were gone. All that I could see was the completed 3900 Level… all 11,500 feet of it.

When I got back to the bolter and my cold coffee, I could see the lights of my shifter's Toyota jeep approaching. As the shifter and foreman got out, I was undecided whether to tell them what I'd just witnessed.

Then I thought, "Why the hell not? It could'a happened."

THE MEDAL FOR BRAVERY: MINING'S VICTORIA CROSS

The Medal for Bravery is recognized as the Canadian mining industry's equivalent to the Victoria Cross, the Commonwealth's highest award for military bravery.

Founded in 1933 by Everett Collins, a past president of the Canadian Institute of Mining, Metallurgy and Petroleum (CIM), to recognize great valour, the medal is awarded only in cases where a miner or other mining worker knowingly risks his life in attempting to rescue a fellow worker.

CIM's Medal for Bravery Committee may recommend "no award" if the evidence submitted does not reveal an outstanding act of bravery. The committee may also recommend two or more awards in a year if circumstances warrant.

The first Medal for Bravery was awarded in 1935; the most recent in 1995. (At the time of writing, no medal has been awarded since 1995.) In total, CIM has awarded 155 medals — 105 of which were awarded in a single year to the Nova Scotia draegermen (mine rescuers) who recovered miners' bodies in the Westray Mine disaster of 1992.

The Medal for Bravery has been awarded to three men from the Sullivan. Here are their stories.

WILLIAM H. "BUD" CHILDRESS AND GUS K. ELIUK

It was February 20, 1953, and Bud Childress and his partner, E. Olson, were drilling a small pillar underground in the Sullivan Mine. They had nearly finished the job. In fact, they were drilling their last hole when the pile of muck they were standing on started to move. Although they didn't know it,

Above: Gus Eliuk; William Childress photo not available.

the muck was hung up, and the water they were using to settle the dust and cool their drills was loosening it.

The pile of muck began to move down into a raise, which had a chute below it. Olson was carried down the raise and into the chute, along with the muck. Fortunately for Olson, as Bud started to slide down, he was able to grab the air hose of the drill and pull himself free of the downward cascade.

Bud shouted down to his partner, "Are you okay?" From far below came Olson's answer, "Yes, okay."

Bud sized up the situation. He decided it would be impossible to bring Olson up the raise. The muck had completely closed over him in the chute. So he went down the man-way, a distance of about forty-five feet, to the drift where the chute was located. There he met Gus Eliuk and told him what had happened.

They went to the chute where Olson was trapped and were able to talk to him, but they couldn't see him because the chute was full of muck. They decided the only way to rescue Olson was through the chute, so they started digging through the muck with their hands. By digging carefully, they managed to make a hole just big enough for a man to crawl through.

Bud and Gus climbed up through the narrow hole and found Olson about fifteen feet up the raise, buried to his waist. The muck had apparently hung up again, thus saving Olson from being buried completely.

Without a thought for their own safety, they started digging to free Olson, knowing that at any moment the hang-up could let go and the muck would cascade down on them. They managed to free the trapped man and take him very carefully out through the escape hole to the chute platform.

Their actions in rescuing Olson from almost certain death were reported to the chairman of the Medal for Bravery Committee. As a result, Bud Childress and Gus Eliuk joined the select group of Canadians who have received the award.

RALPH "SWEDE" WALLIN

Swede started as a labourer at the Sullivan's surface workings in 1946. In December of that year, he was transferred underground as a mucker. Then he became a chuteman on transportation; his job was to load ore cars. That move set the stage for the life-saving rescue he was to perform a year after starting work at the mine.

It was August 19, 1947. David Brown and his partner, Albert "Hap" Richardson, were going about their usual business underground, surveying, when suddenly a surge of wet muck caught them and swept them into a raise.

David Brown was unable to save himself and was carried down to his death. Hap, on the other hand, caught hold of a short piece of protruding pipe near the top of the raise and was able to hang on. As it turned out, the surge of muck was of short duration and, even in his semi-conscious condition, Hap was able to retain his hold until help arrived.

That help came from Swede Wallin, who was working at the muck chute in the drift far below. Swede heard the call for help and, giving no thought to a probable further surge of wet muck, climbed sixty feet up the 45-degree raise, with only the pieces of broken ladders and planks left hanging after the surge to support himself. Through his effort, he was able to relieve Hap and call for further help. Lloyd Searle arrived to help carry the injured man to safety.

Ralph "Swede" Wallin

Swede's quick and courageous action undoubtedly saved Hap Richardson from further and more serious injury. Ralph "Swede" Wallin was awarded the Medal for Bravery in 1948.

MEN WHOSE LIVES WERE
TAKEN IN THE SULLIVAN MINE

According to the Sullivan's archives, seventy-three men were killed underground during the working life of the mine.

The first recorded deaths occurred in 1907 when two miners were killed in an explosion; the last mine fatality took place in 1987 when a miner was killed by a fall of rock.

The greatest number of accidental deaths occurred in the decades between 1920 and 1949. Eleven men were killed in the 1920s, seventeen in the 1930s, and a record twenty-five in the 1940s. In other decades, the number of fatalities never exceeded five in ten years. And, as Mick Henningson points out in the Foreword, the last fourteen years of the mine's operation were fatality-free.

Of the seventy-three recorded deaths, twenty-four were miners, eleven were barmen and four were muckers. Six chutemen and four timbermen died. Five shift bosses and a mine foreman also met their deaths in various accidents, and a mine superintendent was killed by a flying rock.

Men working in non-mining jobs and in trades were not exempt from the dangers of working underground: machinemen, motormen, repairmen, a carpenter, pipeman, trackman, electrician, surveyor's helper, and skiptender all died as a result of accidents at their workplaces. Occupations of four of the dead are not recorded.

The following information is excerpted from the Incident and Accident Reports produced by mine management for the BC Minister of Mines.

1892-1909

WILLIAM ROGERS, machineman. May 1, 1907. Killed by the explosion of a loose piece of powder, which he struck with his pick.

D. McKAY, machineman. May 1, 1907. Killed by the same explosion.

1910-19

HENRY HOGBERG, mucker. June 9, 1919. Deceased caught between the belt and the driving pulley in the rockhouse at the Sullivan Mine; falling down the shaft, cave of ground at the face; run over by skip.

1920-29

E. H. LENDON, mucker. July 18, 1923. Electrocuted when struck by trolley line.

HAROLD HOGBERG, mucker. August 17, 1924. The workman, who was assisting in replacing a tram on the track, crossed between the electric locomotive and a tram. Stepping on the coupling or the bumper, with his carbide lamp in his hat, he came in contact with the trolley wire carrying 550 volts, from which he received the shock which caused his death.

FRITZ STROMBERG, motorman's helper. August 19, 1924. The workman stepped off the electric locomotive while it was in motion, slipped, and was crushed to death.

WILLIAM T. MAW. April 4, 1925. Killed. No details available.

ANGUS LIVINGSTONE, miner. August 3, 1925. The workman died of a fractured skull caused when the top bulkhead fell, crushing his head.

C. PONTONI, miner. October 4, 1926. Mr. Pontoni and others entered a chute because the ore had hung up. A charge was set and they lit the fuse. The ore started to run before Mr. Pontoni could get out of the chute. He was carried sixty feet to the level below. His body was recovered before the blast went off. Mr. Pontoni died of a fractured skull.

ALEX CHISHOLM, helper. December 18, 1926. Alex Chisholm was employed by the Company to clean up the tracks outside the portal. He was an older man, over 70 years of age. Unfortunately, he was slightly deaf and did not hear the ore train coming out of the portal. He was fatally injured when the train ran over him.

JOHN MOEN, miner. September 9, 1927. A fatal accident caused by falling from a ladder. Mr. Moen was using a small plugger about twenty feet off the ground when his ladder broke. The ladder fell, throwing Mr. Moen to the ground and fracturing his skull.

A. PUPPI. November 12, 1927. Killed. No details available.

JOHN MODIC, barman. December 19, 1928. The fatal accident was due to the deceased falling from, or being thrown from, a ladder while barring down. The piece of rock the deceased was working on gave way unexpectedly and either struck him or caused him to lose his balance; the ladder was not moved.

EDWARD KEMP, miner. March 9, 1929. The fatal accident was due to a fall of ground. The deceased was engaged in block holing when a large rock fell from the back and rolled down on the deceased, instantly killing him.

1930-39

THOMAS YOUNG, miner. April 27, 1930. The fatal accident was due to the deceased being crushed by a rock, which rolled down the stope where he was drilling.

EVER BECK, barman. April 30, 1930. The fatal accident was due to the deceased being crushed by a large rock, which he was in the act of barring down.

GUS FRANSO, barman. August 19, 1930. The fatal accident was due to the deceased falling about twenty feet onto the muck pile, fracturing his skull. The deceased was barring down at the time and using a safety rope, which he had secured to a steel, which was inserted and wedged in a drill hole by himself some days prior to the accident. He had been using the rope daily. The wedge had loosened, permitting the steel to pull out of the hole, and so caused the deceased to fall.

ANTONIO F. PELLE, miner. September 20, 1930. The fatal accident was due to the deceased being crushed by ore in a chute. The deceased and his partner had asked the man in charge of the chute drawing to draw the ore from their chute. While this was being done, the chute "hung up." A shot was fired to release it, but without immediate success. Pelle went in to inspect his place and the muck started to run while he was there. The muck carried him down, and it was five and a half hours before he was recovered. He sustained a fractured leg and an injured shoulder; he died of shock* the following day.

(Inspector's additional comments: *While on the subject, it might be permissible to call attention to the masterly manner in which the rescue of Frank Pelle was effected. The man had been carried down into a chute with a sliding mass of broken ore and could not be reached safely from above owing to the possibility of more loose material being brought down on him, while a movement of the ore in the chute would almost assuredly have proved fatal. He could be rescued only after an opening had been cut in the chute bulkhead, which meant that, in addition to six inches of wood, it was necessary to penetrate a steel plate three-quarters of an inch thick. In a very short time, fifty-five men were taking part in the work. Notwithstanding the treatment administered by Dr. Haszard, who had been summoned immediately and climbed in the chute with the rescuers, and excellent hospital care, the man died from shock the next morning.)*

MARK R. COON, barman. August 27, 1931. The fatal accident was due to a fall of ground. The men were engaged in barring down loose pieces of ground and had fired a shot to dislodge a slab. On returning after the shot, they were testing the ground with a pinch bar when another slab broke from directly above them. Coon was killed instantly and Hawke died the following day.

WILLIAM T. HAWKE, barman. August 28, 1931. See previous report.

JOHN OSTERBECK, chuteman. October 14, 1931. The accident was due to the deceased falling down a raise, into which he had gone to recover a pinch bar. This was against the established rules of the Company.

J. DICKSON. June 9, 1932. Killed. No details available.

G. BROWN. June 9, 1932. Killed. No details available.

ALBERT E. WESTNEDGE, miner. November 6, 1933. The fatal accident was due to a fall of ground. The men on the preceding shift had tried to bar down this ground and told the deceased and his partner of its condition. The deceased and partner examined this ground and decided to keep away from the area until the end of the shift, at which time they proposed to blast the loose ground.

NORMAN McIVOR, motorman. January 14, 1934. The fatal accident of December 27, 1933, which resulted in death on January 14, 1934, was due to the deceased being crushed between his motor and the side of the working. His left leg was crushed below the knee. The deceased had stopped his motor to allow another train to switch off his track, then started his motor ahead before the other train had cleared, with the result that the motor driven by the deceased collided with the other train and was derailed. He was crushed as he attempted to jump clear. Normal care on the part of the deceased would have prevented this accident.

JOSEPH A. LEWIS, miner. February 6, 1934. The fatal accident was due to the deceased being carried down a raise where he was engaged in moving loose ore. The ore under him started to move and the deceased was caught and crushed by the moving ore.

ALEXANDER REA, miner. May 10, 1934. The fatal accident was due to a fall of ground when the deceased was engaged in making a trail in a stope. The ground fell from the back, some fifty feet up the slope from the deceased, and some of the rocks rolled down on him.

MELVILLE N. GALLPEN, carpenter. June 25, 1936. The fatal accident was due to the deceased being dragged into a hopper by a conveyor and instantly killed. The deceased had been detailed to make some minor repairs to the bottom of the hopper, and at the same time a mechanic was carrying out repairs on the conveyor, which was shut down for this purpose. The conveyor is driven by an electric motor and all employees engaged in repairs on machinery are required to place a "Not to Go" notice on the switch controlling the machinery on which they are at work. The mechanic removed his notice when he was finished and the electrician threw on the switch, as he was unaware that there was another man still repairing. The deceased had failed to place his own notice on the switch.

ALLAN BRUCE RITCHIE, general superintendent. December 27, 1937. The fatal accident was due to the deceased being struck by a flying rock from a shot in a stope. The deceased had entered the stope by means of a man-way that was not in use, but which was not fenced off, after the men who had spit [lit] the shot had gone to guard the approaches of the regular man-ways into the stope.

HANS A. ANDERSON, miner. August 26, 1938. The fatal accident was due to the deceased falling down a stope and into a raise from a trail. The trail was in good condition and the deceased was not carrying anything to cause him to stumble. His partner heard him approach, singing, and then the noise of him falling down the stope. He was killed instantly.

WILLIAM D. TURNBULL, mine foreman. September 7, 1939. The fatal accident was due to the deceased being carried down a stope by a slide of ore while he and others were examining the place after blasting. His body was recovered the following day.

(Newspaper report of accident: *William Turnbull was caught in a slide of ore that carried him several feet and extinguished his light. Those with him called and he answered that he was alright, but needed a light to see his way out. Before any aid could be given, another slide carried him further down and made rescue difficult. Apprehension spread over the mine and district as time passed until the rescue party was able to get to him. At 4:30 a.m. Friday, he was finally located and it was found that he had passed on.)*

1940-49

MATT PELTO, barman. February 14, 1940. The fatal accident was due to the deceased falling down a raise. He had gone to help another man who had difficulty with large pieces of ore he was barring into the raise. Pelto went on to these rocks to size up conditions and the rocks rolled from under him and carried him down the raise. He was holding a safety rope, but had not secured himself to it and was unable to retain his hold.

JAMES FULTON, barman. November 17, 1941. The fatal accident was due to a fall of ground. The deceased and others were engaged in barring ground that had been blasted when a large slab of ground, which had just been examined and considered safe, fell and killed him instantly and slightly injured two other men. The deceased was an experienced barman and, in addition to his own headlight, was at the time of the accident assisted by another man who operated a special barman's floodlight to make this work as safe as possible.

OIVA SAATELA, miner. March 10, 1942. The fatal accident was due to the deceased being struck by a falling rock while assisting to raise a 33-foot ladder for the purpose of enabling barmen to bar down recently blasted ground. The top of the ladder touched and dislodged some loose rock, which fell on the deceased with immediately fatal results.

DUNCAN WILLIAM McKENZIE, chuteman. March 28, 1942. The fatal accident was due to the deceased being run over by an ore train on which he travelled between transfer chutes. There were no witnesses to the actual accident, but McKenzie was found alongside the train where it was stopped to discharge its load and had apparently fallen off the train or stumbled after stepping off. He died fifteen minutes later.

LEONARD WILLIAM HYSTEAD, chuteman. May 22, 1942. The fatal accident was due to the deceased being crushed between a belt-conveyor and one of its pulleys while engaged in cleaning up spillage from the conveyor. It is believed that his shovel caught in the conveyor and that in trying to recover the shovel, he himself was caught and drawn into the pulley. This conveyor has a speed of only three and one-quarter miles per hour.

MARCO HUMJAN, miner. May 26, 1942. The fatal accident was due to the deceased being poisoned by carbon monoxide in a raise, which had been driven up about forty feet from the 3651 Drift. It was known that the air in this raise was defective and there were notices at the man-way to this effect. The deceased was looking for a timber chain and knew there was one in this raise and went up the man-way despite the notices. He was found unconscious shortly afterwards and given immediate artificial respiration and oxygen but did not recover.

FREDERICK GORDON MEISTER, barman. June 8, 1942. The fatal accident was due to the deceased falling or jumping from a barman's ladder in a stope. A 20-foot ladder was raised and secured by guy ropes and when Meister went up the ladder, he found that one of the guy ropes was tangled at the top of the ladder. When trying to correct the guy rope, the ladder began to sway and the deceased climbed down part of the ladder and jumped off from a height of ten feet to the floor of the stope, where he stumbled and fell over a ledge fourteen feet high. He sustained a fracture of the skull, from which he died shortly after being taken to the hospital.

PETE BUZAN, barman. March 11, 1943. The fatal accident was due to the deceased falling from a ladder and striking his head on a sharp rock. The deceased and his partner were detailed to remove some ore from a hanging wall after a blast. They raised a 30-foot ladder and were drilling a hole with a plugger from the top of the ladder. The hole was in about two feet when the steel stuck in the hole.

The deceased was at the top of the ladder endeavouring to loosen the stuck steel when the ground in front of the ladder came loose unexpectedly, pulling out one of the guy ropes. Due to the broken guy rope, the ladder swung on the back guy rope to the right and fell. The deceased was carried down with the ladder, then thrown clear just before it struck the muck pile. He was killed instantly due to a compound fracture of the skull.

HAROLD SWAN, pipeman. March 11, 1943. The fatal accident was due to a backwards fall into a chute. The deceased was disconnecting a union in a pipeline and was working on the train about ten feet above the edge of the slide into 42124 Raise. He had evidently finished disconnecting the union and had laid his wrenches down then, for some unknown reason, when he stood up, he fell over backwards, slid the ten feet down the slide into 42124 Raise and on down about forty feet to 42124 Chute, where he was found. He died instantly due to a fractured skull.

JOSEPH STARCEVICH, JR., chuteman. June 15, 1943. The fatal accident was due to a collision with a supply train that resulted in severe injuries to the deceased's right thigh. The deceased was driving a single motor pulling six loaded ore cars. He was following a supply train down from the North End to the South End. Both trains were travelling slowly as the supply train intended to stop at 3905. Reports indicate that Starcevich was travelling a little too close and fast behind the supply train and when it stopped was unable to stop in time to prevent a collision.

A large stull (log) extending seven feet over the back end of the last car of the supply train caught and pinned the deceased in the motorman's pit of his motor. He was quickly removed and rendered first aid treatment, which helped to stop the bleeding. The deceased sustained a badly crushed right thigh. He died of shock* ten hours after the accident occurred.

JOSEPH JOHN GRAAS, chuteman. February 20, 1945. The fatal accident was due to loose falling rock striking the deceased. He was barring rocks from the chute when one broke loose and struck him. He was transported to the hospital where he died thirty minutes later.

CLIFFORD LEONARD DEPENCIER, trackman. March 12, 1945. The fatal accident was due to falling down a raise. The deceased was passing by a motor when he slipped and fell down a raise where he died instantly.

MIRKO (MIKE) STARCEVIC, barman. August 27, 1945. The fatal accident was due to falling down a raise. The deceased was barring loose muck on the slide in the course of his duties. He was struck by a rolling rock, which resulted in him falling down a raise.

BRUNO SELLAN, electrician. May 11, 1946. The fatal accident was due to being struck by a timber. The deceased, in the course of his work, stepped off a ladder and was struck by a timber, which had slipped from the hands of miners working in the raise above. His leg was fractured and he died later in the hospital of shock.*

ROLF JOHANSON, miner. October 4, 1946. The fatal accident was due to a fall of rock. The deceased was operating a mucking machine when a large slab of rock fell from the wall behind him and struck him on the head and shoulders, crushing him, which resulted in his instant death.

DANIEL ALEXANDER GILLIS, chuteman. June 23, 1947. The fatal accident was due to misjudgment on the part of the deceased regarding clearance between an ore car and a post. Gillis and the loading crew were instructed to load six cars of muck. Gillis walked ahead of the train and discovered that a high-back flat truck near the switch would have to be shoved clear of the switch in order to load at the chute. The train was moving very slowly and Gillis signalled the motorman to back up. The car had just hit the flat truck when the motorman, who was watching Gillis's light, noticed the light waver and immediately stopped the train.

They heard Gillis groan and on investigation discovered Gillis lying on the right side near a square-set post. He was conscious and asked to be taken to the hospital. He was immediately transported to the surface and was examined and pronounced dead by Dr. J. Haszard. The coroner's jury found the deceased died due to internal injuries caused by a crushing accident.

DAVID HARPER BROWN, surveyor's helper. August 19, 1947. The fatal accident was due to drowning. The deceased and his partner were surveying a diamond-drill hole in the intermediate drift when a rush of mud and water from 39189 Raise caught them. The deceased's body was carried down to the drift below, but the partner managed to hold on to a pipe and remain suspended in the raise, down which the flow ran and which connected the intermediate drift with the main level.

LEONARD ALFRED COND, miner. September 9, 1947. The fatal accident was due to drilling into a hole containing powder. The previous shift had commenced loading the round and had placed a stick of powder in each of three holes. This was not reported to the proper authorities so that it could be brought to the attention of the oncoming shift. The deceased and his partner were instructed to deepen the round and were doing so when the explosion occurred. The deceased was killed instantly.

The miners responsible had their blasting certificates cancelled and were prosecuted and fined for contravention of the provisions of the Metalliferous Mines Regulation Act.

DAVID ERICKSON, timberman. October 22, 1947. The fatal accident was due to a rush of muck and water from the chute at 42119 Raise. The raise was used for storing gravel to be used for concrete underground. The deceased was assisting in drawing the chute and was loosening the packed gravel with a bar when it gave way with a rush, breaking the chute boards, one of which struck him across the abdomen. His body was carried about four hundred feet along 4203 Drift. It is thought that gravel had hung up farther up the raise, damming off a considerable quantity of water, and gave way suddenly, releasing a flow of water and gravel. The deceased was killed instantly.

JOHN CLIFFORD SHEA, repairman. February 4, 1948. The fatal accident was due to the deceased being struck by a travelling crane in the surface crushing plant. The deceased was repairing the chute on the No. 2 Crusher and was lying on the crawl-beam of the crane for this purpose. The crane operator was called to remove a jam in No. 1 Crusher and did not know Shea was on the beam when he moved the crane. The deceased died as a result of his injuries.

GEORGE VICTOR TEWSLEY, inspection crew. February 12, 1948. The fatal accident was due to being crushed. The deceased was a member of the shaft inspection crew. He was instantly killed when he was crushed between the skip and the apron of a loading-pocket in the 3901 Shaft. The deceased and his partner were inspecting the shaft, and he, absorbed in his work, evidently forgot the existence of the loading-pocket.

BRUNO SYLVA PATTYN, stope miner. September 25, 1948. The fatal accident was due to a fall of ground. The deceased and his partner had unsuccessfully attempted to bar a slab down and had decided to blast a hole drilled in it some days before. His partner left to work in another part of the stope, but Pattyn evidently remained behind for a final examination when the slab fell. He perished immediately.

THOMAS SMITH YOUNG, raise miner. November 6, 1948. The fatal accident was due to a fall of ground. The deceased and his partner were barring down the raise, preparatory to drilling, when a piece of rock, estimated at over a ton, fell, striking the deceased and knocking him fifty-seven feet down the raise. He was killed instantly.

ALLAN SCOTT DRUMMOND, engineer/shift boss. March 9, 1949. The fatal accident was due to a fall from a ladder. The deceased fell from a ladder, which gave way while he was descending 39240 Raise. The raise was not a regular man-way but was being examined by the deceased and another shift boss. The deceased fell and rolled about forty feet down a 50-degree slope. He died as a result of multiple injuries.

JOSEPH ALEXANDER CLARK, repairman. April 22, 1949. The fatal accident was due to a cave-in of fine muck. The deceased was buried by a cave-in of fine muck in the No. 1 Fine Chute at the surface crushing plant. He descended the chute on a safety belt to investigate a hang-up when the cave-in occurred. He was dead when extricated, having died of suffocation.

1950-59

DONALD E. McLENAGHEN, skiptender. July 25, 1951. The fatal accident was due to falling into a skipway. The deceased was working at the 3200 Level loading-pocket on the No. 1 Shaft. He was pulling a plank on to the loading platform, when he accidentally struck the control valve, causing the chute gate to drop. He lost his balance, fell into the skipway, and the muck came down on top of him. He died instantly.

LLOYD McLELLAN, timberman. December 4, 1956. The fatal accident was due to carbon monoxide poisoning. The deceased and his partner, Trevor Evans, were assigned the task of removing two old chutes at 36185 Raise. They were provided with a motor and two cars as the muck around the chutes had to be trammed out to the ore dump. The shifter visited the men once and all was well. On his second round, the motor and ore car were gone and he presumed the men were at the dump.

When the men did not report off at the end of the shift, the shifter went in search of them. Following a light, he had to retreat because of bad air. Chemox equipment was put on and the men were recovered from a platform about thirty-six feet up the raise. No pulse was evident but artificial respiration and oxygen therapy were applied until the arrival of the doctor, who pronounced the men dead. All evidence pointed to the fact that the men had thought the platform was a good place to eat lunch as it was out of a strong current of air in the drift below. They had been overcome by a lack of oxygen and had died as a result.

TREVOR EVANS, timberman. December 4, 1956. See previous report.

WILMOT SWANN, timberman. July 28, 1959. The fatal accident was due to injuries sustained in a train collision. An ore train was returning empty with seven ore cars ahead of the locomotive when it was diverted into a side crosscut. The deceased, who was operating a locomotive pushing an explosive car and a flat car in the crosscut, saw the train coming and attempted to run back past his own train to a place of safety after jumping off his locomotive. The collision of the two trains, however, caused the explosive car and the flat car to derail. The deceased was crushed against the side of the roadway. First aid was immediately applied and he was rushed to the hospital, where he subsequently expired.

1960-69

HAROLD DEAN JOHNSON, miner/shift boss. July 3, 1962. The fatal accident was due to a blast caused by drilling into a misfired hole. The deceased was engaged in the development of drawholes above a new scraper drift. The drawhole in which he was working had been driven its full distance before the turnback and the deceased was in the act of drilling the first round of holes on the left side of the drawhole so that a breakthrough could be made to the adjacent drawhole.

He was in the act of collaring the fourteenth hole when the drill apparently entered a bootleg hole approximately four to six inches from the side of the drawhole. This hole had been drilled previously and had been loaded with AN/FO explosive with a primer cartridge and cap, which was struck by the drill. The resulting explosion was heard by a miner working in a nearby drawhole who found the deceased apparently dead from extensive injuries to body and head.

WILLIAM LESLIE PRATT, shift boss. July 18, 1962. The fatal accident was due to a bulkhead on which the deceased was standing being destroyed by a blast from below. He had been supervising the blasting of a bulkhead, which had been placed at a junction. Two miners had been detailed by the deceased to place thirty sticks of explosives below the bulkhead and this charge was connected by primer cord to the stope below. He then left one man at this point to ignite the primer cord while he took the other man to inspect the sublevel, the instructions being he would send word when to blast. While en route to the sublevel, the deceased instructed another miner who was working in the vicinity to warn two miners nearby to retreat to a place of safety. The miner was not aware of where the deceased was going, and assumed he was to inform the blaster when all men were out from the vicinity. This he did, but the blaster took this as a message from the deceased and ignited the charge.

In the meantime, the deceased and the blaster's partner had reached the muck pile where they endeavoured to measure the face of the raise. The other man was back a short distance in the sublevel. When the blast went off, the bulkhead collapsed and the deceased fell with the timber and muck, landing in the stope forty-five feet below. His body was quickly recovered but death must have been instantaneous as there were multiple fractures to the skull with severe brain injury.

MURRAY B. McLEOD, miner. June 8, 1963. The fatal accident was due to burns from the hot muck. The deceased and another miner were working in a scraper drift, which had several draw points to a stope above. The ore in the stope had been broken by forty-five tons of explosives in February 1962, and some heating of the ore had taken place due to spontaneous combustion of the sulphide in the ore. The men were required to wear respirators to protect against any hot dusty conditions and were wearing these on May 15 while they were endeavouring to bar down muck which had hung up in a drawhole. Suddenly there was an outburst of hot air and dust from the drawhole that completely enveloped the two workmen as they attempted to run to safety.

The deceased's mask was momentarily dislodged when he stumbled, but he reported holding his breath while readjusting the apparatus. Both men were burned about the lower part of the body from the knees to the waist and also received severe burns to the hands and face. Both were taken to hospital and responded to treatment and skin grafting.

His partner was discharged about two weeks after the accident, but the deceased, who was burned up to forty per cent of his body, required further treatment. On June 8, he was diagnosed as having an acute hemorrhaging ulcer of the stomach. Blood transfusions were given, but he became progressively worse and died in the evening. It was the medical opinion that this ulcer had been recently formed as a result of the burns.

CYRIL A. GEORGE, barman. February 24, 1964. The fatal accident was due to a fall of rock. The deceased and his partner had been instructed to bar down some loose near a concrete pillar, and they had completed this task and were preparing to leave the area when a quantity of rock, estimated at three tons, fell from the roof and struck him. Medical help was obtained, but it was later determined that death would have been instantaneous and had been caused by multiple skull fractures, crushing chest injuries, and damage to numerous organs.

MICHAEL JOSEPH PETROSKY, miner. June 16, 1964. The fatal accident was due to a fall of rock. The deceased and his partner were in the process of completing the backfilling of a large stope with fill (called float) brought from the sink-float plant on the surface. This float was dumped down a raise near the top of the stope and spread by gravity throughout the stope, except that in the final stages a small tugger hoist and scraper were used to spread the float close to the hanging wall, which had a dip of about forty degrees.

On the day of the accident, the anchor bolts holding the tail block for the scraper cable pulled out and the miners started barring a safe trail so as to reach the location of the anchor bolts, about forty-five feet from the hoist. The back here was about eight feet above the top of the float fill. Several large slabs were barred down by the miners. The deceased had just barred down a slab and was further inspecting the back when another piece of rock fell, hitting him on the head and knocking him down. His partner immediately summoned help, but death must have happened quickly. The deceased was dead on arrival at the hospital. Cause of death was given as due to a crushed skull.

1970-79

MICHAEL LYSOHIRKA, miner. August 30, 1972. The fatal accident was due to a fall of rock. The deceased and his partner had been instructed to continue a short ventilation raise. On arriving at their working place, they found a breakthrough had occurred to the sublevel. The breakthrough had followed a slip plane when the previous round had been placed. In order to render the working place safe, the deceased commenced scaling on the north side of the collar of the raise while the partner, about twenty feet away, was scaling in the vicinity of the breakthrough.

Shortly after commencing scaling, the man at the top of the raise heard a large fall of rock. He called to the deceased to inquire if he was all right, and on not receiving a reply immediately investigated and found his partner partially buried in broken rock. On seeing the deceased was seriously injured about the head and body, he removed him from the fallen ground in order to avoid further injury. The partner obtained assistance without delay, the necessary first aid treatment was applied, and the injured man was taken to the surface and thence to the hospital where he died of his head injuries about five hours after the accident.

JOHN HARRY BROADHURST, electrician. September 22, 1975. The fatal accident was due to injuries received when run over by a moving train. The deceased and his helper were working on day shift and had been servicing electrical equipment on 3700 Level in the vicinity of the track switch to the crushing chamber incline and to the ore-loading chutes. While they were doing this, a locomotive brought in two cars loaded with cement, gravel and a cement mixer. The operator came to a halt at the switch to obtain directions for switching the two cars he was pushing.

The deceased, his partner and a construction foreman entered into discussion with the motorman and decided to shunt the two cars onto a sidetrack. Before moving the train, the motorman switched on the backing headlight and blew the horn on the locomotive. As the train backed up, the deceased attempted to cross the track in front of it. He was knocked down and dragged about fifty feet before it stopped, after the foreman flagged down its motion.

On being removed from under the car, he was pronounced dead by the attending doctor. It is surmised that the deceased was crossing the tracks to go to a small service locomotive standing on an adjacent track. It is also possible that, due to a physical handicap of a lame leg, the deceased may have stumbled and fallen in front of the train as it moved.

BARRY LEE BUCHAN, miner. July 13, 1976. The fatal accident was due to a failed blasting operation underground. The deceased and his partner, Raymond Grebliunas, were employed extending a slusher sub in the No. 2 Shaft Section. In reconstructing the scene of the accident, it would appear the two men had drilled and loaded the necessary three headings and had ignited the fuses, using thermalite igniter cord in the drift and No. 8 draw point, and were in the process of lighting No. 7 draw point when the drift round commenced to detonate.

Both men were severely injured but Grebliunas had managed to crawl about thirty metres south to the man-way while the deceased was lying about three metres south of No. 7 draw point. Both men were alive when found but later succumbed to their injuries. It was conjectured that some difficulty must have been experienced in igniting the holes in No. 7 draw point and the men had stayed to watch the igniter cord light each fuse. This delayed the miners until the other rounds commenced to detonate.

RAYMOND D. GREBLIUNAS, miner. July 13, 1976. See previous report.

JAMES STUART TIFFIN, hot-muck miner. March 2, 1977. The fatal accident was due to falling down an underground ore-pass on 3500 Level. On the day of the accident, the deceased was working where he was bypassing ore from the 207 ore-pass above him into the ore-pass below him. When the lower ore-pass was full, he proceeded to the 3500 Level to bypass this ore down through the ore-transfer system below this level.

The deceased was at the 3500 Level ore-pass bypassing ore when a loaded ore train approached the dump. On passing the remote valve control for the dump door and dump block, the motorman pulled the activating cord to set both objects into the dump operating position. He then continued toward the dump with the train behind him but stopped about three metres north of the dumping position on being flagged down by the deceased. By this time the dump door was fully open. This allowed steam and red dust to billow up on to the level.

The motorman saw the deceased attempting to put on his respirator as he was enveloped in the steam and dust. The motorman left the locomotive and crawled back about twenty-five metres to seek refuge from the cloud in an old lunchroom where he believes he was overcome for about five minutes because of the gas and dust he had inhaled. On reviving, he went out on to the level and closed the dump door by operating the remote control valve. He then backed the train four to six metres when another workman came on to the scene. After a joint unsuccessful search for the deceased, they called their supervisor by telephone to report what had happened.

By then, the supervisor had arrived at the accident scene and instituted a more extensive search for the deceased, who still remained missing. It was then presumed that he must have fallen down the ore-pass so dumping into it was then suspended but this was not until after some eighty cars of ore had been dumped into it after the deceased was first reported missing. After discussion with management and the police, a decision was made to draw down the material in the ore-pass in searching for this missing man. The deceased's body was located and recovered when it became safe to do so.

1980-2001

JOHN HENRY POTVIN, mucker. March 11, 1982. The fatal accident was due to an uncontrollable flow of muck containing mud, water and ore of various sizes up to twenty inches or more. The deceased was assigned by his supervisor to run the jaw crusher on the 2500 Level. It seems clear that the deceased was instructed that the material in the pocket at the crusher was wet and runny and that he should be careful in how he handled it. He was also instructed not to start up until the supervisor arrived.

After sending the deceased to the crusher and rounding up other crew members, the supervisor proceeded down the conveyor belt to the loading station below the 2500 Crusher, where the belt feeder operator caught up to him. They noticed water and muck coming down the man-way from the crusher. Instructing the feeder operator to wait, the supervisor went to investigate.

He found the deceased lying on the operating platform at the top of the crusher, surrounded by muck and boulders, displaying no sign of life. First aid was called and a rescue effort organized to remove the deceased to the hospital. It seems clear that he was killed instantly when struck on the head by one or more large rocks.

GRAHAME BINGHAM, shift boss. April 18, 1987. The fatal accident was due to an underground vehicle colliding with the deceased. The deceased and his partners had been at 0-12 Dump on 4250 Level, preparing the dump for work. He had detailed one partner to build a berm to keep water from going down the muck raise, then left to get a pump and hoses to pump the water to the drainage ditch. A scoop-tram operator on 3770 Level was dumping muck into 3650 Dump with his scoop. When he saw the deceased drive past in the rear lights of the scoop, he waited a moment at the dump thinking that he may come in to talk to him. When he didn't come, the operator backed the scoop into the main scram and saw the deceased walking back down the incline towards him so he pulled into the scram on an angle and stopped to wait.

When he was about two or three feet away from the scoop, the operator saw the movement of the deceased's jeep out of the corner of his eye as it came into the light from the dump. The unoccupied jeep rolled down the incline and hit the deceased, knocking him forward and down, pinning him against the side of the scoop just behind the rear tire.

The operator got off the scoop, ran around to the jeep, got in and moved it ahead about ten feet. He then went back to the injured man and straightened him out to try and make him comfortable. He was having difficulty breathing. The operator saw headlights come into the heading and help soon arrived. First aid was administered and the deceased was transported to the hospital where he later succumbed to his injuries.

LLOYD CHABOT, mechanized miner. November 23, 1987. The fatal accident was due to a fall of ground from the sidewall of the drift. The deceased and his partner, working on 3290 Level in Scram 2, completed preparations for drilling the next development round in the scram and then the partner left to finish mucking out another heading.

The back of Scram 2 had been bolted to the face on a 3-foot pattern with 7-foot Swellex bolts by the previous shift, leaving the pair with scaling, back-blading of the face, exposing lifters and marking up the next round, in readiness for drilling. At the time of the accident, twelve holes had been drilled, and the deceased had stepped off the jumbo on the right-hand side where he was later found under the rock pile, estimated to be ten tons. The deceased received multiple injuries from which he subsequently died.

[Note: "Shock" as a cause of death was sometimes used in years gone by as a catch-all to explain deaths where cause was not identified by autopsy or other means.]

Milestones in the Life of the Sullivan Mine

Much of the following information was compiled by Teck Cominco and is used with permission. Master reports on the Sullivan and North Star mines, published by the BC Ministry of Energy & Mines, Geological Survey Branch, were also consulted.

1892   American prospectors Walter Burchett, Pat Sullivan, Ed Smith and John Cleaver stake the claims that guarantee the quartet enduring fame as the discoverers of the Sullivan Mine.

1896   Col. Ridpath and associates of Spokane, Wash., purchase the Sullivan claims for $24,000 and form the Sullivan Group Mining Company, with head office in Spokane and a local office at Fort Steele, BC. The company does some surface stripping and sinks several small shafts over the next few years.

1898   Original townsite of Kimberley is subdivided on August 12.

1899   Canadian Pacific Railway (CPR) constructs a 19-mile branch line from Cranbrook to Kimberley, making transportation of the ore more cost effective and spurring development of the mine. For the next 40 years, all ore shipments go by rail through the centre of town.

The mine has 20 employees, all male.

1900   First ore shipments by rail go to the Hall Mines smelter at Nelson, BC.

Ore is hand sorted for silver and high-grade lead from a conveyor belt. Ore containing too much zinc, not a marketable metal at this time, is discarded and stockpiled in waste dumps.

1902   Construction begins on the Marysville lead smelter, located beside Mark Creek in the area between what are now the Kimberley and Bootleg Gap golf courses.

1904   Aerial tramline from Top Mine to Mark Creek valley is completed. Ore is hauled out of the mine at the 4600-foot level, conveyed down Sullivan Hill via tram cars, and loaded onto trains at 3900 feet.

1908   Sullivan Mine and Marysville Smelter close. The ore is too complex for known smelting techniques. The lead-zinc alloy will not separate. To protect their interests, mine creditors form the Fort Steele Mining and Smelting Company and acquire the Sullivan property. Opinion is expressed in some quarters that the property is not worth "a plugged nickel."

1909   Consolidated Mining and Smelting Company Ltd. (CM&S), established in the late 1800s by the CPR, acquires a 60% share of the Sullivan and a lease permitting removal of 30,000 tons of ore. CM&S commits to spend $10,000 on development.

1910   23,000 tons of Sullivan ore, from the first CM&S development, are shipped to the smelter at Trail, BC.

North Star Mine closes. It was news of the North Star find, on the hillside where the Kimberley Alpine Resort is now located, that drew Burchett, Sullivan, Smith and Cleaver to the area in 1892. The North Star site was completely staked by the time the four arrived, so they crossed Mark Creek to prospect on the opposite hill. The rest, as they say, is history. The North Star orebody was nowhere near as big as the Sullivan but it was exceptionally rich. Although the mine closed in 1910, various enterprising parties sorted ore from the dumps until 1929, recovering enough silver and lead to make their efforts worthwhile.

1911	First compressor plant is built in Mark Creek valley. It houses a Rand water-driven air compressor purchased from the St. Eugene Mine in Moyie, BC.
1913	CM&S secures complete ownership of the Sullivan property for $75,000.
1914	Sullivan Mine is the largest producer of lead in Canada.
1915	Construction starts on a new mine entrance (the 1915 Portal) at the 3900-foot level. It takes 4 years to drive the tunnel through rock to the southern edge of the orebody, a distance of more than 2 miles.
1916	Mark Creek flood washes away the compressor plant.
1917	A new compressor plant is built. Concentrator is built at Trail to treat Sullivan ore.
1918	Researchers in Trail begin work on developing "differential flotation" technology, which uses the specific gravity of each element to separate

the lead, zinc and iron sulphides to form lead and zinc concentrates. It takes a few years to work out the ground-breaking technology, and when the processes are finally stable and controllable, the decision is made to build a large concentrator between Kimberley and Marysville.

Discovering a way to separate the Sullivan's complex ore is probably the most momentous milestone in the mine's history. Differential flotation makes the mine profitable at last and transforms the Sullivan orebody into one of the world's major producers of lead and zinc. The ore also contains significant quantities of silver and tin, and recoverable quantities of gold, copper, cadmium, antimony and bismuth.

1919	3900 Level tunnel is finished.
	Serious forest fire burns in Mark Creek valley.
1920	Workers strike at mine.
1921	First scraper hoists are installed in 3984 Stope.
1923	Sullivan Concentrator goes into production, processing 2,300 tons of ore a day.
1924	Compressor plant is enlarged to house a 6,500 cubic ft/min Ingersoll-Rand air compressor.
1925	Concentrator production is boosted to 4,000 tons a day.
1928	Concentrator production goes to 6,000 tons a day. The Sullivan is now the largest single producer of lead and zinc in the world.

1931   Production is reduced to part-time due to falling metal prices.

Development below 3900 Level begins.

1932   Construction starts on the third and last compressor plant (the Powerhouse) which still stands in Mark Creek valley.

Top Mine closes down; all operations are now in Mark Creek valley.

Because of the Depression, the Sullivan is the only mine operating in British Columbia.

1935   Gravel filling of mined-out stopes begins.

1939   Metals from the Sullivan are supplied to the British government at below-market prices to help with the war effort.

For the first time in the mine's history, ore is now being taken from below 3900 Level, as well as from above it.

1941   Tin Plant is built. Tin is quite valuable and during wartime it becomes economical to recover a tin concentrate. Small amounts are produced until 1985.

1943   Massive cave-in in North Section: 12,000 square feet, two stopes, and 300,000 cubic yards. The cave-in occurs during the lunch break and no one is in the stope when it collapses, but it spurs efforts to fill all stopes with gravel and forces a much more systematic process of pillar removal, which continues until the mine closes. Development of this system allows a caved area to grow in a controlled way and prevents excessive loading on pillars, which could cause sudden catastrophic collapses. Over the years, pillars are blasted in a very rigid sequence to establish a cave "retreat front." By the 1980s, this places significant limits on production.

1944	Belt conveyors are installed from 3350 Level to 3900 Level.
	Walter Burchett, who found the first piece of float from the Sullivan deposit in 1892, returns to Kimberley for the first time since 1896.
1945	No. 1 Shaft and headframe are completed at 4380 Level. The shaft is used by some mining personnel to access lower levels of the mine, although most crews continue to use the 1915 Portal at 3900 Level to reach their work destinations. This takes a long time and involves using several trains and internal shafts.
1946	3700 Level tunnel is started. The finished tunnel, from the 3800 Level crusher to the bottom of the Townsite hill, will be 10,375 feet long and will emerge on surface near the site of today's Centennial Centre at Coronation Park.
	No. 1 pilot shaft is started.
1948	Mark Creek floods again and has a serious impact on the town.
	Tungsten carbide (Crag) bits are introduced.
1949	3700 Level tunnel and haulage way to the concentrator are completed at a cost of $6.5 million. Ore is no longer shipped by rail through Kimberley's town centre but is transported underground to the 3700 Portal and then on surface to the concentrator.
	Concentrator production is boosted to slightly over 10,000 tons a day.
	The Company adopts a 40-hour work week.
1950	Open-pit excavations start.
	The belt conveyor is extended to 2850 Level.

Float fill material is placed in stopes.

1951	Construction of the Fertilizer Plant begins next to the concentrator. Construction starts on the CM&S hydro power line from Trail to Kimberley.
1952	Open-pit ore production commences. The Trail-Kimberley power line is completed.
1954	Fertilizer Plant begins producing "Elephant Brand" fertilizer using by-products of the ore concentration process.
1955	Sullivan produces a record 2,836,577 tons of ore this year.
1956	Fertilizer Plant shuts down for three months.
1957	Open-pit operations cease. Compulsory eye protection is introduced.
1958	Largest blast in Sullivan's history: 873,000 tons at N-14 Pillar.
1959	Construction begins on the Iron Plant to use another by-product of the concentration process.
1961	Production of pig iron begins.

1962   Installation of the 2500 Level crushing plant and 1,500-foot hoisting conveyor is completed.

Stope production begins on 2850 Level.

A new underground hoist is installed for No. 32 Shaft.

A permanent blending plant is constructed for mixing ammonium nitrate (fertilizer) and fuel oil to make the explosive NCN.

The main support tower for the Trail-Kimberley power line is blown up on the east side of Kootenay Lake by the Sons of Freedom, a radical sect of the Doukhobors. The line, from the Company's dams on the Kootenay and Columbia Rivers in the West Kootenay, supplies electricity for the mine and concentrator. Power is quickly redirected from Alberta and the Cranbrook area via BC Hydro lines.

1963   All stopers, jacklegs and long-hole drills are equipped with noise-suppressing devices, earplugs not yet being in general use.

CM&S has more than 1,000 retired workers on its pension roll for the first time in its history.

New forced-air intake (No. 39 Shaft) is completed to supplement the 3900 Level ventilation circuit.

1964   Three-day strike during Trail-Kimberley contract negotiations.

Another new forced-air intake (No. 41 Shaft) is driven to supplement 3900 Level ventilation circuits.

Construction of a Steel Plant, to use the iron now being produced, is authorized.

1965   Mining of low-grade ore from the open pit is discontinued.

Concentrator treats some ore from Pine Point, Northwest Territories.

1966   Steel production begins.

Temporary plant for crushing Pine Point ore is built above the concentrator.

Consolidated Mining and Smelting Company Limited changes its corporate name to Cominco Ltd.

1967   Sullivan wins the John T. Ryan safety award for best safety frequency record in western provinces and territories.

1969   BC government enacts environmental reclamation legislation.

1971   Iron and Steel Plants close.

1972   Environmental reclamation work begins at the Sullivan Mine.

1974   Four-month strike.

1976   Introduction of "trackless" mechanized mining methods using mobile equipment. The ramps used by these trackless vehicles will ultimately intersect all mine levels and significantly improve access to all mine workings. The decision is made to move all mine access, along with all surface facilities, from 3900 Level (1915 Portal) up to the 4380-foot level.

1979   Drainage Water Treatment Plant beside the St. Mary River is commissioned, a major step towards protecting local creeks and rivers from contaminated mine run-off water.

1980	No. 1 Ramp at 4380 Level is completed and becomes the main mine entrance. Surface buildings, including the mine offices, dry and warehouse, are also opened at this level.

1981	Sullivan Mine Rescue Team wins national championships.

1985	Tin Plant closes.

| 1986 | Production starts to decline significantly due to low metal prices and restrictions in production created by deteriorating ground conditions, which require expensive and time-consuming ground support while getting the "retreat front" properly established.

It is now known the mine will close in 2001. |
| --- | --- |

| 1987 | Fertilizer Plant closes.

Canadian Pacific, headquartered in Montreal, sells its controlling interest in Cominco to a consortium headed by Teck Corporation of Vancouver. |
| --- | --- |

| 1988 | Reclamation of the Fertilizer Plant site begins.

Mine maintenance complex is completed at the Upper Mine.

All activity ceases at 3900 Level in Mark Creek valley.

Column cell flotation technology introduced at the concentrator. |
| --- | --- |

1989	Five-year reclamation plans are developed and submitted to the BC Ministry of Mines.

1990   Computer control system is installed at the concentrator.

        Reclamation of the tailings ponds is well underway.

        Sullivan Mine is shut down for eight months due to depressed
        mineral prices.

1991   Sullivan Mine closure plan is assembled and submitted to BC
        Ministry of Mines.

        Cominco starts deep-drilling on Mark Creek, immediately north of
        the mine, in search of an extension to the Sullivan orebody. The hole
        reaches about 600 feet.

1992   The decommissioning and closure plan is made public this year.

1993   Lead regrind project, using new processing technology, is completed
        at the concentrator, resulting in higher grade zinc concentrates and
        improved lead and zinc recovery.

1995   Unprecedented 7-year collective agreement is signed with the union
        to take the mine to closure in 2001. The agreement provides for no
        lay-offs until the final downsizing takes place near the closure date.
        It also provides for severance provisions.

        The reclamation and decommissioning process increases substantially.
        The 3900 Level buildings, abandoned in 1980, are removed; Mark
        Creek is re-channeled; and Mark Creek waste dumps are re-profiled
        to make a flatter slope. The area is covered with glacial tills and re-
        vegetated. A system of collection and piping of contaminated mine
        drainage and seepage through the old waste dumps is completed
        to the Drainage Water Treatment Plant. Reclamation of some of
        the late tailings area is carried out in the 1990s. In excess of $68
        million will have been expended before reclamation is completed
        in 2005.

The deep-drilling project started in 1991 resumes. The hole goes to 6,350 feet, 700 feet short of its goal, but eventually reaches 8,528 feet in 1996.

2000   Work is started on removing the waste materials at the 4200 Level and above. These acid-generating materials are placed in the old open pit and will ultimately fill it totally. The area will then be recovered with glacial tills and re-vegetated.

Notice of closure goes out to all employees.

2001   Teck Corporation acquires the remaining outstanding shares of Cominco and merges the two companies into one, which is re-named Teck Cominco Ltd. The Sullivan Mine is owned by Teck Cominco Metals Ltd., a wholly owned subsidiary. This company will continue reclamation and environmental monitoring and assessment in the future.

Sullivan Mine ceases operations permanently at the end of day shift on December 21.

2002   Because of the extent of the surface area that has caved in above the mine workings over the years, there is no way to safely fill and restore the area. It is fenced and public access prohibited.

Rain and snow entering the mine through the caved-in area will ultimately flood the mine from the lowest level at 2456-feet elevation up to 3650 feet, taking two or three years to fill to that level. Once the water has reached 3650 feet, it will be pumped annually to reduce it to 3500-foot elevation. The contaminated water pumped out of the mine will go through the Drainage Water Treatment Plant before being released into local water courses. Pumping will be required for about three months each year indefinitely to maintain the water level at 3500 feet.

2003	Having signed an option agreement with Teck Cominco, Stikine Gold Corporation advertises "investor presentations" in local newspapers to promote its Sullivan Deeps project, a deep-drilling program that will pick up where Cominco left off in the 1990s. Stikine wants to drill new deep holes to determine if the Sullivan's "big sister" is in a target area identified by Cominco's earlier geological and geophysical work.
2004	Stikine begins drilling April 6 at a site about 2.5 miles north of the Sullivan.

If a new mine ever does go into production, it will be very different from the Sullivan. Temperatures at the depths already drilled have been recorded at 169°F which would probably require mining by remote control. Miners — the heart and soul of hard rock mining — would be no more underground. There will never be another Sullivan.

Glossary

Note: *Italicized* words in a definition are defined in the Glossary.

Adit	Tunnel driven into the side of a hill or mountain to access an underground mineral deposit.
Anodet	Fast-igniting electric blasting cap.
Anoline	Blasting agent to set off explosives.
B-line	High-explosive detonating cord that ties in all the blasting caps going into holes to be blasted. Burns at 4,000 feet a second.
Back	Roof of any mined-out area, such as a *drift, sub, raise* or *stope.*
Back-holes	Top holes of a round to be blasted.
Bar	Aluminum pole, usually 6 to 12 feet long, with steel chisel-shaped wedges at each end, used to scrape or pry *loose* away from the walls of an area being mined.
Barman	Person whose main job is to bar down *loose* to make the area safe for continued mining.

Barring	Dislodging *loose*.
Bench	Shelf or ledge in a stope or mine working used when the upper section of the face is drilled and blasted. Blasting such a shelf is called "lifting a bench."
Berm	Barrier made out of muck beside a roadway.
Bonus	Extra money or incentive pay that a miner can earn over his hourly wage.
Bootleg	Bottom part of a hole that is left after a blast. Must be examined carefully to make sure no explosive remains. Bootlegs are washed and cleaned out then marked with a chalk circle, indicating not to be drilled in case some powder is left.
Brattice	A sheet of gunnysack material used for building temporary air seals.
Bucket	Lunch pail.
Bulkhead	Wall or partition made of wood or concrete and built across a mine opening to contain gravel, backfill, waste rock, water or to direct air flow.
Bump	Occurs when the ground shifts, usually caused by ground displacement during mining.
Burn or Cut	The first part of a round to be blasted. Includes big hole, square-up, easers and helpers. See diagram 'How to blast a round.'
CM&S	Consolidated Mining and Smelting Company, later Cominco, now Teck Cominco. The Company.
Cage	Device attached to the cable of a hoist to transport men or material to different levels. Usually a cagetender controls the operation and is responsible for getting the men or

materials to the desired level using a system of bell signals to the hoist operator.

Carbide lamp	Used in the Sullivan until 1930. The mixture of water and carbide rock or dust gave off a pungent smell and bright yellow light.
Chert	Hardest ground in the mine, second only to diamonds in hardness.
Chuteman	Person who loads ore into underground train cars by operating a chute gate. Ore is fed into the cars via chutes built over the train tracks.
Chute-loader	Same as chuteman.
Chucktender	Usually a miner whose main job is to line up the drill *steel* on a *jumbo* at the *face* and to change bits on the steel.
Coaches	Enclosed man-cars pulled by an electric *loci*. Each coach had two 6-man bench seats divided by a wall. The Sullivan had four trains, each with about 10 coaches, that travelled to designated areas in the mine. Trains were used underground to transport men and materials until the mine converted to trackless, or *mechanized*, mining.
Collar	Start of a hole when using a drill, or the start of a *raise* or *shaft*.
Continuous miner	Used in coal mines. Similar to a giant chainsaw, the blade moves back and forth across the coal seam cutting coal. The coal goes onto a type of conveyor and moves back to be loaded onto a coal buggy or truck to be taken to dump.
Contract	Bonus pay over and above a day's pay and based on a contract negotiated by the men and the Company.
Crag bit	First tungsten drill bit used underground, harder than steel.

Cross shift	Crew working in the same spot as another crew but on the opposite shift.
Cut	First and main part of the round to be blasted. If the cut doesn't blast properly, the rest of the round will just fracture the rock, not move it.
Cutoff	Loaded blast hole that has not exploded because a blast from another hole has passed through the surrounding ground, by way of fractured ground or a water course, and cut off the fuse in the unexploded hole.
Diamond drill	Machine used on the surface or underground to bore a circular core of rock, which is recovered and examined for mineral content. Powered by compressed air, electricity, gas or diesel motor.
Diggers	Miners' work clothes, often consisting of bib overalls, heavy work shirt, gray wool underwear, and wool socks.
Doghouse	Lunchroom, carved out of rock or built with wood or cement.
Drawhole	Funnel-shaped *raise* driven to allow broken *ore* to feed by gravity into a *slusher sub.*
Drawpoint	Opening in a scram used in mechanized mining where scoop trams draw down the *ore* to be transported to dump.
Drift	Horizontal underground opening driven alongside or through an *ore* deposit to gain access to the deposit.
Drifter	Early-model drill fed forward by hand turning a feed screw or crank mechanism. Usually weighed about 150 pounds. The drill was mounted on a bar and arm. The column bar was stood upright to the back and footwall and was tightened with a screw action, which made it possible to expand the bar for tightening. An arm was

put onto the bar and the drill was clamped to it. Also called a *liner.*

Drill doctor	Person whose job is to repair all underground drills.
Drifting	Track *drifts* mined with *drifters* or *liners* in the early years, later mined with *jacklegs* and *jumbos.*
Dry	Showers and change room, usually with a 20-foot ceiling with suspended baskets and hooks so miners can hang their wet clothes and hoist them up to dry in warmer air.
Dynamite	Early dynamite lacked the chemical and physical stability of modern compounds and separated too readily into its components of inert filler and nitroglycerine. The high freezing temperature of nitro, 52 F, caused the powder to become sensitive to shock. The simple act of throwing it, or even just jarring it, was the next best thing to suicide. A lot of dead miners would confirm that — if they could.
Face	End or wall of a *tunnel, drift, raise* or *stope* at which work is progressing or was last done.
Fault	Break in the earth's crust caused by forces that have moved rock and *ore* in relation to the other. Ore deposits are commonly associated with faults, but not all orebodies contain faults.
Float	Solidified waste by-product produced at the concentrator used for backfill.
Footwall	Lower wall or floor of a *vein* or cavity. It may stand at any angle, from horizontal to vertical.
Footwall steel	Usually old drill *steel*, about two feet long, used to support planks or hold ropes in *raises.* When they had finished drilling a raise round, miners would turn their *stopers* upside down, drill 8-inch holes and put the two-foot steel into the holes. Ropes were tied to the protruding steel to

enable the miners to climb up the raise or planks were placed on the steel to form a platform for *barring* down and setting up the next round.

Galena	The most important *ore* containing lead.
Grizzly	Steel H-beams, usually about 18 inches wide, that are put across a *millhole* to control the size of the *muck* going down the *raise* to the chute that will load the *ore* cars.
Hang-up	*Muck* that has wedged and stopped flowing down a raise.
Hanging wall	Upper wall or roof of a *vein* or cavity. May stand at any angle from horizontal to vertical.
Hat signals	Used to communicate when noise or distance made hearing difficult. The miner would move his hat light up and down to indicate "to you," in a circle to mean "to me," sideways for "stop." Hat signals were used to move trains or when using *tuggers* to move *skips* up and down *raises*.
Haulage drift	Horizontal mine tunnel or *adit* through which *ore* or waste is hauled in mine cars.
Heading	Place where the actual mining, drilling, blasting or scraping occurs.
Hitches	An area dug out by pick or drilled out by stoper, jackleg or plugger where supports such as sprags, posts are placed and wedged tight against opposing walls.
Hogsback	Highest point of two connecting *raises*.
Hoist	Electric or air-driven drum that rotates either forward or backward and is operated by a miner using two hand levers. Each lever has a separate function. One is called the haul down and pulls the scraper down to the *millhole*; the other is the haul back and pulls the scraper back to the end of the *sub* or to the *face*.

Hot muck	Burning *ore*. When a large pillar or multiple pillars were blasted, the broken ore would start to heat up when exposed to oxygen, especially if it contained iron oxides. Spontaneous combustion would occur, resulting in temperatures up to 2000°F and producing sulphur dioxide gas and red-hot dust that turned to sulphuric acid when mixed with water. In these very dangerous conditions, safety gear and caution were a must.
I-cord	Slow-burning igniter cord used to tie in the old safety fuse when blasting. Fuses are tied to the I-cord according to the holes you want to blast first. Miners used their lighters to light the cord.
Jackleg	Pneumatic rock drill that weighs approximately 130 pounds and runs on 100 pounds of air pressure. Drill is mounted on a swivel joint on a pneumatic leg that, when compressed, is about 4 feet long. When given air, the leg will extend telescopically to a maximum of 10 feet to maintain pressure on the drill *steel* as the holes deepen.
Jenny	Hoe-like device with a pointed beak used for mucking or cleaning the *footwall*.
Jumbo	Drill or drills mounted on rail wheels or rubber-tires, and used for drilling on the flat in track *drifts*, mechanized *scrams* or *stopes*.
Level	Horizontal passage or tunnel from which *ore* is extracted. It is customary to mine the orebody from a *shaft* by establishing levels at regular intervals of depth.
Lift	To take a lift, you drill and blast a *face* where no *cut* is necessary. The lower part of the face is drilled and, when blasted, the ground is lifted, not fired back.
Liner	See *Drifter*

Loci	Short for locomotive. Connected to an overhead trolley line powered by electricity.
Loonshit	Slime-like mud usually consisting of backfill *muck* and water, mostly yellow in colour.
Loose	Unstable cracked or hanging ground that needs to be brought down for safety.
Mechanized mining	Mining with rubber-tired equipment, powered by diesel engines, such as *jumbos*, *scoops*, jeeps or trucks.
Man-way	Passageway for miners on foot, usually a ladder in a *raise*.
MSA canister	Full-face mask used for protection against low concentrations of gases. Separates small amounts of gas into breathable air.
Millhole	*Raise* that is driven up from a chute to a *slusher sub* for the specific purpose of scraping blasted *ore* down it so the ore can be loaded into cars.
Motor	Trolley-driven electric locomotive running on tracks.
Muck	*Ore* or rock that has been broken by blasting.
Mucker	Person who does clean-up work, usually involves a shovel.
Mucking machine	Machine that runs on railway track and is used for cleaning up after a round has been blasted in a *drift*, or for clean-up around chutes. It throws *muck* over the top of itself into a car attached behind.
NCN	Explosive made from a combination of fertilizer and coal oil. It can be blown into a drilled hole using a special grounded plastic hose and compressed air. It packs into a solid mass and is ignited with a blasting cap connected to *B-line*.
Nipper	Labourer whose job includes clean-up, fetching and carrying supplies and equipment (nipping), usually a rookie.

Ore	Mineralized material in the ground that can be mined and processed for recovery of contained minerals at a profit.
Pig snout	Small breathing mask that fits over the mouth and nose and filters only dust.
Plugger	Drill with handles, uses body weight to advance the drill into the hole, similar to jackhammer.
Portal	Entrance into the mine from outside.
Rails	Train tracks
Raise	Vertical or inclined underground tunnel which has been excavated upwards from one level to connect to a *level* above. Usually mined to convey personnel, *muck* or ventilation.
Rock	Aggregate of minerals.
Rock bolt	Used to stabilize blocky or slabby ground. Rock bolts are installed after a hole has been drilled. Most are about six feet long but some are longer, depending on the depth of the slabs. Can be used to put up screen or wire mesh. Bolts are held in the hole with either an expansion shell or a split bolt, which is a bolt that widens from top to bottom as it is driven in.
Rockhouse	Building just below the 3900 Portal where *ore* was dumped into bins and loaded into CPR cars for transport through the town centre to the concentrator. Later bypassed when the Company installed the 3700 Portal haulage system using their own rail system.
Round	The area to be drilled and blasted.
RDO	Round that is drilled off but not yet blasted.

Safety lamp	Used to indicate where gas may be present or oxygen is low. The lamp's flame burns brighter in the case of some gases or burns lower in the case of low oxygen.
Scoop tram	Rubber-tired front-end loader used in mechanized mining.
Scram	Travel-way for *mechanized mining* equipment, average dimensions 15 by 20 feet.
Scraper	Hoe-like device, weighing up to 1.5 tons, that uses a dragline operation to scrape *ore* or waste.
Section	The Sullivan Mine had five sections at one time, and each section had its own foreman, shift bosses and general roll call. The South End, Centre Section and North End were called the upper sections because they operated above 3900 Level. No. 1 Shaft and No. 2 Shaft were the lower sections; they operated below 3900. At one time, four underground hoists delivered men and materials either up or down, depending on the section. No. 1 Section's hoist was the only one on surface. This shaft went down 4500 feet at 45 degrees.
Shaft	Opening cut downwards for the transportation of men and materials, and *ore* and waste. Also used for ventilation and as an auxiliary exit. Often equipped with a surface hoist system that lowers and raises a cage in the shaft, as well as *skips* or containers for bringing up *ore* or waste.
Shift	An eight-hour work period.
Shift boss	First-line supervisor responsible for a number of workers and their duties.
Shifting	The act of supervising men during their *shift* or work period
Shotcrete	Combination of cement, gravel and water sprayed on using a hose hooked to a machine that mixes the material

and uses compressed air to apply it where needed to secure the ground.

Sidewall rock   *Rock* adjacent to the *vein*, usually distinguished as the *hanging wall* on the upper side and *footwall* on the underside.

Siwash   Idlers or blocks used to direct *hoist* and *scraper* cables to different angles, or to provide more pulling power.

Skip   Moves men and equipment vertically from one *level* to another. Varying in size, the larger ones are used to transport men and *ore* in main *shafts* while the smaller ones move material and tools in *man-way* raises.

Slash   Any small additional widening of an excavation, usually drilled and blasted.

Slickers   Rubber jacket and bib overalls worn over your work clothes to keep them dry.

Slough   When loose muck moves by gravity, pronounced sluff.

Slusher miner   Miner who scrapes broken pillar *ore* into an ore pass, usually a job for an older miner as it is less labour intensive and does not require climbing on ropes or handling drills.

Slusher sub   A horizontal or slightly inclined *sub-level* down which broken *ore* is scraped.

SO$_2$ Sulphur dioxide gas, a product of burning iron sulphides, see *hot muck*.

Spare-board   A blackboard or notice board listing the names of less senior miners who don't have a regular heading in which to work.

Sprags   Logs 4 to 6 inches in diameter used for drill set-ups, framing seals or for construction.

Spit (to spit)	To light a blasting fuse or igniter cord with matches or a lighter.
Steel	Rod of steel 1 to 12 feet long, with a fine hole through its length and a drill bit attached to one end. As a drill rotates the steel and bit, a water needle forces water through the steel and up into the bit. The water, expelled through openings in the bit, cuts down on the dust, cleans cuttings out of the hole being drilled, and cools the bit.
Stope	Mining area, established on an underground *level*, where *ore* is blasted and broken. Varies in size according to the size of the ore *vein*, can be as big as 100 by 300 feet.
Stoper	Self-rotating drill, approximately 130 pounds, used for drilling holes inclined above the horizontal. Mainly used in *raises*, it has a telescopic leg fed by air.
Stulls	Logs 8 to 16 inches in diameter, used in construction or for ground support.
Sub or Sub-level	Tunnel, located between two main *levels*, which may be used as a *man-way* or for a long-hole drilling location.
The Shaft	No. 1 and No. 2 Shafts, below 3900 Level.
Trail	City about 165 miles from Kimberley where Sullivan *ore* was sent to be smelted, site of many of the Company's administration offices.
Trammer	Person whose job includes hauling ore by train, *scoop* or truck to the main *ore* passes that go to the underground crushers.
Top Mine	Early townsite for miners and families, near the original portal at 4600 Level.

Tugger	Air *hoist*, consisting of a drum with cable wrapped around it, used for hauling a *skip* up and down a *raise* to transport materials.
Turn-back	*Raise* that is turned to go in another direction while being driven, may turn back over itself.
Turn-over	Top of *raise*, where it flattens out.
V-car	Train car with a V-shaped bottom.
Vein	An opening, fissure or crack in *rock* containing mineralized material.
Winze	Vertical or inclined *shaft* sunk from one *level* to another.

Postscript

I n many ways, I suppose, I'm glad this book is finished but in many ways I will miss it. It's like losing a family member since it's been with me for so long, almost eighteen years. But now it's time for it to leave home.

I feel that I have done the best that I could writing this book and together with those that chose to go with me on this journey, we have produced something that we can all be proud of.

Kimberley is a proud community, proud of its heritage, proud of the mine and the miners that chose to work in the Sullivan. The Sullivan not only provided for local families but also provided for British Columbia and, during the war years when the country needed metals, it provided for Canada. The mighty Sullivan was truly the biggest and best mine of its time.

I walk a lot and so does my mind. I've pretty much concluded that my mind seems to travel farther than the rest of me. My walks take me up and down the streets of Kimberley and as I pass houses, I peek into the windows. I remember those who once lived there and thanks to the Sullivan, memories live there also, plenty of them.

It's funny how sound carries on a clear cold winter night. As I walk I hear the laughter and the noise that kids make, perhaps sledding, and the excited bark of the ever-present dog. These are the sounds that have been heard on the streets of Kimberley for over a hundred years, thanks to the Sullivan and its miners. I hope those that have moved on will never forget where they came from. I tell myself that they haven't.

My walk will usually take me past the old portal with its mantle proudly displaying "1915." The memories I have when I'm at this part of my journey are immense. I can still see the grimy faces with only the whites of eyes and teeth showing through as a glimmer and a smile were shared. And if I tell you I can still hear voices and laughter, you may look at me with question, but, yes, I can still hear them. That's just the way it is. I wouldn't want it any other way.

There is a moment when I go by that I'll turn and see the coaches all lined up to go underground. There are a hundred years' of faces watching as I pass and with a slight wave and nod, they're gone.

Mining was the greatest job and I worked with the greatest guys. I, like Bud Hart, am proud to call them "The Best Miners in the World." I do miss it. It was good work.

About the Author

W.R. (Bill) Roberts was born in Alberta, raised in British Columbia and is an alumnus of Athol Murray College of Notre Dame in Saskatchewan. He worked for Teck Cominco for thirty-eight years, thirty-six of those underground, as a miner with a short stint as a shift boss. He is proud of being a hardrock miner and his association with his fellow workers. He feels in his heart that these stories are told the way they should be. Bill has written several published short stories and this is his first book. Bill and his wife, Sandra, are both retired and live in Kimberley, BC.

INDEX